Sun

S0-DUV-083

# CALIFORNIA
# WATER RESOURCES DEVELOPMENT

| | EXISTING or under CONSTRUCTION | AUTHORIZED | POSSIBLE FUTURE |
|---|---|---|---|
| Reservoirs, lakes | 1-180 | 181-192 | 193-233 |
| Aqueducts, tunnels | 1-32 | 33-40 | 41-58 |
| Urban areas | | | |

#4800

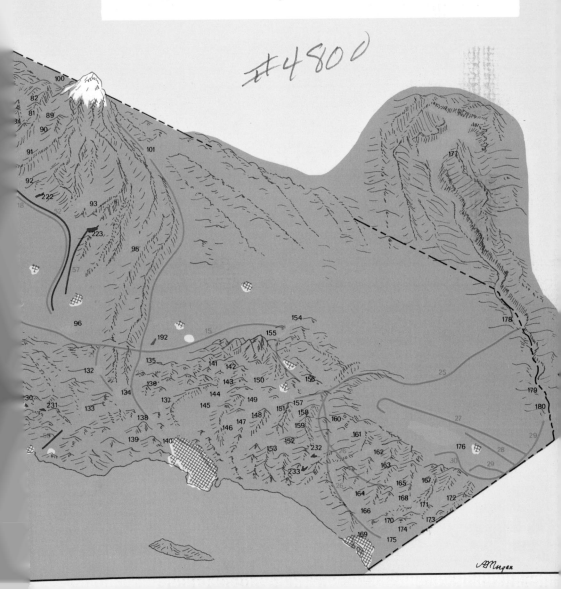

# KEY TO ENDSHEET MAP

RESERVOIRS AND LAKES (EXISTING OR UNDER CONSTRUCTION)

1. Copco Lake
2. Iron Gate Res.
3. Dwinnell Res.
4. Clair Engle Lake
5. Lewiston Res.
6. Lake Pillsbury
7. Lake Mendocino
8. Lake Sonoma
9. Nicasio Res.
10. Lake Hennessy
11. Clear Lake
12. Lake Berryessa
13. East Park Res.
14. Stony Gorge Res.
15. Black Butte Res.
16. Whiskeytown Res.
17. Keswick Res.
18. Shasta Lake
19. Box Canyon Res.
20. McCloud Res.
21. Pit #7 Res.
22. Pit #6 Res.
23. Iron Canyon Res.
24. Lake Britton
25. Tule Lake
26. Clear Lake Res.
27. Goose Lake
28. Eagle Lake
29. Honey Lake
30. Mountain Meadows Res.
31. Lake Almanor
32. Butt Valley Res.
33. Antelope Lake
34. Bucks Lake
35. Lake Oroville
36. Frenchman Lake
37. Lake Davis
38. Little Grass Valley Res.
39. Sly Creek Res.
40. Thermalito Forebay and Afterbay
41. Jackson Meadows Res.
42. New Bullards Bar Res.
43. Bowman Lake
44. Lake Spaulding
45. Scotts Flat Res.
46. Englebright Res.
47. Merle Collins Res.
48. Rollins Res.
49. Camp Far West Res.
50. French Meadows Res.
51. Hell Hole Res.
52. Loon Lake
53. Auburn Res.
54. Folsom Lake
55. Lake Natoma
56. Union Valley Res.
57. Ice House Res.
58. Silver Lake
59. Stampede Res.
60. Prosser Creek Res.
61. Lake Tahoe
62. Lower Bear River Res.
63. Salt Springs Res.
64. Pardee Res.
65. Camanche Res.
66. New Hogan Res.
67. Salt Springs Valley Res.
68. Farmington Res.
69. Woodward Res.
70. Donnells Res.
71. Beardsley Res.
72. New Melones Res.
73. Tulloch Res.
74. Lake Lloyd
75. Lake Eleanor
76. Hetch Hetchy Res.
77. New Don Pedro Res.
78. Turlock Lake
79. Lake McClure
80. McSwain Res.
81. Lake Florence
82. Lake Edison
83. Mammoth Pool Res.
84. Huntington Lake
85. Shaver Lake
86. Redinger Lake
87. Bass Lake
88. Millerton Lake
89. Courtright Res.
90. Wishon Res.
91. Pine Flat Res.
92. Terminus Res.
93. Success Res.
94. Tulare Lake
95. Isabella Res.
96. Buena Vista Lake
97. Mono Lake
98. Grant Lake
99. Lake Crowley
100. Tinemaha Res.
101. Haiwee Res.
102. San Pablo Res.
103. Briones Res.
104. Upper San Leandro Res.
105. San Antonio Res.
106. Calaveras Res.
107. Lake Del Valle
108. Clifton Court Forebay
109. San Andreas Res.
110. Crystal Springs Lake
111. Lexington Res.
112. Calero Res.
113. Chesbro Res.
114. Uvas Res.
115. Anderson Lake
116. Coyote Lake
117. San Luis Res.
118. O'Neill Forebay
119. Los Banos Creek Res.
120. Little Panoche Creek Res.
121. San Antonio Res.
122. Nacimiento Res.
123. Salinas Res.
124. Whale Rock Res.
125. Lopez Res.
126. Twitchell Res.
127. Jameson Lake
128. Gibralter Res.
129. Cachuma Res.
130. Matilija Res.
131. Casitas Res.
132. Pyramid Lake
133. Piru Lake
134. Castaic Lake
135. Fairmount Res.
136. Bouquet Res.
137. Hansen Res.
138. San Fernando Valley Res
139. Chatsworth Res.
140. Sepulveda Res.
141. Cogswell Res.
142. San Gabriel Res.
143. Morris Res.
144. Santa Fe Res.
145. Whittier Narrows Res.
146. Brea Res.
147. Fullerton Res.
148. Carbon Canyon Res.
149. Puddingstone Res.
150. San Antonio Res.
151. Prado Res.
152. Irvine Lake
153. Villa Park Res.
154. Mojave Res.
155. Silverwood Lake
156. Lake Perris
157. Lake Mathews
158. Railroad Canyon Res.
159. Elsinore Lake
160. Auld Valley Res.
161. Vail Res.
162. Lake Henshaw
163. Sutherland Res.
164. Lake Hodges
165. San Vicente Res.
166. Miramar Res.
167. Cuyamaca Res.
168. El Capitan Res.
169. Murray Res.
170. Sweetwater Res.
171. Lake Loveland
172. Morena Lake
173. Barrett Lake
174. Upper Otay Res.
175. Lower Otay Res.
176. Salton Sea
177. Lake Mead
178. Imperial Res.
179. Senator Wash Res.
180. Laguna Res.

# KEY TO ENDSHEET MAP (continued)

### RESERVOIRS AND LAKES (AUTHORIZED)

181. Butler Valley Res.
182. Knights Valley Res.
183. Lakeport Res.
184. Indian Valley Res.
185. Dixie Refuge Res.
186. Abbey Bridge Res.
187. Marysville Res.
188. Sugar Pine Res.
189. County Line Res.
190. Buchanan Res.
191. Hidden Res.
192. Buttes Res.

### RESERVOIRS AND LAKES (POSSIBLE FUTURE)

193. Helena Res.
194. Schneiders Bar Res.
195. Eltapom Res.
196. New Rugh Res.
197. Anderson Ford Res.
198. Dinsmore Res.
199. English Ridge Res.
200. Dos Rios Res.
201. Yellowjacket Res.
202. Cahto Res.
203. Panther Res.
204. Walker Res.
205. Blue Ridge Res.
206. Oat Res.
207. Sites-Funks Res.
208. Rancheria Res.
209. Newville-Paskenta Res.
210. Tehama Res.
211. Dutch Gulch Res.
212. Allen Camp Res.
213. Millville Res.
214. Tuscan Buttes Res.
215. Aukum Res.
216. Nashville Res.
217. Irish Hill Res.
218. Cooperstown Res.
219. Figarden Res.
220. Little Dry Creek Res.
221. Owen Mountain Res.
222. Yokohl Res.
223. Hungry Hollow Res.
224. Kellogg Res.
225. Los Banos Res.
226. Jack Res.
227. Santa Rita Res.
228. Sunflower Res.
229. Lompoc Res.
230. Cold Springs Res.
231. Topatopa Res.
232. Fallbrook Res.
233. De Luz Res.

### AQUEDUCTS AND TUNNELS (EXISTING OR UNDER CONSTRUCTION)

1. Clear Creek Tunnel
2. Whiskeytown-Keswick Tunnel
3. Bella Vista Conduit
4. Muletown Conduit
5. Corning Canal
6. Tehama-Colusa Canal
7. Putah South Canal
8. Cache Slough Conduit
9. Folsom South Canal
10. Mokelumne Aqueduct
11. Contra Costa Canal
12. South Bay Aqueduct
13. Hetch Hetchy Aqueduct
14. Delta Mendota Canal
15. California Aqueduct
16. Pleasant Valley Canal
17. Madera Canal
18. Friant Kern Canal
19. San Luis Obispo Conduit
20. Whale Rock Conduit
21. West Branch California Aqueduct
22. Angeles Tunnel
23. Los Angeles Aqueduct
24. South Coast Conduit
25. Colorado River Aqueduct
26. San Diego Aqueduct
27. Coachella Canal
28. East Highline Canal
29. All American Canal
30. West Side Canal
31. Santa Rosa Conduit
32. Sonoma Aqueduct

### AQUEDUCTS AND TUNNELS (AUTHORIZED)

33. Stony Canal
34. Folsom-Malby Conduit
35. North Bay Aqueduct
36. Peripheral Canal
37. Pacheco Tunnel
38. Santa Clara Canal
39. Hollister-Watsonville Conduit
40. Coastal Branch California Aqueduct

### AQUEDUCTS AND TUNNELS (POSSIBLE FUTURE)

41. Clear Creek Tunnel #2
42. Trinity Tunnel
43. South Fork Tunnel
44. Cottonwood Tunnel
45. Westside Conveyance System
46. Grindstone Tunnel
47. Stony Creek Conveyance Channel
48. Garrett Tunnel
49. West Sacramento Canal
50. Cache Creek–Sacramento River Canal
51. Knights Valley–Lake Hennessey Canal
52. Sonoma–Marin Conduit
53. Hood–Clay Canal
54. Eastside Canal
55. Contra Loma Canal
56. Tuway Canal
57. Porterville–Bakersfield Canal
58. Sespe Conduit

SOURCES: *California Water Resources Development*, Irrigation Districts Association of California, 1968
and
*Water Resources Development in California*, California State Department of Water Resources, 1970

# CALIFORNIA WATER

A STUDY IN RESOURCE MANAGEMENT

Research Library
Natural History Museum
Los Angeles County

# CALIFORNIA WATER

A STUDY IN RESOURCE MANAGEMENT

EDITED BY

# DAVID SECKLER

UNIVERSITY OF CALIFORNIA PRESS
BERKELEY, LOS ANGELES, LONDON 1971

UNIVERSITY OF CALIFORNIA PRESS
BERKELEY AND LOS ANGELES, CALIFORNIA
UNIVERSITY OF CALIFORNIA PRESS, LTD.
LONDON, ENGLAND
COPYRIGHT © 1971, BY
THE REGENTS OF THE UNIVERSITY OF CALIFORNIA
ISBN: 0-520-01884-2
LIBRARY OF CONGRESS CATALOG CARD NUMBER: 76-139773
PRINTED IN THE UNITED STATES OF AMERICA
DESIGNED BY DAVE COMSTOCK

# CONTENTS

# THE CONTRIBUTORS

BIRDLEBOUGH, Stephen C., Attorney at Law, Redding, California.

BOLLMAN, Frank H., Postgraduate Research Agricultural Economist, Department of Agricultural Economics, University of California, Berkeley.

BOOK, David L., Staff Physicist, Lawrence Radiation Laboratory, University of California, Livermore.

DEAN, Gerald W., Professor, Agricultural Economics; Agricultural Economist in Experiment Station and on Giannini Foundation, University of California, Davis.

GILL, Gurmukh, Research Assistant, Department of Agricultural Economics, University of California, Berkeley.

GOLDMAN, Charles R., Professor of Zoology and Research Limnologist, University of California, Davis.

GRAY, Edward, Postgraduate Research Agricultural Economist, Department of Agricultural Economics, University of California, Berkeley.

HARTMAN, L. M., Professor of Economics, Colorado State University, Fort Collins.

KING, Gordon A., Professor, Agricultural Economics; Agricultural Economist in Experiment Station and on Giannini Foundation, University of California, Davis.

LAIRD, A. D. K., Director, Sea Water Conversion Laboratory; Professor, Mechanical Engineering, Thermal Systems Division, University of California, Berkeley.

McGAUHEY, P. H., Director, Emeritus, Sanitary Engineering Research Laboratory; Professor, Emeritus, Sanitary and Public Health Engineering, Civil Engineering, University of California, Berkeley.

RAUSSER, Gordon C., Associate Professor, Agricultural Economics; Acting Assistant Agricultural Economist in Experiment Station and on Giannini Foundation, University of California, Davis.

REX, Robert W., Professor of Geology, University of California, Riverside.

SECKLER, David, Acting Associate Professor of Agricultural Economics, Agricultural Economist in Experiment Station and on Giannini Foundation, University of California, Berkeley; now Professor of Economics, Colorado State University, Fort Collins.

TAYLOR, Paul S., Professor of Economics, Emeritus, University of California, Berkeley.

TODD, David K., Professor of Civil Engineering, University of California, Berkeley.

WALLACE, L. T., Agriculturist, Agricultural Extension Service, University of California, Berkeley.

WILKINS, Alfred, Attorney at Law, Weaverville, California.

WOOD, Lowell D., Chairman and Assistant Professor, Department of Agricultural Economics, Brigham Young University, Provo, Utah.

# INTRODUCTION

By 1972 the State of California will have completed the basic features of one of the most complex and ambitious water development projects undertaken by man. This State Water Project will carry 4.2 million acre-feet of water per year from the Sacramento Delta to agricultural, urban, and industrial users in the central and southern areas of the state. The Project includes 444 miles of aqueducts. Over 2 million acre-feet of this water will be pumped nearly 2,000 feet over the Tehachapi Mountains into the Los Angeles basin. The initial features of this project will cost over $2.8 billion.

The State Water Project is matched by an equally ambitious project of the federal government in California. The United States Bureau of Reclamation began its Central Valley Project in 1933 and has been expanding it more or less continuously to the present. It also draws water from the Sacramento Delta for primarily agricultural uses in the Central Valley. Some $1.3 billion have been spent to date on construction for this project. It currently delivers 4.7 million acre-feet of water per year to some 1.5 million acres of land in the Central Valley. Rapid expansion of the Central Valley Project is planned over the next several decades.

The Delta Pool is thus the heart of a vast arterial system fed by the rainfall in the north and transported to users in the southern and central areas of the state. But the fact is that there is not enough water in the Delta Pool to meet all the increasing demands being made upon it. Herein lies the essence of the problem of California water.

If planned withdrawals from the Delta Pool are to be realized, several consequences must necessarily follow. First, the sheer volume of water withdrawn will significantly change the level and rates of flow of water through the Delta itself. The consequences of this to the quality of water in the Delta and to its ecological balance are many and complex, but certainly not good. Secondly, the flow from the Delta through San Francisco Bay will be significantly reduced. Recent evidence suggests that the Bay depends on this freshwater flow to flush pollutants and sediments out to sea. There is a very real danger that the Bay could "die" in the manner of Lake Erie. Third, partly in order to offset these effects and partly to provide for shortages of water in the Delta itself, further sources of water will have to be developed upstream to augment Delta supplies. This means, in brief, that the now rather undeveloped, "wild river" systems of the Klamath, the Trinity, and the Eel rivers on the northern coast of California must be dammed and diverted. Again, such development will substantially affect the ecological balances in those systems with consequent damage to fish, wildlife, and people.

These are the basic features of California water. The state now stands poised to take a major step in its planning. Since the Delta Pool cannot simultaneously meet all the conflicting demands placed upon it now and in the near future, some decision has to be made. On this everyone seems to agree. But, of course, hardly anyone agrees with anyone else about exactly what decision should be made.

This book does not pretend to offer a solution to the dilemma of California water. Several of the contributors no doubt have strong opinions on what should be done, but we have not attempted to voice these opinions here. Rather, what we have attempted to do is to provide a spectrum of consequences, alternatives, and ways of thinking about this problem. The ultimate solution must inevitably rest on personal assessments of the conflicting values involved, and that is a matter beyond our intent here. The book will, hopefully, enable the reader to make a more informed evaluation of his own: that is our main objective.

Most of the papers were written specifically for this book. We agreed from the very start to write in a way that would be intelligible to the intelligent layman. This because we were ourselves only intelligent laymen with respect to each other's fields, and because our purpose is not to prescribe but to inform. In this we have been aided by Mr. Jerome Fried, whose editorial and writing skills were made available through the generosity of the University of California Press and the Giannini Foundation of Agricultural Economics.

In looking over the several chapters, it seems that one theme emerges quite clearly: the enormous strides in technology over the past few years have introduced a new era in water resources management. Before these technological developments occurred, water resources management—for all practical purposes—was involved simply with the question of how best to gather water in areas of "surplus" and transport it to areas of "deficiency." Now, however, the problem is much more complex.

First, it is not easy to define what "surplus" and "deficiency" mean any more. As technology progresses, the sectoral balances of the economy change and population mobility becomes the order of the day. As the populations of areas rise and fall, past patterns of growth and needs become more or less irrelevant to future requirements. Similarly, the progress of technology in agriculture substantially changes both its productivity and the relations between agricultural yields and water requirements. The technology of water conservation and "waste-water" reclamation require a whole new look at our concepts of water needs. In sum, there simply are no "fixed requirements" for water in any meaningful sense, either by economic sectors or by geographic regions.

Second, for a variety of reasons too complex to go into here but intimately related to the drift of recent technology, the value of water in place—as a free-flowing stream for recreational and aesthetic purposes—is rising very rapidly. It is no longer simply a question in abstract economics, one of taking water that has no value or that is "wasted" and allocating it to a higher value. Rather, it is a question of allocating water among high-valued uses in all directions under conditions in which it is virtually impossible to tell just what the magnitudes of these values are.

Third, the advances in technology have provided an impressive array of alternative means of supply for meeting what demands arise. No longer is it merely a matter of gathering and transporting from one place to another. Now we have desalting technology, waste-water reclamation, groundwater utilization and management, and the use of geothermal steam as additional and alternative methods of supply.

In a word, the range of choices in water management has expanded as the difficulties of choice have become more profound. The rise of technology in this new era has been accompanied by an explosive rise in the level of risk and uncertainty in water resources management. It is quite likely that, unless our old ways of thinking about water are adapted to these new conditions, some very bad mistakes will be made. That, it seems, is the general theme emerging from these various chapters.[1]

This book began in early 1970 when several people in the University of California formed a small, informal study group for purposes of exchanging information about the California water situation across our several areas of expertise. It was soon decided that the most efficient means of getting started would be for each person to write a brief paper on his particular area for the others to read. Two things then happened. First, it became apparent that the original group would have to be substantially expanded to give a more comprehensive picture of this complex problem. Second, as word got out, there was some demand for these papers around the campuses, from legislators, from the general public. One thing led to another and here, after rather more work than anticipated, we are.

The book is divided into four parts. Part One outlines the past, present, and future expectations of the California Water Plan and reviews some of the major points of criticism regarding it. Part Two surveys various aspects of the demand for water in California, urban and agricultural, its value in a natural setting, and, finally, the demand for water as an element in the ecology of the Bay-Delta region. Part Three covers the various means of water supply, from desalting to waste-water reclamation through conjunctive use of groundwater and surface-water supplies and geothermal steam. The last chapter of this part examines the use of water for the production of electrical energy in light of alternative means of energy supply. Finally, in Part Four we turn to brief examination of the process of decision-making in water resources. We begin with the very important problem of decision-making under uncertainty. Because of the importance of this problem in the new era of water management, a more detailed, technical statement is included as an appendix. The chapter after that discusses the "160-Acre Limitation," one of the most influential laws in the history of water resources management; this is followed by an

---

1. After this book was in galley proof form, the California Department of Water Resources issued Bulletin No. 160-70, *Water for California, The California Water Plan Outlook in 1970,* Summary Report, December 1970. This new report reflects a basic change in the Department's thinking, a change much more in accord with the thinking in this book. See also footnote 25, Chapter 3, below.

examination of the legal background of conjunctive use of ground water and surface water in the state. Next, the evaluation procedures of the Army Corps of Engineers are examined in terms of a case study, the Dos Rios Project. The book concludes with an overview of the problems of evaluation and decision-making in water resources generally, with reference to the particular problem of California water.

PART ONE
# THE CALIFORNIA WATER PLAN

# 1 THE CALIFORNIA WATER PLAN AND ITS CRITICS: A BRIEF REVIEW

GURMUKH S. GILL, EDWARD C. GRAY, AND DAVID SECKLER

I

California covers an area of 158,693 square miles. It is the third largest state in the union in area and the largest in population, with more than 20 million people. It is a land of contrasts. Within its boundaries are situated Mount Whitney, the highest mountain in the contiguous United States, 14,495 feet above sea level, and Death Valley, 282 feet below sea level, the lowest point in the western hemisphere. The eastern part of the state is dominated by the Sierra Nevada, nearly 400 miles long and some 70 to 80 miles wide, with 12 peaks over 14,000 feet high — a rampart against whose bulk the moist winds from the Pacific Ocean break to drop an average of between 300 and 400 inches of snow every year. West of the Sierra and along its entire length lies the great Sacramento–San Joaquin Valley, into which drain the streams carrying the runoff from the mountains — Pit, Feather, Yuba, American, Stanislaus, Tuolumne, Merced, Kings, Tule, Kern — to form the two large rivers that meet at the Sacramento Delta and thus reach the sea through San Francisco Bay and the Golden Gate, the only outlet along the entire length of the Valley that lets water out to the Pacific through the Coast Ranges.

The Los Angeles–Long Beach region ranks as the third largest metropolitan area in the United States; San Francisco–Oakland stands sixth. Yet, at the same time, the north coastal region of the Trinity Alps contains the largest primeval area in the United States; and when to this are added the High Sierra redwood forests and the national parks, including Yosemite Park, California is seen also as a land of unique wilderness resources.

California is the nation's leading agricultural producer. Cash receipts of California farmers totaled $4.4 billion in 1968. The state ranks second largest in the nation in manufacturing and is also second largest in commercial fishing.

California began its development as an agricultural state. Yet most of the agricultural lands of California receive less than 15 inches of rainfall per year. Therefore, from Spanish mission days, the development of irrigation has been one of the principal concerns of the state. The total irrigated acreage of California is now 8.5 million acres; projected irrigated acreage for the year 1975 is 9.7 million acres used in agriculture.

In California, normal annual precipitation varies from as high as 58.94 inches in Blue Canyon to as low as 3.14 inches in the Imperial Valley. The total annual runoff of water in California is 70 million acre-feet.[1] This not only far exceeds the present estimated demand of 30 million acre-feet for agricultural and urban water but also comfortably exceeds the projected demand of 50 million acre-feet per year. However, there is a problem. About two-thirds of California's annual runoff originates north of the Sacramento–San Francisco area, whereas two-thirds of the present use occurs south of that region. This is the setting for our study of California water. As *Time* magazine recently observed: "California has everything — usually in the wrong place."

II

The California Water Plan is a master plan for the control, conservation, protection, and distribution of the waters of California, to meet present and future needs for all beneficial uses and purposes in all areas of the State to the maximum feasible extent. It is a comprehensive plan which would reach from border to border both in its constructed works and in its effects. The Plan is a flexible pattern susceptible of orderly development by logical progressive stages, the choice of each successive incremental project to be made with due consideration to the economic and other pertinent factors governing at the particular time.[2]

1. The acre-foot, one of the standard measures of water, is the amount required to cover one acre of land with one foot of water, 43,560 cubic feet, or 325,851 gallons.
2. California Department of Water Resources, *The California Water Plan*, Bulletin No. 3 (Sacramento, 1957), p. 37.

Instead of examining all the multifarious aspects of the California Water Plan in detail, attention will be concentrated in this chapter on the two principal organizational components of the Plan and their major projects: the Central Valley Project of the United States Bureau of Reclamation and the State Water Project of the California Department of Water Resources.

At the very outset, it is necessary to understand one cardinal point: Water resources planning in California has been formulated in terms of the "surplus" of water in the northern part of the state and the "deficiency" of water in the south. Consequently, the problem of water planning in California has reduced to the question of how to transport water from the north to the south. As Michael W. Straus, Commissioner of the U.S. Bureau of Reclamation, said in 1950:

The requirement for this study develops fundamentally from full recognition of the unequal distribution of vital water resources in the Western States and the vast and increasing influx of population into those States with little regard to water supplies available to sustain such populations and their resulting economies and civilizations. In view of the known huge surplus of water washing into the sea to the north and the existing and potential shortage in the Southwest, those inevitable instructions were given to look into the future possibilities of transporting surplus waters to satisfy the Southwest deficiencies . . .[3]

Similarly, an annual report of the California Department of Water Resources in 1968 observed:

California is currently in the midst of constructing an unprecedented water project for one essential reason—the State had no alternative. Nature has not provided the right amount of water in the right places at the right times. Eighty percent of the people in California live in metropolitan areas from Sacramento to the Mexican border; however, 70 percent of the State's water supply originates north of the latitude of San Francisco Bay. Throughout the State, the bulk of rainfall occurs in a few winter months, while the summers, when water needs are greatest, are long and dry.

The solution to California's maldistribution of water resources has been one of conserving the sporadic stream runoff in surface

3. U.S. Bureau of Reclamation, "United Western Investigation: Interim Report on Reconnaissance, California Section," Report UW1-2 (Salt Lake City, January 1951), Introduction, Letter to the Secretary of the Interior, p. 2.

storage reservoirs and transporting the regulated supplies to areas of use. Progressively larger storage works and longer conveyance systems have been required to meet the continuing growth in demands for water . . . [4]

Given this central premise, a certain set of programs inevitably follows. If one wishes to quarrel with the programs, his argument must center on the premise. It is as simple as that.

## III

The United States Bureau of Reclamation's Central Valley Project was designed as an undertaking of the State of California in its initial State Water Plan in 1930. Primarily, it was intended to develop the agricultural potential of the Central Valley. That first Plan was authorized by the California Legislature in 1933, and voters approved issuance of $170 million of state bonds to finance it. However, the situation in financial markets in that Depression year was not optimistic for investors, and the bonds found no takers. The Bureau of Reclamation was then invited to undertake the development of water supply for the Central Valley. According to the Bureau's "capsule" history of of its achievements in the Central Valley for 1930 through 1963:

Investigation and development of irrigation in the Central Valley date back to the 1850's, when private parties first constructed canals to serve local areas near the rivers. Efforts to develop a comprehensive plan for the Valley date back to 1873, when a Board of Commissioners prepared a report on irrigation in the San Joaquin, Tulare, and Sacramento Valleys.

The initial units of the overall plan for water development within the basin were first defined in a report issued by the State in 1930 and entitled "State Water Plan." This plan envisaged the transfer of an overabundant water supply from the northern part of the Sacramento Valley to the southern part of the San Joaquin Valley, where a deficiency existed. The units proposed as the first phase toward the solution of this problem included Shasta Dam, Delta Cross Channel, Delta-Mendota Canal, Friant Dam, Madera Canal, Friant-Kern Canal, Contra Costa Canal, and a power transmission system.

4. California Department of Water Resources, *The California State Water Project in 1968, Appendix C: Description and Status,* Bulletin 132-68 (Sacramento, 1968), p. 3.

The initial units proposed in the State report are essentially those authorized for construction under Reclamation law by the Congress in 1937 and since built by the Bureau of Reclamation. In addition to the units mentioned above, Keswick Dam was authorized and built to regulate the fluctuating power releases from Shasta Dam and add to the power capacity of the project. In 1949 Congress authorized the construction and operation of the American River Division, including Folsom Dam and Power plant, Nimbus Dam and Powerplant, and the Sly Park Unit as part of the Central Valley Project. In 1950, the Sacramento Valley Canals were authorized, including the Corning Canal, Red Bluff Diversion Dam, and the Tehama-Colusa Canal. The Corning Canal is now operating and the Red Bluff Diversion Dam is under construction. The Trinity River Division, authorized in 1955, was scheduled for completion in 1963. The latest authorized addition (1960) is the San Luis Unit. This unit, a joint Federal-State venture, consists of the San Luis Dam and Forebay Dam, 123 miles of canal, a pumping-generating plant, and three pumping plants. This unit is under construction. All features of the project have been integrated into a unified operations system.[5]

All these units have now been completed except the Tehama-Colusa Canal, a long-term project designed to transport Sacramento River water down the west side of the Sacramento Valley from the vicinity of Red Bluff. Work is progressing on this unit, which is meant to continue south as the West Sacramento Canal Unit, the subject of continuing investigation.

5. U.S. Bureau of Reclamation, "Central Valley Project, California," 1963.

No history of the California Water Plan is complete without mention of the 1963 Pacific Southwest Water Plan with which the then Secretary of the Interior, Stewart Udall, was closely associated. It proposed, *inter alia,* further water development on the Colorado River in the form of Bridge Canyon and Marble Canyon dams and a water-salvage operation along the mainstream of the Colorado; this was to be in association with a major transfer of northwestern California water (Trinity and Eel rivers) through enlarged State Water Project facilities to Lake Havasu (behind Parker Dam) on the Colorado River. It sought to provide the people of the entire southwest with a water development plan that "transcended" state and water-basin boundaries.

Because partial "drowning" of the Grand Canyon would have followed building of the two dam structures, a storm of protest from throughout the nation greeted the plan. The cries were particularly loud in California where conservationists were being affronted by an issue both intra- and extrastate. The proposal to export California water to the Colorado River was especially anathematic coming, as it did, to the water industry so soon after the "unfavorable" United States Supreme Court adjudications of Colorado River water rights. To all intents and purposes, the original formulation of the Pacific Southwest Water Plan is now moribund.

For the eastern side of the Central Valley, a large water storage and conveyance system is in prospect. It encompasses two parts: the Auburn-Folsom South Unit of the American River Division, and the East Side Division. The major features of the first, now under construction, are the Auburn Dam and Reservoir on the North Fork American River and the Folsom South Canal to run southward and link with the East Side Division. This Division is designed to provide supplemental water service to some 3 million acres along the east side of the San Joaquin Valley as far south as the Tehachapi Mountains. When completed, these facilities would deliver some 1.5 million acre-feet of water annually.

There are other expansion proposals. The Tuscan Buttes Project would store large amounts of Sacramento River water pumped from the stream during flood periods. The Kellogg Unit would divert additional water from the Delta to the Contra Costa Canal. At present under construction are the Pleasant Valley Canal, leading off the California Aqueduct, and the San Luis Drain, both on the west side of the San Joaquin Valley. The Drain will run from near Kettleman City northward to the Delta and will provide drainage service for "federal" lands newly irrigated with "San Luis" water.

The joint-use facilities of the San Luis Unit will substantially increase water deliveries by the Central Valley Project over the ensuing years. In 1969 total deliveries of the project exceeded 4.9 million acre-feet. Of this total, the Bureau of Reclamation reported, some 4.7 million acre-feet were for agricultural use and the remainder for municipal and industrial use and for waterfowl conservation.[6]

IV

The activities of the United States Bureau of Reclamation in California were not universally applauded; indeed, considerable friction developed between the Bureau and various Californians over the course of time.[7] In 1944 the State Legislature approved a move to

6. U.S. Bureau of Reclamation, "Central Valley Project: 1969 Annual Report" (Sacramento, 1970), p. 11. Of the total deliveries of 4.9 million acre-feet, 2.5 million was classified as "water sold" and 2.4 million as "water rights" deliveries.

7. Erwin Cooper, *Aqueduct Empire* (Glendale, Calif.: The Arthur H. Clark Co., 1968), p. 159.

reestablish the state's interest in the Central Valley by buying out the federal government's equity in the Project. The Federal government discouraged the idea.[8]

In 1945 the State Water Resources Act was passed, creating the State Water Resources Board. First under the leadership of State Engineer Edward Hyatt and then of A. D. Edmonston, the state investigated the feasibility of diverting water from the Feather River to the south in state-owned, state-operated facilities.

In 1951 a very important element entered the California water picture with the publication of the Bureau of Reclamation's "United Western Investigation: California Section," referred to earlier. This study contemplated diversion of over 6 million acre-feet of water per year from the Klamath River in northern California, conveying it through an elaborate aqueduct system "to irrigators, industries, and municipalities in the Central Valley of California, and the central- and south-coastal areas of that State."[9] Of this amount, only 286,000 acre-feet of water was intended for municipal use; the remainder was to be allocated for "irrigation and other uses." Further, it proposed diversion of 1.2 million acre-feet to the Colorado River Basin for unspecified purposes. Water conveyed by the Los Angeles Aqueduct from the Owens Valley was to be allocated to the Mojave Desert region. Finally, the flow of the American River to California was to be partially diverted to Nevada. The investigation, naturally, sparked a good deal of agitation among water planners in California.

In 1951 the idea of purchasing the Central Valley Project from the federal government was reexamined, and in 1952 the state made an offer and was refused.

The Feather River study made in 1951 envisaged a diversion of some 4 million acre-feet of water from the Sacramento Delta south-

8. At the time, Secretary of the Interior Harold L. Ickes commented: "It is the age-old battle over who is to cash in on the unearned increment in land values created by a public investment. . . . their principal objective is to avoid application to the Central Valley of California of the long-established reclamation policy of the Congress which provides for the distribution of the benefits of great irrigation projects among the many and which prevents speculation in lands by the few." The policy to which Ickes alluded is, of course, the provision that irrigation water developed by the United States Bureau of Reclamation can only be used on 160 acres or less (320 acres in the case of joint proprietorship of a man and his wife).

9. U.S. Bureau of Reclamation, "United Western Investigation," *op. cit.,* p. viii.

ward. Because the sources feeding the Delta were to be regulated through a large dam on the Feather River in the vicinity of the town of Oroville, the study was called the Feather River Project. Many of the features of the Feather River Project matched those of the Bureau of Reclamation's "Investigation." Of course, a basic difference lay in the sources of water contemplated: the federal report focused on diversions from the Klamath River; the state's, from the Feather River. Also, there were no provisions in the study for water exports to Nevada (or implications of diversion to Mexico); neither was it envisaged that northern water should substitute for water received in the south from the Colorado River, nor was it intended that Owens Valley water should be exchanged and diverted to the Mojave region. The Feather River Project was approved by the California State Legislature in 1951.

After further intensive study and detailed programming to make it specific enough for budgeting, the Project was resubmitted in 1955 to the State Legislature, which voted for an independent review by the Bechtel Corporation, an engineering consulting firm. This review, completed by the end of the same year, was generally favorable.[10] When the "preliminary edition" of the over-all California Water Plan appeared in May 1956, the Feather River Project was designated explicitly as its initial unit:

> Financing and construction of the authorized Feather River Project, the initial unit of the California Water Plan, should be expedited to permit its early completion and operation in order that urgently needed flood protection will be provided, and in order that supplemental water supplies can be made available to areas of dangerous water deficiency in the San Joaquin Valley, in the vicinity of San Francisco Bay, and in southern California.[11]

In the late 1940's and early 1950's it was beginning to be felt "that a greater measure of State leadership and participation in planning and construction is required if the water resources of California are to be properly controlled and utilized to meet rapidly increasing needs of the people."[12] This attitude grew during the first half-decade

10. Cooper, *op. cit.*, p. 204.
11. California State Water Resources Board, *Report on the California Water Plan,* Bulletin No. 3, Vol. III (Sacramento, 1956), pp. 14–7.
12. *Ibid., Water Resources of California,* Bulletin No. 1 (Sacramento, 1951), p. 22.

and culminated on July 5, 1956, in the establishment by the State Legislature of the Department of Water Resources, as successor to the State Water Resources Board.

In May 1957, the Department published "The California Water Plan" as Bulletin No. 3 in the series that had begun after the founding of the State Water Resources Board some dozen years before. This plan essentially represented a resolution of the needs perspective of Bulletin No. 2 (1955) by looking back to the supply potential and other inventory data of Bulletin No. 1 (1951). Though the question of transporting water from the extreme north to the extreme south along the "surplus-deficit" axis of the state was thoroughly examined and articulated, the plan was not a strict timetable for construction or a rigid program of future development. Rather, it served to define various physiographic-hydrologic units and to specify how they might be incorporated into or related to projects constituting parts of an integrated water system that would best serve the long-term needs of the state.

During 1957-1958, further intensive engineering investigations proceeded, essentially along the lines of selecting among alternatives within the framework of the original Feather River Project concept of transporting surplus water southward from the Delta. Decisions were made on rough "size" and "location," but not on fundamental objectives and the broad strategy for achieving them. Bulletin No. 78, of February 1959, reported the final determination: a main aqueduct would take water from the south of the Delta down the west side of the San Joaquin Valley and across the Tehachapi Mountains. Here the aqueduct would fork, a west branch terminating south of the San Fernando Valley and an east branch crossing the Antelope and Mojave Plateaus, piercing the San Bernardino Mountains, and ending in a reservoir near the city of Riverside. From the terminal near Riverside, connections to the Coachella Valley and existing Colorado River aqueduct distribution systems would be made. Coastal areas in the vicinity of Santa Barbara would be served by a branch leaving the main aqueduct from near the boundary between Kings and Kern counties. When fully operational, the project would transport over 8 million acre-feet of water annually, of which over 5 million would be delivered to the Coastal Branch and facilities further south. It was estimated that the project would cost $1.9 billion, exclusive of any part of the Oroville Dam and San Luis Reservoir complexes, the Delta "crossing" (Peripheral Canal), and the North Bay and South Bay Aqueducts. With the state's share of these facilities added to the basic cost, the total estimated requirement for the State Water Project increased to some $2.5 billion.

By the close of the 1959 session, the Legislature had authorized, by the Burns-Porter Act, the issue of $1.75 billion in general obligation bonds to provide the main financial base of the Project. This amount was, of course, considerably less than the original $2.5 billion contemplated, but it was felt that this was the most that could be feasibly offered at the time. The bond issue was approved by the voters in the election of November 8, 1960, by a vote of 3,008, 328 for and 2,814,384 against. Thus began the State Water Project.

In the words of the Department of Water Resources:

The State Water Project is an amazing venture. It is the first statewide water resources development in the United States, and is the largest single water development in the world to be financed at one time. It is the first water project which will construct four reservoirs having recreation as their primary purpose. The Project contains the highest dam in the United States. Oroville Dam will tower 770 feet above its foundation when completed late this year. The Project will have the largest underground powerplant in the nation—the Oroville Powerplant—which, in conjunction with its companion powerplant downstream at Thermalito, will produce power enough for a city of one million people. The Project's largest pumping plant will lift more water higher than any other in existence, raising 110 million gallons an hour in a single lift up the Tehachapi Mountains.[13]

The following facilities now are part of the State Water Project:
a. The dams and reservoirs on the upper tributaries of the Feather River at the Frenchman, Antelope Valley, Grizzly Valley, Abbey Bridge, and Dixie Refuge sites.
b. The Oroville Dam and Reservoir.
c. The North Bay Aqueduct.
d. The South Bay Aqueduct.
e. The California Aqueduct.

13. California Department of Water Resources, *The California State Water Project in 1967, Appendix C: Description and Status,* Bulletin 132–67 (Sacramento, 1967), p. 287.

f. The San Luis Dam and Reservoir.

g. The Coastal Aqueduct.

h. Works in the Delta.

i. Drainage facilities in the San Joaquin Valley.

j. Water development facilities for local areas provided for under the Davis-Grunsky Act.

k. Additional facilities to meet local needs and to augment supplies in the Delta.

l. Electric power facilities.[14]

In recent years (a) has come to be known as the Upper Feather Division and (e) through (g) are grouped and known collectively as the California Aqueduct. A main line of the latter comprising six sections or divisions is distinguished from the branches (West Branch and Coastal Branch).[15] "Works in the Delta" (h) is mainly the Peripheral Canal.

These facilities accord approximately with the "State Water Facilities," which constitute a portion (the first stage) of the State Water Resources Development System. Both names derive from the California Water Code, Section 12934(d), which describes the State Water Facilities as comprising the equivalent of the listed items (a) through (l), except (k). Three main divisions of the State Water Facilities are recognized in the Water Code. The first is a dam and reservoir system on the Feather River, (a) and (b) combined. The second is an aqueduct system "which will provide for the transportation of water from a point or points at or near the Sacramento-San Joaquin Delta . . .," i.e. (c) through (g). The third is a system to transfer water across the Delta for flood and salinity control there and for related functions (h).

Additional to the main objective of supplying irrigation and municipal water, State Water Project facilities provide flood control and recreation benefits, and generate power. These facilities are also important in regulating stream flows down the Lower Feather and Sac-

14. *Idem, The California State Water Project in 1963*, Bulletin 132-63 (Sacramento, 1963), p. 1.

15. The mainline sections are North San Joaquin Division, San Luis Division, South San Joaquin Division, Tehachapi Division, Mojave Division, and Santa Ana Division. Sometimes the Mojave and Santa Ana Divisions are combined and called the East Branch.

ramento rivers into the Delta. As the Department of Water Resources observes:

> The gentle, nearly sea-level terrain of the Delta forms a natural pool of fresh water through which all excess water in the Central Valley drains prior to wasting to the ocean. The State Water Project diverts a portion of this excess water. Eventually, increasing water use in the Sacramento Valley will so deplete the natural drainage to the Delta that the Middle Fork Eel River Development will have to be added to the Project. This development will supplement Delta flows with Eel River water which would otherwise waste to the ocean.
>
> Water withdrawn from the Delta will be conveyed to areas of need by a system of project aqueducts totaling almost 700 miles in length.
>
> The Peripheral Canal will facilitate the transfer of water across the Delta, will improve water quality in the interior channels of the Delta, and will enhance recreation in the area.[16]

The State Water Project is designed to deliver, by about the year 1990, 4.23 million acre-feet of water annually for agricultural, municipal, and industrial use. When this level of delivery is reached, the Project will be in full operation.

The water will be delivered to thirty-one agencies throughout the state under long-term contracts which specify the annual entitlements. The sum of these entitlements in about 1990 will amount to the "full operation" level of 4.23 million acre-feet, the total for which the Project is designed.

The contracting agency with by far the largest maximum annual entitlement is the Metropolitan Water District of Southern California — over 2 million acre-feet, considerably more than the next contractor, the Kern County Water Agency with 1.15 million acre-feet. The "adverse" adjudication of Colorado River water rights by the United States Supreme Court in 1963 resulted in the Metropolitan Water District renegotiating its contract from a previous level of 1.5 million acre-feet.

According to the Department of Water Resources:

> About 59 percent of the project water (2,497,500 acre-feet annual maximum) will be delivered south of the Tehachapi Mountains in

16. California Department of Water Resources, *The California State Water Project in 1969, Appendix C: Description and Status,* Bulletin 132-69 (Sacramento, 1969), p. 2.

Southern California. This is enough water to satisfy the needs of about 12 million people.

About 32 percent of the project water (1,355,000 acre-feet annual maximum) will be supplied to the San Joaquin Valley — one of the major agricultural regions of the nation. This is enough water to irrigate the equivalent of 600 square miles of land in the Valley.

About 4½ percent of the project water will be delivered to users South of San Francisco Bay for a combination of agricultural, municipal, and industrial uses.

The remaining 4½ percent of the project water will be delivered for municipal and industrial use north of San Francisco Bay, in the Central Coastal area, and in areas near the Feather River.[17]

Apart from benefits represented by water deliveries, the State Water Project will exercise a flood-control function and create new recreation opportunities (but, of course, destroy others). As to the former, the Lower Feather River flood plain is now protected by the Oroville and Upper Feather Division facilities; and the flood plain of Alameda Creek by a dam that is part of the South Bay Aqueduct. In addition, salt-water intrusion into the Delta Region has been turned back through releases from Oroville Dam.

The Project will generate an estimated annual total (state share) of 5.35 billion kilowatt-hours of electricity, well short of the state share of the estimated annual energy requirements for pumping of 13.88 billion kilowatt-hours. That part of power generated in "recovery plants" (on the California Aqueduct) that is state-owned will be used directly and entirely for pumping water on the Tehachapi Division.

The main source of finance for the State Water Project has been general obligation bonds, of which some $1.1 billion have been sold. As noted above, this method of financing was made possible by passage through the 1959 Legislature of the California Water Resources Development Bond Act, popularly known as the Burns-Porter Act.

Apart from funding through the sale of general obligation bonds, the 1959 Legislature created the California Water Fund. The Fund initially received some $200 million in accrued state Long Beach oil revenues transferred from the then existing Investment Fund. It has since received specified portions of state tideland oil and gas revenues.

17. *Ibid.*, p. 3.

These royalties have been an increasing source of Project finances.[18]

In addition, the operating costs of recreation and fish and wildlife enhancement are paid out of the state's General Fund. The federal government pays Project costs allocated to flood control. For example, the federal government is paying a share of the capital costs of Oroville and Del Valle dams as part of its flood control program. It is also meeting part of the cost of San Luis Division and Peripheral Canal facilities, which will be jointly used by the state and the U.S. Bureau of Reclamation.

The 1969 estimate of capital expenditure for the Project through 1985 was some $2.8 billion.[19] This figure allows about $163 million for Middle Fork Eel River development (of which Dos Rios is a part) and $8 million for San Joaquin drainage facilities. It excludes both assumed payments to the Corps of Engineers for Dos Rios storage after 1985 and post-1968 costs of the San Joaquin drainage facilities. The total is comparable with the estimate made by a special survey committee appointed in 1967 by Governor Reagan shortly after he took office. In March 1970, Deputy Director Teerink of the Department of Water Resources stated that over $1.66 billion had been spent on construction of the State Water Project. He further stated:

> Oroville Dam and Reservoir . . . is built and operational. . . .
> Almost 350 miles of the aqueduct system have been constructed in
> the San Joaquin Valley and San Francisco Bay Area. Water deliveries are presently being made in Stanislaus, Kings, Tulare, and
> Kern Counties in the San Joaquin Valley and to Alameda, Santa
> Clara, and Napa Counties in the San Francisco Bay Area, and
> Plumas County in the Upper Feather River Area. Construction over
> the Tehachapi Mountains through the Antelope Valley in Southern
> California is advancing with delivery to commence in 1971.[20]

18. For example, the 1968 Legislature provided for the appropriation of $14 million annually of these revenues, commencing in the 1970–1971 fiscal year, for continuing additional funds for the Project. In addition, the capital cost of recreation and fish and wildlife enhancement is being reimbursed at the rate of $5 million annually from oil and gas royalties. Likewise, these tideland revenues are now the source of the grants disbursed under the Davis-Grunsky Program, which is designed to provide financial assistance for the construction of water development facilities for local areas.

19. California Department of Water Resources, *The California State Water Project in 1969, op. cit.*, p. 6.

20. John R. Teerink, "The California Water Plan as It Relates to Water Resources Management," Paper presented to the Subcommittee on Science, Research, and Development of the House [of Representatives] Committee on Science and Astronautics, San Francisco, California, March 17, 1970, p. 1.

In 1969 and the first part of 1970, the state faced a serious financial obstacle to completing the State Water Project. Because of a legal provision, California was unable to promise more than 5 per cent interest when incurring indebtedness. In the "tight money" market, the going interest rate on bonds was substantially above this. Consequently, the state was unable to sell some $650 million of authorized water bonds for financing the project. In June 1970, the voters of the state passed, by a narrow margin, "Proposition 7" which enabled California to raise its legal borrowing rate to 7 per cent — even more with legislative approval. With this enabling action, the principal features of the State Water Project are financially assured of completion.

## V

The Delta Pool is the heart of the two major projects in the California Water Plan. It is from the Pool that all diversions stem, and it is into the Pool that new supplies are planned to flow. For this reason, the following chart, compiled by the Department of Water Resources, provides a fitting summary of our discussion of the California Water Plan. The chart is self-explanatory; in it lies, essentially, the future of the Plan as envisaged by its proponents. Two things should be noted: the increasing proportion of the Delta supply that will be used by the Central Valley Project, and the parity between the North Coast imports and the Delta outflow in the year 2020, so that if there is no North Coast development Delta outflow into San Francisco Bay will be practically nonexistent.

## VI

The California Water Plan has encountered a heavy barrage of criticism from its beginning in the 1930's to the present day. Rather than attempt to cover in detail all the critical points of view, we concentrate here on some of the major engineering, economic, and environmental criticisms of the State Water Project. As we shall see, this body of criticism is sufficiently extensive to occupy to the full the brief space allotted here; it is also representative of the broad grounds of criticism leveled against such other constituents of the Plan as the Central Valley Project.

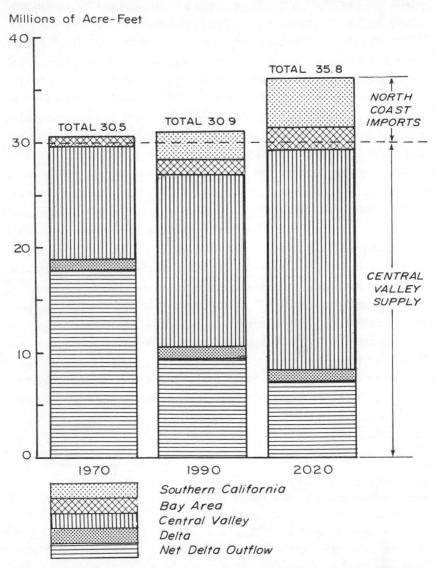

FIGURE 1.1. Utilization of Central Valley Water Supply (average water year—1935–1936). SOURCE: John R. Teerink, Deputy Director, California Department of Water Resources, "The California Water Plan as It Relates to Water Resources Management," Paper presented to Subcommittee on Science, Research, and Development of the House Committee on Science and Astronautics, San Francisco, California, March 17, 1970 (Washington: U.S. Government Printing Office, 1970), p. 673.

The criticisms fall into two broad and often overlapping categories: (1) the State Water Project is economically and financially unsound, and (2) it will severely damage the environment of California.

Economic and financial criticism began with the early work of Paul S. Taylor and an article in 1957 by James C. DeHaven and Jack Hirshleifer.[21] In 1958 occurred an important event in the history of the criticism, the appointment of a board of consulting engineers to review the aqueduct systems of the Feather River Project. All members but one agreed to a favorable report, the lone dissenter being Adolph Ackerman, the only non-Californian on the review board. His minority report anticipated most of the criticisms that have been leveled against the State Water Project since that time. In 1960 Hirschleifer, DeHaven, and Milliman published the book *Water Supply,* and in 1966 Joe S. Bain, Richard Caves, and Julius Margolis published the book *Northern California's Water Industry.* Both books were critical of the Project. In 1968 Gardner Brown wrote an article praising certain features of the State Water Project and condemning others. There have been, of course, many other critics, but those mentioned here are a fair sample of the major body of criticism.

The economic-financial arguments may be conveniently grouped into four basic categories:

*Supply and demand.* The idea of southern "deficiencies" and northern "surpluses" has been exaggerated. Thus, Bain *et al.* called population projections for California and the south "sometimes incredible."[22] Hirshleifer *et al.* said:

Forecasts of population growth are almost in every case called upon by "practical" planners to justify large water-supply projects in excess of currently visible needs. The most crucial point to appreciate in reference to population predictions is that there is no such thing as a "scientific" forecast. . . . all techniques currently in use represent crude extrapolations of existing trends, and the startling unreliability of such projections in the past should make us wary of placing excessive reliance upon them now. By "excessive reliance"

21. James C. DeHaven and Jack Hirshleifer, "Feather River Water for Southern California," *Land Economics,* Vol. XXXIII, No. 3, August 1957, pp. 198–209.
22. Joe S. Bain, Richard E. Caves, and Julius Margolis, *Northern California's Water Industry: The Comparative Efficiency of Public Enterprise in Developing a Scarce Natural Resource* (Baltimore: The Johns Hopkins Press, 1966), p. 562.

we mean commitments to expensive building programs designed to meet needs supposed to arise in the relatively far-off future, and we certainly would consider anything beyond twenty years as "far off."[23]

Many economists are of the opinion that various institutional obstacles are interposed between the supply of and the demand for water. For example, prices cannot respond to relative scarcities and preferences. Large misallocations of water between users result, and users are encouraged by artificially low prices to consume far more than they would were prices to reflect true values. Thus, Hirshleifer *et al.* remark: "No matter how conclusively refuted by observed sensitivity to prices (e.g., the all-too-common experience of inability to sell high-priced water) the belief that the demands are absolutely inelastic continues to dominate all planning in this field."[24]

Not surprisingly, there is confirmation of this in Hirshleifer *et al.*: ". . . rationalization of use would not only reduce agricultural acreage but would undoubtedly involve a reduction in industrial and residential consumption as well, as the rising cost of water served as an incentive to curb excessive low-valued water uses."[25] Again, "Urban water use is depicted as rising from 1,500,000 acre-feet in 1960 to 5,300,000 acre-feet in 2020 — with per-capita use rising from 160 gallons a day in 1960 to 210 gallons a day in 2020, in the face of rising water costs. All this would seem to call for a careful discussion of the crucial economic assumptions involved."[26]

Finally, Bain *et al.*, remarking upon the beneficial use of water in the north for local agricultural and municipal uses, and for recreation and the like, conclude: "It appears in general . . . that by the early 1960's the water resources of Northern California had reached the ceiling of full usage. That is, water from all sources was economically

23. Jack Hirshleifer, James C. DeHaven, and Jerome W. Milliman, *Water Supply: Economics, Technology, and Policy,* 2d ed. (Chicago: The University of Chicago Press, 1969), p. 310.

24. Jack Hirshleifer and Jerome W. Milliman, "Urban Water Supply—A Second Look," Paper presented at the annual meeting of the American Economic Association, San Francisco, December 1966. (Reproduced by the Rand Corporation, Santa Monica, California.)

25. Hirshleifer, DeHaven, and Milliman, *op. cit.,* p. 311.

26. *Ibid.,* p. 315.

a scarce good, and water-facilities development at, within, and beyond the present margin tended mainly to reallocate scarce water supplies among types, places, and times of use."[27]

*Evaluation.* Evaluation procedures too come under criticism. DeHaven and Hirshleifer criticized the original Feather River Project on the ground that the 2.7 per cent discount rate used in its evaluation was too low. Rather, they suggested a figure of between 5 and 8 per cent. They also indicated certain "advantages" of this project which would make it appear very favorable vis-à-vis a comparable investment in the private sector. These were hidden subsidies arising from federal income tax advantages of the state bonds, use of general state credit rather than revenue bonds, and the exemption of state properties from all local and federal taxes.[28] Assuming a 5 per cent rate of interest and average incremental costs for southern California, these critics estimated the state subsidy to be of the order of $27.89 per acre-foot in the form of transfer of risk from beneficiaries to the public at large.[29]

Brown, however, later pointed out that at least compared to U.S. Bureau of Reclamation projects the State Water Project carried fairly low subsidies. He also noted that the actual discount rate used in the evaluation of the State Water Project was 4 per cent, a figure he did not consider entirely unreasonable.[30]

Ackerman said:

Financing of the Project has been proposed by issuing general obligation bonds, with "the full faith and credit of the State of California pledged for the punctual payment of both principal and interest thereof." An examination of the proposal calls for a review of recent reports by Legislative Committees which contain such warnings as: "The existing rate of increase in the State's general obligation bond indebtedness is presently reaching problem proportions even without any bonds for water projects," and "It thus can be seen that the financial position of the State is not encouraging," and "In recapitu-

27. Bain, Caves, and Margolis, *op. cit.,* p. 573.
28. *Op. cit.,* p. 203.
29. *Op. cit.,* p. 206.
30. Gardner Brown, "The California Water Project: Is Public Decision Making Becoming More Efficient?" *Water Resources Research,* Vol. 4, No. 3 (June 1968).

lation, California in the 1959-60 Fiscal Year finds itself on the brink of one of its most serious financial crises."[31]

He also observed:

At this stage no adequate demonstration is available to show the "financial feasibility" of the project as now proposed. The adoption of a project under these circumstances would contribute to damaging the state's credit position for many years to come. In my opinion any inference, that the current proposal has been developed to a stage where the public can repose full confidence in it, is wholly unwarranted.[32]

Many critics questioned the neglect of cost increases that were almost certain to occur either because of underestimation or inflation.

Finally, Bain *et al.* computed that

It [the Feather River Project] promises approximately to pay for itself only if operated at least until about 2039 and only if capital investment is asked to bear an interest charge not appreciably in excess of 4 per cent. With higher interest charges (or a shorter life) it would definitely be a loser; for example, with a time horizon of eighty years and interest charge of 5 per cent the present value of its net deficit would be about $339 million. Four per cent is appreciably lower than the going marginal borrowing rate on private funds.[33]

We note that 4 per cent is also appreciably lower than the 7 per cent now proposed.

*Alternatives.* It is said that both the present and future alternatives to the State Water Project have been ignored. Hirshleifer *et al.* observed:

Summing up, then, we find that the Feather River Project is a very expensive source of water for the South Coastal Area. . . . the Feather source is much more expensive than a number of alternatives. Reduction in local evaporation, a small amount of additional local entrapment, reclamation of sewage, . . . additional Owens water, and purchase and transport of a fraction of other areas' Colorado River allocations (primarily Imperial Valley) all appear definitely cheaper. . . . economic considerations indicate that the

31. Adolph J. Ackerman, "Feather River-Southern California Aqueduct," Madison, Wisconsin, 1959, p. 9.
32. *Ibid.,* p. 4.
33. Bain, Caves, and Margolis, *op. cit.,* p. 570. Brackets supplied.

marginal values in use of water in the South Coastal Area does not currently justify jumping to such an enormously expensive new source [Feather River Project].[34]

Because of these present alternatives and future technological developments, many recommended postponing the State Water Project. Brown pointed out future technological possibilities in these words: "If by the late 1950's competitive, inexpensive (20 cents per one thousand gallons) desalinated water did not seem imminent, surely the State's nuclear engineering staff was aware of the sharp exponential decline in the cost of desalination. Between 1953 and 1961 costs had dropped from $5 to $1 per thousand gallons."[35]

DeHaven and Hirshleifer observed: ". . . there is the possibility of important changes in technology before 1976. The conclusion seems inescapable, therefore, that Southern California interests should not bind themselves to take project output starting 1976. They should request that all project components incremental to Southern California be indefinitely postponed until an economic demand develops."[36]

Bain *et al.* said:

A possibly feasible alternative would have been postponement of some version of the present FRP by two or three decades. . . . it would be more economical first to exploit less costly alternatives. It would also be more prudent, because several decades from now changes in technologies and developments in population patterns not presently anticipated may indicate the desirability of different solutions to any problem of water deficiency in the Southern part of California. The unseemly haste which has marked the early undertaking of the Feather River Project can probably be attributed more to the desire of Southern California interests to secure rights to Northern California water while they are still available than to any misapprehension on their part concerning the fact that the Project is being undertaken prematurely from an economic standpoint.[37]

Ackerman advocated step-by-step incremental planning consistent with the development of demand for water:

Instead of determining the most economical and financially feasible

34. Hirshleifer, DeHaven, and Milliman, *op. cit.,* pp. 350–351.
35. Brown, *op. cit.,* p. 468.
36. *Op. cit.,* p. 206.
37. Bain, Caves, and Margolis, *op. cit.,* pp. 571–572.

"first stage" which would meet the demands for water in the foreseeable future, with provisions for expansion as and when justified by future circumstances, the concept of "global" or "total planning" of a project to meet demands in the year 2020 has been introduced. I do not consider it feasible to make a sound appraisal of a project concept based on conditions which are presumed to materialize more than half a century from now.[38]

Finally, it was also recommended that the project be scaled down in size:

. . . it cannot be argued that the FRP is an indivisible unit, with no features which could economically be left out or scaled down. All features of the Project except Oroville Dam, the Delta Pumping Plant and the main Aqueduct as extended only by its West Branch to Los Angeles clearly could be eliminated.

. . . the FRP is generally oversized or includes large uneconomical segments, or both.

. . . An economically much more feasible or justifiable project would delete entirely the Eel River dams and transmission facilities, the North Bay Aqueduct, and the East Branch Aqueduct serving the Mojave Desert and the Palm Springs-Coachella Valley area. And the Central Coastal Aqueduct would be a clearly marginal inclusion.[39]

*Capital gains.* Many critics have voiced concern over the capital gains that will accrue to large landowners because of the State Water Project. These objections are based on two considerations: first, a public project that subsidizes the wealthy is bad in itself; and second, the U.S. Bureau of Reclamation, it is contended, would have undertaken at least the agricultural segment of the State Water Project had the state not done so. Thus, California has given up valuable federal subsidies by choosing to go it alone in order, they say, to escape the 160-acre limitation clause.

Three critics closely associated with this point of view are Paul C. Taylor, an economist at the University of California, Berkeley; Erwin Cooper, an ex-Department of Water Resources employee; and George Ballis, an associate of the Public Affairs Institute, Washington, D.C.

Taylor says of those interests in the Central Valley aligned against the 160-acre limitation that they wish to provide "water for the landed,

38. *Op. cit.,* p. 8.
39. Bain, Caves, and Margolis, *op. cit.,* pp. 570–571.

THE CALIFORNIA WATER PLAN

the more land the more water, opening the purses of taxpayers and power consumers to furnish it."[40]

Cooper regards the motivation behind the State Water Project thus:

The idea of moving the Feather River out of its own watershed began as the brainchild of the big San Joaquin Valley land powers: the corporate farms, land management firms, railroads with huge acreages. Bloodless, efficient organizations, they were geared to compounding dollars for their owners and stockholders. Their future lay in irrigated farming. The men who controlled them along with much else in California, were unanimously dedicated to the proposition that the only way to beat the Bureau of Reclamation's 160-acre limitation on water for farmers was to have the state, rather than the federal government, operate a water distribution system. In this way their lands would escape fragmentation by the acreage auctioneer.[41]

Ballis estimated that approximately 30 per cent of the agricultural land in the southern and western portions of the San Joaquin Valley in the vicinity of the State Water Project is owned by only six large corporations. For example, he figures Kern County Land Company holds 348, 026 acres (8.7 per cent of the total), and Standard Oil, 218,485 acres (5.5 per cent). About two-thirds of all this land, he says, is in farms exceeding 1,000 acres.[42]

The economist Kenneth Boulding summed it well:

> All benefits that are dispersable
> Should be, perhaps, non-reimbursible
> But people should be made to pay
> For benefits that come their way—
> Unless we want to subsidize
> The good, the needy, or the wise.
> (It would be well to be quite sure
> Just who *are* the deserving poor,
> Or else the state-supported ditch
> May serve the Undeserving Rich).[43]

40. Paul S. Taylor, "The Excess Land Law: Legislative Erosion of Public Policy," *Rocky Mountain Law Review*, Vol. 30, No. 4 (June 1958), p. 37.

41. Cooper, *op. cit.*, p. 201.

42. George Ballis, "The California Water Plan—An Evaluation" (Washington, D.C.: Public Affairs Institute, 1960), p. 32.

43. Kenneth Boulding, "The Feather River Anthology or 'Holy Water'" (unpublished).

The environmental critics of the State Water Project include, prominent among others, the Sierra Club. The Sierra Club has been joined by many other organizations—the Planning and Conservation League, for example, the Committee of Two Million (a fisherman's organization)—and by a number of individuals, such as Alvin Duskin and Frank M. Stead. Briefly, because the specific ecological problems are too complex to treat at all adequately here, and because some of the problems are treated in detail elsewhere in this book, we shall attempt simply to indicate some of the outstanding features of controversy.

1) The feeling exists that Los Angeles has already grown beyond supportable dimensions; and either further growth should not be encouraged by State Water Project water, or it should be curbed by withholding water, or—most often—both.

2) The impact of the Project on the Delta and San Francisco Bay is not known, but it is most likely dangerous. It could lead to loss of the fishing resource and the wildlife marshes in the Delta, and to chemical changes of the waters of the Bay-Delta leading to disturbance of the biological balance (with consequent growth of algae and oxygen reversal).

3) With continued withdrawals of water from the Delta, additional sources of water will have to be found. This means that the dam builders will turn their attention to the rivers of the north coastal area, specifically the Eel, the Klamath, and the Trinity. These rivers and their valleys constitute one of the last refuges of nature in California. In addition to destroying the region's natural amenities and its economic base in the recreational use of its resources, these dams will destroy the periodic flushing action of floods through the river systems. The deep pools in the rivers will thus silt full, destroying breeding grounds and therefore the valuable fishery resources of the area. Weeds and brush will encroach onto the banks of the rivers, supplying a base for further silt accumulation and destroying the accessibility and beauty of the rivers. Because the silt will accumulate in the river beds and reservoirs, the ocean beaches will lose their source of replenishment and decay back into the sea. These effects are already observable from existing water "development" projects in the region; further development will generate an ecological disaster.

## VII

The future of the California Water Project is unclear. However, two factors are sufficiently established to permit the statement to be made with some assurance that things will not be entirely as they have been. First, developing concern over the environment will almost certainly influence decisions about water development to a far greater extent than in the past. Second, the accelerating pace of technological change has provided a spectrum of alternatives hardly imagined at the time the basic features of the Project were taking shape in the 1940's and 1950's.

Among the more outstanding technological horizons in the future are waste-water reclamation, nuclear desalination, the exploitation of newly discovered thermal water resources in the south, and ground-water utilization. Both the state's Department of Water Resources and the federal Bureau of Reclamation have played active roles in developing these technologies. For example, means have been discovered for eliminating nitrates and other nutrients from agricultural and urban waste waters. The Department of Water Resources has operated an experimental desalting plant at Point Lobos for several years and plans to build a large 50-million-gallon-per-day nuclear prototype in the near future. The U.S. Bureau of Reclamation is designing development projects based on irrigation by sprinkler rather than by furrow, which is expected to improve substantially the efficiency of water use in agriculture. Finally, staff members of the Department of Water Resources have conducted massive exploration and research in the area of ground water utilization and have become acknowledged world experts in the field.

Thus, the California Water Project at the beginning of the 1970's is in a rather mixed situation. Though there is a firm grasp on the traditional commitment to north-south diversion, exploratory moves are being made to incorporate the new perspectives of environmental quality and recent technology. The strong push of environmentalists may be sufficient to direct California into a new and altogether different approach to water planning in the years ahead.

# PART TWO

# WATER USE

# 2 THE ECONOMIC DEMAND FOR WATER IN URBAN AREAS

L. T. WALLACE

Some people think that since water is a necessity for life, it is priceless. Sometimes this is true. A man dying of thirst would be willing to pay any amount for some water. But the same would be true also for many other necessities of life: oxygen, food, trace minerals, vitamins, space, and so on.

The question is hardly ever whether or not a man, or a region, or a city, is to have water at all; rather, the question is whether more or less water will be made available. And indeed, the total value of water may be very high, but at the same time the value of an additional thousand gallons may approach zero. In fact, often the reason people "need" so much water is that it is cheap. For example, in some places people do get by on an average of 2 to 3 gallons of water per day, but the average inhabitant of Los Angeles uses approximately 160 gallons per day. Should the people of Los Angeles be made, or taught, to use less water per capita since they use over 50 times as much as is "required" to meet basic necessities? The answer to the question of water "requirements" is based on a solution of the problem of its economic demand and value. If more water is needed, will the additional benefits of obtaining this water equal or be more than the additional costs of providing it? If water prices are high enough, less water might be used and any extra money might be spent on something else. On the other hand, if someone can persuade you that water is priceless, you will probably pay him a lot of money to get some of it for you. However, if you think water has

Many thanks are due J. Barron, M. Brewer, L. Clement, C. Howe, A. Peterson, R. Sargent, S. V. Wantrup, and W. Wood for their comments on an earlier draft.

a price just like other commodities, that someone's talk may not be so effective.

Let us look more closely at some of the dimensions of urban water demands. The subject is much too large and complex to be covered in detail here, but we can go into some of the relevant economic considerations and provide some introductory data, hopefully laying the groundwork for those who wish to pursue the matter further.

## DEMAND

In the literature on water use, the words "demand," "use," "requirement," and "need" are often used interchangeably. However, they are not synonymous.

To begin with, some differentiation can be made between *economic demand for water, water use, water requirement,* and *need for water,* terms that recur frequently. *Economic demand* for water is the sum of what all the water buyers will purchase at different prices within a given market area, as for example Los Angeles. *Water use* is the amount of water consumed, simply the sum of the population times per capita water use. *Water requirement* is most often considered a projection of water use, assuming a certain level of prices and population growth. Finally, *need* as it relates to water is often used interchangeably with *requirement,* and is assumed to be a minimum level below which it is poor strategy to fall.

A demand curve, *DD*, for a commodity is shown in Figure 2.1. It slopes downward from left to right. The curve *DD* shows the amount of a commodity buyers will purchase at different market prices. The slope shows an inverse, or negative, price-quantity relationship, that is, as the quantity that is offered increases, the price per unit has to be lower to clear the market.

There are three main reasons for this relationship to exist. First, preferences are not the same; some people simply do not care to buy an item others are willing to purchase. Second, since incomes are not equal, some people can afford to pay higher prices for something than other people. And third, some people do not get as much value or use from an item as other people might and therefore will not pay as much for it.

If a commodity is said to be priceless, what is really meant, us-

Price per Unit

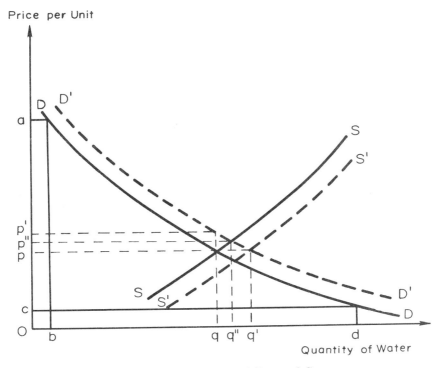

FIGURE 2.1.    Hypothetical Demand Curve.

ually, is that very little of it can be sold and therefore the price has to
be high. Thus, in Figure 1, selling amount $b$ (very little) is at price $a$
(quite high). If the use value of, or returns from, the commodity is low,
then it will take a low price to be able to sell much of it. This is the case
when, as in Figure 1, the amount $d$ can be sold only by putting the
price at $c$.

A supply curve is different. It has a positive price-quantity relationship: the higher the price the greater the amount of the commodity
offered on the market. A supply schedule is shown as the curve $SS$ in
Figure 1. The equilibrium price of water is at the intersection of the
demand and supply schedules, at the point $pq$ in Figure 1.

As population grows, as incomes increase, or as necessity becomes
greater, the demand curve for water can shift, for example to $D'D'$ in
Figure 1. This increased demand means that a higher price may be
charged for the same amount of water sold as before (quantity $q$ now
brings price $p'$). In this situation, if population growth was the main

reason behind the increase in demand, the same amount of water ($q$) sold at a higher price ($p'$) would mean less water per capita. On the other hand, if a water development project were initiated, supply could increase along with demand, shown by the shift in the supply curve from $SS$ to $S'S'$, so that on a per capita basis people might have the same amount of water at the same price ($p$) as before. Or, finally, the supply curve may remain at $SS$, but prices may rise to an equilibrium at $p''$, where people get somewhat more water, $q''$, on the whole, though per capita use may be reduced.[1] The main point is that the economics illustrated in Figure 1 tells us that water development projects may not be necessary if needs can be satisfied at higher water prices.

While we assume that the demand schedule for urban water resembles that of a typical commodity, it may have particular characteristics which are not yet clarified because of the nature of water-supply organizations and the stability of most water prices within a given market. Because historical data on price-quantity relationships for major water uses are fragmentary,[2] most empirical estimates of the economic demand for urban water have been indeterminate, never having been given the market price tests accorded other commodities.[3]

There is usually no restriction to the entry of new water users, or suppliers, in areas already being serviced. However, in practically all urban areas the number and size of the buyers have little or no effect on price; the physical supply of water is rarely a limiting factor; and new suppliers are subject to public utility price regulation. Once a hookup has been made to water-service lines, there is little or no price differential between neighbors or neighborhoods. Further, the fixed costs of providing and distributing water are closely tied to the physical facilities constructed (or projected) to handle the population-use load.

Urban water in many communities is considered a public good, its supply financed by public funds. Market performance is generally judged on the ability to provide water at all times, regardless of peak loads or seasonality, rather than on some criterion of price efficiency.

1. If the supply curve were completely vertical, the implication would be that all available water was being used at utmost efficiency. Then, unless new supply shifted the curve, any increased demand could only result in a price rise.

2. J. S. Bain, R. E. Caves, J. Margolis, *Northern California's Water Industry* (Baltimore: The Johns Hopkins Press, 1966), pp. 161, 184–185.

3. The discussion that follows is taken in large part from Bain *et al., ibid.,* pp. 3–10.

Technical efficiency of supply organization, ability to function in the bond markets, level of new hookups, and extent of reserves to maintain and replace equipment also enter into judging water-supply agency effectiveness. Profit maximization alone is seldom used to evaluate performance, although maintenance of "reasonable" profits for utilities is considered essential.

ELASTICITY OF DEMAND

Elasticity of demand refers to the extent to which quantity changes in response to some given price change, or vice versa, a relationship that is always negative in demand analyses. For example, an elasticity of demand of −.5 means that for a 10 per cent increase in price there will be a 5 per cent decrease in quantity sold; conversely, putting 5 per cent more of the commodity on the market (increasing supply by 5 per cent) will lower the price by 10 per cent. Since price can be a major factor influencing the amount of water that is bought, elasticity of demand describes both market conduct and performance.

However, it has been extremely difficult to identify a price-demand elasticity factor for a particular water use in any market,[4] and it has never been satisfactorily done in a market served by two or more water-supply agencies. The principal reason elasticities for water use are so difficult to determine is that price changes that test effective demand rarely occur in the same city.[5] Although some evidence can be marshaled that shows a quantity response to price changes over time, it is difficult to know if these changes are cause and effect.[6]

Most elasticity estimates range between −.3 and −1.2, depending on the use analyzed (primarily residential). Higher coefficients have been found in relatively small cities; large cities tend to have lower

4. S. H. Hanke, "Demand for Water Under Dynamic Conditions," *Water Resources Research*, Vol. 6, No. 5, Oct. 1970, pp. 1253–1261, reports a study for Boulder, Colo., in which residential water prices were changed from a flat-rate price structure to a metered one, thereby permanently reducing domestic water demands by over one third.

5. For planning purposes, the effects of both short-run and long-run price-quantity changes are needed. The main problem continues to be the lack of comparable data for all categories of water use for the various areas included in a regional or statewide analysis.

6. Some discussion of this aspect can be found in California Department of Water Resources, "Water Use by Manufacturing Industry in California, 1957–59," Bulletin 124, 1964, pp. 66–73. See also Bain *et al., op. cit.,* p. 17.

TABLE 2.1
*Water Price Elasticity Estimates, Selected Geographic Areas*

| Location | Water use | Price elasticity estimate | Price-quantity relationships resulting from the elasticity estimate | |
|---|---|---|---|---|
| | | | Increase in price (percentage) | Decrease in quantity used (percentage) |
| United States, cross section | Residential (indoor) | − .23 | 10 | 2.3 |
| California, south coastal | Urban (residential, commercial, and industrial) | − .31 | 10 | 3.1 |
| Georgia | Residential (all) | − .67 | 10 | 6.7 |
| California, coastal | Residential (outdoor) | − .70 | 10 | 7.0 |
| California, northern | Residential (all) | −1.10 | 10 | 11.0 |
| Kansas | Residential (all) | _1.24 | 10 | 12.4 |

SOURCE: See footnote 8.

elasticity estimates.[7] In almost all such studies for urban water, all uses were aggregated and it was hard to separate demand elasticity estimates for any one use.[8] Table 2.1 lists some water price elasticity

7. See Bain *et al., op. cit.,* pp. 188-189, and Manuel Gottlieb, "Urban Domestic Demand for Water: A Kansian Case Study," *Land Economics,* May 1963, pp. 204–210.

8. An estimate for residential water demand elasticity was made by Louis Fourt in "Forecasting the Urban Residential Demand for Water," an unpublished Agricultural Economics Seminar paper delivered at the University of Chicago, February 14, 1958. His estimate was −.40 at the 5 per cent level with an $R^2$ of .61–.84, depending on the specific model used. For higher elasticity estimates, see H. F. Seidel and E. R. Baumann, "A Statistical Analysis of Water Works Data for 1955," *Journal of American Water Works Association,* XLIX, December 1957, p. 1541. Other price elasticity estimates can be found in C. W. Howe and F. P. Linaweaver, "The Impact of Price on Residential Water Demand and Its Relation to System Design and Price Structure," *Water Resources Research,* first quarter 1967; R. M. North, "Consumer Responses to Prices of Residential Water," University of Georgia, November 1967; B. D. Gardner and S. H. Schick, "Factors Affecting Consumption of Urban Household Water in Northern Utah," Bulletin No. 449, Agricultural Experiment Station, Utah State University, November 1964; California Department of Water Resources, "Unit Urban Water Use Model for the South Coastal Area," Technical Memorandum No. 27A, January 1968.

demand estimates and shows the estimated decrease in quantity of water used for each estimate given a 10 per cent increase in water prices.

## OTHER FACTORS AFFECTING DEMAND

The ability to provide continuously effective water service despite daily and seasonal variations is important because most customers look upon water suppliers as fulfilling a public trust. This, in turn, establishes permanence and responsibility for a rather special customer-supplier relationship.[9]

Climate has little effect on industrial and commercial water use, although residential and municipal demands can and do vary as a result of temperature, humidity, and precipitation.[10] Environmental characteristics such as soil, vegetation, and altitude also play a role, although little work has been done to establish definite numerical relationships.

Water quality, number of people and kind of uses, costs of water treatment for recycling or reclaiming, and aesthetic factors such as recreational uses, visual perception, odor, turbidity, toxicity, and extent of aquatic life are among the many other factors that have been mentioned as affecting the demand for water.[11] Qualitative factors bring into focus another dimension of demand for urban water: What is the economic demand for water given a particular use and a possible variation in water qualities? It is evident that there is a certain range of opportunities for water substitution depending on the "salinity" of the water, the amount available, and the purpose to which it will be put.

Timing of water availability can become an important influence, as well as method of delivery, because these factors may affect cost or convenience. If water becomes available only at specified times, the uses made of it, and thus the demand for it, will be somewhat limited, as has been demonstrated in some agricultural areas. On the other

9. Bain *et al., op. cit.,* p. 9.

10. See State of California, The Resources Agency, Department of Water Resources, "Municipal and Industrial Water Use," Bulletin 166–1, August 1968 (reprinted May 1969), p. xii.

11. For a particularly good discussion of water quality factors affecting economic and use demands for water, see A. V. Kneese and B. T. Bower, *Managing Water Quality: Economics, Technology, Institutions* (Baltimore: The Johns Hopkins Press, 1968), pp. 31–39.

hand, if such limitation is publicly accepted as a meaningful rationing device applied to all, demand may increase, as it did in Baltimore when residential lawn watering was restricted to alternate days on opposite sides of the street!

Another important aspect of demand depends on whether the total cost of water is large or small in the production or consumption processes of the four major water-use groups: industrial, commercial, residential, municipal. Since most water costs for residences tend to be relatively small compared to other home-owners' costs, there is little incentive to conserve water. Commercial establishments in industries with high water use are usually not too much affected in this regard. Most municipalities are in the position of buying water from themselves. It is only when water use is great in an industry, or when water costs or water-treatment costs become an important budget item, that economic concern and interest are aroused.

Domestic water use is an act of economic consumption. Demand for domestic water is direct, not "derived" as in the case of acquiring a production input. Accordingly, environmental factors, household-appliance technology, population density, income levels, and the price of water, all exert some influence.[12]

Demands for commercial and industrial water, however, are derived demands. Market forces, including market access and sale conditions, per capita incomes of buyers, level of commercial and industrial services purchased locally as compared to those bought elsewhere, and the general level of economic confidence and activity, become important factors, which are reflected in their economic demands for water. (It should be acknowledged that the largest use of industrial water is for cooling; of this most is self-supplied, and the majority of that comes from brackish sources.[13])

Factors affecting the demand for municipal water depend primarily on the level of expected services rather than on prices. However, this is probably because of the Peter-Paul relationship in the supply-use situation for public water.

In all the instances mentioned here, but to a varying degree for each, water-use requirements will depend on the kind of technology

12. For further discussion see Bain *et al., op. cit.,* pp. 182–184.
13. State of California, Department of Water Resources, Bulletin 166-1, *op. cit.,* p. 25.

used, its technical efficiency, and changes in water-treatment costs. In the industrial sector, a demand response might be made as a result of changing industrial patterns, such as in the structure of the industry, in industrial processes and organization, in plant design, and in the degree to which recirculating fresh or salt water is possible.

## ESTIMATES

From 1960 to 1965, total water use increased about 15 per cent in the United States, up from 1,500 gallons per capita per day to 1,600.[14] Urban water use took approximately 10-15 per cent of this amount, the remaining 85-90 per cent going mainly to agriculture. Within total urban water use, residential use claimed 50-60 per cent, public use took 3-7 per cent, commercial use 20-30 per cent; industry used less than 5 per cent.[15]

Population, water production, and per capita water use are the factors analyzed in most studies of urban water demands.[16] Although there are regional differences in per capita water use, a study of California counties showed an annual average of 172 gallons per capita per day based on average daily water use by month in the years 1961-1965.[17] This sample covered cities including 55 per cent of the population served with water.

Because of increases in both the use of water-utilizing appliances

14. C. R. Murray, "Estimated Use of Water in the U.S., 1965," Geological Survey Circular 556, U.S. Department of the Interior, Washington, D.C., 1968, p. 1. This also contains an excellent water-use bibliography.

15. Bain *et al.*, *op. cit.*, p. 180, and J. Hirshleifer, J. C. DeHaven, and J. W. Milliman, *Water Supply: Economics, Technology, and Policy* (Chicago: University of Chicago Press, 1960), pp. 303–309.

16. State Water Resources Board, "Water Utilization and Requirements of California," Bulletin No. 2, Vols. I and II, June 1955. These documents present an "analysis of present and probable ultimate use of water in California for irrigated agriculture, domestic, industrial, and other beneficial purposes." These publications, the result of a program of investigation adopted at the Board's regular meeting September 5, 1947, were the basis of determining the amount of water needed for "supplemental water required for satisfaction of present and probable ultimate needs" in California. However, the Department of Water Resources no longer estimates "ultimate" requirements. Instead, all projections are for definite periods of time, i.e., to the year 2020, etc. See also California Department of Water Resources, "Investigation of Alternative Aqueduct Systems to Serve Southern California," Bulletin No. 78, Appendix D, "Economic Demand for Imported Water," March 1960, p. 155.

17. California Department of Water Resources, Bulletin No. 166–1, *op. cit.*, p. 38, Table 2.

TABLE 2.2.
*Total and Per Capita Urban Water Requirements, South Coastal Area,*[a] *California, by Decades*

| Year | Total acre-feet (in thousands) | Per capita (gal./day) |
|---|---|---|
| 1950 | 874 | 140 |
| 1960 | 1,564 | 160 |
| 1970 | 2,282 | 170 |
| 1980 | 2,978 | 176 |
| 1990 | 3,601 | 186 |
| 2000 | 4,312 | 199 |
| 2010 | 4,876 | 207 |
| 2020 | 5,289 | 210 |

SOURCE: Hirshleifer *et al., Water Supply: Economics, Technology, and Policy,* p. 313, Table 40. See also Department of Water Resources, Bulletin 78, II, pp. 31–33.

[a] This area includes the drainage line counties to the coast extending from Ventura County to the Mexican border.

and the technological water requirements of household appliances and industrial processes, many studies show an increasing per capita consumption over time. Table 2.2 indicates this trend, as well as imputed population estimates for total acre-feet of urban water use.

One study holds forth the possibility of constant, or possibly declining, daily per capita water use. In a study of sixty-one cities and areas, thirty-four had no change in water use over a period of five years, thirteen had decreases, and fourteen had increases.[18] These differences may be due to data limitations as well as to different trends in the observable economic factors.

At one point, the California State Department of Water Resources made a projection of the growth of applied water requirements in millions of acre-feet for the entire state (see Table 2.3). A report published by the Los Angeles Chamber of Commerce for the South Coastal Area

18. California Department of Water Resources, Bulletin No. 166–1, *op. cit.,* p. 2. This report presents per capita water use values for cities, counties, and hydrographic areas in California. See also a report of the California State-Federal Interagency Group (Department of Water Resources; U.S. Department of Agriculture, Soil Conservation Service; U.S. Department of the Interior, Bureau of Reclamation; U.S. Department of the Army, Corps of Engineers), "Twenty Years Ahead in California Water Resource Development," November 1965; Table 1 and Figure 1 itemize the primary and secondary purposes by project and location of a proposal for the next twenty years (1966–1985) of California's water resource development program.

TABLE 2.3.
CALIFORNIA WATER CONSUMPTION ESTIMATES, 1960, 1990, 2020
(ACRE-FEET — AF — IN THOUSANDS)

|  | 1960 | | 1990 | | 2020 | |
|---|---|---|---|---|---|---|
|  | AF | % | AF | % | AF | % |
| Urban | 3.26 | 10 | 8.48 | 21 | 14.00 | 28 |
| Agricultural | 28.48 | 90 | 32.32 | 79 | 35.70 | 72 |
| TOTAL | 31.74 | 100 | 40.80 | 100 | 49.70 | 100 |

SOURCE: State of California, The Resources Agency, Department of Water Resources, "Implementation of the California Water Plan," Bulletin No. 160–66, March 1966, p. 55, Fig. 5.

alone indicates that, with a range of 134-240 gallons per capita per day within the area, the projected municipal and industrial use is estimated to be 2.46 million acre-feet in 1970, increasing to 5.43 million acre-feet by 2020. Agriculture's demands for water in this area are projected to decline from 0.97 million acre-feet to 0.37 million acre-feet, corresponding to a decline in irrigated acreage from 350,000 acres to 140,000 acres.[19] Another estimate for California south of the Tehachapis projects one million acre-feet per year in 1980, 1.75 million acre-feet per year in 1990, and 3.5 million acre-feet per year by 2020.[20] Despite the variance in estimates covering different areas, a lot of water is projected to be used in southern California in urban areas. (It is certain that the above data are overestimates, since the population base assumed is now acknowledged to be much too large. However, no new estimates had been cleared and made publicly available at the time this was written. Thus, though the estimates have historic value, many of the projections have, or will, become obsolete because of revised projections of population, per capita demand, etc.)

Industrial uses of water have lent themselves to more detailed analysis on a physical basis than have other types of water use. However, industrial water-use projections have been determined in much the same manner as those for urban use: per employee use times total employment compared to per capita use times population.

Based on existing industrial technology, industrial water use esti-

19. Los Angeles Chamber of Commerce, "Report of Water and Power Committee, Los Angeles Area Chamber of Commerce, on Water Demands and Supplies for Southern California Coastal Area," June 1968, Tables 2 and 2A.
20. California Department of Water Resources, Bulletin 78, *op. cit.*, Appendix D, p. 18.

TABLE 2.4.
*Water Use per Employee per Annum by Industrial
Subsector (1957–1959 average)*

| Industrial subsector | Use per employee per annum (acre-feet) |
|---|---|
| 1. Food and kindred | 0.713019 |
| 2. Textiles | 0.190592 |
| 3. Apparel | 0.027234 |
| 4. Lumber | 0.349573 |
| 5. Furniture | 0.039699 |
| 6. Paper | 1.553275 |
| 7. Printing | 0.069461 |
| 8. Chemical | 1.082675 |
| 9. Petroleum | 4.735634 |
| 10. Rubber | 0.291075 |
| 11. Leather | 0.034440 |
| 12. Stone, clay, and glass | 0.650090 |
| 13. Primary metals | 0.381792 |
| 14. Fabricated metals | 0.349127 |
| 15. Instruments | 0.080078 |
| 16. Miscellaneous | 0.202267 |
| 17. Machinery | 0.134367 |
| 18. Electrical machinery | 0.067192 |
| 19. Transportation equipment | 0.081422 |
| 20. Weighted average | 0.335134 |

SOURCE: Drawn from work sheets of Leon Danielson's unpublished Ph.D. dissertation, University of California at Berkeley.
Many thanks are due to Dr. Danielson for his significant help in
locating source materials for this chapter. His sources for this
Table were California Department of Water Resources, "Water
Use by Manufacturing Industries, 1957–59," Bulletin No. 124,
1964, Table 6, p. 73, and population estimates based on census
data. (Particular note should be made of the study's data limitations noted on p. 12 of the Bulletin.)

mates have been made for the southern California area for a specific
time period (Table 2.4). The apparel industry shows the least water
use per employee (textiles being a relatively capital-extensive and
labor-intensive industry) while petroleum shows almost 5 acre-feet
per employee per year (the petroleum industry being capital-intensive
and labor-extensive). These estimates are only averages based on the
existing management-capital-labor-technology system in use during
the period surveyed. These averages would not be relevant if any one,
or all, of the components of this system were to change significantly.

A comparison (Table 2.5) of water used for public supplies in the
United States and in California for 1965 shows proportional differences between the two areas (even though California is included in the

TABLE 2.5.
*Selected Water Use Categories, 1965*

|  | Per capita (gal./day) | Industrial & commercial (million gal./day) | Domestic, public losses (million gal./day) |
|---|---|---|---|
| California | 231 | 680 | 3,300 |
| United States | 155 | 7,800 | 16,000 |

SOURCE: C. R. Murray, "Estimated Use of Water in the U.S., 1965," Geological Survey Circular 556, U.S. Department of the Interior, Washington, D.C., 1968, p. 17, Table 5.

U.S. data). While these comparisons are far from conclusive, they indicate some of the "intuitive" reasons for California's concern over water use and water supplies.

Despite inadequacies of data and analysis, several water-use studies provide historic facts and offer rules of thumb that may be useful in making urban industrial water-use estimates for "near future" planning horizons on a regional basis.[21] Several facts emerged in 1965, among them that over one-fifth of the water used by industry was self-supplied, and of this about 25 per cent was saline. This proportion is increasing rapidly, while the relative use of fresh water diminishes.[22] Only 2 per cent of industrial water was consumed; the greater part of the remainder (except for losses) was returned for subsequent reuse.

From 1960 to 1965, there was about a 17 per cent increase in fresh water used in industry as against a 35 per cent increase in saline water. With fresh water increasingly difficult to obtain, and increasingly more costly, Table 2.6, which shows self-supplied water for all industrial uses in 1965, may soon have to be modified. The estimated increase in the annual rate of water use for industrial purposes is approximately 2 per cent, which may rise to 2.5 per cent after a peak of 3.5 per cent in the next two decades.

About 75 per cent of the industrial water used in 1965 was used for thermoelectric power plants. Of this water, about 97 per cent was

21. See N. W. Rollins, D. J. Allee, and B. Lawson, "Industrial Water Use in the North Atlantic Region – Projections and Methodology," Technical Report No. 17, Cornell Water Resources and Marine Sciences Center, Ithaca, New York, October 1969 (A. E. Res. 302). In the words of its preface: ". . . broad aggregated area planning tool . . . not applicable to specific projects within a watershed. . . . presents industrial water use estimates and projections for the northeastern U.S., as well as the methodology used."

22. Murray, *op. cit.*, pp. 4–12.

TABLE 2.6
*Self-Supplied Industrial Water, All Industrial Uses by Major Source,
U.S. and California, 1965 (million gal./day)*

|  | Fresh | Saline | Sewage | All Water |
|---|---|---|---|---|
| California | 1,500 | 11,000 | .5 | 13,000 |
| U.S. | 130,000 | 45,000 | 140.0 | 170,000 |

SOURCE: Murray, *op. cit.*, p. 30, Table 14.

used for cooling as compared with an approximate weighted average of 70 per cent for other industries. Water used for cooling is mostly just run through the plant with little or no net consumption.

Pricing urban water is a complicated task. For instance, there is little or no price or quality competition within a geographic market area, and water uses within a market are not homogeneous, even though there may be a single supply source. Water-industry markets are not continuous in either time or space. In addition, the justification for the existence and continuance of most water markets is made on a legal, rather than an economic, basis. Further, the urban water supplier at retail level is most often a department of local government, or an agency with special functions (up to and including powers of eminent domain, taxation, and resource sales); the water wholesaler is usually a federal, state, or county agency.[23] In addition, if the state sells water only to wholesalers, it may have limited influence on pricing policies of the retail agencies.

This public perspective in the water industry suggests a different approach to pricing than the usual market orientation and economic motivation of pricing to maximize profit. Instead, the price of water seems more oriented to getting the resource used and toward welfare goals rather than monetary payoffs.

We have a situation in which ". . . urban pricing systems generally rest on formulas and procedures which are well-known and widely used within the public utility companies; . . ."[24] In essence, utility pricing establishes rates high enough to recover service costs (variable plus fixed costs, including a try at a reasonable rate of return on in-

23. Bain *et al.*, *op. cit.*, pp. 8–10, 352.
24. *Ibid.*, p. 353.

vestment) through fixed charges, or minimum bills, plus a schedule of
declining block prices for actual delivery or use.[25]

Marginal cost pricing for urban water is rarely if ever done.[26] If
marginal cost (the cost of the last increment of water produced or
provided) was used in determining water prices, different prices
could be charged for similar uses in the same community depending on
the timing, ease of hookup, and capacity of the water system itself. In
actual practice, average costs are used to establish water prices. An
average-cost method of valuing water permits uniform pricing throughout a community and is probably easier to implement. However, it does
have a drawback in that relatively high costs of expanding or modify-
ing the water system are shared by everyone rather than borne only
by those who have caused the change in water facilities. The theoretical and operational pros and cons of marginal versus average-cost
approaches have been argued inconclusively for many years. However,
it is quite clear that little consideration is given to actual costs when
pricing water.[27] Hardly ever do water rates actually equate marginal
values to customers with different uses under equal cost conditions.[28]

If emphasis is put on a use approach to pricing, water rate schedules tend to be based on an average-cost concept with some price dis-
crimination to "users" outside a prescribed jurisdiction, as for example,
the city limits.[29] These discriminatory higher rates for outsiders are
sometimes accused of encouraging urban annexation. However, they
are usually imposed out of a sense of "fairness," because city residents
do pay fixed meter charges with tapered tolls, urban water does cost
something, the commodity is usually free to the municipal depart-
ments, and revenues must be made up somewhere.

It is still a matter of debate whether marginal cost pricing is more
economically efficient than some other method. The goals and motivation within the entire water source-use-distribution system must be
identified and weighted before such a determination can be made.
Evidence shows that water prices per unit are higher in an urban

25. Hirshleifer *et al., op. cit.,* p. 99.
26. Bain *et al., op. cit.,* pp. 350–361.
27. *Ibid.,* p. v-vii.
28. Hirshleifer *et al., op. cit.,* p. 87.
29. Bain *et al., op. cit.,* p. 349.

economy than they are for irrigated farming, and therefore the demand for water tends to be more inelastic in an urban area than in a rural one. For this reason urban water prices can be higher than cost, with any excess going to the general treasury.[30] Examples of such a situation can currently be found in the southern end of the San Joaquin Valley, where urban water rates are set high enough to subsidize the agricultural use of water in the county. The city's ability to bond, or use the property tax, to help agriculture pay for the water it uses is justified on the ground that the gross economic activity generated by agriculture within the county results in general benefits from employment and income multipliers that offset the imposed costs.[31]

Present and projected urban water uses can be calculated only under specified price conditions. Where water is cheap, it is applied liberally to all uses. Water-use priorities are without meaning if the marginal value in use is not relevant and the price of water is not a deterrent to low-valued water uses. Thus, in many cases the price of water is assumed to be its average least cost, with more emphasis on reducing idle capacity in the system through promotional pricing than on long-run marginal costs of the typical system to be covered.[32]

Where urban water rates substantially understate effective marginal costs, profligate water uses create an apparent need for new supplies when what is more urgently required is more economical use of existing supplies.[33] This situation is at least partly responsible for the projected increase in total and per capita urban water "requirements" and "demands" in California.

The cost of supplying urban water is certainly subject to economies of size criteria. Cost factors include sources of water supply and con-

30. *Ibid.*, p. 347.

31. One authority goes so far as to suggest that most cities in southern California subsidize urban and/or agricultural water via the property tax. See Hirshleifer *et al.*, *op. cit.*, p. 311.

32. For an interesting discussion of these points, see Hirshleifer *et al.*, *op. cit.*, pp. 29, 87, 304–313. See also Bain *et al.*, *op. cit.*, pp. 350–361.

33. California Department of Water Resources, Bulletin 78, *op. cit.*, p. II-5, states an assumption of making up the water price and cost difference in the service area of Metropolitan Water District of Southern California by "its present procedure of taxation or otherwise"; and *ibid.*, Appendix D, p. 15, implies that, since the price of water is assumed to be its cost in estimating growth in demand for imported water, a least-cost price is the prime pricing motivation.

duit pipes to distribution sites, storage facilities, wells (if needed for underground storage or for salt-water barriers), pipe or canals, and number of hookups. More complicated distribution systems and more refined treatment processes are always available at increased costs. Private investment in recycling water is becoming more important as a very real expansion of the local water supply.

Capital investments for supplying urban water are seldom made to maximize profits. Instead, the criteria for public investment in a water supply usually include a supply that must be available at all times after the announced date of initial delivery, a supply that must be of high quality and must be adequate for anticipated long-run needs, provision made for peak seasonal or daily periods, and a system that should minimize the cost of water delivered to a common point, while capital outlays are shared through revenues and other methods of public financing.[34]

Misinterpretation of these criteria often leads to either under- or overinvestment in water supply facilities. Planners, engineers, and responsible elected officials need discussion and analysis to minimize the chances of unwise investments.

"Externalities" of one kind or another are common influences on urban water-use and demand estimates. One common externality occurs when the use of water by one group changes the value or cost of water to other users.[35] As an example, suppose upstream users pollute and thus reduce the quality of water supplied to downstream users, who in turn may reduce the water quality still further for subsequent downstream users. External costs are called external diseconomies, while external benefits (when water quality is improved or pollution reduced) are called external economies.

External diseconomies are probably more apparent than economies in our society and, in the instance of water, usually take the form of increased levels of necessary water treatment. Although the origin of water-quality standards is sometimes authoritatively obscure,[36]

34. For a more detailed discussion, see Bain *et al., op. cit.,* pp. 367–368.
35. *Ibid.,* p. 11.
36. For an interesting article on the obscurity of water quality standards, including the 500 parts per million standard for drinking water, see P. H. McGauhey, "Folklore in Water Quality Standards," *Civil Engineering,* Vol. 35, No. 6, 1965, p. 71.

it is certainly true that the amount and character of water treatment before domestic use are related to the quality of water intake.[37]

External diseconomies are likely to become increasingly evident when growing urban populations become more densely concentrated within single, or basin-connected, watersheds. Supply costs of urban water will be forced upward and will subsequently have to be offset either by increased prices or by other forms of charges or taxation.

While the economics of water use is a complex subject, it is clear that the amount of water used in an area is affected by its price. Too, while we need to know more about the historical development of urban water use in relation to water rights and water districts, we can see that the water supplies are potent tools of regional economic growth. Many questions can be asked about "new" supplies versus more intensive recycling, the imposition of higher water costs to reduce low-valued water uses, and the possibilities of financing alternative water sources. Further discussion on the development and use of water in California is made even more appropriate at this time because of significant revisions downward in estimates of California's future population levels, and the continued requests for increased funds to finance what might be an unneeded Water Plan.

37. For a good discussion of economic concepts related to water quality and resource use, see Kneese and Bower, *op. cit.,* pp. 75–142.

# 3 AGRICULTURAL DEMANDS FOR WATER

G. W. DEAN AND G. A. KING

Further development of irrigated agriculture on the west side of the San Joaquin Valley will be a principal feature of water development projects in California now under way. The newly constructed California Aqueduct will serve about 1.2 million acres of land on the west side by 1990, over 300,000 acres of which will be irrigated for the first time. In addition, it will permit much more intensive production in some areas heretofore severely limited in their underground water supplies.

The timing of these developments and the cropping patterns adopted are of vital interest to individual producers and industry groups in the state, especially producers of fruits, nuts, grapes, vegetables, and certain field crops, since only high-value crops have the "capacity to pay" the high water costs of the state project. Because population will grow and incomes will rise, the demand for these commodities undoubtedly will increase as time goes on. This chapter will raise the question of whether the timing of these development plans is consistent with estimates of future demand for agricultural production in California.

The demand for water for irrigation originates in the demand for food and fiber products by consumers. The price paid for water, as well as those paid for labor, capital, and fertilizer, and the prices obtained for the commodities produced on the farm determine the quantity of water demanded by any individual producer. (In addition to controllable inputs such as fertilizer, demand for water also is influenced by noncontrollable elements such as weather.) Thus, the demand for water for irrigation in any region or water basin is basically the summation of the demands of individual producers.

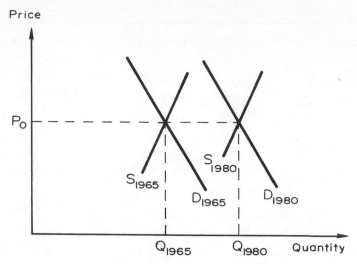

FIGURE 3.1. Hypothetical Demand Curve for Water.

In recent years, water agencies have begun to accept the concept of demand functions for water. Feasibility studies for individual irrigation projects in particular water basins have begun to derive explicit demand curves for water of the type shown in Figure 3.1. Such a demand curve must be constructed under the assumption of "everything else held constant"; that is, technology, product prices, and input prices other than water are held constant at a specified level, usually an average of such factors in the recent past. The demand curve for water can then be used to estimate the quantity of water that would likely be used at various water prices and, in turn, to make calculations of "payment capacity" and "ability to pay" for use in project analysis.

In planning water resources development, a rationale other than convenience underlies the assumption that relative prices remain constant. While appraisals of projects are typically based on the efficiency criteria of benefit-cost analysis, attention must also be given to the equity, or income redistribution, aspects of these projects. Not only is it difficult to imagine a governmental investment project which does not redistribute income but, in fact, this may be a prime reason for the project. When it comes to water resources, however, income redistribution from one set of producers to another is seldom, if ever, intended as an explicit purpose of the project.[1] Constant prices, of course, do not guarantee that there will be no income redistributions as a result of a project. Comparison of incomes, by group, "with" and "without" the project would show some redistribution, even at constant prices. But the constant-price assumption eliminates the kind of income-redistribution effect among producers that would occur if the newly irrigated acreage produced supplies that could be sold only at substantially lower prices.[2]

We assume here that the intent of the California Water Plan is to increase, over time, the quantities of agricultural products at a rate that matches shifts in demand, so that prices remain constant in real terms. Figure 3.2 reflects such a situation, in which the supply and demand functions in, say, 1965 (before the project) and 1980 (after the project) intersect at the same price, PO. Generally, the factors that shift demand (population, income, tastes) can be projected with some accuracy. The ones that shift supply are principally technology and new acreage. Technology, resulting in increased yields per acre, is assumed to be exogenous. Therefore, new acreage is the major variable in the area of public decision that affects supply.[3] As noted above, our supposition is that the intent of the California Water Plan is so to stage agricultural irrigation developments that the added supplies of products can be sold at constant prices. Essentially, this assumes a competi-

1. See James Bonnen, "The Absence of Knowledge of Distributional Impacts: An Obstacle to Effective Public Program Analysis and Decisions," Joint Economic Committee, U.S. Congress, *The Analysis and Evaluation of Public Expenditures: The PPB System* (Washington, D.C.: Government Printing Office, 1969), pp. 434–436; and Charles Howe and K. William Easter, *Interbasin Water Transfers — Economic Issues and Impacts*, Resources for the Future (Baltimore: The Johns Hopkins Press, 1969), Chapter 4, for strong evidence that water-resource projects have redistributed incomes from the South to the West and from nonreclamation farmers to reclamation farmers.

2. The income redistribution is, of course, much more complex if the irrigation water to the new district is provided below cost as a public subsidy. A subsidy would involve income transfers from the consumers (taxpayers) as well as from other producers. Whether consumers experience a net gain or loss is, in this case, dependent upon the size of the subsidy relative to the benefits obtained from lower prices for agricultural products.

3. Public investment in experiment-station research is an important variable affecting technology and, thus, increased yields. Such research may be of continued importance in maintaining the backlog of new inventions, methods of pest control, fertilizer application, and the like, consistent with societal goals of low food prices and preservation of environmental quality.

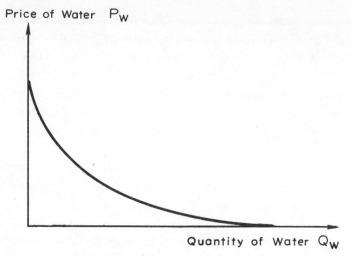

Price of Water  $P_W$

Quantity of Water  $Q_W$

FIGURE 3.2. Supply and Demand Shifts Resulting in Constant Price.

tive model where average costs for individual producers are equal to market price for each product, both before and after demand and supply shifts.[4]

The constant-price assumption may be maintained for most irrigation projects because their individual output is too small to affect prices. The projected development on the west side of the San Joaquin Valley as part of the California Water Plan is, however, so large that assuming it will have no effect upon prices is dubious. Rather large acreages of tree fruits, nuts, grapes, and vegetables are planned in proportion to the size of the markets for those products in the United States.

## California Crop and Livestock Projections to 1980 and 2000

All long-range economic forecasting techniques are limited by the fact that economic variables, such as prices and production, are heavily dependent on exogenous factors, such as population growth and tech-

4. If new technology can be applied more fully in the newly irrigated areas as compared with existing areas, as seems likely, the competitive model would eventually result in lower prices for products and a relative shift in production from existing to new areas, along with a redistribution of income from the old to the new areas. In addition to strict efficiency criteria, this type of income redistribution should be explicitly recognized by water planners if prices are not held constant.

nological change, which are themselves impossible to forecast with accuracy. Thus, economic forecasts are really projections conditional on assumed levels of these basic exogenous variables. The results reported in this section are based on a more detailed study by the authors,[5] itself subject to all such usual limitations. However, the general approach used is fairly standard and, in fact, corresponds closely to methods used by water resources agencies in making their market outlook studies. We have made crop projections as follows:

The estimate for U.S. production "required" to meet demand at equilibrium prices in 1980 and 2000 is taken from a Department of Agriculture study;[6]

California's share of the U.S. production of each product or commodity category is then projected, based on the state's historical share of the market. If that share has been changing either upward or downward over time, the share is projected to continue changing in the same direction but at a decreasing rate, reaching a stable percentage by 1980. In essence, this procedure is based on the premise that economic forces have favored a change in shares of the market by region but that, in an exchange economy, counterforces such as changing prices for resources will in time tend to stabilize the system. If there is no discernible trend in California's share, the projection is taken to be equal to its 1961-1965 average share of the market;

Levels of probable future yield of individual California crops are estimated based on historical trends and the judgment of crop specialists;

Finally, projections of the acreages "required" for crop production in California are found by dividing the projected output requirements by projected yields per acre.

5. G. W. Dean, G. A. King, C. Richard Shumway, and H. O. Carter, *Projections of California Agriculture to 1980 and 2000.* University of California, Berkeley, Agricultural Experiment Station Bulletin 847, September 1970.

6. The U.S. Department of Agriculture study (U.S. Department of Agriculture, Economic Research Service and Forest Service, *Preliminary Projections of Economic Activity in the Agricultural, Forestry, and Related Sectors of the United States and Its Water Resource Regions, 1980, 2000, and 2020,* August 1967, processed) is based on a series of specific assumptions as to U.S. population, employment, per capita income, income elasticities, trends in consumer tastes, exports and imports, and price levels. For our purposes, we note only that the U.S. population assumption is 308.1 million in the year 2000 (Series C estimates of the Bureau of the Census) and that projected prices for farm products fall in the range obtaining in recent years (essentially constant prices).

TABLE 3.1
*Projected Irrigated Acreage Planted in California*

| Crop | Total irrigated acreage planted (1,000 acres) | | | | | |
|---|---|---|---|---|---|---|
| | 1960 | 1961-65 average | 1965 | 1968 | 1980 | 2000 |
| *Field crops* | | | | | | |
| Sugar beets | 216 | 298 | 323 | 264 | 338 | 460 |
| Wheat | 84 | 93 | 92 | 130 | 93 | 92 |
| Rice | 297 | 328 | 337 | 445 | 297 | 264 |
| Dry beans | 210 | 207 | 199 | 207 | 213 | 250 |
| Potatoes | 110 | 107 | 114 | 98 | 100 | 108 |
| Safflower | 103 | 161 | 176 | 102 | 232 | 222 |
| Alfalfa seed | 147 | 119 | 116 | 103 | 170 | 240 |
| Cotton | 965 | 781 | 740 | 701 | 855 | 864 |
| Corn | 138 | 109 | 152 | 196 | 206 | 200 |
| Oats | 26 | 24 | 24 | 22 | 28 | 28 |
| Barley | 881 | 852 | 857 | 859 | 773 | 843 |
| Grain sorghum | 243 | 264 | 337 | 384 | 403 | 428 |
| Alfalfa hay | 1,179 | 1,161 | 1,188 | 1,164 | 1,175 | 1,321 |
| Other hay | 379 | 380 | 408 | 451 | 466 | 539 |
| Miscellaneous field crops | 168 | 160 | 131 | 138 | 160 | 160 |
| Total | 5,146 | 5,044 | 5,194 | 5,264 | 5,509 | 6,019 |
| *Vegetables* | 767 | 737 | 690 | 878 | 886 | 1,019 |
| *Tree fruits, nuts, and grapes* | 1,345 | 1,379 | 1,436 | 1,518 | 1,776 | 1,968 |
| *Irrigated pasture* | 1,203 | 1,122 | 1,044 | 1,046 | 1,046 | 1,046 |
| *Double-cropped acres* | − 330 | − 330 | − 330 | − 355 | − 462 | − 504 |
| TOTAL | 8,131 | 7,952 | 8,034 | 8,351 | 8,755 | 9,548 |

SOURCE: Dean *et al., op. cit.*

Table 3.1 summarizes the estimated total irrigated acreage in the state actually planted to particular crops in certain years, with projections to 1980 and 2000. The data in this table are conversions from projections partly based on U.S. Department of Agriculture, Economic Research Service and Forest Service figures.[7] Table 3.1 projects that the "required" irrigated acreage in the state (on which some crop is planted) will increase from about 8.35 million acres in 1968 to about 8.76 million acres in 1980 and 9.55 million acres by 2000. (These projections will be commented on later.)

Table 3.2 summarizes projections for California's livestock. These are not particularly critical for the irrigated acreage projections except for alfalfa hay and "other hay." The original projections for alfalfa

7. For details of these procedures, see Dean *et al., op. cit.*

TABLE 3.2.
*Projected California Livestock and Livestock Products*

| Type of product | Unit | 1961–65 | 1980 | 2000 |
|---|---|---|---|---|
| Milk | Number of dairy cows and heifers over 2 years old (1,000 head) | 877 | 965 | 1,208 |
| Beef | Number of cattle fed in feedlots (1,000 head) | 1,957 | 2,500 | 3,200 |
| Lamb | Number of ewes, 1 year and over (1,000 head) | 1,293 | 1,150 | 1,150 |
| Pork | Number of pigs saved (1,000 head) | 308 | 250 | 250 |
| Eggs | Number of layers, annual average (1,000 birds) | 29,943 | 35,835 | 49,270 |
| Broilers | Number of broilers produced (1,000 birds) | 60,115 | 67,520 | 87,454 |
| Turkeys | Number of turkeys raised (1,000 birds) | 16,386 | 26,254 | 34,215 |

SOURCE: Dean *et al., op. cit.*

hay and "other hay" acreages are based on feed requirements of the California livestock industries, rather than on the "share of the U.S. market" used for other crops, since hay is a low value, bulky product which does not figure significantly in interstate trade.

The projections of fluid milk and eggs are tied to growth in California's demand, because interstate flows are expected to remain small. However, a suitable basis for projection is less evident for meat products. California now imports about 40 per cent of its beef, 98 per cent of its pork, and 70 per cent of its broiler meats; the state exports only turkeys. All of these products are easily shipped between states and, with the exception of turkeys, California's share of total U.S. production is relatively small. For this reason, the projections of beef cattle, sheep, hog, broiler, aad turkey production in Table 3.2 are based on recent trends, modified by judgment concerning possible new developments.

The crop and livestock projections in Tables 3.1 and 3.2, together with changes in feed efficiency, permit a comparison of expected future feed supplies (feed grains, hay, and other feeds) in California with expected livestock feed requirements. Briefly, feed-grain imports into California in 1961-1965 averaged about 2.1 million tons; feed-grain production in the state averaged only about 2.6 million tons annually over this period. Thus, imports were around 80 per cent of California's own production. Even if California increases feed-grain production to

3.3 million tons in 1980, imports of feed grains would need to remain at current levels to meet demands. Imports would increase to 2.3 million tons by the year 2000 under the projected conditions. Thus, projections indicate that California will remain a substantial deficit area in feed grains. The beef-feeding industry in the state is probably the key to future feed-grain import levels. However, the projections for beef-cattle feeding in California are extremely uncertain. The future would appear to hinge on the rate of further development of large, efficient cattle-feeding operations now emerging in the Great Plains and other areas and on relative freight rates for feed grains, live animals, and dressed meat to California.

## Comparisons with California Department of Water Resource Projections

From the standpoint of the over-all demand for irrigation water, a useful summary figure is the "required" net irrigated land acreage in California. Table 3.3 compares estimates from Dean *et al.* with two studies of the California Department of Water Resources. The "irrigated acreage planted" of the Dean *et al.* study summarized in Table 3.1 appears comparable with "net irrigated land" of the California Department of Water Resources studies cited in Table 3.3. Neither estimate includes the "associated noncropped area" (farmsteads, fallow, roads, ditches, rights-of-way, fences, turn areas, and the like) which, when added to net irrigated acreage, determines gross land area (irrigable land required). While, as expected, the data in 1960 and 1965 from the two types of study are not identical because of slight differences in definitions, data sources, and the like, the acreages are of a similar order of magnitude — about 8.1 million acres. For 1980, Dean *et al.* estimates about 0.3 million acres less than the 1966 DWR study and about 0.8 million acres less than the 1969 DWR study; for 2000, the estimates of Dean *et al.* are respectively about 0.4 million acres and about 0.6 million acres less.

The major difference in the two sets of studies is in the acreage in field crops. The 1969 DWR study projects considerably higher acreages of rice and alfalfa hay and somewhat higher acreages of cotton and sugar beets. The acreages of tree fruits, nuts, grapes, and vegetables are quite similar. It is well recognized that field crop acreage is the

TABLE 3.3.
*Comparisons of Irrigated Acreage Projections*

| Source | Definition | 1960 | 1965 | 1980 | 2000 |
|--------|-----------|------|------|------|------|
| | | | | (1,000 acres) | |
| Dean *et al.*, 1970 | Irrigated acreage planted | 8,131 | 8,034 | 8,755 | 9,548 |
| DWR, 1966 | Net irrigated land | 8,085 | n.a. | 9,060[a] | 9,970[a] |
| DWR, 1969 | Net irrigated land | n.a. | 8,148 | 9,584 | 10,154 |

SOURCES: Dean *et al., op. cit.* DWR, 1966 — California Department of Water Resources, *Implementation of the California Water Plan,* Bulletin No. 160-66, March 1966, Table 4. DWR, 1969 — California Department of Water Resources, *Market Outlook for Selected California Crops — 1965–2020,* Office report prepared by Donald K. Cole and Robert M. Ernst, September 1969, Tables 15 and 18.
[a] Interpolated here from data for 1960, 1990, and 2020.

most difficult to project because of the uncertain impact of government programs and, in the case of all grains except rice, the extremely small percentage of U.S. production grown in California. However, as will be pointed out below, there are reasons to suggest that even the Dean *et al.* projections of field crop acreage may be high.

The total amount of new land to be irrigated in California depends not only on the "required" acreage but on the rate of urbanization of currently irrigated land. Dean *et al.* have accepted the 1966 DWR projections of urbanization, which show urbanized acreage increasing from about 2.1 million acres in 1960 to 3.6 million in 1980 and 4.8 million in 2000 (the latter figures are our interpolations from DWR data for 1960, 1990, and 2020). The annual rates of urbanization implied by these estimates are considerably lower than some alternative estimates, but appear quite reasonable based on the intensive studies of Ruth and Krushkhov and the Economic Research Service of the U.S. Department of Agriculture.[8] The annual rate of shift of lands to urban uses implied by the DWR estimates is about 75,000 acres per year to 1980. Shumway *et al.*, relying primarily on an extension of the Ruth-Krushkhov study, estimates the shift at about 60,000 acres per year.[9]

8. H. D. Ruth and Abraam Krushkhov, *Urban Land Requirements in California, 1965-1975,* California State Development Plan, Phase II, Urban Expansion Requirements Study, item 201.2 (Berkeley: University of California, 1966). U.S. Department of Agriculture, Economic Research Service, *Urbanization of Land in the Western States,* ERS–428, January 1970.

9. C. Richard Shumway, Gordon A. King, Harold O. Carter, and Gerald W. Dean, *Regional Resource Use for Agricultural Production in California, 1961-65 and 1980.* University of California, Berkeley, Giannini Foundation Monograph No. 25, September 1970.

The recent Economic Research Service study, while based on data for only twenty-six urbanizing counties of California, implies a similar, although perhaps slightly lower, rate of shift. Preliminary data from an unpublished Soil Conservation Service study suggest that about 27 per cent of the land shifted to urban use is prime agricultural land (defined as SCS capability Classes I and II), and 37 per cent is land with lower agricultural capabilities (Classes III and IV). The remaining 36 per cent is land not suited for cultivation (Classes V through VIII).[10]

The major conclusions of these comparisons are that the projected increases in "required" irrigated crop land acreage in California from the Dean *et al.* study are somewhat less than those of the Department of Water Resources, that urbanization does not appear to be moving faster than the Department's projection, and, therefore, that the planned rate of increase in irrigated acreage called for by the California Water Plan is more than adequate to meet demand. In fact, the planned rate of development may result in price declines for certain specialty crops.

## POTENTIAL IMPACT OF THE WEST SIDE DEVELOPMENT

The most important area of new irrigation development in the state in the next decade will be on the west side of the San Joaquin Valley. By a rather inclusive definition, the west side includes approximately 1.5 million acres. However, for our purposes here, the region is defined as San Joaquin Valley land that is to be served by water from the California Aqueduct. This is the area included in the thirteen irrigation districts on the west side which now receive, or will receive, according to plan, state or federal water from the California Aqueduct. Irrigated acreage in these districts is projected to increase from about 864,000 acres in 1968 to 1,156,000 acres in 1980 and 1,194,000 acres in 1990 — an increase of about 330,000 acres by the latter year. The major increases will be in the west of Fresno and Kings counties (Westlands Water District) and in the Kern County districts (primarily

10. It should be pointed out that estimates of urbanization by the Soil Conservation Service (California Conservation Needs Committee of the Soil Conservation Service, *California Soil and Water Conservation Needs Inventory,* November 1961) are consistently higher than those of the sources relied on here.

the Lost Hills, Berrenda Mesa, and Belridge districts on the west side
and the Wheeler Ridge-Maricopa Water Storage District at the southern end of the San Joaquin Valley).

These two major areas differ in important respects. Westlands
Water District will be served exclusively by federal water at a relatively low price; the Kern County districts receive state water at extremely high prices.[11] Also, much of Westlands Water District is already developed from expensive underground water supplies, so that
the federal water will supplement or substitute for ground water;[12] the
Kern County districts, on the other hand, are new districts receiving
water for the first time and are developing large areas of new land.

The figures on newly irrigated land alone, however, underestimate the total impact of the new water supply, since the new water
supplements or replaces groundwater supplies in several districts. One
method of roughly assessing the total increase in effective irrigated
acreage resulting from the additional water supply is to compare the
acreage capable of receiving 3 acre-feet of water in 1968 with that expected in 1980 and 1990. (A supply of 3 acre-feet of water is approxi-
magely sufficient to allow intensive cropping, including summer crops.)
Projections show that the acreage capable of being intensively cropped
could increase by about 426,000 acres between 1968 and 1980 and by
another 27,000 acres by 1990. By far the largest single area involved
is Westlands Water District with 190,000 acres, most of it land now
only partially irrigated which will receive supplemental water. These
calculations of additional intensively cropped acreage take into account all sources of water supply—state, federal, and other surface
sources, and ground water.

PROJECTED CROP ACREAGE

There is considerable interest, as well as some concern expressed
by growers elsewhere in the state, in the type of cropping pattern that
will develop on the West Side. Water costs, particularly in the areas

11. The current price for California Water Project deliveries is much lower than what
will be charged when the project is completed. This encourages early development of
land at favorable water prices, resulting in a faster development rate than otherwise
might be economically feasible.
12. If new water supplies had not been developed, long-term irrigation agriculture in
certain districts would have been questionable.

served by state water, will be extremely high. The economic financial feasibility studies prepared for the various districts show that only the higher valued crops—fruits, nuts, grapes, vegetables, and such field crops as cotton and alfalfa seed—have the "capacity to pay" the high water charges. Therefore, projected acreages for many of the districts are dominated by such crops. It is extremely difficult to forecast with any accuracy to what extent the actual acreages will follow these projections. However, these projections would appear to be the logical starting point in trying to forecast.

Plans call for an additional 65,000 acres of fruits, nuts, and grapes between 1968 and 1980; 108,000 additional acres of vegetables; 36,000 more of alfalfa seed; 28,000 more of sugar beets; and 51,000 more of cotton. So far as soils and water supply are concerned, these projections appear quite plausible. (The economic feasibility of such plans is discussed below.) About 100,000 acres of additional land (Class A soils) are well suited to deep-rooted, sensitive tree crops without a reclamation period, well in excess of the 65,000 acres projected for these crops. In addition, about 125,000 acres of B soil (suitable for all crops but those very sensitive to salt and boron, and capable of being corrected to A soil within about three years) could be used for vegetables or other sensitive crops. A large portion of this acreage is double-cropped; so the actual net is less than 108,000 acres.

A similar picture emerges for the period 1968-1990, with an added 286,000 acres projected for fruits, nuts, grapes, and vegetables; 60,000 for alfalfa seed; 47,000 for sugar beets; and 86,000 for cotton. The quality and quantity of soils and water again appear adequate.

## Projected Specialty Crop Acreage

The acreages of the specialty crops—defined here as fruits, nuts, grapes, and vegetables—shown in Table 3.1 were projected on the basis of "requirements" to meet demand at constant prices. Now we attempt instead to project "probable" aggregate acreages of these crops in the state on the basis of trends in the state for the past fifteen years. Rather remarkable shifts in the location of production have occurred over this period as urbanization pressures have caused sizable relocations of acreage of specialty crops from the Central Coast and South Coast regions of the state into the Central Valley. Tree fruits (most

TABLE 3.4.

High-Quality Soils in California, by Region, 1965 Land Use and 1980 Projections[a] (1,000 acres)

| Region | Total high-quality soils[a] | 1965 land use | | | | 1980 projected land use | | | |
|---|---|---|---|---|---|---|---|---|---|
| | | Urban land | Public and semi-agricultural land | Net potential agricultural land | Tree fruits, nuts, grapes, and vegetables[b] | Urban land | Public and semi-agricultural land | Net potential agricultural land | Tree fruits, nuts, grapes, and vegetables[b] |
| North Coast | 77 | 3 | 11 | 63 | 13 | 5 | 11 | 61 | 15 |
| Central Coast | 862 | 177 | 98 | 586 | 397 | 272 | 89 | 502 | 370 |
| South Coast | 1,177 | 541 | 78 | 558 | 279 | 746 | 58 | 372 | 220 |
| Sacramento Valley | 745 | 33 | 83 | 629 | 237 | 56 | 80 | 608 | 380 |
| San Joaquin Delta | 580 | 72 | 63 | 445 | 371 | 102 | 60 | 418 | 470 |
| San Joaquin Valley | 3,031 | 114 | 354 | 2,563 | 682 | 167 | 348 | 2,515 | 1,204 |
| West Side | — | | — | — | — | — | — | — | (1,050) |
| Non-West Side | — | | — | — | — | — | — | — | ( 154) |
| Desert | 1,471 | 20 | 221 | 1,231 | 108 | 41 | 219 | 1,212 | 90 |
| Intermediate elevation valleys | 170 | 6 | 33 | 132 | 37 | 10 | 32 | 128 | 24 |
| State acreage projected | 8,112 | 965 | 940 | 6,207 | 2,124 | 1,400 | 897 | 5,815 | 2,773 |
| State acreage "required" | — | — | — | — | — | — | — | — | 2,646 |
| State "excess" acres: | — | — | — | — | — | — | — | — | 127 |

SOURCE: Shumway et al., op. cit., and California Crop and Livestock Reporting Service, California Vegetable Crops, Acreage, Production and Value, and Acreage, 1965-66, 1966, and California Fruit and Nuts Statistics, 1954-67, 1967.
[a] "High-quality soils" defined as recent alluvial fan and flood-plain soils of medium texture; specifically, defined as soil classes 01, 02, and 03 used by Shumway et al., op. cit., Table B.1. Data rounded to nearest 1,000 acres; totals may not check exactly because of rounding. Data from high mountain valleys excluded.
[b] Based on county data. Not all acreage of these crops is located on high-quality soils, although nearly so.

deciduous fruits and oranges) and tree nuts (almonds and walnuts) have experienced substantial relocations during this period. Processed vegetables have also shifted, although unique climatic factors in the coastal and southern California areas have permitted those areas to retain much of their traditional fresh-vegetable acreage.[13]

The projected shifts in location of specialty-crop production are apparent from Table 3.4. Acreages of the specialty crops decline in the important regions, except the Central Valley, where they increase sharply, particularly in the San Joaquin Valley.[14] Table 3.4 also shows that there is sufficient high-quality land well adapted to specialty-crop production in each region to meet the projections even after deducting for urban and other nonagricultural acreages.[15]

### Effects on Specialty Crops

It is now possible to compare the aggregate projected state acreage of specialty crops with the projected acreages that would be "required" from California to meet demand at constant prices. The bottom portion of Table 3.4 shows an "excess acreage" of 127,000 acres of tree fruits, nuts, grapes, and vegetables, that is, the projected acreage in excess of what will be required to meet demand at constant prices. In addition, there are estimated "excess acreages" for early spring potatoes of 19,000 acres and of alfalfa seed of 36,000 acres — a total of 182,000 excess acres.

Initial plantings on the West Side suggest that the feasibility studies may have overestimated the acreages of potatoes, alfalfa seed, and cantaloupes and underestimated the acreages of fruits, nuts, and grapes. The first column of Table 3.5, therefore, shows a reallocation,

13. For further details on shifts of location within the state, see Warren E. Johnston and Gerald W. Dean, *Trends for Major California Crops: Yields, Acreages, and Production Areas,* California Agricultural Experiment Station Circular 551, November 1969.

14. For each region, the projections to 1980 are simply linear extrapolations of the trends taking place over the 1954–1968 period. Specifically, the average aggregate acreages for the three-year periods 1954 to 1956 and 1966 to 1968 were calculated. The average rate of annual change between these two dates was then extrapolated to 1980.

15. Only the San Joaquin Delta projection appears dubious. However, this is primarily a statistical problem because of the difficulty of using county data on crop acreages when the Delta boundaries do not follow county lines. That is, some of the specialty-crop acreage assigned to the Delta is actually in the Sacramento Valley and the San Joaquin Valley.

TABLE 3.5.
Projections of Price and Gross Income Changes to 1980 (Specified Specialty Crops in California)

| Crop category | 1980 projected "excess acres" | | Percentage of "excess supply" relative to relevant market size, 1980 | Estimated price elasticity of demand | Percentage change in price to 1980 | Percentage change in gross return to industry to 1980 |
|---|---|---|---|---|---|---|
| Fruits, nuts, and grapes | 107,000 | | | | | |
| Deciduous fruits | | 30,000 | 4.6 | −0.65 | − 7.1 | − 2.8 |
| Almonds | | 30,000 | 10.7 | −1.31 | − 8.2 | 1.6 |
| Grapes | | 20,000 | 4.0 | −0.23 | −17.4 | −14.1 |
| Oranges | | 27,000 | 2.3 | −0.66 | − 3.5 | − 1.3 |
| Vegetables | 50,000 | | | | | |
| Cantaloupes | | 5,000 | 4.9 | −0.50 | − 9.8 | − 5.4 |
| Other vegetables | | 45,000 | 2.3 | −0.35 | − 6.6 | − 4.5 |
| Potatoes, early spring | 10,000 | | 13.3 | −0.31 | −42.9 | −35.3 |
| Alfalfa seed | 15,000 | | 3.8 | n.a. | — | — |
| TOTAL | 182,000 | | — | — | — | — |

SOURCE: Dean and King, *Projections of California Agriculture to 1980 and 2000: Potential Impact of San Joaquin Valley West Side Development.* University of California, Berkeley, Giannini Foundation Research Report No. 312, September 1970.

on a judgment basis, of the 182,000 "excess acres" among the specialty crops. The next column shows the percentage of "excess supply" that would be created by these additional acres. The relevant market size was taken to be the U.S. market in each case. The third column provides estimates of the price elasticity of demand for each commodity.[16] In general, demand is quite inelastic (absolute value less than 1.0). Given the excess supplies and demand elasticities, Table 3.5 shows that deciduous fruit prices would decline about 7 per cent and almond prices about 8 per cent.[17] Because of a low price elasticity for grapes, the small excess supply results in price declines of about 17 per cent, which is probably an overestimate if the new acreage is in wine grape varieties of high demand. Orange prices show a decline of only 2 to 4 per cent, but this would hold only with continuation of the present allocation between fresh and processed sales. According to industry projection, an increasing proportion of the crop will be allocated to the lower-return, processed markets, since acreage is increasing both in Florida and in other parts of California. Therefore, a much greater price decline is expected for California oranges than is noted in Table 3.5.

Cantaloupe prices would drop about 10 per cent if the projected acreages develop and the demand assumptions are valid. Other vegetable prices would drop by about 7 per cent. The acreage projected for early spring potatoes is so far in excess of demand that, given low price elasticity, prices would drop precipitously. In fact, envisioning price declines of this magnitude casts serious doubt on the levels of potato acreage projected. No price elasticity is available for alfalfa seed. However, the projected excess production is sufficiently high to suggest sizeable price reductions.

The demand elasticities used in Table 3.5 are at the retail level. Generally, demand is less elastic at the farm level. If this holds true,

16. The price elasticity of demand is defined as percentage change in quantity demanded divided by percentage change in price, all other factors held constant. For example, the price elasticity of −0.5 for cantaloupes implies that a 5 per cent increase in quantity placed on the market would lead to a 10 per cent decline in price, other things constant.

17. Almond prices could perhaps decline somewhat less, depending on the degree of substitution between walnuts and almonds. However, prices could decline substantially more if the export market is less price-elastic than assumed here, which seems quite likely for the future.

the price effects in Table 3.5 probably would be somewhat more serious at the farm level.

The last column of Table 3.5 shows the projected percentage change in gross returns for each industry based on the other data in the table. If the demand for a commodity is price inelastic (less than 1.0 — negative sign ignored), a given percentage increase in quantity marketed will lead to a larger percentage drop in price, and gross returns to the industry will therefore decline. Only almonds in Table 3.5 show an elastic demand; however, the trend over time has been toward a lower elasticity for almonds, so that even here the demand may be inelastic at 1980 levels of supply.

Rather substantial reductions in gross returns are shown in Table 3.5 for several industries.[18] Since the production costs per unit for higher levels of output are not expected to drop significantly even with higher yields per acre, the impact of falling prices on net returns to growers is likely to be more severe than the gross returns figures indicate. Also, the impact on growers will be felt in all areas, not just the West Side. Established growers, producing (in some cases) with older rootstocks, wider tree spacing, and the like, may be particularly affected by price declines.

## Further Examination of Particular Markets

If the assumptions underlying the preceding analyses are valid, the supplies of specialty crops will lead to lower prices in the next decade. Although the assumptions are highly uncertain, closer examination gives little cause for optimism. First of all, the U.S. Department of Commerce population projection used in the analysis, while itself a reduction from earlier projections, apparently is in the process of being officially lowered. If the latter projection were substituted for the one used — that is, a reduction in estimate from 308 million to 283 million people in 2000 — the "required" supplies of all commodities would drop by roughly 8 per cent.

A second critical component of the price projections is the assump-

18. The drop in potato returns is not to be taken seriously as a forecast, since growers would undoubtedly react to lower prices by reducing acreages. However, this points out the inconsistency in projecting high potato acreages at favorable prices in project planning.

tion that trends in the acreage of specialty crops in each region of the state will continue to change at the rates of the past fifteen years. One may argue that lower prices would lead to a supply response on the part of growers, resulting in lower acreages and supplies. However, the pressure for finding high-income crops in all parts of the state suggests that the projected levels of supply are not unlikely. The West Side acreage, particularly that part served by state water, faces extremely high water costs. Extensive production of feed grains and most other field crops under these conditions is of questionable economic feasibility. At current price-cost levels, the land is more likely to be developed for trees, grapes, and vegetables, which offer a higher probability of profit in the face of high water costs.

A closer examination of market outlook on a crop-by-crop basis within the specialty-crop category also is not encouraging. One study [19] shows only limited potential for expanded acreages of the five principal deciduous fruits; in fact, if 1961-1965 prices are to be maintained despite the projected increased yield, a *decrease* in acreage is required for the aggregate of these five crops. Serious problems in marketing California oranges are apt to arise in the next decade because of the expanded acreage both in California and in Florida. D. F. McMillen[20] of Sunkist Growers projects that an increasing percentage of navel oranges will be processed in the next decade. He emphasizes the problems facing the industry in marketing in the future, at favorable returns to the growers, the levels of production implied by current bearing and nonbearing acreages of both navels and Valencias. In recent years, net returns to producers have declined sharply. In fact, growers suffered losses (negative net returns) in 1967, the latest data now available. Essentially, population and income effects have not shifted the demand for oranges at a sufficiently rapid pace to allow the increased production to be sold at favorable prices.

There have also been sharp increases in both nonbearing and bearing acreages of almonds in California. The export market will become of greater importance to the economic position of the industry as large

19. Ergun Kip and Gordon A. King, *The Demand for Selected California Deciduous Tree Fruits with Implications for Alternative 1980 Production Levels.* University of California, Berkeley, Giannini Foundation Research Report 309, June 1970.

20. D. F. McMillen, "The Citrus Industry in the Decade Ahead," *Citrograph*, Vol. 55, No. 3, January 1970, p. 93.

blocks of nonbearing acreage come into production. In 1969, large exports were possible as a result of low foreign production, especially in Italy, where production dropped from 47,000 tons (shelled) in 1968-1969 to 25,000 tons in 1969-1970. Total foreign production decreased from 107,500 tons to 69,000 tons, according to preliminary estimates published in the *Almond Control Board Report,* 1969, exhibits A and B. However, with normal levels of foreign production, there will be increased competition in the export markets. It would appear that further expansion of almond acreage would result in a level of production in excess of what is consistent with current prices to producers. With yield levels similar to the favorable 1969 crop, overproduction appears likely with current levels of domestic and export demand.

The economic position of the grape industry has been relatively unfavorable for several years. Raisins are quite strongly influenced by the uncertain export market; domestic per capita fresh grape consumption declined from 4.7 pounds (retail) in 1949 to 3.1 pounds in 1968. The market for wine is the only relatively bright spot; per capita consumption has increased from 0.89 gallons in 1958 to 1.03 gallons in 1967.[21]

While it is not practical to discuss individual vegetable crops in a similar manner, the markets for each are relatively small. Thus, it is unlikely that there is much potential for profitable vegetable production beyond the levels indicated in this chapter.

These observations and impressions confirm the conclusions of the previous analysis that specialty crops are likely to be in excess supply in the next decade. Price declines of the order suggested would have several rather predictable impacts: a revaluation of farmlands toward lower levels; requests for additional or stronger marketing orders, quantity controls, or price and income supports; and requests for lower water prices.

Among field crops a particularly critical commodity is cotton, since it is the dominant stable high-income crop in most parts of the San Joaquin Valley. The West Side districts plan to increase land planted in cotton by about 50,000 acres by 1980. The cotton-acreage projection for the state used here is based on the demand for U.S. cot-

21. California Wine Institute, *1968 Economic Research Report,* No. ER-3 (San Francisco: California Wine Institute, 1968).

ton reported by Daly and Egbert.[22] Since their report, however, the competitive position of cotton has continued to decline in relation to competitive fibers in all end-use markets. Based on more recent trends in the cotton industry, Dean and King[23] provide an alternative estimate showing cotton in California declining from 765,000 acres in 1961-1965 to 748,000 acres in 1980 rather than increasing to 838,000 acres as had been projected earlier. The lower acreage figure for cotton is also more in line with experience since 1961-1965. Should the government program for cotton be altered, it is almost certain to be in the direction of lowering income to cotton farmers (lower support prices, payment limitations, and the like). While the changes in cotton acreage resulting from modification or elimination of the cotton program are difficult to predict, it seems clear that many cotton growers, as a result, will be searching for high-value crops to replace cotton. The result could be extensive additional plantings of tree nuts, oranges, grapes, and other permanent crops, as well as expansion of vegetable acreages.

Other key field crops affected by federal farm programs are rice and sugar beets. Both depend to a great degree on the international situation and they could change markedly. Government programs for feed grains and wheat would also affect California farmers. The future position of feed grains (including Mexican wheat) in California's agricultural economy is important in the over-all state crop acreage projections. As discussed above, California is now and will almost certainly continue to be strongly deficient in feed-grain production. Feed-grain prices in California are, therefore, determined primarily by Midwest and Great Plains prices plus transportation costs to California. As a result, feed-grain prices and feed costs to the California livestock industry are little affected by rather large percentage changes in feed-grain acreage in California. The question is primarily whether feed grains will give sufficiently high returns to find an expanding role in California cropping systems.

22. R. F. Daly and A. C. Egbert, "A Look Ahead for Food and Agriculture," *Agricultural Economics Research,* Vol. 18, January 1966, pp. 1–9.

23. G. W. Dean and G. A. King, *Projections of California Agriculture to 1980 and 2000: Potential Impact of San Joaquin Valley West Side Development.* University of California, Berkeley, Giannini Foundation Research Report No. 312, September 1970.

## Projections of Land and Water Use

As pointed out above, the projected rate of irrigation development in the next decade appears more than adequate to offset conversion of agricultural land to nonagricultural uses. However, many people are questioning the longer-term relationships. Questions involving the interrelationship of food and population are receiving considerable attention in the public press. Therefore, perhaps it is relevant to ask: What if urbanization expands at a faster rate than now projected, new irrigation development increases at a slower rate than now projected, currently irrigated land is lost to salinity because of inadequate drainage, or yield increases are overestimated? The first three factors would reduce the land "available" for agricultural use in California; the last would call for an increase in the acreage "required" to satisfy the new projected demands for agricultural products. What would be the implications of such developments? Would they mean food shortages? Would serious damage occur to the California economy?

The key lies in returning to the basic assumptions of this study, stressing that the projections for California are made within the framework of projections of total national demand and interregional competition. If the land available for agriculture in California is restricted below the levels "required" by the projections, the most likely development is that the acreage planted in lower valued field crops would show up in other regions of the United States.[24] However, higher valued crops such as fruits, vegetables, nuts, and grapes – for which California has a general interregional comparative advantage – would likely remain at or near the projected levels. Livestock projections would also be little affected. California is already a strongly deficit area in feed grains and a larger feed-grain deficit would not further raise feed-grain prices to the disadvantage of livestock production.

The projections imply that a food shortage for California or the

24. There are many other areas of the United States with ample resources to produce such commodities. To illustrate: California currently devotes about 2 million of her 8.5 million harvested acres to feed grains. Yet California produces slightly less than 2 per cent of the feed grains in the United States. If, therefore, California's entire feed-grain acreage were to be given over to other crops (an extreme assumption to illustrate the point), the necessary acreage could be found by an insignificant percentage increase in the other feed-grain-growing regions of the United States.

United States is not in prospect in the foreseeable future. In fact, the more pressing problem in California in the next decade or two appears to be oversupply of particular specialty crops. It would appear incumbent on water-resource planners to reassess the agricultural demand for water in California carefully. A lower demand for water would have serious implications for both the magnitude and the timing of the California Water Plan.

In summary, there is no "shortage" of agricultural land in California for the foreseeable future, as is sometimes claimed. Still, a good case can be made for land-use and resource planning from at least two points of view: to provide an attractive and livable physical environment (for example, establishment of greenbelts and control of air and water pollution), and to provide a contingency of agricultural land against extremely long-range changes in the demand for food nationally and internationally. This planning might include such measures as redirection of urban growth onto land with low agricultural potential, establishment of new towns in nonagricultural areas, and higher density urban development.[25]

25. After this chapter was in galley proof form, a revised set of projections for the California Water Plan was published by the California Department of Water Resources which is more consistent with the conclusions of the University of California study reported in this chapter. (See California Department of Water Resources, Bulletin No. 160–70, *Water for California, The California Water Plan Outlook in 1970,* Summary Report, December 1970.) The tone of the new report is reflected in the following quotation from the Foreword by William R. Gianelli, Director, Department of Water Resources: "Fortunately, the projected slower growth of statewide population, together with the additional water supplies being made available by projects under construction or authorized, will provide a 'breathing spell' in the development of California's water resources. This will afford additional time to consider alternative resources of water supply and develop policies for the maximum protection of the environment."

# 4 WATER SUPPLY AND IRRIGATION EFFICIENCY IN THE WEST

EDWARD C. GRAY

For many, the essence of the water problem for the western states is summed up in the oft-quoted reference to California: "Over 72 percent of the runoff occurs north of a line drawn roughly through Sacramento. In contrast, an estimated 77 percent of the present water requirement and 80 percent of the forecast ultimate requirement is found south of the same line."[1] While the various schemes to move newly "developed" water from the "surplus" north to the "deficit" south might bear repeating yet once more, here we shall examine the role that improved irrigation efficiency might play in increasing the effectiveness of existing water developments.

Analysis of the possibilities naturally falls into two parts. In the first, a firm estimate of the percentage of water withdrawn by irrigated agriculture in the western states is derived. In the second, the question of irrigation efficiency is introduced through a comparison of gross farm water use and the evapotranspiration or consumptive-use requirements of crops, that is, the amount of water an area planted in a specific crop basically needs (see note 14 below). Prima facie, a consideration of both parts permits actual irrigation water "losses" in the western states to be calculated.

Because water losses do not inevitably equal the difference between quantities applied and quantities required, we do not go so far

This paper is substantially the same as one entitled "The Efficiency of Irrigation in the Western States," to be published in the 1970 Annals of Regional Science, Western Regional Science Association.

1. California State Water Resources Board, *Water Utilization and Requirements of California*, Bulletin No. 2, Vol. 1, June 1955, p. 220.

TABLE 4.1.
*Water Delivered by Irrigation Organizations for Various Uses, 1959*

| State | Farm irrigation (million acre-feet) | (per cent) | Other than farm irrigation (million acre-feet) | (per cent) |
|---|---|---|---|---|
| California | 12.35 | 90.8 | 1.26 | 9.2 |
| Oregon | 2.89 | 97.8 | .06 | 2.2 |
| Washington | 3.70 | 98.2 | .07 | 1.8 |
| Nevada | .82 | 98.7 | .01 | 1.3 |
| Utah | 2.96 | 93.3 | .21 | 6.7 |
| Arizona | 2.49 | 94.8 | .14 | 5.2 |
| New Mexico | .90 | 97.1 | .03 | 2.9 |
| Colorado | 5.94 | 95.0 | .31 | 5.0 |
| Wyoming | 3.28 | 99.2 | .03 | .8 |
| Idaho | 10.88 | 97.9 | .24 | 2.1 |
| Montana | 4.33 | 98.7 | .06 | 1.3 |
| TOTAL[a] | 50.54 | 95.5 | 2.41 | 4.5 |

SOURCE: Derived from U.S. Bureau of the Census, *U.S. Census of Agriculture: 1959, Vol. III, Irrigation of Agricultural lands, The United States,* State Tables 1.
[a] Totals may not add because of rounding.

as to estimate these quantities. Further, we recognize the obvious need for "excess" applications of irrigation water where problems of high soil salinity exist. Nevertheless, we feel that presenting estimates of irrigation efficiency and the relative importance of irrigated agriculture in each of the western states permits a very significant aspect of the western water problem to be seen in perspective.

I

The predominant use of fresh water in the west is for irrigated agriculture.[2] The extent to which this is true is partially reflected by the figures of Table 4.1.

It should be noted that the term "irrigation organization" is much

2. It is important to clarify what we mean by "use." In this section the term is employed in relation to deliberate withdrawal from groundwater or surface water sources, except that "withdrawal" for hydroelectric-power generation is not counted a "use." The use itself may be intrinsically "consumptive" to a greater or lesser degree, that is, differ in the *general* extent to which the water is available for further use. However, the amount of water actually available for subsequent reuse without treatment may depend, for example, upon disposal and collection methods for handling "used" water. The purpose for which the withdrawal is made may or may not be distant from the point of diversion; evaporation and seepage losses from conveyance systems can thus be greater or lesser to this extent.

TABLE 4.2.
*Land Irrigated (by Source of Water) and Water for Irrigation Use (Calculated as Percentage of Total Estimated Water Withdrawal),*[a] *1959*

| State | Total acres irrigated[b] | Source of water | | Irrigation use |
| | | Irrigation organizations | On farm | |
| --- | --- | --- | --- | --- |
| | | (1,000 acres) | | (percentage of total) |
| California | 7,395.6 | 2,914.8 | 4,480.7 | 90.9 |
| Oregon | 1,384.3 | 671.5 | ·712.8 | 95.5 |
| Washington | 1,007.0 | 745.1 | 261.8 | 91.0 |
| Nevada | 543.0 | 243.1 | 299.9 | 97.5 |
| Utah | 1,061.7 | 859.8 | 201.9 | 95.6 |
| Arizona | 1,152.4 | 476.4 | 676.1 | 96.3 |
| New Mexico | 731.8 | 236.0 | 495.8 | 94.6 |
| Colorado | 2,684.8 | 1,571.2 | 1,113.5 | 97.0 |
| Wyoming | 1,469.9 | 713.3 | 756.6 | 99.2 |
| Idaho | 2,576.6 | 1,862.4 | 714.2 | 99.5 |
| Montana | 1,874.5 | 933.8 | 940.7 | 99.0 |
| TOTAL | 21,881.5 | 11,227.4 | 10,654.1 | 95.0 |

SOURCE: Derived from U.S. Bureau of the Census, *op. cit.,* State Tables 3.
[a] Withdrawals for hydroelectric-power generation only and by industry using its own sources are excluded. Conveyance losses are also excluded.
[b] Totals may not add because of rounding.

more inclusive than the name itself suggests. For the 1959 U.S. Census of Agriculture, "irrigation organization" could denote an enterprise whose main purpose was not the supply of water for irrigation, provided that at least some of the water stored or conveyed was ultimately used for farm irrigation.[3]

However, the important question remains: How nearly does Table 4.1 represent the total picture in the western states for 1959? Calculations of nonirrigation use based on reasonable per capita data indicate that the table underestimates use for other than farm irrigation.[4] The last column of Table 4.2 reflects adjustments made on this account.

For a more satisfactory picture of the pattern of water use, two additional factors must be taken into account. The first and most important concerns the extent to which irrigated agriculture relies upon

3. For a more detailed definition, see U.S. Bureau of the Census, *U.S. Census of Agriculture: 1959, Vol. III, Irrigation of Agricultural Lands,* Introduction, pp. xx–xxi.

4. As a first approximation, we assume per capita use of water in urban and rural territories to be 200 and 50 gallons per day, respectively. The urban figure represents withdrawals from "public" water supply systems. It reflects public, commercial, and (most) industrial uses, in addition to domestic use.

ground- and surface-water sources found on the farm itself.[5] Again for 1959, census data reveal that, for seven of the eleven western states, land irrigated by water supplied by irrigation organizations was less than that irrigated by water from on-farm sources. Table 4.2 gives a detailed account of these acreages by state. The percentages of the combined total of water withdrawals calculated to be for farm irrigation are also given in the table.

The second factor concerns the extent to which industry is a self-supplier of water and, thus, is responsible for withdrawals that would already have been counted in the urban "per capita" calculations previously mentioned. Data in this area are difficult to obtain. However, from estimates prepared by MacKichan for 1950, industrial withdrawal use from private sources in the eleven western states can be calculated as approximately 2.2 percent of "irrigational withdrawal use."[6] Thus, for 1959, irrigated agriculture in the western states was responsible for some 92.5 per cent of water use.

There has probably been little change in these patterns since 1959. If, therefore, it can be shown that the art of supplying water in crop production is highly inefficient, then, prima facie, a potential exists for the "creation" by irrigated agriculture of substantial amounts of additional water simply by becoming more efficient.[7]

It should be noted that the final figure for irrigated agriculture above is net of "losses" from conveyance systems, reservoirs, and natural stream channels. If the losses experienced (and reported) by irrigation organizations in their canals and conveyance systems were

5. The significance of self-supply in the irrigated agriculture of the United States and of California is stressed by S. V. Ciriacy-Wantrup in "Water Economics: Relations to Law and Policy," Chapter 5 of *Waters and Water Rights,* Vol. I, Robert Emmet Clark, ed. (Chicago: The Allen Smith Company, 1967).

6. Kenneth A. MacKichan, *Estimated Use of Water in the United States – 1950,* U.S. Department of the Interior, Geological Survey Circular 115, May 1951. The author specifically excludes withdrawal for the generation of water power from industrial withdrawal use. His estimate for California of 330,000 acre-feet in 1950 is substantially in agreement with a calculation of 541,000 acre-feet as an average annual use during the period 1957–1959, which can be made from the basic data provided in California Department of Water Resources, *Water Use by Manufacturing Industries in California, 1957–1959,* Bulletin No. 124 (Sacramento, April 1964).

7. A given water supply can be made more effective, of course, by other means. For example, storage can be drawn down; final discharge can be reduced; and supply can be augmented through reuse, with treatment if necessary.

allocated in proportion to their deliveries to final use, there would be virtually no change in the relative status of irrigated agriculture as a water use in the west. On the other hand, however, the potential for further increasing the water supply vector would obviously exist to the extent that part of these losses was avoidable.

There is also the important question of the recovery of such losses. Whether they occur in storage, in conveyance (or in natural stream channels), or through extravagant irrigation or other wasteful practices in use, these losses can largely become additions to ground water and, therefore, available at some future time. For irrigation, can we, therefore, infer that efficiency is of no great import, even allowing for the dominant position of irrigated agriculture among use categories? There are several reasons why we cannot.

In the first place, low-efficiency irrigation normally requires greater surface-storage and conveyance-system capacity. Consequently, there is justification for its bearing a share of seepage and evaporation losses from these facilities. These losses are likely to be very variable. For example, they depend upon climatic factors such as the dependability of rainfall. They depend, too, upon whether or not canals and laterals are lined and, if they are, upon the materials used and the standards of construction. Another important variable is transportation distance. But even though there is variability, we can, nevertheless, be reasonably sure that evaporation from surface reservoirs in semiarid regions is substantial.[8] Where long-distance transportation of water is involved, it is likewise probable that seepage is significantly high and often collects in groundwater basins where no recovery is possible.[9]

Secondly, irrigation effluents are not necessarily of a quality that permit them to be reused in agriculture without treatment. This is the

8. For example, the annual evaporation loss from Lake Mead (behind Hoover Dam) on the Colorado River can easily be calculated to exceed 750,000 acre-feet.

9. Daily seepage through the concrete lining of a main aqueduct was estimated by the Bureau of Reclamation at .08 cubic feet per square foot of wetted perimeter (*United Western Investigation, Interim Report on Reconnaissance,* January 1951). For an aqueduct about the size of the All American Canal (but concrete lined!), this is equivalent to a loss exceeding 25 million gallons or nearly 80 acre-feet per mile per year. With a canal flow greater than 500 second-feet, leakage through gates, wasteways, etc., was estimated to amount to an additional 50 acre-feet per mile per year.

case, for example, in California's Imperial Valley, where irrigation return (drainage) waters contain total dissolved solids considerably in excess of levels that would make them suitable as irrigation water for even the most salt-tolerant crops. More specifically, the average total dissolved solids during 1962-1966 in the two major irrigation return systems draining the Imperial Valley—the Alamo and New rivers—was reported respectively as 2,700 and 3,900 parts per million. The California Department of Water Resources in its Bulletin No. 1, *Water Resources of California* (Sacramento, 1951), suggests a figure greater than 2,100 as sufficient for water to be relegated to Class III status—"injurious to unsatisfactory, unsuitable under most conditions." However, the low quality of drainage water here is a function of the relatively high salinity of irrigation water from the Colorado River and also of the arid climate of this irrigation district.[10] Circumstances can so greatly influence the quality of effluents that any generalization about reuse prospects becomes tenuous. In arid areas where water is of relatively high salinity to begin with, we might often be able to conclude that inefficiencies in irrigation are more apparent than real. In such instances, low-quality drainage water cannot be identified with avoidable waste.

The recovery of deep percolation water of satisfactory quality by pumping represents an expenditure of energy that is, however, otherwise avoidable—a third reason for attaching importance to irrigation efficiency. Such expenditure may be condoned only when there is a need for additional storage capacity, and when the advantage of storage in underground basins over storage in surface facilities is sufficiently great.

Finally, excess applications of irrigation water do not inevitably become additions to ground water or return to natural stream channels. For example, the discharge of irrigation tail waters to points outside the available phase of the hydrologic cycle corresponds to a real decrease in potential water supply.[11]

10. In an arid climate, there is normally no removal of salt accumulation in the soil by natural precipitation; leaching is an entirely artificial process.

11. To the extent that water distribution depends upon gravity flow, the available phase of the hydrologic cycle is reduced. Thus, drainage water entering the lower reaches of streams may effectively be "lost." If the return were further upstream, the same water might be reused.

## II

Independent research made possible a comparison of the efficiency of irrigation among the eleven western states. This involved estimating the quantity of water "consumed" by irrigated agriculture in each state during each of the four agricultural census years since 1949.[12] Comparison of these estimates with actual farm water supplies (gross use) will give some indication of irrigation efficiency.[13]

In the study in question, the annual consumptive use of water by a specific irrigated crop in a state was derived as the simple product of the acreage of that crop harvested from irrigated land in a year and its statewide unit consumptive water use (expressed as a water depth or acre-feet per acre). Whether the water occurred as moisture in the soil in which the crop was growing, as a free surface, or as natural precipitation intercepted by the crop, for the purposes of the study consumptive use of water by crops was defined as the depth of water (1) transpired, (2) used in the building of plant tissue according to some optimal goal, and (3) evaporated from a cropped area in any specified time.[14]

Irrigated-crop acreage data for each state were obtained from census publications. Unit consumptive water use by a crop was estimated

12. Edward C. Gray, "Water Requirements of Irrigated Agriculture in the Western States of the Continental United States" (Berkeley: Department of Agricultural Economics, University of California, 1969), 95 pp. (mimeographed).

13. More specifically, "irrigation efficiency" is defined as the percentage of irrigation water consumptively used. When the water is measured at the farm head gate, the term "farm irrigation efficiency" is used. For measurements at the field and at the point of diversion, the terms "field irrigation efficiency" and "project efficiency," respectively, are employed.

14. As defined, "consumptive use" is thus synonymous with "evapotranspiration." It is necessary to introduce the concept of some objective to be optimized because of the possibility of applying different total quantities of irrigated water over a growing season (and employing different irrigation cycles) in such manner that plant growth proceeds with the available soil moisture content somewhere between field capacity of the soil and the permanent wilting point. For the purpose of the definition, the assumption is made that sufficient water is available for the optimum to be achieved. The relation between plant growth and soil moisture is discussed by a number of authors. For reviews of literature in this area, see Robert A. Young and William E. Martin, "Modeling Production Response Relations for Irrigation Water: Review and Implications," *Conference Proceedings*, Western Agricultural Economics Research Council, Committee on the Economics of Water Resources Development, San Francisco, California, December 12–13, 1967, pp. 1–21, and J. C. Flinn and W. F. Musgrave, "Development and Analysis of Input-Output Relations for Irrigation Water," *Australian Journal of Agricultural Economics*, Vol. 11, No. 1 (June 1967), pp. 1–19.

at the state level by obtaining what per-acre consumptive-use data were available in the literature and deriving a weighted average by employing crop acreages as densities.[15] In general, for the western states, per-acre consumptive-use data are sketchy; numerous difficulties had to be overcome in applying them to acreage data to compute quantities of water "consumed" by irrigated agriculture in a state.

The search of the literature for evapotranspiration data for crops grown in the western states revealed common application of the Blaney-Criddle formula for estimating water use. For short-period consumptive use by a crop in a given locality, the formula is given simply as $u = k.f$ where $k$ is the consumptive-use coefficient for that crop for the period; $f$ is a short-period, consumptive-use factor ($= t.p/100$); $t$ is the mean short-period temperature (degrees Fahrenheit); and $p$ is the short-period percentage of annual daytime hours (obtained from tables for various latitudes). The formula is empirical, relying on measurements of $u$ and $f$ for the determination of $k$. For the full growing season, the formula is restated as $U = K.F.$, where $F$ is the sum of the $f$'s corresponding to each of the short periods (a monthly unit is usual) composing the full growing season. Again, $K$ is determined from measurements of $U$ and $F$.[16]

The essential appeal of the formula lies in an assumed constancy of $K$ for plantings of a specific crop over a fairly wide geographic area. This permits an extrapolation, by simple calculations of $F$, of $U$ to localities other than those in which field measurements were originally taken. It is beyond our scope here to discuss the merits of this formula or any others that attempt to estimate evapotranspiration by simple formulations employing climatic elements as independent variables.[17] Suffice it to say that the determinants of evapotranspiration are many.[18]

15. The consumptive-use data were usually applicable to small physiographic subregions, but sometimes to larger hydrologic subregions.

16. See Harry F. Blaney and Wayne D. Criddle, *Determining Consumptive Use and Irrigation Water Requirements,* U.S. Department of Agriculture Technical Bulletin No. 1275, 1962, 59 pp.

17. Formulas developed by Penman, Thornwaite, Quesnel, Hedke, and Lowry and Johnson are of this kind.

18. Colin Clark would deny that crop variety or species (as opposed to plant vigor and stage of growth) was independently important; see Colin Clark, *The Economics of Irrigation* (London: Pergamon Press, 1969), p. 4.

For nine of the eleven western states, bulletins that relied on Blaney-Criddle data and dealt with per-acre consumptive use of the main crops of the state in its principal growing areas were located and their data used.[19] For northern California, however, recent consumptive-use data exist for use in the framework study of water requirements coordinated by the Pacific Southwest Inter-Agency Committee. These data were based on soil-moisture depletion studies of the University of California at Davis.[20] A second exception to exclusive use of the Blaney-Criddle formula was Arizona, where there were also available consumptive-use data derived by use of "K" factors determined by Erie from moisture-depletion measurements over many years in the central parts of the state.[21] These data were utilized independently of and for comparison with the older Blaney-Criddle data.

Gross farm water use data[22] were obtained from the 1959 Census of Agriculture; the quantity of water delivered for use by farm irrigation water users in each state was inflated by a factor reflecting the proportion of delivered (off-farm) water as against water from on-farm sources. These figures were then compared with estimated water consumption by irrigated agriculture (as described above), both with and without allowance made for effective precipitation. Table 4.3 records these comparisons under the heading "Efficiency of Irrigation," the latter as "Crude," the former as "Refined."[23]

Because per-acre consumptive-use data for Utah were adopted for Nevada in the absence of data for the latter state, too much significance should not be attached to the high crude-irrigation efficiency of 71.3 per cent for Nevada.

19. For Oregon, Washington, Utah, Arizona, New Mexico, Colorado, Wyoming, Idaho, and Montana.

20. These are reported by Halkias *et al.*, "Determining Water Needs for Crops from Climatic Data," *Hilgardia*, Vol. 24, No. 9 (December 1955).

21. L. T. Erie, Orrin F. French, and Karl Harris, *Consumptive Use of Water by Crops in Arizona*, Arizona Agricultural Experiment Station Bulletin 169 (Tucson, 1965).

22. Gross farm water use may be called "farm delivery demand" in the literature. For an individual farm the proportion of water that is actually "delivered" from sources outside the farm will depend upon the extent of on-farm water development. In many cases water requirements will be met completely from on-farm sources of supply. To this extent, the use of the term "delivery" is misleading.

23. The term "crude" is employed because no allowance is made for effective natural precipitation. If it were allowed, efficiencies would fall accordingly. It must be stressed that these efficiencies are state-wide averages. Theoretically, efficiency may be appreciably higher (or lower) in any given locality.

TABLE 4.3.

*Comparison of Estimates of Water Consumption and Gross Farm Water Use,*
*Irrigated Agriculture, 1959*

| State | Estimated | | Efficiency of irrigation | |
|---|---|---|---|---|
| | Water consumption | Gross farm use[a] | Crude[b] | Refined[c] |
| | 1 | 2 | 3 | 4 |
| | 1,000 acre-feet | | percentage | |
| California | 21,684 | 31,335 | 69.2 | 59.2 |
| Oregon | 2,322 | 5,947 | 39.0 | 33.5 |
| Washington | 1,913 | 4,996 | 38.3 | 32.0 |
| Nevada | 1,314 | 1,842 | 71.3 | 67.7 |
| Utah | 2,494 | 3,651 | 68.3 | 51.7 |
| Arizona | 3,082 | 6,017 | 51.2[d] | 45.0[d] |
| Arizona | 3,982 | 6,017 | 66.2[e] | 60.0[e] |
| New Mexico | 1,736 | 2,792 | 62.2 | 50.5 |
| Colorado | 4,831 | 10,155 | 47.6 | 35.5 |
| Wyoming | 2,095 | 6,756 | 31.0 | 23.5 |
| Idaho | 4,115 | 15,059 | 27.3 | 23.7 |
| Montana | 2,890 | 8,699 | 33.2 | 22.2 |

[a] Because these are estimates of actual use, they are net of natural precipitation.
[b] Column 1 as a percentage of column 2.
[c] Column 1 less effective precipitation as a percentage of column 2.
[d] Based on Blaney-Criddle methods.
[e] Based on Erie "K" factors.

The figures for Arizona are interesting in that two estimates of consumptive use were employed. A difference of 15 per cent resulted.

Part of the research referred to comprised comparison of estimated theoretical and actual gross farm water use in selected parts (regions) of five of the eleven western states. The intention was to have a more-or-less random evaluation of the methods and data being used. However, it must be stressed that there never was any expectation of definitive results. This follows from the plurality of factors that impinge upon the agreement of theoretical with actual gross farm use, among them the accuracy of measurement of actual water use and of assumptions made in connection with unit consumptive use, the methods of determining actual amounts of effective natural precipitation, and the reliability of available irrigation efficiency data.

The decision to evaluate the method and data sources using areas smaller than the state rested primarily on the belief that "regional" data were more reliable. For the regions selected, there was certainly

TABLE 4.4.
*Comparison of Theoretical and Actual Gross Farm-Water Use,
Five Selected Regions, 1959*

| State in which region located | Farm irriga- tion efficiency assumed | Gross farm-water use | | Theoretical *as percentage* of actual |
|---|---|---|---|---|
| | | Theoretical | Actual | |
| | 1 | 2 | 3 | 4 |
| | percentage | 1,000 acre-feet | | percentage |
| California | 71.6 | 11,914 | 12,144 | 98 |
| Oregon | 60.0 | 1,245 | 1,699 | 73 |
| Arizona | 58.0 | 4,013[a] | 4,195 | 96[a] |
| Arizona | 58.0 | 5,737[b] | 4,195 | 137[b] |
| New Mexico | 50.0 | 778 | 877 | 89 |
| Idaho | 40.0 | 3,091 | 4,309 | 72 |

[a] Consumptive-use data Blaney-Criddle derived.
[b] Consumptive-use data based on Erie "K" factors.

greater coverage in available consumptive-use data of the range of crops grown than was the case for the state as a whole. This enabled estimates of water theoretically consumed to be derived by piecemeal aggregation.[24]

Essential details of the comparisons are given in Table 4.4. On the basis of column 1 efficiencies, which are estimates found in the literature, we find very good agreement in two instances — the California and the Arizona "test" regions.[25] On the other hand, theoretical gross farm water use is significantly overestimated when Erie "K" factors are used to derive consumption for the Arizona area. It is underestimated for the Idaho, Oregon, and New Mexico areas where data are Blaney-Criddle derived.

In the four instances of considerable disagreement between theoretical and actual, we confess to a temptation to change column 1 efficiencies to those presented in column 4 of Table 4.3 and then to observe the effect of the change on the comparison. For Oregon and Idaho (where the difference in efficiencies between column 4 of Table 4.3 and Table 4.4 was most marked), the change resulted in an improvement

24. It will be recalled that weighted averages were used for state calculations. This was operationally convenient because incomplete data virtually precluded piecemeal aggregation.

25. For only the Arizona region where consumptive use was determined using Blaney-Criddle data.

in the theoretical-actual comparison from 73 and 72 per cent to 109 and 121 per cent, respectively. Change of this kind has no substantive basis, however. For instance, we might just as readily have assumed the source of disagreement between theoretical and actual to lie with underestimation of unit consumptive use. In this respect the percentage adjustments in consumptive use that gave perfect agreement for the Oregon and Idaho "test" areas (in conjunction with Table 4.4 efficiencies) produced efficiencies of 46.0 and 33.1 per cent, respectively, when they were applied to statewide data. These are in fair agreement with Table 4.4 efficiencies of 50 and 40 per cent, respectively.

## Conclusion

In view of the disparities and deficiencies that exist in the available data and the plurality of variables that are involved in a theoretical-actual comparison, can we, in fact, draw any conclusions of substance? Does the additional information from the regional testing give us confidence to make a general statement on the state of the art of irrigation in the western states? We feel that we can answer both with a qualified "yes" and venture the following opinions, albeit somewhat reluctantly.

Consumptive-use data at present employed in framework studies of irrigation water requirements are excellent approximations for the California region but overestimate farm-water needs for the lower Colorado region (the state of Arizona, principally).

Water requirements calculated from consumptive-use data developed through measurement and application based on the Blaney-Criddle method will generally be underestimated.

For the state of California, the over-all average farm irrigation efficiency is of the order of 60 per cent, but 70 per cent efficiency can attain as an average in water-deficient areas.

For the state of Arizona as a whole, evidence would point to average farm irrigation efficiency being less than 50 per cent in 1959.

There is a wide variability in average irrigation efficiency among the western states. For 1959, the likely range was from a "high" of 60 to a "low" of 25 per cent.

Finally, we stress some of the points made earlier. We point to the predominant position of irrigated agriculture among uses of water in the western states. We emphasize the potential for "creating" additional water resources as the combined consequence of this and the possibility of improving the efficiency of irrigation. However, we recognize that irrigation water "wasted" at a point in the hydrologic cycle is not inevitably water "consumed." If it were, efforts to improve the efficiency of irrigation might be more effective.

# 5 ON THE DEMAND FOR WATER IN ITS NATURAL ENVIRONMENT

FRANK H. BOLLMAN

A changing scene requiring emphasis on different uses has always confronted the development and management of California's
water resources. First there was hydraulic mining and an embryonic
agriculture; then, closer settlement; expansion of irrigated agriculture; emerging industrialization; and, at the present and latest day, a
highly developed and urbanized economy – an affluent society with its
diverse and heavy attendant water requirements: hydropower; municipal, agricultural, and industrial supply; flood control, and navigation.
The conflict in demands for water in its various uses is certainly not
new, for arguments over legal water rights so prominent in western
history did not miss California, nor did extensions of those arguments
as emphasis shifted.

What is a relatively new element in the competition for the limited
freshwater supplies of the state is the rising demand at many different
places throughout the state for quantity and quality of water that will
ensure that the natural environment, in all its dimensions, is protected
and enhanced.

Recreation, particularly water-associated outdoor activities,
pollution abatement, the many and diverse instream uses of water for
fish and wildlife, and preservation of scenery, of places of scientific
and historical interest, and of wild rivers, are rapidly assuming the
role of major social needs, with obvious implications for official water
and land policy. For the State Water Plan and the state and federal
agencies responsible for water resources development and management the implications seem clear – the storage of water for agricul-

tural, industrial, and urban use must be critically appraised anew in view of these emergent demands. In this chapter we shall first look at some of the general problems associated with the demand for water in its natural environment. Then we shall look specifically at the situation in California from this perspective.

## THE PROBLEM OF VALUE

In California, rapid increases in population, urbanization, per capita income, and leisure time are forces which, in one way or another, cause not only large increases in water use but also shifts between uses.

The gradual diminution in the number of natural areas and free-flowing streams in California, as in the rest of the nation, has meant a steady rise in the value of those remaining. In addition, a greater appreciation of the recreational and aesthetic qualities of the natural environment makes society sensitively aware that these social values should be accounted for in any future sizeable manipulation of water and land. Not only is our affluent society now able to afford including aesthetics in planning, in many recent instances it has signified its willingness to pay for the preservation and enhancement of the recreational and aesthetic qualities of water *in situ*. In other words, water in its natural setting has appreciated in value, and the ability to bear the costs of keeping water in this setting has likewise increased considerably.

There is, therefore, a strong a priori argument that these social values be incorporated into any comprehensive plan of water development. Earlier plans, which may have been comprehensive for the essentially market products of water — power, irrigation, industrial and municipal water supplies — have to be reformulated to include these essentially extramarket values. While these comments also apply to "deficit" water areas, they are especially pertinent for the nonconsumptive instream uses of the water of the North Coast region of the state — an area still relatively rich in amenity resources, largely because it is the area of the largest remaining water "surplus." These uses must be given a value commensurate with the changing preferences of society.

The problem of value is fundamental to the planning of water use and development; it is, therefore, important to appraise the relative importance of the various demands and evaluate the benefits to be received from different uses.

The "needs of society," indeed, take priority in this process of weighing diverse and conflicting demands. However, the needs of society today are not the sole guide in the decision process, but rather future needs, decades ahead. Projections of the demands for water in its many uses — aesthetic and recreational, industrial, municipal, and agricultural — help point to the likely future social values, the objective being that water will be allocated in a way that will maximize social welfare of the state in the future as well as in the present.

Even given the shortcomings of many of the projections which have been made, it is evident that there has been a considerable increase in demand for the bundle of recreational services associated with streams in one way or another. The demand for water sports and for those activities made more enjoyable by natural beauty and scenery, including free-flowing streams and natural lakes, is expected to increase significantly in the next decade. Water sports activity specifically is projected to grow by some 126.3 million participation days. Much of this increase will occur in visits to and active recreation in natural streams and lakes. By 1980 sightseeing and nature walks where the attractive beauty of water in a natural setting looms large is anticipated to grow by 93 million days. More than 27 million more days will be spent in fishing and camping where natural streams play an important role in providing the aesthetic setting. The relevant statistics for California are given in Table 5.1.

Projections, then, are vital and relevant for water policy; and, although inherent conceptual and technical difficulties exist in deriving and formulating projections, they are basic to informed decisions as to future uses within and between regions.[1] Of course, future demands, irrespective of how accurately they are projected, have to be supplemented by benefit-cost and other types of economic analysis and reasoning. The problem is how to allocate water in its various uses over

1. For a definitive and critical appraisal of the relation between water requirements and water demands and its significance for water policy, see S. V. Ciriacy-Wantrup, "Projections of Water Requirements in the Economics of Water Policy," *Journal of Farm Economics,* Vol. XLIII, No. 2 (May 1961), pp. 197–214.

TABLE 5.1.
*Estimated Total Potential Demand for Outdoor Recreation in California*

| Activity | Participation days | | | |
|---|---|---|---|---|
| | 1950 | 1960 | 1970 | 1980 |
| *Water sport* | | | | |
| Swimming | 68.4 | 154.3 | 262.1 | 354.1 |
| Boating | 23.0 | 37.5 | 56.0 | 79.2 |
| Water skiing | 4.9 | 11.9 | 21.2 | 29.0 |
| Sailing and canoeing | 3.3 | 5.4 | 7.9 | 11.2 |
| Total | 99.6 | 209.1 | 347.2 | 473.5 |
| *Back-country recreation* | | | | |
| Fishing | 33.6 | 51.8 | 69.3 | 84.5 |
| Camping | 13.1 | 31.3 | 47.8 | 60.0 |
| Total | 46.7 | 83.1 | 117.1 | 144.5 |
| *Passive outdoor pursuits* | | | | |
| Sightseeing | 81.1 | 133.1 | 197.7 | 273.2 |
| Nature walks | 24.6 | 34.2 | 45.7 | 63.3 |
| Total | 105.7 | 167.3 | 243.4 | 336.5 |

SOURCE: Stanford Research Institute, *Recreation and Parks Study*, Part 1, prepared for State of California Department of Parks and Recreation (Pasadena, California, 1965), p. 70, Table 34.

time to obtain the highest net social value. Future demands have to enter the calculus of allocative decisions, including, of course, the decision to defer allocations.

Projections and assumptions must be made about future trends in demand for the water (both quantity and quality) in a single stream, total watershed, or hydrological system, and these projections and assumptions are consequently involved in the decisions to develop or manage the water resource. Since projections do influence public opinion and thus ultimately decisions about where and to what extent public monies are invested in management of and research dealing with water, the assumptions, underlying projections, and more particularly the decisions themselves should be explicitly stated. For example, common assumptions in estimates of fifty years ahead are that technology will not change the methods of augmenting supply or that improved methods of saving water will not be found.[2] One very useful exercise would be to assess, on the basis of current projections of water demand, the number and miles of undeveloped streams that would re-

2. A description and meaning of water requirements and the derivation of these requirements for agriculture, industry, and municipalities as employed in the California Water Plan are given in California Department of Water Resources, "Implementation of the California Water Plan," Bulletin No. 160–66, Appendices A–F (Sacramento, August 1967).

main in California in the year 2020. It would be even more revealing to ascertain the streams and miles of stream in the state for which no development is planned. While this residuum of streams may be increased as detailed feasibility studies show that some projected developments are not economically feasible (especially if the cost of alternative water supply is reduced), it would be a timely measure for taking stock of riverine environment.

While it is recognized that the extramarket values of aesthetic and recreational uses of water must be considered in explaining possible alternatives in water management and development, the social values of such uses are not easily expressed, much less converted to economic terms. Although there are several defects in the market, even for the so-called economic products of water power and water supplies, in the case of outdoor water-associated recreation — particularly those activities associated with a flowing stream — price, the value established in monetary terms in the market place, is not available.[3]

That the task of attaching useful values to extramarket services has proved intractable should not diminish the merit of individual contributions to the improvement of economic analysis and procedures for approximating the demand for these services and for measuring their benefits.

The state of the art was neglected until the late 1940's and 1950's when Ciriacy-Wantrup, Hotelling, and Clawson suggested ways of simulating a market demand function for outdoor recreation by attempting to determine what people were "willing to pay."

Ciriacy-Wantrup advocated the direct approach of interrogation to obtain demand schedules for these services.[4] The ingenious idea of

3. The implications for resource policy of these defects, which make prices for various uses of water "unreliable as indications of social welfare," have been discussed in S. V. Ciriacy-Wantrup, "Philosophy and Objectives of Watershed Policy," *Economics of Watershed Planning*, G. S. Tolley and F. E. Riggs eds. (1961); and *idem*, "Conservation and Resource Programming," *Land Economics*, Vol. 37, No. 2 (May 1961), p. 105.

4. S. V. Ciriacy-Wantrup, "Capital Returns from Soil-Conservation Practices," *Journal of Farm Economics*, Vol. XXIX, No. 4, Part II (November 1947), pp. 1181–1196. See also U.S. Bureau of Reclamation, "Report of the Committee on Problem 11," *California: Central Valley Project Studies—Payments by Beneficiaries, Problems 10 to 13*, 1947, pp. 81 and 89; U.S. Department of Interior, National Park Service, *The Economics of Public Recreation: An Economic Study of the Monetary Evaluation of Recreation in the National Parks*, Section II, Views of the Consultants (specifically Harold Hotelling), 1949; Marion Clawson, *Methods of Measuring the Demand for and Value of Outdoor Recreation*, RFF Reprint Number 10 (Washington, D.C.: Resources for the Future, 1959), 36 pp.

Professor Hotelling in 1949, pointing out a possible technique for evaluating benefits of national parks, was the genesis of the indirect approach. Hotelling's idea was subsequently extended and refined by Clawson in 1959. Both have been instrumental in guiding research endeavors into simulating demand for outdoor recreation services along a line of inquiry which has come to be known as the "travel-cost-proxy approach." In this approach, demand for recreation services is imputed through studies of expenditures on travel to recreation sites.

Building on these ideas in recent years, a number of investigators have advanced the state of the art of benefit evaluation and clarified a number of issues.[5]

Notwithstanding these recognized advances and this synthesis of ideas, there still exist large areas of disagreement between economists, and between economists and administrators and managers of recreational services and amenity resources, as to both the relevance and the comprehensiveness of benefit evaluation studies. In other words, the benefits of those services which have been variously called nonmarket, intangible, or incommensurable though not readily measurable in monetary terms are, nevertheless, real – of worth to society and increasing as natural areas diminish throughout the state. These benefits cannot be assumed to be negligible.

The rational choices in the potential use of any stream or system of streams, as envisaged in comprehensive water planning, are dependent on assaying all the values that various communities place upon specific uses of water.[6] In the conflict between what have been termed "preservation values" and "development values," planning has been hopefully viewed as eventually attaining the status in which all values involved are so presented that "decisions to develop are made after consideration of the preservation values which will be lost and so that

5. See Lionel J. Lerner, "Quantitative Indices of Recreational Values," *Water Resources and Economic Development of the West: Economics in Outdoor Recreational Policy*, Report No. 11, Conference Proceedings of the Committee on the Economics of Water Resources Development, Western Agricultural Economics Research Council jointly with the Western Farm Economics Association (Reno: University of Nevada, 1962), pp. 55–80. See also Marion Clawson and Jack L. Knetsch, *Economics of Outdoor Recreation*, Resources for the Future, Inc. (Baltimore: The Johns Hopkins Press, 1966), 328 pp.

6. For a definition of comprehensive river-basin planning, see *Policies, Standards, and Proceedings in the Formulation, Evaluation, and Review of Plans for Use and Development of Water and Related Land Resources*, 87th Congress, 1st Session, 1961, S. Doc. 97.

decisions to preserve are made with awareness of the development values foregone."[7]

In the state, indeed throughout the nation, the widespread concern with preserving the opportunity for outdoor recreation, natural beauty, and quality of the environment signify that the public is willing to forgo development values; the public is willing to pay for the extramarket benefits of preservation. The onus thus falls upon the evaluators to inform the public of what the cost is of realizing these extramarket benefits.

The value of natural scenery, such as river gorges and rapids, is not gauged simply from its recreational use. For many of these natural features, it does not follow that value is proportionate to the number of visitor-days of use. Though visitors to a particular stretch of wild river may be only few, the enjoyment of the rugged site is probably valued quite highly. This value cannot be assumed to be zero, of no consequence, when development plans are drawn for the river. Under current criteria, the value of a rugged and remote site may be estimated at up to $4 per day, as the value of specialized recreation, for example, nature photography. In many instances, valuation of specialized recreation at one site on a river does not encompass all the values associated with the miles of pristine river scenery lost by inundation by the waters backing up from the construction of a dam.[8]

In assessing the net value of slack-water recreation created by a reservoir, the value of the site for other types of recreation that existed on that stretch of stream before the dam was built should not be omitted.

It cannot be assumed automatically that the same standard value for the recreational use of a flowing stream and its adjoining land applies both before and after it is altered to a slack-water facility. The evaluation of the net benefits from slack-water recreation development in the Thermalito Forebay and Thermalito Afterbay of the Oroville Reservoir, however, employs this type of reasoning:

> The evaluation of a project for recreation benefits is usually made in terms of visitor-days of use converted to and expressed as a mone-

7. Roger Tippy, "Preservation Values in River Basin Planning," *Natural Resources Journal,* Vol. 8 (April 1968), p. 259.

8. Under the same criteria, the value for general recreation varies from $0.50 to $2.50 per recreation day.

tary value. The net number of visitor-days of use of a project is determined by deducting the number of visitor-days of use expected without the project and without additional recreational facilities, from the number of visitor-days of use anticipated with the project. The net economic worth or benefit of recreation use is derived by multiplying visitor-days of use by the assigned value of a visitor-day of use.[9]

In this instance the value of a visitor-day of recreation use does not alter; the same "assigned value" applies regardless of how or where it is used.[10]

There are other points at issue that are of more than academic interest. Expected use for the free-flowing stream before development must be based on past actual use of all services of the site — visits for sightseeing, fishing, trail-walking, or any other reason. This implies surveillance and an accounting for all instream uses. The actual trend in use over time should be known. How do the local community and visitors value this "neck of the woods," this "stretch of river"? The information is basic.

The next and more difficult step, a necessary one that has to be taken with extreme care, is to perceive just how scarce such under-developed sites can become when other proximate stretches of stream are developed. Expected use cannot be projected independently of what is known to be happening, and is reasonably certain to happen, to other stretches of the river that are substitutes for the site in question. Does this particular site, in the qualities and services it offers, complement what is available at other sites, developed or undeveloped, nearby?

As other river sites are developed, an undeveloped site will likely not only increase in value per visitor-day of use, but expected use will increase at a rate much greater than that predicted from a simple trend of past use. Scarcity has this accelerating effect on value, and wild stretches of river are, after all, growing more scarce.

9. California Department of Water Resources, *Oroville Reservoir, Thermalito Forebay, Thermalito Afterbay,* Bulletin No. 117–6 (Sacramento, 1966), p. 13. Net benefits are estimated as $P_a (D_w - D_{wo})$ where $P_a$ is the value assigned and $D_w$ and $D_{wo}$ are the visitor-days with and without the project.

10. In current procedures of the California Department of Water Resources, the concept of "visitor-day" has been replaced by "recreation day." A recreationist may engage in several different activities on one such day.

Likewise, the estimation of anticipated use requires a meticulous accounting for all factors influencing future use of the slack water made available by development.

Extrapolations of average state-wide or large-region characteristics are clearly inadequate and distorting. A more subtle omission, however, must be guarded against: anticipated use cannot be gauged without reference to all the other slack water in development or projected for development in the same vicinity. It might be anticipated that, with the supply of reservoir and dam water surface increasing, anticipated use at any particular site based on projecting its use independent of likely supply will fall short of the mark. If so, net benefits are not what they were made out to be.

Bias, therefore, can easily enter expected-use and anticipated-use estimations. What is necessary at this stage of the State Water Project, and as a guide for future development, is a series of strategic post-mortems in which actual use at certain developed water sites is compared with use previously projected, and reasons sought for any disparities. If economic justification is to serve its role, better knowledge of factors to which net benefits are sensitive seems mandatory. And why not? For are they not extremely sensitive to the difference between expected use before and anticipated use after? The effects of past water-development decisions should be more intently studied.

The results of such study could help insure that the public will not have to bear a consequence that they would have liked otherwise to avoid. Too little natural instream environment in the future is a consequence of no small magnitude.

Too, recreational benefits at such a site, assessed on the current standard dollar value per visitor-day, usually encompass a valuation of one recreational activity. There are other extramarket aspects not included in such evaluations — scenery, the sound of rushing water, isolation. Measuring the value of the many joint advantages of a site has so far eluded efforts. Another intractable problem in measurement is the value of a site as assessed by certain people who, although not directly enjoying the pleasures it has to offer, derive satisfaction from knowing that it is preserved so that they or other members of society, including future generations, might visit it. Unvisited natural resources are certainly not valueless. That many Americans sanction the use of tax monies for the purchase and upkeep of wilderness areas and natural seashores they have no intention of visiting supports the argument that a natural unique resource has value apart from that accorded by its actual use.

The problem of the value of a free-flowing stream is, therefore, extremely complex. Its over-all value cannot be derived by dismembering it in quantity-of-use terms for its few or many recreational uses. Many of the aesthetic services are joint products. This, of course, does not imply that evaluation should not be attempted; it rather suggests that evaluation is all the more desirable when, as is the case now with North Coast streams, industrialization and urbanization – in their derived demands for water – are encroaching on the aquatic environment. It is essential, as Scott points out, "to know what recreational values are being destroyed and when their value at the margin is sufficient to buy off further encroachment . . . or to buy out existing users in favor of extending the [undeveloped] recreation area."[11]

Many of the enhancement features associated with large upstream dams and impoundments (for example, they make it possible to regulate downstream flows for fish life) quite possibly could be obtained at greatly reduced costs if supplemental water were stored at strategic small-scale facilities which did not alter the nature of the free-flowing but seasonal stream. It is all a question of net benefits in project selection, but too often enhancement is incidental to a project which initially may cause fish and wildlife losses. Enhancement has now come of age; it has an independent right to consideration as the best and most valuable use of a stream.

The marginal value product of water, that is, the value of the last unit of water produced in each use – acre-foot of water supply and mile (or yard, for that matter) of flowing stream for fish-spawning and nursery – is the guide to its allocation and, hence, reallocation over time. Neither total value nor average value product (average value of all units of water produced) plays a role in allocating water to its different uses. The idea that water is priceless because it is essential to life is nonsense economically.

11. Anthony Scott, "The Valuation of Game Resources: Some Theoretical Aspects," Department of Fisheries of Canada, *Canadian Fisheries Report No. 4* (Ottawa, May 1965), p. 42.

In actual practice, it is extremely difficult to derive empirically the marginal value product for each use of water. Different qualities of water, at very different stages of delivery, apply to different uses. Besides, indivisibility of the resource intrudes; not one mile of water is involved, but perhaps thirty miles of stream are altered from flowing to slack water, when a dam is constructed at the most efficient storage site on a river. S. V. Ciriacy-Wantrup has sufficiently summed up the central issue for water policy: "The relevant criterion is not whether misallocation exists at the moment [as many studies profess to show] but whether continuous reallocation is too slow." [12]

The cost in terms of uses forgone — power, water supply, and the like — to preserve a river in its pristine condition can be very high. That extramarket benefits have in the past been incompletely assessed does not mean that, in any future development decision greatly affecting the instream environment, extramarket benefits should be considered the sole guide to its preservation. This extreme position is no more valid than that placing sole reliance on assessed market values. Until satisfactory methods are evolved to measure extramarket values, there are bound to be cases where these values are either underestimated or overestimated.

In Crutchfield's summary:

> We [economists] must be in on plans [involving decisions on fish and wildlife] and we must be in on the plans using economic evaluation techniques that fall within the confines of the accepted practices of other water uses. If you do not use economic evaluations at all your case is hopeless. If you use phony evaluations it is not much better. I think we have to work at the problem in these lights. . . . Those days [of no conflict] are gone and I think we are going to have to face the evaluation problem and do a better job than we have in the past if these values are to be preserved at all. [13]

The need exists to devise methods of objectively scrutinizing extramarket values and of weighing the market and extramarket values.

Another lesson for planning emerges from the consideration that

---

12. Ciriacy-Wantrup, "Projections of Water Requirements in the Economics of Water Policy," *op. cit.,* p. 208.

13. James Crutchfield, "Can We Put an Economic Value on Fish and Wildlife," *Colorado Outdoors* (March-April 1965), p. 2.

all market and extramarket costs and benefits be presented. This process requires that all practicable alternatives must be appraised. To
achieve a purpose, planning should evolve around alternatives rather
than the project itself. For planners to concentrate on a project could
mean the neglect of nonproject alternatives which may also achieve
the purpose. In the past, there have been instances in which, with one
project only in focus, the objective became too narrowly defined as a
justification for benefits for that particular project—in some cases, a
simple minimization of costs without reference to benefits.

In general, the tendency for plans to center on individual projects
in basin or interbasin development, or to be concerned too narrowly
with obtaining additional pure sources of water for a limited range of
commercial uses, has to be countered. Alternatives in locating projects,
and options, both for timing and size of projects, tend to be overlooked.[14] The California Water Plan and the State Water Project are
not beyond reproof on these grounds.

The substitution of slack-water recreation does not necessarily
compensate for the loss of the many recreational services of a free-
flowing stream—white-water canoeing, float-trip boating, fishing from
the bank, wading, and the like—even though statistics show that use
of the slack-water types of recreation on a reservoir is usually far
greater than for those associated with a flowing stream on the same
site. In many instances, the recreational uses of the stream prior to
development are insufficiently measured and sometimes not appraised
at all.

Such arguments as ". . . it is possible that a reasonably abundant
supply of game fish [other than anadromous fish like salmon] can be
produced in the Columbia system in spite of the construction of dams
authorized or completed. However, these fish will be mainly of the species considered inferior by most resident sportsmen although they
have been acceptable to fishermen in reservoirs elsewhere in the
country"[15] illustrate the tendency to ignore preferences, particularly

14. The history of the projected Dos Rios Project on the Eel River illustrates the tendency in the planning process to overlook or not search thoroughly enough for practicable and feasible alternatives in location, size, and timing even within one river basin.

15. *Ten Rivers in America's Future,* The Report of the President's Water Resources
Policy Commission, Vol. 2, Part 1, No. 1 (1950), p. 47.

where these preferences obstruct development for other purposes. Obviously, in this instance sportsmen preferred salmon and steelhead fishing. Their preference should be taken into account. It is, therefore, basic to any water management program that the consumer and his preferences be ascertained and that agencies virtually managing and developing aquatic habitats in their many dimensions provide as wide a range of services as possible and endeavor to ensure that the broad spectrum of consumers' tastes is satisfied – the white-water canoeist as well as the slack-water powerboat enthusiast; no group should be excluded simply because their use will be minimal. Obviously, decisions concerned with water allocation have to be taken not only with as complete a knowledge of the conditions and consequences of change in water use as may be discovered but together with a comprehensive assay of society's preferences. The absence of a pricing system for many of the services of a free-flowing stream should not deter attempts, direct or indirect, to assess such preferences.

That the consumer of these services has not been identified sufficiently and the means to satisfy his tastes elicited adds to the difficulties of agencies managing the aquatic environment. For whom are they managing those resources? Gross participation figures alone are no guide to the quality or type of activity which should be preserved or developed in a program that will satisfy recreationists' preferences. The consumer should not remain anonymous and preferences should be solicited.

To project what demands will be in the future entails as a minimum the latest and best information on preferences and recent trends in substitution between recreation activities. Many of these preferences are not recorded in visitors' data alone. This is particularly true of the many nonconsumptive recreational and aesthetic pursuits.[16] If projections are to be a guide to allocation of water, to municipal and industrial as well as recreational uses, then in the next several de-

16. To assess the total demand for all recreational and aesthetic services of a flowing undeveloped stream would entail estimating the "market" as a whole, the pattern of user demands, and the pattern of demand for competing and complementary activities. The type of information to be collected is set out in Frank H. Bollman, "A Prospectus for the 1970 National Survey of Fishing and Hunting" (Berkeley: Giannini Foundation of Agricultural Economics, University of California), 31 pp.

cades changes in taste will be important factors to be reckoned with.

The projections of the demands for water-associated outdoor recreation developed for the California Region of the Framework Study
which are termed "directly dependent upon the availability of a running stream or body of water" relate to only five activities — swimming,
boating, water-skiing, sailing and canoeing, and fishing.

These projections give little insight into the need for natural free-
flowing streams to meet requirements in other than these five activities. Indeed, it would appear that it is the aggregate supply of running
streams or bodies of water naturally or artificially stored that is to
meet the requirements of what amounts to very few activities. The
proportions envisaged for artificial and natural stored water in this
mix are certainly not ascertainable from such calculations.

Estimated average statewide per capita participation is not the
most reliable indication of future needs, and regionally the use of such
a measure could be quite distorting.[17]

The precise cluster of joint products or services of free-flowing
streams and natural lakes must first be identified, and the latest information on trends in demand for these activities incorporated into
consumption predictions. Even a reconnaissance-type study, as the
Type I Framework Study of the California State-Federal Interagency
Group, must fall far short of its objective if these preconditions are not
met. "The basic objective in the formulation of framework plans is to
provide a broad guide to the best use or combination of uses of water
and related land resources of a region to meet foreseeable short- and
long-term needs." As already emphasized, "the best use" of free-flowing
streams cannot be based on cursory analyses of the demands for their
services or on the assumption that slack water artificially stored will
meet these demands; the quality of the recreational experience has to
be taken into account. Admittedly, demand studies undertaken for

17. For a summary of the preliminary projections for water-associated recreation
demand, see California Department of Parks and Recreation, "Present and Future Recreation Demand for the California Region of the Framework Study," mimeographed, 25
pp. For a description of this study, see California State-Federal Interagency Group for
Pacific Southwest Interagency Committee of the Water Resources Council, "Plan of
Study: California Region — Comprehensive Framework Study" (May 1967), p. 1, from
which the sentence quoted in the next paragraph is taken.

particular projects are more detailed than those in the Framework Study. Recognition of these needs has wide-ranging implications for preservation and development. In the next section we shall briefly review the situation in California in light of these principles.

## RECREATIONAL USE IN CALIFORNIA

In ten years of construction of major reservoirs in California, 1956-1965, some 16,271,730 gross storage acre-feet were added at projects where recreation was planned as one of the uses. Exclusive of reservoirs having less than 2,000 acre-feet and of those constructed by private individuals (farm ponds and dams provide recreational services — fishing, boating, and swimming — in addition to home and stock and irrigation water), the total gross storage in acre-feet for the 79 major reservoirs developed from 1956 to 1965 for all uses was 16,608,270. How many miles of shoreline or surface acres resulted (better measures of the recreational opportunity at these reservoirs) is at present not available.

In the State Water Project, at 21 dams and reservoirs projected for construction by the early 1970's, there is a total of 57,900 surface acre-feet and 525 miles of shore line.[18] There is certainly no deficit in terms of the present and projected supply of developable slack water.

Table 5.2 gives some of the physical dimensions of the 21 major dams and reservoirs included in the State Water Project. What should be subjected to more detailed scrutiny is the appraisal of costs involved in developing recreation at reservoirs and dams against the cost of providing recreational services with the stream in its natural state. A flowing stream may be so valuable in providing recreational services that this use precludes all other uses.

Total disbursements reported through 1969 for recreation and fish and wildlife enhancement at 12 of the 21 dams and reservoirs in the State Water Project was $25,551,740. Disbursements are made up of the costs of acquiring land and the joint cost allocable to recreation and fish and wildlife enhancement. Including the costs attributable to the California Aqueduct Delta to Dos Amigos Pumping Plant, approxi-

18. California Department of Water Resources, *The California State Water Project Summary: Nineteen-sixty-nine*, Bulletin No. 132–70 (Sacramento, 1970), Appendix C, p. 31.

TABLE 5.2.
California State Water Project—21 Dams and Reservoirs

| | Dams | | | | | Reservoirs | |
|---|---|---|---|---|---|---|---|
| | Structural height | Crest elevation | Crest length | Volume | Gross capacity[a] | Surface area | Shore line |
| | feet | feet[b] | feet | 1000 cubic yards | acre-feet | acres | miles |
| Frenchman[c] | 139 | 5,588 | 720 | 536 | 55,417 | 1,580 | 21 |
| Antelope[c] | 105 | 5,002 | 1,320 | 380 | 22,513 | 931 | 15 |
| Grizzly Valley[c] | 115 | 5,775 | 800 | 230 | 84,371 | 4,025 | 32 |
| Abbey Bridge | 110 | 5,468 | 1,150 | 500 | 45,000 | 1,950 | 21 |
| Dixie Refuge | 100 | 5,754 | 1,050 | 400 | 16,000 | 900 | 15 |
| Oroville[c] | 770 | 900 | 6,920 | 80,000 | 3,537,577 | 15,805 | 167 |
| Thermalito Diversion[c] | 161 | 225 | 1,300 | 154 | 13,328 | 323 | 10 |
| Thermalito Forebay[c] | 71 | 225 | 15,900 | 1,580 | 11,768 | 630 | 10 |
| Thermalito Afterbay[c] | 37 | 136 | 41,600 | 5,038 | 57,041 | 4,302 | 26 |
| Clifton Court Forebay | 34 | 14 | 36,500 | 2,440 | 30,000 | 2,200 | 8 |
| Bethany | 80 | 243 | 3,240 | 1,040 | 4,804 | 173 | 5 |
| Del Valle[c] | 223 | 745 | 880 | 4,200 | 77,106 | 1,060 | 16 |
| San Luis[c] | 385 | 544 | 18,600 | 77,645 | 2,038,008 | 12,700 | 65 |
| O'Neill Forebay[c] | 88 | 225 | 14,350 | 3,000 | 56,426 | 2,700 | 12 |
| Los Banos Detention | 167 | 384 | 1,370 | 2,100 | 34,562 | 623 | 12 |
| Little Panoche Detention | 152 | 676 | 1,440 | 1,210 | 13,236 | 354 | 10 |
| Buttes | 140 | 2,780 | 2,230 | 3,130 | 21,800 | 580 | 6 |
| Cedar Springs[c] | 213 | 3,378 | 2,250 | 7,400 | 78,000 | 995 | 13 |
| Perris[c] | 120 | 1,590 | 11,600 | 17,200 | 100,000 | 2,080 | 6 |
| Pyramid | 381 | 2,606 | 1,080 | 6,763 | 179,000 | 1,360 | 21 |
| Castaic[c] | 335 | 1,535 | 5,200 | 43,000 | 350,000 | 2,630 | 34 |
| TOTAL | | | 169,500 | 257,946 | 6,825,957 | 57,900 | 525 |

SOURCE: California Department of Water Resources, The California State Water Project Summary: Nineteen-sixty-nine. Bulletin No. 132-70 (Sacramento, 1970), Appendix C, p. 31.
[a] State share of the joint-use canal.
[b] Above sea level.
[c] Projects partly or fully developed for recreation and fish and wildlife.

TABLE 5.3.

Area and Costs of Specific Recreation Lands at State Water Project Facilities[a]

| | Acres acquired | Costs[b] | Acres to be acquired | Total acres | Cost per acre acquired |
|---|---|---|---|---|---|
| | | dollars | | | dollars |
| Frenchman Lake | 719 | 41,367 | 0 | 719[c] | 58 |
| Antelope Lake | 1,342 | N.A. | 0 | 1,342[c] | N.A. |
| Lake Davis | 733 | 186,385 | 0 | 733[c] | 254 |
| Lake Oroville | 2,448 | 1,585,186 | 24 | 2,472[c] | 646 |
| Thermalito Forebay and Afterbay | 200 | 172,349 | 31 | 231 | 862 |
| Lake Del Valle | 1,206 | 485,208 | 0 | 1,206 | 402 |
| San Luis Reservoir and O'Neill Forebay | 132 | 22,742 | 671 | 803 | 172 |
| California Aqueduct (excluding reservoirs) | 535 | 549,123 | [d] | 535 | 1,026 |
| Castaic Lake | 779 | 851,803 | 399 | 1,178[c] | 1,093 |
| TOTAL | 8,094 | 3,894,753 | 1,125 | 9,219 | — |

SOURCE: California Department of Water Resources, *The California State Water Project in 1969: Appendix D — Costs of Recreation and Fish and Wildlife Enhancement*, Bulletin No. 132–69 (Sacramento, 1969), p. 11.

[a] Includes recreation lands for only those project facilities with an established Recreation Land Use and Acquisition Plan.

[b] Total reported costs through 1968.

[c] In addition to these lands, federal lands have been acquired at a nominal cost to the state.

[d] Additional land needs are to be identified by future studies.

TABLE 5.4.
*State Water Project Potential for Water-Oriented Recreation*[a]

| New lakes | Acres of water surface | Miles of shore line |
|---|---|---|
| Upper Feather River area | 9,400 | 104 |
| Oroville area | 21,300 | 213 |
| San Francisco Bay area | 3,100 | 29 |
| San Joaquin Valley, West Side | 17,000 | 99 |
| Southern California area | 7,600 | 80 |
| TOTAL | 58,400 | 525 |

SOURCE: California Department of Water Resources, *The California State Water Project Summary: Nineteen-sixty-nine,* Bulletin No. 132–70 (Sacramento, 1970), Appendix C, p. 9.
[a] Plus water supplies for new recreation developments constructed by the state and by local governmental agencies.

mately $25.5 million has been expended to provide partial or full recreation use and fish and wildlife improvement at 12 project sites with a total shoreline of 421 miles and a combined surface area of 44,520 acres. Recreation and fish and wildlife enhancement costs apply to those reservoirs and dams shown fully or partly developed for recreation.[19]

The costs of acquiring specific recreation land at the various State Water Project facilities and the acreage involved are shown in Table 5.3; the potential for water-oriented recreation is shown on a regional basis in Table 5.4.

The recreational use of State Water Project facilities from 1962 to 1969 is shown in Table 5.5. A total of 1,554,800 visitor-days were recorded in 1969 at these sites. The large amount of reservoir surface in the state does not reinforce the argument that more reservoirs are required for recreation purposes.

Gross-use estimates do not reveal who receives the direct recreational benefits of State Water Project facilities. Thus, another basic consideration in the evaluation process is to identify the beneficiaries of all water uses. Water decisions, when based upon economic efficiency criteria, relate to the total net benefits to the nation irrespective of who gains these benefits, who may be adversely affected, and who should share these costs. This is another way of saying we need to know more about the regional effects of water development and to evolve measures

19. Table 2, note c.

TABLE 5.5.
*Summary of Project Services, 1962–1969*

| Year | Water delivered Municipal and industrial use | Irrigation | Recreation use | Electrical energy generated |
|------|------|------|------|------|
| | acre-feet | | recreation days[a] | kilowatt-hours |
| 1962 | 4,594 | 4,312 | 30,000 | N.A. |
| 1963 | 6,686 | 5,959 | 105,000 | N.A. |
| 1964 | 11,292 | 9,619 | 332,000 | N.A. |
| 1965 | 17,642 | 16,384 | 500,000 | N.A. |
| 1966 | 27,529 | 27,384 | 465,000 | N.A. |
| 1967 | 28,736 | 28,027 | 438,000 | N.A. |
| 1968 | 51,474 | 241,769 | 932,000 | 628,000,000 |
| 1969 | 37,436 | 246,810 | 1,554,800 | 2,614,000,000 |
| Total[b] | 185,389 | 580,264 | 4,356,800 | 3,242,000,000 |

SOURCE: California Department of Water Resources, *The California State Water Project in 1969, Appendix D,* Bulletin No. 132–69 (Sacramento, 1969), p. 11.

[a] A recreation day is the visit of one person to a recreation area for any part of one day.

[b] In addition, dams of the State Water Project have prevented millions of dollars in flood damage, the most notable to date being an estimated $30,000,000 in probably damage prevented by operation of partially completed Oroville Dam during the storm of December 1964 and January 1965.

of the probable impacts of the regional changes that are bound to result from further development of rivers in the North Coast region.

As shown in Table 5.6, there are, as would be expected, great disparities between opportunity for recreation at major reservoirs and dams and the state's population distribution. Butte, Merced, and Trinity counties, relatively distant from large population centers (together they contain only 1.07 per cent of the state's population) have, in all, 9 dams which hold 51.36 per cent of the water stored in the state's major dams and reservoirs. Los Angeles County, with 35 per cent of the state's population, at present does not have even one large storage dam for recreational use.

### IRREVERSIBILITY: SOME IMPLICATIONS

Implicit in the consideration that all values be accounted for is a highly significant question for water policy in the state—that of avoiding irreversibilities. What is the extent of the social loss in the irreversible development of reaches, tributaries, or main-flowing streams in the North Coast region? Further, if the decision should be made to zone some of these streams or portions of them as sanctuaries for fish and wildlife, as wild rivers for white-water canoeing, and for their scenic grandeur, what would be the resultant costs? An excerpt from Professor Ciriacy-Wantrup's cogently reasoned argument for preservation of prime irrigable land in California is pertinent and possibly has transfer value for reservoir sites and natural areas along these streams which are now few in number and growing increasingly scarcer. Many stream environments might be classed as irreplaceable assets. He proposes, as a tenet of resource policy, a strategy for decision that would insure against experiencing extreme regrets, that is to say, a strategy that has the minimum such maximum.

. . . in accordance with our reformulation of the objectives of land policy we are mainly interested in the order of magnitude of maximum possible losses as compared with that of the insurance premium that must be paid to guard against them.[20]

As in the case of California's prime irrigable land, the maximum possible losses occasioned by an irreversible decision for a particular stream habitat may be quite high. Other (undisturbed) streams would continue to exist but one particular stream might be regarded as "unique" in the type of scenic attraction recreational services it offers.

There are a number of decision criteria for selecting a strategy under uncertainty; the choice of the minimax has a perfectly good rationale to justify it in the case of unique natural resources.[21]

As can be inferred from the growth in demand for the services of the natural environment, particularly those associated with streams and natural lakes, the specific needs of the future are difficult to forecast. With technological possibilities expanding for water reuse, desalting of brines and sea water, and nuclear power, there is a reasoned case for maintaining flexibility toward the future. The removal of the aquatic habitat, or part of it, of salmon and steelhead in the North Coast streams, even though costly fish passages and hatcheries are

20. S. V. Ciriacy-Wantrup, "The 'New' Competition for Land and Some Implications for Public Policy," *Natural Resources Journal*, Vol. 4, No. 2 (October 1964), p. 259.

21. L. J. Savage, "The Theory of Statistical Decision," *Journal of the American Statistical Association*, Vol. 46, No. 253 (March 1951), pp. 55–67.

TABLE 5.6.
*Major Reservoirs Constructed in California with Recreational Use, 1956–1965;
Recreation Opportunity Compared with Population; by Counties*

| County | Number | Gross storage | Estimated population, June 30, 1970 | Population ratio: county to state | Storage ratio: county reservoirs to total, all state reservoirs[a] |
|---|---|---|---|---|---|
| | | acre-feet | | percentage | percentage |
| | 1 | 2 | 3 | 4 | 5 |
| Alameda | 1 | 78,500 | 1,052,500 | 5.22 | .48 |
| Alpine | 0 | 0 | 500 | [b] | 0 |
| Amador | 0 | 0 | 12,800 | .06 | 0 |
| Butte | 4 | 3,637,780 | 99,500 | .49 | 22.36 |
| Calaveras | 3 | 457,900 | 14,100 | .07 | 2.81 |
| Colusa | 1 | 67,500 | 12,200 | .06 | .41 |
| Contra Costa | 0 | 0 | 573,700 | 2.85 | 0 |
| Del Norte | 0 | 0 | 16,800 | .08 | 0 |
| El Dorado | 5 | 433,760 | 46,500 | .23 | 2.67 |
| Fresno | 2 | 251,300 | 420,500 | 2.09 | 1.54 |
| Glenn | 0 | 0 | 20,500 | .10 | 0 |
| Humboldt | 0 | 0 | 102,000 | .51 | 0 |
| Inyo | 0 | 0 | 83,300 | .41 | 0 |
| Imperial | 0 | 0 | 16.100 | .08 | 0 |
| Kern | 0 | 0 | 343,700 | 1.70 | 0 |
| Kings | 0 | 0 | 68,900 | .34 | 0 |
| Lake | 1 | 3,500 | 20,300 | .10 | .02 |
| Lassen | 0 | 0 | 18,300 | .09 | 0 |
| Los Angeles | 0 | 0 | 7,061,700 | 35.03 | 0 |
| Madera | 1 | 4,700 | 45,400 | .23 | .03 |
| Marin | 1 | 22,500 | 208,300 | 1.03 | .14 |
| Mariposa | 2 | 1,035,480 | 6,100 | .03 | 6.36 |
| Mendocino | 1 | 122,500 | 54,400 | .27 | .75 |
| Merced | 2 | 2,153,000 | 108,400 | .54 | 13.23 |
| Modoc | 0 | 0 | 7,200 | .04 | 0 |
| Mono | 0 | 0 | 5,400 | .03 | 0 |
| Monterey | 1 | 350,000 | 247,700 | 1.23 | 2.15 |
| Napa | 1 | 1,600,000 | 82,900 | .41 | 9.83 |
| Nevada | 4 | 169,000 | 26,900 | .13 | 1.04 |
| Orange | 0 | 0 | 1,438,800 | 7.14 | 0 |
| Placer | 3 | 492,100 | 82,600 | .41 | 3.02 |
| Plumas | 4 | 252,010 | 12,500 | .06 | 1.55 |
| Riverside | 0 | 0 | 451,500 | 2.24 | 0 |
| Sacramento | 0 | 0 | 642,100 | 3.18 | 0 |
| San Benito | 1 | 18,000 | 19,100 | .09 | .11 |
| San Bernardino | 0 | 0 | 703,600 | 3.49 | 0 |
| San Diego | 2 | 10,500 | 1,401,300 | 6.95 | .06 |
| San Francisco | 0 | 0 | 699,800 | 3.47 | 0 |
| San Joaquin | 1 | 431,500 | 298,200 | 1.48 | 2.65 |
| San Mateo | 0 | 0 | 95,900 | .48 | 0 |
| San Luis Obispo | 2 | 600,000 | 558,200 | 2.77 | 3.68 |
| Santa Barbara | 0 | 0 | 264,100 | 1.31 | 0 |

| County | Number | Gross storage | Estimated population, June 30, 1970 | Population ratio: county to state | Storage ratio: county reservoirs to total, all state reservoirs[a] |
|--------|--------|---------------|-------------------------------------|-----------------------------------|-------------------------------------------------------------------|
|        |        | acre-feet     |                                     | percentage                        | percentage                                                        |
| 1      | 2      | 3             | 4                                   | 5                                 |                                                                   |
| Santa Clara | 1 | 10,000 | 1,065,600 | 5.29 | .06 |
| Santa Cruz | 1 | 8,400 | 121,700 | .60 | .05 |
| Shasta | 1 | 250,000 | 82,800 | .41 | 1.54 |
| Sierra | 0 | 0 | 2,400 | .01 | 0 |
| Siskiyou | 1 | 58,000 | 35,500 | .18 | .36 |
| Solano | 0 | 0 | 176,100 | .87 | 0 |
| Sonoma | 0 | 0 | 210,900 | 1.05 | 0 |
| Stanislaus | 0 | 0 | 205,000 | 1.02 | 0 |
| Sutter | 0 | 0 | 42,500 | .21 | 0 |
| Tehama | 2 | 161,900 | 30,300 | .15 | .99 |
| Trinity | 3 | 2,566,400 | 7,700 | .04 | 15.77 |
| Tulare | 3 | 353,000 | 196,100 | .97 | 2.17 |
| Tuolumne | 2 | 365,500 | 21,400 | .11 | 2.25 |
| Ventura | 1 | 250,000 | 382,500 | 1.90 | 1.54 |
| Yolo | 0 | 0 | 88,400 | .43 | 0 |
| Yuba | 1 | 57,000 | 47,800 | .24 | .35 |
| TOTAL | 59 | 16,271,730 | 20,161,000 | 100.00 | 99.97 |

SOURCES: Cols. 1 and 2: California Department of Water Resources, *Implementation of the California Water Plan,* Bulletin No. 160–66 (Sacramento, 1966), Table 2, pp. 11–15. Col. 3: California Chamber of Commerce, Research Department, "Population by Counties 1940, 1950 and 1960 Census and Estimates, 1967 Through 1970," Economic Series (January 15, 1970). Col. 4: Calculated from column 3. Co.. 5: Calculated from column 2.

[a] Reservoirs which include recreation use.

[b] Negligible.

provided to maintain the run, with no certainty of long-run success, is irreversible. There is a case for reasoned delay — time in which to demonstrate thoroughly the need for the products or services of development (in this case, water exports) and to acquire the knowledge that will permit the consequences to the environment of project construction to be predicted more reliably. The revision of water-demand projections downward is one opportunity for delay. An "insurance premium" is paid to keep such an option open if immediate benefits are foregone. These benefits may not be inconsiderable in some instances; they should be identified and measured in all instances.

There is some evidence (whether it is sufficient still awaits impartial judgment) that cost-reducing techniques for freshwater recovery and reuse techniques can substantially supplement water supplies, particularly for the densely populated coastal metropolises.

The cost, therefore, of preserving water *in situ* in the North Coast may not be too high.

Where unique natural resources are involved, economic analysis has to cope with defining economic and technological irreversibility. What is the optimum amount of river or estuary to maintain today, tomorrow, and in the future? Quite probably society can afford the first yard or first mile with much less loss in scenic grandeur and marine life than that involved in taking a subsequent segment. But to determine the point at which the values foregone (including future values) are greater than those gained is extremely difficult, demanding a good knowledge of the total ecosystem and its over-all production possibilities.[22] Where the line of demarcation is to be drawn is difficult to gauge, but various kinds of analyses can give useful insights.

In making a decision as to how much, if any, of a river or estuary is to be given up for development purposes, certain things should be taken into account. The relative scarcity of the aquatic habitat — for instance, the remaining miles of spawning streams for anadromous fish in the state — and the relative scarcity of the flora and fauna it supports, or the associated scenery, are compared with the relative scarcity of what will be obtained by development. Are there substitute opportunities (including technical possibilities) for the development of products elsewhere which, although more costly, are not so costly in terms of loss of biological resources and aesthetic qualities?

Analyses ascertaining the fundamental biological relationships of the ecosystem show the relation of a part to the whole and are a necessary prerequisite to devising measures which are safeguards against irreversibility. In other words, interest centers on what happens to the whole when a part of the system is modified or converted to other than its natural use.

Investigation of the relation of the part to the whole (or the role of stream habitat to the over-all aquatic environment) presents the biologist and ecologist with a very complex problem, one which is further complicated by the planning and engineering studies that frequently deemphasize these interrelationships. At present, research staffs in agencies are largely oriented to the engineering viewpoint, even to the

22. What is the social loss to mankind for the extinction (by human action) of one species of bird, animal, or fish?

assessment of social values, although these are rightfully fashioned in the political process. It is now obvious that biological, ecological, and social viewpoints should not be subordinate to that of engineering efficiency. A partnership is urgently required, and this will mean adequate staffing with competence and capability in those three professional categories.

The type of research advocated would serve to unmask "the tyranny of small decisions," in which one decision taken is relatively unimportant at the time it is made but, given time and additional decisions, the system is completely altered.[23]

In many rivers, small increments in water pollution and the obstacles created by dams have eventually resulted in extinction of anadromous fish. Theoretically the resource damaged, such as a fishery by project development, could be made whole again at perhaps lower cost at another site. In practice, attempts to replace the resource elsewhere have not been outstandingly successful. The systems approach is violated when fish and wildlife agencies are requested to evaluate a project, or a portion of a project, or a section of stream when there are plans for additional water developments on the same stream. In many instances, these agencies do not have the choice of proposing an alternative to the project they have been asked to evaluate, nor do they have the research capability and manpower to investigate and sponsor other alternatives. A multipurpose water agency ideally would propose all feasible alternatives; the fish and wildlife agency could indicate the appropriate measure for mitigation and enhancement. Such an ideal arrangement seems remote.

In summary, it is demonstrable that water in a free-flowing stream provides many unique services which have an increasing economic value. Water instream is an appreciating asset, and some development decisions are irreversible. Although current estimating methods do not adequately encompass all social values, without a detailed scrutiny a reasonably accurate picture of the social costs and benefits of maintaining a river or tributary in its wild state cannot be assessed.

The difficulty of forecasting the effects and consequences of manipulating a watercourse — particularly the ecological consequences —

23. A. E. Kahn, "The Tyranny of Small Decisions: Market Failures, Imperfections, and the Limits of Economics," *Kyklos,* Vol. 19, No. 1 (1966), pp. 23–47.

for a valley, delta, or estuary is compounded by the lack of research findings in the biological and social spheres. This situation is nation-wide and an indirect result of past failure to recognize extramarket benefits. The criterion of engineering efficiency has to be modified to account not only for biological consequences but also for distributional effects on the welfare of communities. The preferences of communities have to enter into planning decisions. Better information and knowl-edge in these fields place greater responsibility on the natural and social sciences to reveal ways in which society can reconcile competing demands on the water resources in the state. Safeguards against the obscuring of conflicts between objectives by planning agencies are needed.

While much more can be said on the subject, one of the acceptable guides to the further allocation of water in the state is an elaboration of all feasible alternatives that can achieve the objective. All details of these alternatives should be made public; the varying costs, benefits, and effects for each alternative should be publicly scrutinized and de-bated. This is one fundamental safeguard to insure that the water resources of the state will be managed and developed in a way that will contribute to the "greatest good for all."

# 6 BIOLOGICAL IMPLICATIONS OF REDUCED FRESHWATER FLOWS ON THE SAN FRANCISCO BAY-DELTA SYSTEM

CHARLES R. GOLDMAN

The great California Delta area formed inland at the confluence of the Sacramento and San Joaquin rivers by the anastomosis of their sloughs and meandering tributaries is part of a continuous natural water system that begins in the Cascades and the Sierra Nevada and terminates in the Pacific Ocean. The portion of this system consisting of just the Delta and San Francisco Bay is referred to as the Bay-Delta System. This System may be viewed as an ecological unit even though its margins are as indistinct as the ebb and flow of its tides and the freshwater flows that advance and retreat with the annual runoff. An important characteristic of this portion of the total mountains-to-Pacific system that distinguishes it from either its river sources or its ocean terminus is its estuarine nature, that is, its condition of being intermediate in salt content between fresh and salt water. Indeed, it is sometimes referred to as the Bay-Delta estuary. More often, however, the term "estuary" is applied to the Bay alone. According to the National Estuary Study of the U.S. Department of the Interior transmitted to Congress on January 30, 1970, an estuary is "a semi-enclosed coastal water body having free connection with the open sea within which sea water is measurably diluted with fresh water drained from the land."

The degree of saltwater intrusion into an estuary is regulated primarily by the tidal cycle and the magnitude of freshwater discharge, and somewhat by the direction and velocity of the wind. The waters of

Net Delta Outflow (million acre-feet/month)

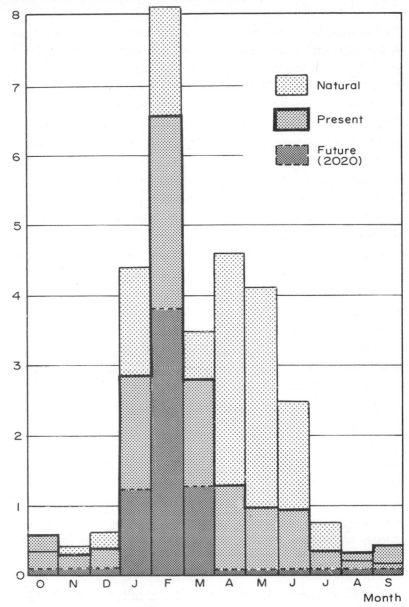

FIGURE 6.1. Average Delta Outflow: Natural, Present, and Future,[a] Hydrologic Year 1936. SOURCE: Kaiser Engineers, "Final Report to the State of California, San Francisco Bay-Delta Water Quality Control Program," 1969.

[a] Natural outflow based on California Department of Water Resources estimate. Present and 2020 figures based on U.S. Bureau of Reclamation and Department of Water Resources, 1968. Assumption: Delta lowlands water use remains the same as it is today.

the Bay and Delta exist in a dynamic balance that reflects the totality of the physical, chemical, and biological dimensions of the entire watershed. Natural changes in the discharge of fresh water into the Bay-Delta System have been observed to alter the character of both the Delta and the estuary below. Therefore, some of the changes resulting from intentional manipulations of the freshwater flow will be readily detectable and roughly predictable. Other more subtle changes will take longer to occur and will go undetected except by the trained observer. Figure 6.1 shows the estimated average Delta outflow before the State Water Project construction began, at present, and in the year 2020. The total flow will not only be greatly reduced in the future, but there will be only three months each year when the flow will be at all significant. Predictions as to the precise nature of the changes taking place and their rate of occurrence cannot yet be determined, since the exact magnitude of the physical changes and strategies for their implementation are not yet known. One thing is certain, however. Changes will occur in physical, chemical, and biological relationships — the ecology — if the freshwater flow is reduced. The following pages summarize some of the ecological implications of reduced freshwater discharge for the Bay-Delta System.

The terms "eutrophication" and "nutrient trap" are particularly important to an understanding of what follows. Eutrophication has gained rather wide general usage in both the scientific and the news media and the concept is particularly applicable to the Bay-Delta System. It refers to an increase in the abundance of nutrients utilized by aquatic plants. This increase may occur naturally in bodies of water over long periods of geologic time, but it is greatly accelerated by discharges of domestic and agricultural wastes. Eutrophication, or nutrient enrichment, is therefore *pollution* in every sense of the word, since it promotes the growth of undesirable aquatic plants, particularly of algal species, sometimes causing population explosions called "algal blooms." These dense algal mats greatly reduce the penetration of sunlight to submerged flora, eventually causing their death. Bacteria and other lower organisms that feed on dead matter thus undergo population increases paralleling the increase in their food supply. The combined respiration of these organisms consumes a greater amount of the dissolved oxygen in the water than was the case when their

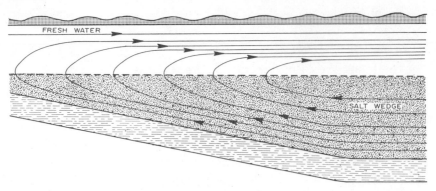

FIGURE 6.2. Estuaries form natural nutrient traps with the salt wedge (below dashed line) returning nutrients to the system. SOURCE: Based on D. Pritchard, "Salinity Distribution and Circulation in the Chesapeake Bay Estuarine System," *Journal of Marine Research*, Vol. II, 1952, pp. 106–123.

numbers were less, sometimes reducing it to a concentration below what is required to support higher forms of aquatic life. Such is the nature of the recent "fish kills" that have been occurring throughout our nation's waters. The disastrous and extremely rapid degradation in the environmental quality of Lake Erie is probably the best publicized example of eutrophication in North America. Lake Tahoe, on the California-Nevada border, although still of high water quality, is similarly threatened.

Nutrient traps are characteristic features of estuaries and result from the natural physical phenomenon occurring when sea water and fresh water meet. Where the volume of fresh water flowing into an estuary is large compared to the tidal effect, as is the case in the Bay-Delta during heavy runoff, a "salt wedge" is created. The lighter, warmer water travels seaward over the heavier, colder salt water moving shoreward, like a wedge, beneath it (see Figure 6.2). The degree of mixing occurring between the two layers and the extent of upstream intrusion of the salt wedge depend primarily upon whether the tidal movements or the freshwater flow exerts the dominant influence. During a low flow, the salt wedge extends far upstream, for example over a hundred miles in the Mississippi River, and very little mixing may occur. During a high flow, the salt wedge extends a much shorter distance, only one mile in some cases, and mixing is greater. When nutrients being carried seaward by the fresh water settle into the region of the salt wedge, they are returned upstream until eventually they are borne seaward again by the force of the inflowing fresh water. The consequence of this phenomenon is an accumulation of nutrients and other materials within the estuary, since they are returned to the system rather than immediately carried out to sea. This circulation of nutrients within an estuary by the opposite directions of the salt and freshwater flows is what has given rise to the term "nutrient trap." It is because of this concentration of nutrients that estuaries have long been valued for shellfish production in their enriched brackish waters.

## Physical and Chemical Consideration of Reduced Flow

Data provided by the Kaiser Engineers[1] in 1969 show the importance of the freshwater inflow in resisting saltwater penetration. The relationships between the Delta outflow and total dissolved solids content and chloride content were studied at several different locations. It was found that during the spring, if the flow is 3,000 cubic feet per second, the total dissolved solids level is higher than accepted standards in over 50 per cent of the Delta. If the flow is 4,000 cubic feet per second, this percentage is reduced considerably. The volume of freshwater flow is directly related to the degree of dilution of pollutants as well as the extent to which they are flushed from the system.

The U.S. Geological Survey released a report on July 1, 1970, on the effects of water circulation in San Francisco Bay.[2] The report emphasized the importance to the ecology of the Bay of freshwater inflows entering from the Sacramento and San Joaquin rivers. The importance of these inflows is based on the fact that the South Bay (that part of the Bay south of the San Francisco-Oakland Bay Bridge) has no significant freshwater source discharging into it. The flushing action occurring in geometrically simple estuaries, by which materials accumulated in the estuary are carried out to sea, is controlled by the volume of inflowing fresh water and tidal movement. In the South Bay,

1. Kaiser Engineers, "Final Report to the State of California, San Francisco Bay-Delta Water Quality Control Program," 1969.
2. D. S. McCulloch, D. H. Peterson, P. R. Carlson, and T. J. Conomas, "A Preliminary Study of the Effects of Water Circulation in the San Francisco Bay Estuary," Geological Survey Circular 637-A, B. U.S. Department of the Interior, 1970.

the freshwater inflow component of flushing therefore depends upon water entering from the North Bay. Two major water-quality concerns in the South Bay critically affected by flushing are salinity and phosphate concentration. The concentration of salt in water is increased naturally by evaporation. Maintenance of a constant salinity requires a renewal of fresh water equivalent to the amount of water evaporated. San Francisco Bay loses a layer of water about four feet thick every year through evaporation and, in the absence of freshwater renewal, the salinity of the Bay would increase within a year by approximately 25 per cent. Such a condition, in which the evaporative loss exceeds the freshwater inflow, has been termed an "inverse estuary." The Geological Survey report stresses the possibility of this phenomenon occurring in the South Bay during years of low freshwater inflow from the Delta. The adverse consequences of a dry year are therefore twofold, since the effect of decreased flushing action is coupled with the effect of increased evaporation. High rainfall years were found to correspond with periods of lower salinity and lower concentrations of undesirable materials, such as phosphates. Conversely, low rainfall years corresponded with higher bay salinities and higher concentrations of various pollutants, which sometimes produced "deleterious" effects.

In his foreword to the Survey report, Dr. W. T. Pecora, Director of the Geological Survey, concluded:

> Water-quality characteristics of south bay are influenced primarily by inflow of fresh water, manmade wastes, and tidal exchanges of water of varying salinity. Changes in any of these controls could have significant effects on the overall quality of the bay. This report qualitatively demonstrates that high and low seasonal inflows of fresh water to the bay's Sacramento River delta correlate inversely with salinity and phosphate concentration in the south bay. It suggests that net fresh water flow to the bay from this source is a major quality control under present conditions. Additional investigations are warranted to establish long-term significance of this suggested coupling.[3]

A decrease in the volume of freshwater flow into the San Francisco Bay-Delta will result in a greater intrusion of salt water, since

3. *Ibid.,* p. iii.

Annual Sediment Outflow (millions of tons)

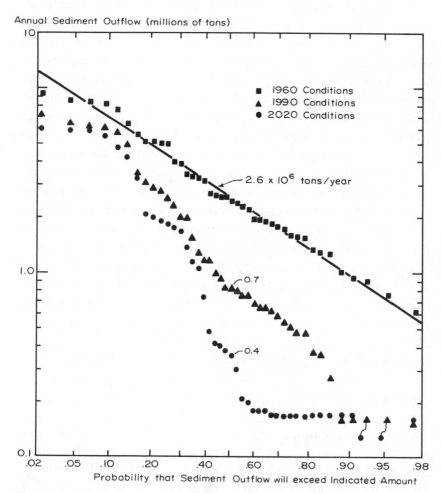

FIGURE 6.3. Annual Suspended Sediment Outflow from the Delta to the Bay System. SOURCE: R. B. Krone, "Predicted Suspended Sediment Inflows to the San Francisco Bay System," September 1966. Federal Water Pollution Control Administration, Southwest Region, U.S. Department of the Interior.

the salt wedge will extend much further upstream than it normally does, being less impeded by the reduced downstream flow. Thus, the salt water will reach a broad band of the Delta that is now fresh water. At the same time, plant nutrients brought down from the Delta or discharged into the Bay will be retained in the System for a longer time, enhancing the growth of vegetation. Further, a sluggish flow in the Delta will promote a higher mean water temperature, since a unit volume of water will have longer to absorb solar heat. Professor R. B. Krone[4] (see Figure 6.3) predicts that a diversion of fresh water from the estuary will greatly reduce the sediment inflow. Although a lesser amount of sediment means increased transparency of the water, inorganic turbidity in the Bay waters provides certain distinct ecological benefits. Decreased turbidity would result naturally from decreased inflow of sediment-bearing water, a longer time for sedimentation to occur, and decreased water turbulence which aids in maintaining sediment in suspension. Figure 6.3 illustrates this point and is based on historical flow data of the Sacramento-San Joaquin River System and a month-by-month diversion schedule corresponding to that of planned diversion projects existing by the years 1990 and 2020. The figure indicates that the sediment inflow now exceeds 2 million tons per year 60 per cent of the time. In the year 2020, when the planned diversion systems would be in full operation, the sediment inflow which would be expected 60 per cent of the time drops to only 0.18 million tons per year. The most important consideration is that the sediment and water inflow to the Bay System from the Delta will for 40 per cent of the year be kept close to its minimum value.

A rather broad spectrum of chemical effects can be anticipated from reduced flow into the Bay-Delta. They go well beyond the simple increase in salinity for the lower portion of the System. As already noted, estuaries owe much of their fertility to the nutrient inflow that is trapped for a considerable time by upstream movement of the tide. Before man and his activities played so prominent a part on the world scene, a reduction in flow would have meant essentially a lower nutrient discharge. Under present circumstances, a reduced volume of

4. R. B. Krone, Statement to the Conservation of Natural Resources Subcommittee of the Committee on Government Operations, Congress of the United States, House of Representatives, on Future Sediment-Related Environmental Changes in the San Francisco Bay and Sacramento-San Joaquin River Estuary. San Francisco, August 20, 1969.

TABLE 6.1.
*Total Nitrogen and Total Phosphorus in Municipal, Industrial,*
*and Agricultural Waste Flows, 1966, Bay-Delta Counties*

| County | Waste Loads (thousand pounds/day) | |
|---|---|---|
| | Total Nitrogen | Total Phosphorus |
| Napa | 0.8 | 1.2 |
| Solano | 3.7 | 4.7 |
| Yolo | 3.0 | 1.4 |
| Sacramento | 19.0 | 24.5 |
| San Joaquin | 9.7 | 14.2 |
| Contra Costa | 42.0 | 13.8 |
| Alameda | 24.9 | 39.0 |
| Santa Clara | 26.5 | 20.0 |
| San Mateo | 11.2 | 11.7 |
| San Francisco | 20.4 | 19.6 |
| Marin | 2.2 | 3.6 |
| Sonoma | 1.0 | 1.4 |

SOURCE: Kaiser Engineers, "Final Report to the State of California, San Francisco Bay-Delta Water Quality Control Program," 1969. Table V-10.

flow also means an increased concentration of various nutrients and pollutants. Of greatest concern is the increase in such algal growth-promoting substances as nitrogen, phosphorus, and the essential trace elements.[5] As mentioned previously, these are derived in part from natural drainage of the watershed but are greatly supplemented by input from domestic sewage and agricultural and industrial drainage (Table 6.1). Only with a thorough knowledge of whether or not a significant portion of the sewage and agricultural drainage will be diverted from the Delta in an ocean outfall, more information on improved stripping of nutrients by tertiary sewage treatment, and data on new patterns of currents that might be established can we predict what final nutrient concentrations to expect in the Bay-Delta System as a result of the proposed future freshwater diversions.

Petrochemical and other industrial wastes have already posed serious pollution problems in the San Francisco Bay-Delta. Evidence of this can be seen from the air by even the casual observer. Low concentrations of some pollutants destroy the flavor of sea food while others, including insecticides, may reach lethal or fecundity-reducing

5. C. R. Goldman, "Micronutrient Limiting Factors and Their Detection in Natural Phytoplankton Populations," in C. R. Goldman, ed., *Primary Productivity in Aquatic Environments. Memorie dell' Istituto Italiano di Idrobiologia,* 18 Suppl. (1965), pp. 121–135.

levels for animals, birds, and fish if the present dilution of these pollutants is reduced. Many of the inorganics entering the System are properly classed as fertilizers, since they cause eutrophication, and may have originated as such in the agricultural areas of the Sacramento and San Joaquin valleys.

A method for determining the amounts of various chemicals that constitute biostimulatory levels has been proposed.[6] It involves a determination of *in situ* (actual) growth rates for algal populations as related to different concentrations of algal nutrients. Such a survey has not yet been extensively performed on the Bay-Delta waters, although some bioassays have been made by the author, by Engineering Science, Inc., and by the U.S. Federal Water Quality Administration.

Investigations by the California Department of Water Resources from 1962 to 1964 have indicated that nitrogen and phosphorus exist in the Bay-Delta in concentrations 10 to 100 times greater than necessary to support substantial growths of algae.[7] Summer plankton counts were found to range typically from 3 to over 30 million cells per liter (a half-million cells per liter is considered indicative of an algal bloom, although proper interpretation from an algal count requires considerations other than just the total number). There is strong evidence that this fertility has continued to increase during the past four to six years, and fish kills which are probably the result of oxygen depletion during blooms are now a common occurrence in the System.

Inorganic particulate matter provides much of the present turbidity in the System. A decrease in inflow is certain to drastically reduce the present seaward movement of sediment from the Sacramento and San Joaquin valleys and decrease inorganic turbidity. One of the properties of the fine particles in solution, such as clays, is that they act as ion exchangers for a variety of chemicals. In the Bay-Delta System, the particles causing the inorganic turbidity may act to remove phosphorus and heavy metals from the aquatic system by first collecting them on their surfaces (adsorption) and then sedimenting them by settling to the bottom. It is most difficult to predict the overall importance of this scavenging activity, but it would be folly not to study its potential importance, since many heavy metals, such as mer-

6. Kaiser Engineers, *op. cit.*, pp. XIX-17; XXIII-5, 6.
7. *Ibid.*, p. IX-4.

cury, cadmium, lead, zinc, and copper, find their way into the Delta. Further, sediments tend to maintain a chemical equilibrium with overlying water and can recharge it with nutrients or poisons.

Dissolved organic matter in natural waters takes almost as many forms as there are particulate organic forms to provide it. The problems of surfactants, which were great foam-producers before the advent of biodegradable detergents, are in this broad category. Among those organics of most generally recognized importance are the insecticides, including the DDT, DDD, and DDE varieties of chlorinated hydrocarbons. Some are growth-promoting substances called metabolites, which include the vitamins, and may be in part responsible for blooms of undesirable organisms like the dinoflagellates which produce the highly toxic "red tide" periodically occurring off our coasts and even observable in Clear Lake, California.[8] A contrasting antimetabolite group may inhibit the growth of aquatic plants and animals. Any dissolved organic molecules are likely to be adsorbed to the surface of inorganic particles and are thus related to the problems of a reduced Bay-Delta sediment load in the same way as phosphorus and the trace elements. In any event, the inorganic and organic chemistry of the System will undergo a marked change if there is a reduced flow.

## ADDITIONAL BIOLOGICAL CONSIDERATIONS OF REDUCED FLOW

So far, probable biological consequences have been touched only lightly. To the average citizen of the Bay and Delta area, biological change will be the most noticeable and potentially objectionable aspect of reduced flow through the System. Obviously, fouling organisms will spread and the waters will be less attractive as well as less useful. Barnacles will be able to extend their range upstream to waters now considered safe mooring. Attached plants will thrive and are likely to become a nuisance as they clog the shallower waterways. Algae and bacteria are likely to become so plentiful that they will put a serious strain on the water's oxygen content, perhaps making it impossible for other organisms, especially fish, to survive.

For a better grasp of the relationships in the aquatic ecosystem, it

8. A. Horne, P. Javornicky, and C. R. Goldman, "A Freshwater 'Red Tide' on Clear Lake, California" (manuscript).

is necessary to have some understanding of the aquatic food chain of the Bay-Delta System. Admittedly far too little research has been done on the biology of deltas and estuaries to give us a really precise knowledge of their intricacies. But much more is becoming known, and in recent years the California Department of Fish and Game, the federal government, the University of California, and private research organizations have done much to further our biological knowledge of the Bay-Delta System. Because of the sluggish flow through the System, it has many of the characteristics of a lake, as well as those of a stream. The base of the food chain in this ecosystem is formed by planktonic algae as well as higher aquatic plants which must grow up through the turbid Delta water for their sunlight. Some of this "primary productivity" is consumed directly by fish. A large portion, however, dies and undergoes partial decomposition by a rich flora of bacteria. This dead vegetable matter, called "detritus," is a major source of food for the progression of animals that feed upon it. The particles of detritus are borne along by the currents and in part returned upstream by the tides. The animals, such as oysters, clams, and zooplankton (animal plankton), which feed on this detritus utilize both the organic particles and their bacterial coating as food. These animals in turn feed the fish which serve an important sports fishery in the Bay-Delta. As already noted, the dissolved organic matter from further decomposition may adsorb to clay particles, which can also serve as food to bottom organisms such as bottom fish feeders like sturgeon and filter-feeding animals low in the food chain.

I have already mentioned that a decrease in flow will greatly reduce the total sediment input into the Bay-Delta System. Even if the turbidity per unit volume of water were the same, a reduced rate of flow would bring less sediment into the Bay and Delta during the same period of time. This alone would increase the transparency of the water. In the unlikely event that nutrient conditions could remain unchanged, we would then have a large increase in the growth of higher aquatic plants such as pond weeds and bulrushes, which are now shaded out in deeper water by the sediment and algae in suspension. But in all probability, the decrease in inorganic turbidity would be accompanied by an increase in planktonic algae in response to higher nutrient levels, increased temperature, increased light penetration, and the longer retention time of an average unit of water in the System. Professor E. P. Odum[9] explained the high productivity of coastal water off Sapelo Island, Georgia, in a similar fashion. Within the salt marsh nearby, nutrients are plentiful but cannot be utilized because the extensive sediment, combined with organic matter, effectively reduces light penetration. As soon as the nutrients reach the clearer waters offshore, they support a high plankton population. Unless a very high percentage of agricultural drainage as well as domestic pollution actually bypasses the Delta in a sewer with an ocean outfall, we can expect a general eutrophication of the Delta's waters. This will certainly mean a further general decrease in the quality of both the Bay and Delta environment. If the System becomes high enough in dissolved nutrients, it will no longer be a suitable aquatic habitat for the striped bass, or for the salmon which must migrate through it to complete their life cycles.

Definite evidence exists that striped bass populations are reduced by a lower outflow. The California Fish and Game Department suggests several possible causes, including a decrease in turbidity (although it does not consider this the most probable cause). The Department points out that, since the bass live in open water, the turbidity gives them important shelter from predators.

In addition to fish kills, "dead zones" may be found below the effluent outfalls of pulp and food-processing industries. The reason for these occurrences has already been mentioned as attributable to the removal of oxygen from the water by bacteria whose abundance has been increased through eutrophication. But even without these events, depleted oxygen levels near the bottom will convert insoluble chemicals to soluble forms (as in the change of ferric phosphate to ferrous phosphate) which serve as nutrients for increased algal growth.

The threat to salmon and striped bass emphasizes the urgency of research on the Bay-Delta before significant alterations are made that will reduce the volume of freshwater input. We cannot afford to lose the valuable salmon fishery. The king salmon of the Bay-Delta streams provides a commercial catch of some 6 million pounds annually; some 160,000 salmon are caught by anglers, too. Striped bass caught by anglers, almost entirely in the Bay-Delta region, number some 750,000

9. Eugene P. Odum, "A Research Challenge: Evaluating the Productivity of Coastal and Estuarine Water," *Proceedings,* Second Sea Grant Conference, 1968, Graduate School of Oceanography, University of Rhode Island, Newport, R.I.

annually.[10] These fish, dependent upon their freshwater environment, are sensitive to changes in it. It is essential that we determine if they can be maintained in a reduced-flow environment and, if so, what strategies will be employed to accomplish that result. At this time, moreover, there is a desperate need to prove the effectiveness of new screening devices so the young will not be transported to irrigation projects instead of to the sea.

The Pacific Flyway remains one of the great migratory routes for waterfowl. Containing a significant percentage of California's wetlands, the Suisun Marsh provides 54,000 acres of habitat for mid-winter populations that at times reach over a million waterfowl. The relationship of salinity to production of food species in the Marsh has been carefully reviewed by R. E. Mall. This study concludes that:

> Department of Fish and Game studies have indicated that alkali bulrush is the most used and selected plant food of waterfowl wintering in the Suisun Marsh. Its availability and productivity as a food source is limited largely by its growing season submergence requirements and its response to salinity during the month of May. In order to secure good seed production of alkali bulrush it is desirable that the soils' salinity be below 16 °/∞ and preferably in the vicinity of 9 °/∞ TDS [total dissolved solids] at that time. To accomplish that now normally requires that marsh soils flooded in October remain submerged until mid-June. This maintains low salt concentrations by providing high soil moisture and impeding the upward movement of salt which would otherwise occur. Benefit may also be obtained from brief periods of pond water removal just after the waterfowl season in order to take advantage of the salt leaching by spring rainfall and a lowered water table.[11]

Reduced freshwater flow can do much to reduce the productivity of the Marsh. Marshes are extremely sensitive ecosystems. Their capacity for support of overwintering waterfowl can easily be lost. Mr. Mall concludes that waterfowl displaced through habitat loss are unlikely to find new areas for survival:

10. Department of Fish and Game, State of California, "Report to the State Water Resources Control Board on the Impact of Water Development on the Fish and Wildlife Resources of the Sacramento-San Joaquin Delta and Suisun Marsh," State of California, The Resources Agency, Department of Fish and Game (G. Raymond Arnett, Director), 1969.
11. *Ibid.*, pp. 5–21, 22.

Initially, birds may shift to other feeding areas creating potential problems of crop depredation. But with the expected outright loss of an additional 20 percent or 84,000 acres of the remaining marshland within California by 1980, the survival of such displaced waterfowl in California would finally become impossible.[12]

There is general awareness that the Sacramento and San Joaquin rivers already carry a heavy load of various pollutants. If the amount of these materials entering the Delta remains nearly the same but the diluting volume is reduced, higher concentrations are certain to result. Greater saltwater intrusion will cause the estuary nutrient trap (including pollutants) to extend further upstream. As an illustration of the consequences such an event might have, let us consider pesticide pollution. In 1965 approximately 10,000 to 20,000 pounds of chlorinated hydrocarbons reportedly entered the Bay-Delta System and are now detectable in almost all aquatic organisms.[13] Though present concentrations are not lethal, many of the higher level organisms, such as fish, carry concentrations that even now might be causing sublethal damage and that, if increased, could possibly reach a lethal level. Another source of pollution is the sewage discharged from watercraft in the Bay-Delta. The daily flow from commercial, military, and pleasure watercraft was 234,600 gallons in 1965.[14] It almost goes without saying that the amounts of pollutants entering the System are so large that any reduction in flow that would tend to increase their concentrations will greatly alter the whole ecology of the Bay-Delta System, producing a general decline in environmental quality.

Man's manipulation of the environment has often before this spawned biological disaster. We need not go beyond our own shores to consider such unfortunate events as the introduction of the European starling, the invasion of the Great Lakes by the sea lamprey, and perhaps even the importation of the alewife which has recently fouled the beaches of Lake Michigan. Without extremely careful study beforehand, the chances are great that environmental manipulation will bring irreparable damage. Notable progress has recently been made to

12. *Ibid.*, p. 5–21.
13. Kaiser Engineers, *op. cit.*, p. XII–7.
14. *Ibid.*, p. XV–9.

"Save the Bay." But it is possible to save San Francisco Bay only to lose it through deterioration of the quality of the Delta above.

There is still an urgent need to assess the degree of deterioration and to develop techniques for lessening the detrimental effects of reduced flow in the Bay-Delta System. Certain areas of the Delta could be manipulated now on an experimental basis to assess the consequences of reduced freshwater flow before these consequences are incurred. Synoptic studies of the entire Bay-Delta should be undertaken now to assess the variations in fertility already existing to provide baseline knowledge against which to match any future change that may take place. Agricultural land as well as natural terrestrial marsh and aquatic ecosystems need more detailed study if we hope to make the best future use of both water and land from California's ever-diminishing resources.

In its report on the Bay-Delta Water Quality Control Program, the Kaiser Engineers stated, "Although many of the biological effects due to water quality changes are understood in a qualitative way, there is a serious lack of quantitative methods to evaluate the relationships between water quality and aquatic ecology."[15] This problem is typical of all aspects of our present understanding of the Bay-Delta and is perhaps the most important reason for refraining from manipulation of the water flows within the System before first determining their probable effects. The lack of data permits us to make no more than broad, subjective predictions about what might happen as a result of reduced flows. Probably, changes would occur that had not been foreseen, and the magnitude of the changes might be considerably different from what we now predict. We therefore run the risk of producing not only the deleterious effects described in this chapter, but also other as yet unknown and potentially more serious effects.

The importance of obtaining much more quantitative data on all aspects of the Bay-Delta System cannot be overemphasized. No project should be undertaken that would significantly alter the San Francisco Bay-Delta ecosystem until all of the most essential facts are known. In the long run, it is easier and more economical to preserve the quality of an environment than it is to attempt to restore it after it has been lost.

15. *Ibid.,* p. XII-1.

# PART THREE

# THE TECHNOLOGY OF WATER SUPPLY

# 7 DESALTING TECHNOLOGY

A. D. K. LAIRD

Because water is essential to the existence of man and an abundance of it makes his life more pleasant, he expends much effort in securing dependable supplies. Until recently, he was limited to managing natural water supplies. Now he can use his technology and resources to greatly extend his water collection and transportation schemes, to modify the weather, to reclaim his waste waters for further use, and to take water from the sea and make it fresh to augment or replace his natural supplies.

The branch of technology dealing with making fresh water from saline waters embraces many processes and methods, the function of which is referred to alternatively as "saline water (or sea water) conversion," "demineralization," "desalinization," "desalination," or simply "desalting."

Desalination is reduction of the dissolved salt content of water. The amount of reduction will depend on the intended use of the water. Acceptable salt concentrations cover a wide range. Water for power boilers and for some food- and drug-processing industries has to be ultrapure, containing only traces of impurities. Water from snow-fed reservoirs frequently contains less than 50 parts per million by weight of total dissolved solids (ppm TDS). The maximum TDS content recommended for drinking water by the U.S. Department of Public Health is 500 ppm, although many city-water supplies contain significantly more. Water tastes objectionable to most people at 1,200 ppm, and is probably unhealthy for them at 2,000 ppm. On the other hand, very pure water may have deleterious effects on many soils; for example, through chemical action it compacts clay soils. Otherwise, agricultural water, containing no more than traces of plant poisons, is acceptable to most plants up to 600 ppm TDS, is acceptable to some plants at

1,200 ppm, and is unacceptable to most land plants at 2,000 ppm. Normal sea water averaging about 35,000 ppm, or 3.5 per cent, is extensively used as cooling water and for some flushing operations. In addition, many relatively saline waters are used as sources for a wide variety of chemicals.

Most of the world's vast inventory of water, 97 per cent of which is in the seas, is too salty to be used by terrestrial plants and animals, or for cleaning and chemical processes. Consequently, the bulk of the water used by man has been desalted. In fact, the hydrologic cycle is a gigantic natural desalination system using evaporation-condensation-precipitation processes driven by solar energy aided by winds. Man and other freshwater users intercept the water on its way back to the sea. This is the only water supply heretofore available to man on a long-term basis. Large as this supply is, it is not limitless, and its distribution is uneven relative to areas in which man chooses to live. Consequently, serious questions are being raised concerning man's ability to supply the increasing water needs he is generating in many regions. Man also has the ability in the long run to bring on global shortages by expanding his demands beyond the total amount of water that falls on land. Then, regardless of his efforts at redistribution of natural freshwater supplies, he will be faced with increasing his supply or reducing his demands.

In California, serious shortages relative to demands now exist in limited areas, and are predicted for large areas by the end of this century. Since midcentury, much consideration has been given to whether and how these demands should be satisfied. Suggested means of curtailing demands include limitations to be imposed on populations and their water-degrading activities, a significant water-use tax, and much higher prices to reduce waste and inefficiency.

Nine-tenths of the yield of the natural hydrologic cycle falls on inaccessible land areas or directly back into the sea. Therefore, a desirable future method of augmenting natural water supplies might be the global management of weather to satisfy regional needs. However, this way of increasing the effectiveness of the natural desalination system is still in the developmental stage, with little prospect of reliable operation for several decades. More complete utilization of natural waters we now receive could meet heavy demands in the immediate future. The storage of excess runoff in natural underground aquifers or in multiuse surface reservoirs shows promise. Large storage facilities and inventories of water, in conjunction with reclamation and desalting plants, would help supply short-term peak demands and long-term average requirements, while greatly increasing the over-all availability of good water. Waters that become too degraded — by the addition of wastes, by their uptake of soluble solids, or by their greater salinity due to surface evaporation — could be made usable by desalination.

There are many possible desalting methods, each taking advantage of a variety of basic phenomena. All require a source of energy to force the separation of salts from their solvent and to move the various streams through the processes. There must be means of disposing of effluent waste brine and of thermal energy. Also, chemical processes must be controlled to avoid corrosion and excessive deposition of scale minerals. Consequently, there are many facility requirements and operating procedures common to all desalting methods. All desalination plants need intake and outfall structures, and most require pretreatment of feedwater and stabilization of the freshwater product.

Details of processes, plants, construction methods, economics, and financing are available in several texts and in numerous reports and publications.[1] Many processes and components of systems are proprietary. The extensiveness of present desalination knowledge precludes its summarization here. However, a brief account of the principal methods will be useful as technical background for the discussion of the present status and the outlook for the future.

## PRINCIPAL DESALTING METHODS

Of the most successful desalination methods developed to date, distillation is the most advanced and will be used as the principal example of the interplay of research, technology, and experience behind the evolution of desalination. Alternatives to distillation that

1. California State Department of Water Resources, "Saline Water Demineralization and Nuclear Energy in the California Water Plan," Bulletin No. 93, December 1960; "Implementation of the California Water Plan," Bulletin No. 160–66, March 1966; "Desalting — State of the Art," Bulletin No. 134–69, June 1969; "The California State Water Project in 1970," Bulletin No. 132–70, June 1970.

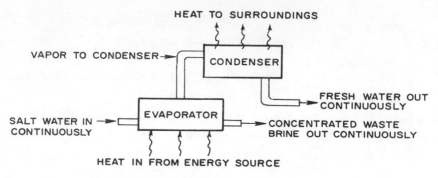

FIGURE 7.1. Elementary Distillation System.

may be more appropriate for a given set of conditions and have wider application as they become better developed will be briefly examined as well.

Since the separation of salt and water by distillation depends on the insolubility of salt in water vapor, the rudiments of the method consist of supplying heat to evaporate water from a saline solution and condensing the vapor on a cool surface to form fresh water. As illustrated in Figure 7.1, heat supplied to the evaporator causes some of the water to vaporize. The vapor flows to the condenser where it gives up heat to the surroundings and changes back to water. Since the salts do not vaporize, we have produced pure water, but in so doing we have increased the concentration of salts in the evaporator. If the concentration became high enough, solid salts would form and cause serious operating difficulties. Therefore, under operating conditions, saline feedwater is added and concentrated brine drawn off to keep the concentration in the evaporator at a desirable constant level.

Although distillation can be done simply, it becomes complicated when the requirements of long-term, trouble-free, reliable operation are combined with a demand for the utmost in economy. To meet all these conditions, advantage must be taken of many other basic physical principles and an extensive technology. There are also certain natural and man-made constraints on the system. The cost of heat to drive the process is high enough that heat-saving devices and methods should be used to keep down operating costs. On the other hand, the cost of financing suggests that capital investment should be kept down, which, in turn, implies simple devices and methods. Since nothing can be done or built without affecting the environment, compromises must

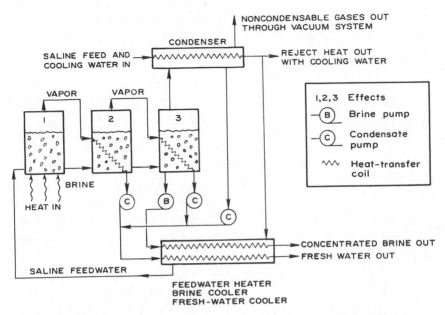

FIGURE 7.2. Multiple-Effect Distillation (showing only three effects).

be made between gains for the general welfare and losses to parts of
the environment.

It is a fact of thermodynamics that the extraction by evaporation
of one pound of pure water from a body of sea water requires roughly
1,000 times more energy than its extraction by a reversible process.
Making this apparently inefficient process economically feasible has
been a challenge to distillation-plant designers. So far, they have
raised this 0.1 per cent apparent efficiency to only 2 per cent but, even
so, have maintained distillation's dominant position in sea-water
conversion.

One of the earliest improvements resulted from the realization
that the heat required to evaporate water from brine could be used
repeatedly. When the water vapor condenses to form fresh water, it
gives up the heat (technically, thermal energy[2]) that it has absorbed
during its vaporization. This thermal energy is taken up by somewhat
cooler salt water on the other side of the condensation surface (metal
wall). If this heat-receiving salt water is held at a lower pressure than
the condensing vapor, it can be partially evaporated (because water

2. In thermodynamics, the word "heat" is reserved for thermal energy in transit, as
specific as the word "rain" is for falling liquid water.

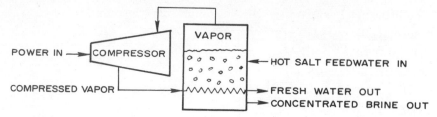

FIGURE 7.3. Vapor-Compression Distillation.

boils at lower temperatures as pressure decreases) to form another almost equal mass of water vapor which, in turn, can be condensed on a second condensation-evaporation surface to evaporate yet another roughly equal quantity of water at a still lower pressure. Each such evaporation and condensation is called an "effect." Many effects are possible. Five to forty may be economical, depending on the specific application. This scheme is the basis of the multiple-effect (or multi-effect) distillation process used by many small plants (see Figure 7.2). The principle can be combined with other schemes to improve the efficiency of large plants.

Good use can also be made of the corollary principle that water boils and its vapor condenses at higher temperatures as the pressure rises. In the simple apparatus depicted in Figure 7.3, vapor drawn from the top of a chamber partly filled with boiling brine is compressed; that is, its temperature and pressure are raised. This stream is fed into a coil immersed in the boiling brine. Since the pressure and consequently the temperature of the vapor are higher than those of the brine, the vapor condenses on the relatively cool walls of the coil and is drawn off as fresh-water product. The heat from the condensing vapor enters the brine and causes it to evaporate. It will be recognized that this scheme is the equivalent of an effect turned in upon itself, for the condensing vapor evaporates the brine from the same, rather than from another, chamber. Since the thermal energy released during condensation is nearly the same as that absorbed during evaporation from the brine, the system operates on the energy supplied by the compressor. This apparently "bootstrap" operation requires relatively little energy per unit water produced and can be made thermodynamically very efficient. Only enough increase in pressure is required to make the higher pressure side of the condenser warmer than the suction side to allow heat to flow from the condensing vapor to evaporate the brine. The relative simplicity, compactness, and intrinsically high thermal efficiency of the vapor-compression process are very attractive. The process is used extensively for small to medium-sized plants. Until recently, its use in large plants has been inhibited by the unavailability of practical compressors of the unprecedented capacities required for economical operation in large installations. A test plant is being readied by the Office of Saline Water, U.S. Department of the Interior, and large vapor-compression distillers should soon be helping to produce low-cost water.

Because the temperature difference in the vapor-compression process is relatively small, another thermodynamic fact must be taken into account: the boiling temperature of a brine is higher than the condensing (boiling) temperature of pure water vapor at the same pressure. This generally amounts to a degree or two for sea water. Consequently, the vapor from sea water must be compressed to a temperature that is a degree or two higher than would be needed if the distillate were pure water. This effect, though not usually serious, must be taken into account when distilling much more concentrated brines and using heat-transfer surfaces intended to operate with small temperature differences across them.

For a given temperature difference available between the condensing and evaporating fluids, there is a maximum salt concentration beyond which no more evaporation will occur. To drive off more vapor, it would be necessary to increase the temperature differences. In the evaporation of salts to dryness, this may be a serious problem because of the expense of special equipment and high thermal-energy requirements.

Since, in a distillation plant, evaporation generally starts above the sea-level boiling point of sea water, thermal energy can be conserved by heating the incoming sea water while cooling the effluent brine and product water. In continuous operation, the mass of the incoming feed is about equal to the combined mass of the two outflowing streams. Consequently, the feed is heated about as much as the other two streams are cooled. A simple apparatus to accomplish this economy scheme is one in which the brine and product are run through separate tubes surrounded by the counterflowing feed, which is enclosed in a large tube (see Figures 7.2 and 7.6A). Such a heat-transfer device is generally known as a heat exchanger, and in this application as a liquid-liquid feedwater heater.

This method of transferring heat directly between two liquids on opposite sides of a wall is relatively ineffective. A much more economical feedwater heater (described more fully below in connection with Figures 7.4 and 7.6B) has been developed in which the thermal energy is transferred, or carried, from the cooling brine and product water to the warming feedwater by evaporating some water from the brine and distillate and condensing it on the feedwater tubes. This transfer is accomplished by using the fact that a liquid boils at lower temperatures as the pressure is reduced. Thus, the brine and product water, almost at their boiling point, are allowed to escape through orifices into a space at lower pressure, where they partially vaporize.

Some of this vaporization is generally so explosively rapid that it is called "flashing." The relatively low temperature of the incoming feedwater allows condensation at a small fraction of the atmospheric pressure, thus providing a substantial pressure drop for the hot brine. The approximately fivefold increase obtainable in the heat-transfer rate results principally from the large heat of vaporization that transfers readily from the brine on evaporation, and to the condenser-tube surfaces on condensation. A practical feedwater heater of this type consists of a series of flash chambers, each at an increment of pressure and temperature lower than the one before (see Figure 7.4). The incoming sea-water feed is carried in the direction of increasing temperature through a bundle of tubes running the length of the series of chambers. The hot brine then enters the bottom of the first (warmest) chamber through a restricting passage or orifice, and some of it evaporates. The vapor rises, condenses on the tubes carrying the sea-water feed, and falls as distilled water into a trough below the tubes. A fraction of the brine evaporates and condenses similarly in each of the chambers, thus reducing the volume and increasing the salinity of the remainder as it flows toward the cold end of the series. Part of the condensate also evaporates and recondenses along with vapor from the brine in each chamber, thus increasing in volume as it, too, flows toward the cold end. The brine and fresh water are pumped separately from the last chamber.

This form of feedwater heater has an additional important advan-

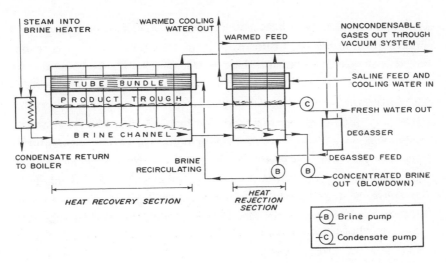

FIGURE 7.4. Multistage-Flash Distiller with Brine Recirculation.

tage over the previous one in that the fresh water it produces more than pays for the necessary pumping and complication. Because the flashing process is performed in stages, this scheme is known as "multistage-flash distillation." If its purpose is to produce water rather than serve primarily as a feedwater heater for some other process, a heater must be provided to heat the brine as it leaves the tube bundle. This enables the heated feedwater to assume the role of the hot brine stream as it reenters the series of chambers.

The thermodynamic effectiveness of this kind of process improves as the number of chambers is increased. This is because the larger the number of chambers, the larger the number of temperature-drop increments there will be, and the smaller each increment must be. Therefore, the temperature of the evaporating brine in the warmest chamber (which is one increment lower than the temperature of the hot brine as it approaches this warmest chamber) is increased as the number of chambers is increased. The feedwater is also warmed through the same number of increments to a final temperature close to that of the brine in the warmest chamber. Thus, more thermal energy is recovered by being transferred from the waste brine to the saline feed because the feed is heated more as the number of chambers is increased. Another way of explaining this increase of effectiveness with increase in the number of chambers is to note that the temperature difference between the vapor and the cooler salt water inside the tubes decreases with the increase in number of chambers. This means that heat is being transferred with less temperature drop, and thus less thermodynamic loss is involved.

The scheme outlined is called a once-through cycle. It will remove about one-tenth of the water from the brine. If more water removal from the brine is desired, most of the brine is recirculated through the condenser chambers to give it a chance to evaporate. Some concentrated brine is rejected from the system continuously and is made up by feedwater (see Figure 7.4). Most multistage-flash plants operate this way, and they provide over 85 per cent of the world's supply of artificially desalted water.

Being dependent on the local sea-water temperature, the lowest temperature in the multistage-flash process is a constraint on the system. The highest temperature, however, may be chosen to give the best economy subject to technological and economic restraints. If the number of stages and the lowest temperature remained the same in the process but the highest temperature were increased, under favorable conditions more product water could be produced in each flash chamber because the temperature difference that is the driving potential would be larger. Consequently, the same investment in equipment would produce more water, thus tending to lower the product cost. Alternatively, if the temperature drop between stages were kept constant when the highest temperature was increased, there would be more stages, resulting in higher thermodynamic efficiency but more investment in equipment. Depending on the interplay of these changes with other variables, the product cost might come to more or less. Extensive economic studies have shown that, if mineral scale deposits could be prevented from forming on the brine side of heat-transfer walls, the optimum highest temperature for an independent water plant would be some 400° F. Currently, plants operate around 230° to 250° F. Experimental plants work at temperatures over 300° F. and much research, with a good chance of success, is directed to controlling mineral scale formation to allow the use of higher, more economically desirable temperatures.

Large savings in water costs can be made if the cost of fuel can be shared with another product. Waste steam from some other chemical process would be cheaper but, generally, is not readily available at

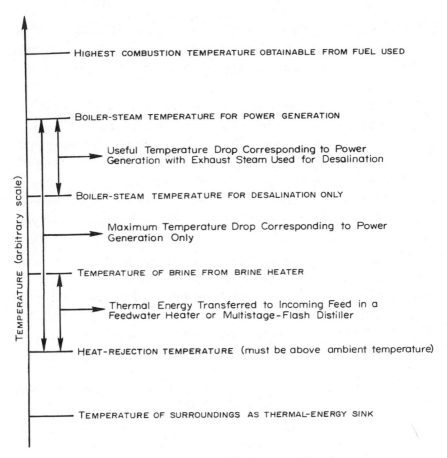

FIGURE 7.5. Systems Temperature Levels.

suitable temperatures. It happens, however, that needs for electrical power and water generally coincide in California, and combinations of water- and electricity-generating plants are feasible. Steam does not generally flow uninterrupted through a big power turbine. It is withdrawn, reheated or otherwise conditioned, and readmitted to the turbine at several pressure levels. Thus, it is relatively simple to design a turbine so that suitable steam can be extracted from it to run a thermal distillation plant. The result is a dual-purpose plant operating more efficiently in the production of electrical power and water than either plant would function by itself. The principal advantages are those of size and the sharing of fuel cost, facilities, and services.

To reduce distillation costs, methods of improving the transfer of thermal energy between heating and cooling media are being sought constantly. Savings result from reductions in size and in related costs of heat-transfer equipment, and from more effective use of thermal energy.

The rate of transfer of heat between fluids is proportional to the product of the area in which they are in thermal contact and the difference between their temperatures. The proportionality constant, called the "over-all heat-transfer coefficient," is a function of a variety of conditions involved. The product indicates that, if one factor is small, the other must be large to allow a given rate with given equipment and conditions. Thus, to minimize cost, a trade-off is made between temperature drop (fuel costs) and area (capital cost), and attention is directed to increasing the effectiveness of heat transfer represented by the over-all heat-transfer coefficient.

Improvements in this coefficient have been made by introducing phase change, by causing closer approaches to thermodynamic equilibrium, and by changes in flow conditions and surface configurations. Knowledge of the relevant phenomena comes from many sciences and technologies and is still far from complete. The chances of improvement in economy are good, since there are many possibilities yet to be discovered and explored. Several proven schemes are already awaiting incorporation into distillation plants. Others are under investigation or development.

The relatively poor performance of liquid-liquid feedwater heaters, noted earlier, is due to the low thermal conductivity of liquid water. A fluid adheres to the inside surface of a tube in which it is flowing. Its velocity increases from zero at the wall to approximately the average velocity of all the fluid in a short distance from the wall. Within the first few thousandths of an inch of the wall, the flow is referred to as "laminar" because movement is practically all parallel to the surface. Across this layer, heat is transferred only by conduction. Because of the poor conductivity of the water, this layer has high thermal resistance and acts as an insulator. With very low liquid flow rates in the tube, the entire flow may be laminar, a condition normally avoided in heat-transfer equipment. At faster flows, the core, or inner part, of the liquid stream becomes turbulent, a condition characterized by the effective mixing of different parts of the core and by much better heat transfer. The more rapid the flow, the more of the tube is filled with turbulence, and the thinner is the laminar layer of high thermal resistance next to the wall. A large increase in heat-transfer rate may be obtainable by increasing the flow velocity.

Figure 7.6A illustrates a liquid-liquid feedwater heater that requires a large temperature drop to provide an economical heat-flow rate because of high thermal resistance in the two laminar liquid layers. Note that flowing the liquids in opposite directions (counterflow) opens the possibility of heating the feed to a temperature higher than that of the effluent brine.

The roughly fivefold increase in over-all heat-transfer coefficient that can be realized when condensation is made to take place on one side of the heat-transfer surface, as illustrated in Figure 7.6B, is due largely to the high heat of vaporization liberated as thermal energy directly into the water film on the tube surface. Note that the heat transfer in Figure 7.6B is similar to that between the vapor and the tube bundle in Figure 7.4.

There can still be significant thermal resistance if the film of condensate is not thinned in some way. If a fatty material can be deposited on the tubes, the film tends to bunch up into droplets with relatively thin films or bare metal between the droplets. This artifice, known as "dropwise condensation promotion," results in an additional increase of heat-transfer effectiveness, and may soon become practical in saline-water distillation plants.

Mechanical wipers are extremely effective in reducing thermal resistance when they are used to lay on thin films of evaporating brine or to wipe off condensate films. A method of obtaining over-all heat-transfer coefficients sixty times those for liquid-liquid exchangers with practical apparatus is being tested. The relatively high cost of rotating equipment has, so far, prevented its adaptation. However, its high thermal efficiency recommends it for small to medium-capacity vapor-compression plants. An economical way of combining much of the effectiveness of relatively thin liquid films and high velocities close to the tube walls is to spray water directly onto the outsides of the tubes in which vapor is condensing. Over-all heat-transfer coefficients vary widely, but they are substantially higher when spraying is used rather than flowing liquids in or around tubes. This method is standard practice in sprayed-coil cooling towers and has been used successfully in desalination for evaporator-condensers.

Deaerators are used to strip dissolved gases from incoming feed-

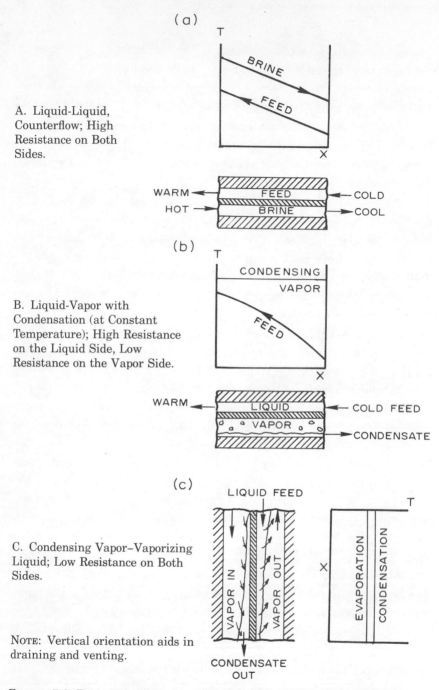

A. Liquid-Liquid, Counterflow; High Resistance on Both Sides.

B. Liquid-Vapor with Condensation (at Constant Temperature); High Resistance on the Liquid Side, Low Resistance on the Vapor Side.

C. Condensing Vapor–Vaporizing Liquid; Low Resistance on Both Sides.

NOTE: Vertical orientation aids in draining and venting.

FIGURE 7.6. Basic Heat-Transfer Apparatus, Showing Variation of Temperature, $T$, with Distance, $X$, Along the Flow Passages, to Arbitrary Scales, and Indicating the Effects of Phase on Heat Transfer.

waters to forestall corrosive effects on metal parts and blanketing effects on condensers (see Figure 7.4). Since gases are practically insoluble in boiling water, heating and pressure reduction are usually combined to cause boiling and thus to remove them. Deaeration can be carried out at near atmospheric pressure to minimize or eliminate the need for vacuum pumps, although it can be combined with the low-pressure chambers of a multistage-flash system to take advantage of vapor-condensing and gas-removing equipment already needed in these chambers.

Figure 7.6C illustrates the vertical-tube-evaporator system in which evaporation occurs on one side of the heat-transfer wall, and condensation on the other. It operates with much higher effectiveness than the liquid-liquid or the liquid-vapor heat exchanger illustrated in Figures 7.6A and 7.6B.

A recent improvement, of the nature of a breakthrough in heat transfer, results from the addition to the feedwater of minute quantities of an ecologically acceptable detergent. In many cases, this treatment doubles the effectiveness of almost any vertical-tube-evaporator system, helps stabilize plant operation, and encourages the release of vapor in multistage-flash chambers. It is under test and should be adapted for plant design soon.

Further improvements in over-all heat-transfer coefficients are apt to be hard-won. To match the low thermal resistance of thin condensing and evaporating films, the solid wall between the two films must be carefully chosen. Of the metals, titanium seems to provide an economical combination of thermal resistance and service life. A particularly corrosion-resistant aluminum alloy also appears economical. Very thin plastic films are being tested for some heat-transfer duties and may prove practical.

Because of thermal resistance, initial cost, and maintenance problems of solid heat-transfer surfaces, much research has been done on distillation methods in which heat is transferred without their aid. Most methods involve direct contact of a relatively insoluble liquid or solid as a means of transferring heat. So far, these methods have proved uneconomical. Most of this work has been suspended, at least until better materials and processes become available.

A more promising approach to the elimination of solid walls is the

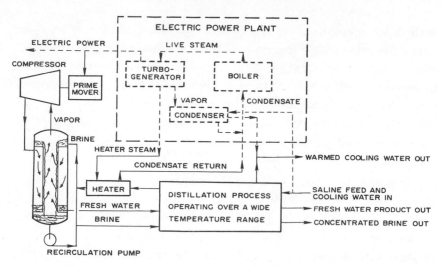

FIGURE 7.7. Hybrid Distillation Plant that Becomes Dual Purpose When an Electric Power Station Is Added. The vapor-compression cycle, incorporating vertical-tube evaporation (Figure 6C) with brine recirculation, is fed saline water heated in a distillation plant (such as multistage-flash) operating between the vapor-compression temperature and the cooling-water temperature.

condensation of vapor evaporated from hot brine directly into a cooler stream of product water instead of onto tubes. This form of vapor-reheat distillation is called "direct-contact condensation, multistage-flash" and, under some circumstances, it may prove economical enough to replace the multistage-flash system.

A vapor-compression distillation plant operates most economically at temperatures well above ambient, which necessitates the use of a feedwater heater. Consequently, it is economical to use a multistage-flash distiller as the feedwater heater to form a hybrid distillation plant (see Figure 7.7). The vapor-compression plant would be operated at a temperature higher than the highest thermal-distillation-plant temperature and serve as the brine heater while producing fresh water. Since such plants operate over a relatively small change in temperature, it is possible to keep their highest temperatures below those causing scale depositions.

The thermal distiller may be multistage-flash; direct-contact condensation, multistage-flash; multiple-effect flash; multiple-effect-multistage-flash, or other process.

It is evident that the energy from a fuel can be used economically with this combination, since the vapor-compression plant uses power either from an electric motor supplied by a turbo-electric generator or directly by a steam turbine. The staging and effect concepts can be incorporated into vapor-compression distillers and are important considerations in hybrid-plant schemes. Wherever practical, hybrid plants would be combined with large electric-power generating systems to take advantage of the size and other economies of dual-purpose operation.

It should be emphasized that all energy added to any system, including desalination plants of all kinds, will be degraded to thermal energy and must be rejected to the surroundings. Consequently, all the thermal energy associated with distillation processes must be rejected in their vicinity, because steam cannot be transported far from the plant producing it. Processes driven by electricity, such as electro-dialysis, can, however, operate far from the power plants supplying them, because electricity can be transported over great distances. This separation of plant from principal heat-disposal area gives such processes an advantage for inland locations because they reject relatively little thermal energy at the water-plant site where it is generally uneconomical to dispose of heat.

Thermal energy rejected from desalination plants is carried away mostly in the used cooling water, the reject brine, and the product water. Whether this waste heat is regarded as "thermal enrichment" or "thermal pollution" depends on whether it is considered beneficial or detrimental to the environment.

The effects of large amounts of rejected thermal energy have become important in rivers and estuaries and along sea coasts. To attain maximum thermal efficiency and cause no disturbance to the thermal environment, the rejected heat would have to be at the temperature of the surroundings. However, even a close approach to this ideal condition would be economically impossible. Practically, unless the effluent cooling water is at least a few degrees above ambient temperature, large cooling-water rates are required and pumping costs are prohibitive. A small cooling-water-temperature rise also implies excessive cost for outsize heat-transfer areas in heat-rejection equipment. Thus, if the greatest over-all public benefit requires a large plant, its environment would have to receive large quantities of reject thermal energy at temperatures above ambient. If the resultant warming is considered thermal pollution, the harm it causes would have to be balanced against the additional capital and operating costs necessary to reduce the warming. In some areas, legal limits have been set on the temperature rise of waters receiving reject heat, so that societal regulation rather than economic considerations may fix the associated costs.

If rivers or bays cannot assimilate the reject heat, atmospheric coolers are used. In humid areas, evaporative coolers are frequently objectionable because they cause local mists and, sometimes, icy roads. Nonevaporative coolers are more expensive, but they heat only the air and, so far, the heating of the air is not viewed as cause for alarm. On the coasts, deleterious heating effects can be avoided by extending cooling-water outfalls well out to sea.

Certainly not all heating of the environment is bad. Several fish farms and oyster beds are more productive because the water is heated by reject thermal energy. Many such uses are likely to contribute to our future food supply and may improve our otherwise-too-cold recreational waters. Careful planning could make thermal enrichment out of much of the predicted thermal pollution.

The best scheme for making use of the relative insolubility of salt in the solid phase of water (ice) is vacuum freezing with vapor compression (see Figure 7.8). Cooled deaerated salt water is admitted to an insulated chamber, called a "crystallizer." The pressure is kept reduced to the point at which the brine vaporizes, cooling itself so that ice crystals form. This ice is carried with recirculating brine into a vertical chamber, from which the brine passes through side screens and returns to the crystallizer. A small portion of the fresh-water product is used to wash the ice pack from the top down and is lost into the brine flowing through the screens. The ice pack is continuously scraped off at the top as it rises. A compressor raises the pressure of the vapor from the crystallizer so that its condensing temperature will be above the melting point of the ice. Because energy is added by the compressor and heat flows in from the surroundings, a refrigeration system must be used to remove excess thermal energy. The vapor is then brought into contact with the ice. Both become product water as the ice melts and the vapor condenses. The fresh water and reject brine go through a heat exchanger to precool the feedwater.

Since it rejects but little heat locally, and the heat of fusion of ice is only about one-seventh the heat of vaporization of water, this scheme is thermodynamically attractive compared to distillation. It also has potential advantages over distillation in the possibility of using relatively cheap materials for construction because of its freedom from scaling and severe corrosion. It may be adaptable with advantage where ice is a more important product than water for, say, a crushed-ice plant. However, sufficient development has not yet occurred to make it competitive with distillation of sea water—and it may never be. So far, it operates best on brackish water. Improvements are to be expected, as the many mechanical problems that remain are solved. It should always have an advantage when feed waters are unusually troublesome for other processes.

Electrodialysis, still another basic process, removes the salts rather than the pure water from the saline solution. It depends on the natural ionization of salts in solution and the use of membranes that are selectively permeable to ions. To give one example of ionization, common salt (sodium chloride, NaCl) in aqueous solution breaks up into positive sodium ($Na^+$) and negative chloride ($Cl^-$) ions. A selectively permeable membrane is a thin sheet of organic material that allows the passage through it of some ions but not of others. The development of suitable membranes is a continuing challenge.

The common electrodialysis method of desalination employs two kinds of membranes. One passes positive ions (cations) much better than negative ions (anions), the other passes anions much more readily than cations. Alternate cation and anion membranes are arranged as walls to separate parallel channels, along which saline water is flowed and across which electric current is passed (see Figure 7.9). The direct electric current carries ions of opposite sign through the membranes on opposite sides of each channel. Consequently, the concentration of ions—and thus of total dissolved solids—in every second channel is reduced, but in the channels in between the concentration of total dissolved solids is increased. The channels are made long enough so that the required purity in the product water is obtained. It should be noted that, since the membranes are selectively permeable, impurities other than the ionized salts passing through the membranes remain in the product water. The concentrated brine in the alternate channels is

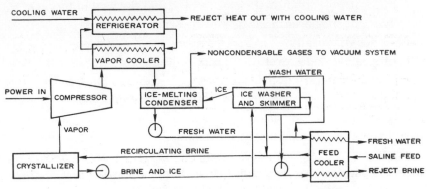

FIGURE 7.8. Vapor-Compression Freeze-Separation.

discarded. The electrical current flowing across the channels is proportional to the number of ions it transports and, therefore, to the required reduction of salinity. Consequently, more concentrated saline water requires proportionately more electrical energy for its desalination. Thus, electrodialysis is used mainly for treating brackish water with concentrations up to 4,000 parts per million of total dissolved solids. Although this process is not yet fully developed, it has the potential of high economy-efficiency for desalting low-salinity waters. It is favored for inland sites because it gives off little thermal energy.

Osmosis is the passage of the solvent of a less concentrated fluid into a more concentrated fluid through a membrane between them which does not allow the passage of the dissolved substance. Under natural conditions, the flow is from the more dilute to the more concentrated solution. Osmotic pressure is the pressure that would have to be exerted on the more concentrated solution to prevent this flow. Pure water can be produced when a pressure higher than osmotic is exerted on saline waters contained by semipermeable membranes that permit water to pass but hold back most of the salts and other solids. This process is known as "reverse osmosis" or "hyperfiltration" (see Figure 7.10). Because the osmotic pressure increases with the concentration difference across the membrane, the energy required by the process depends on the salinity of the feedwater. As with electrodialysis, the process rejects very little heat to the surroundings.

Although it is a new process, reverse osmosis has already been established for reclaiming sewage water, and has proved to be the most economical process for purifying relatively concentrated (over 5,000

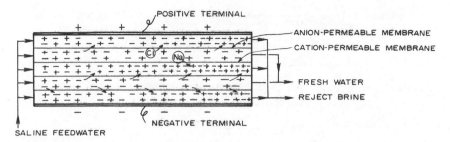

FIGURE 7.9. Electrodialysis Process. Note that the channels next to the electrodes contain more ions of one sign than of the other. The intermediate channels shown are typical of the many found in actual plants.

parts per million of total dissolved solids) brackish water. If the expected improvements in effectiveness and service life materialize, reverse osmosis may supersede all other processes for all services, except possibly in making ultrapure water and desalting sea water in the billions-of-gallons-per-day capacity range.

Ion exchange is essentially an ion-substitution chemical process. The water to be purified is trickled slowly among organic resin particles containing suitable ions that can be exchanged for unwanted ions in the feedwater. For example, the resin might contain hydrogen ions ($H^+$) that exchange places with the positive ions in the dissolved salts of the water, which thus becomes a dilute acid. The solution is then passed through a second resin column that replaces the negative ions of the dissolved salt with hydroxyl ions ($OH^-$), which combine with the $H^+$ ions to form $H_2O$, pure water. Thus, the salt is with the resin and the water is free of it. When, after several hours of operation, the $H^+$ and $OH^-$ ions of the resins have been used up, the columns must be regenerated by passing appropriate solutions through them. The cost of the large quantity of chemicals required for regeneration generally precludes the use of this method for the treatment of highly saline water. The ion-exchange process is generally used for making extremely pure water and could be used also for selectively removing impurities, such as boron from agricultural water.

## USES FOR DESALINATION

Foreseeable needs in California for desalted water range from small-capacity units for individuals or small groups, to millions of

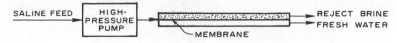

FIGURE 7.10. Reverse Osmosis.

acre-feet per year in reclaiming waste water and providing new water supplies for cities, industries, and agriculture. California water planners have included desalination among potential alternatives to supply large quantities of water when presently scheduled facilities become inadequate. The methods to be used will depend on their competitive positions at the time and place needed.

One of the greatest advantages of desalination is its ability to redistribute salt. But this can also be a detriment. For example, if water were removed from a stream and desalted to improve its quality, the salt would not be eliminated; it would just be concentrated in a waste brine. The salt of the region would be reduced if the brine were disposed of in the ocean or placed permanently in suitable underground storage—or if the salt were dried and shipped away. If, however, the brine should be returned to that stream minus the desalted water, the water downstream would be degraded by having its salinity increased. Thus, to reduce the amount of salt reaching the waters of an area, desalination must be combined with some form of disposal.

Maintaining the salt balance in the state can be expected to make extensive use of demineralization. Controlling the salinity of agricultural soils in several regions of California is becoming a serious problem that desalination may help to solve.

In the Imperial Valley, crops are already suffering from too much salt. Since this is a closed drainage area, imported irrigation water escapes by evaporation, but the equivalent of roughly 1,400 acre-feet of solid dry salt, spread over the cropland each year with the water, must remain in the Valley. Saline ground water tends to move upward into the plant-feeding zone. Drain pipes laid under the fields carry off the salty drainage water to the Salton Sea, which is the sump pool at the low point of the Valley. Since over a million acre-feet of water a year evaporate from this salt lake, its salinity is rising, which threatens to kill the game fish in it and eventually render it unsuitable for water-contact sports. In addition, the level of the Salton Sea has been rising and further damaging the facilities and the economy of this important recreational area. At the same time, the rising water aggravates drainage problems, thus causing significant areas of otherwise good farmlands to be abandoned each year because they become too salty. Long-term relief by the use of more Colorado River water is not likely because of its increasing salinity and short supply. A scheme that would solve these problems – piping water from the Salton Sea to the Pacific Ocean or to other receiving areas outside the Valley, and importing better water from northern California – is beyond the resources of the region. Direct injection of the water into subterranean storage under the Valley is impossible because the underground area is already full of water.

Conceivably, desalination could alleviate these conditions. Fortunately, there are very large amounts of very hot salt water underlying the Valley to a depth of some three to four miles. This geothermal brine appears to be a vast natural resource with a power production potential of about twenty 1,000-megawatt nuclear-power plants. Indications are that this source could power a desalted-water supply and salt-disposal system, and provide salable electric power to help defray the costs of developing and operating a large project to turn back the salt menace in the Valley.

Planning for such a project is still in the reconnaissance stage. Different possibilities exist, depending on the choice of whether the Valley of the future is to be a barren desert, an urban and industrial region, an agricultural area, or some combination of these. However, there appear to be several technologically possible benefits: large blocks of electric power for general use or for desalination where needed; good water to meet any foreseeable needs of agriculture, industry, and urban areas in the Valley; lowering of the water table to relieve drainage problems; stabilization of the surface level and salinity of the Salton Sea; and diversion of some Colorado River water to other regions.

The realization of any or all of these possibilities will depend on the economical production and use of geothermal brines, the desires of the public, and the cooperation of many groups. The Mexican government has shown the way with their power plant just south of Calexico, where wells produce millions of pounds per hour each of brine and steam. The Imperial Valley could support enough such wells to produce at least 20,000 megawatts of electrical power and upward of 2 million acre-feet per year of distilled water — the upper limit being set by the amount that could be marketed at the price set. It is anticipated that implementation would proceed on its own financing as markets develop.

Other salt-control schemes are possible, for example, like the one in conjunction with sewage reclamation in the Los Angeles area, where freshwater barriers are maintained against the intrusion of sea water into agricultural districts. There are many places in California and throughout the world where salt control by demineralization and salt disposal would be beneficial.

A program of water-inventory recycling could sharply reduce the need for enlarged water works to supply projected requirements of growing cities and industries. The present outlook is that it will become economical to recycle roughly one-quarter of the total water used in a large city. For continuous operation, large and varied demineralization facilities will be required. Some reclaimed water is used directly for recreational purposes but, so far, most is put into aquifers for later agricultural or urban uses, as in Los Angeles. Since reverse osmosis does not allow the passage of organic and particulate matter into the product water and economically desalts industrial waste waters and sewage, it could be used as the necessary desalination step in the improvement of such waters for reuse. Desalting and clarification procedures can make the quality of reclaimed water better than that of the new water supply in many cases. Besides reducing the cost for new water works, reprocessing from waste streams affords additional economies because of reduced needs for sewage-disposal facilities and treatment.[3]

It must be observed that, frequently, the materials in industrial waste waters are potentially valuable if they can be concentrated. The recovery of water concentrates solutions and suspensions and may change them from wastes to assets. Many natural saline waters contain valuable minerals and metals. Reverse osmosis is used to concentrate fruit and vegetable juices and to de-water food waste from packing plants. One of its biggest successes has been in concentrating milk solids in waste streams from the dairy industry. Frequently, such

3. See also the chapter herein on Waste Water Reclamation, by P. H. McGauhey.

recovery of valuable materials, including water, helps pay for—and frequently brings a profit from—pollution-control measures. The concentration of wastes by desalination makes their disposal more manageable and economical. Downstream users profit also from improved water supplies. Reject heat, discussed above, is a potentially serious form of pollution or an important asset, depending on how it is handled.

The disposal of reject brine is an important part of desalination. The cost of disposal must be included in the cost of the water, and disposal figures prominently in the effect of desalination on its environment. Enormous quantities of salt will have to be removed when significant quantities of desalted water are produced. A million acre-feet of sea water contain about 50 million tons of salt. Since the production of desalted water results in the salt concentration being doubled or tripled, the production of a million acre-feet of usable water from sea water requires the rejection of about 70 to 100 million tons of salt in the effluent brine. Thus, the conversion of enough sea water to supply an urban complex such as the San Francisco Bay area for one year would entail the production of reject brine containing roughly as much salt as is used on the entire North American continent in one year. Almost anywhere except on the sea coast, the disposal of even a small fraction of this much salt would be prohibitively expensive unless, or until, there is a master sewer in the area with an outlet to the sea.

Inland waters of interest for desalination have dissolved solid contents from just beyond the threshold of acceptable purity to saturation with a variety of compositions, and with salt-disposal problems roughly in proportion. The rejected salts from the more concentrated feedwaters, however, would be largely in the solid state and thus much more difficult to handle than just brines.

Practically, the means of disposing of brines are conduits to the sea; injection into leakproof, otherwise-useless surface basins or aquifers deep underground; safe storage as solids; and commercial sale for their chemicals. Small amounts of some of the salts could be sold after concentration, but the bulk of the salts would have to be removed from the active environment. Fortunately, there are enormous void volumes in strata underlying many of the arid regions where desalting might be practiced. These aquifers could be used to store concentrated brines so long as there was no chance of the salt migrating into useful waters. Enough space would be available to accept brine for many years and to hold it indefinitely — or until it might become a desirable source of chemicals.

The alternate method of locally disposing of salts by drying and storage in artificial ponds is less attractive, because of the probability that pond linings would deteriorate and allow the salts to contaminate local waters. In addition, local surface areas are generally insufficient for long-term disposal. The consequent eventual transportation of veritable mountains of salt to suitable natural storage sites would be relatively expensive.

During desalination some saline waters produce sulfurous gases in such quantities that they cannot be released into the atmosphere. Available for the abatement of this problem are several processes that produce sulfur for sale. However, the quantities of sulfur that may be produced from all pollution abatement processes may be sufficient to oversupply the world's requirements and make it necessary to dispose of part of the sulfur along with the salts.

The Office of Saline Water and many private concerns are working on the extraction of useful chemicals from brines and the disposal of the solids in overabundant supply. Progress made so far indicates that mineral recovery may become an important factor in the reduction of water costs.

Man is just developing nuclear-power plants that bountifully supply energy and make such small and infrequent fuel demands that they can be operated anywhere. Further, they will soon be able to produce very low-cost energy. Successful breeder reactors may be less than ten years away. Other very economical fission processes are in the offing. With the arrival of the fusion process, expected in a few decades, there will be low-cost nuclear energy available beyond presently practical limits.

Consequently, most plants that would be capable of supplying significant fractions of areal needs for water are being planned as nuclear-powered dual-purpose (electricity-water) plants, or as multipurpose integrated systems referred to as agro-industrial complexes. Such systems are planned to make best uses of resources for the general welfare and economic stability.

A conjunctive-use system is another potentially profitable complex, generally combining a desalted-water supply, a power source, and a pumped-storage facility. The resulting flexibility of water-and-power use and storage, and the sharing of facilities, makes for economical operation.

A reasonable estimate of the future cost of desalination, compared with other methods for augmenting natural supplies, must be based on present product cost, net benefit, and the expected development of each method. Water supplies should be considered as parts of a system operating as integral parts of our environment and serving our society.

Although the monetary cost of water is generally the major factor in the choice between desalting methods and other methods of producing it, the cost to a project's total environment is important. Very large water systems of any type are so expensive that they tend to divert resources from other desirable objectives. It is not difficult to imagine the simultaneous construction of enough desalting plants to supply the 5 billion gallons per day in additional water supply to satisfy requirements that may well develop in southern California before the turn of the century. Such construction could cause severe shortages and price increases in certain metals and services, thereby inflating plant costs. Careful planning would be needed to avoid disruption of the material, labor, and money markets.

In considering future costs of desalination plants, the development and cost histories of other technologies may give useful clues. Possibly, the present desalting technology is analogous to that of the automobile sixty years ago. Then there were cars operating on several processes because none was demonstrably better. Manufacturing materials and methods were relatively primitive. Some of the coming improvements were predictable, but those depending on invention were not. Cars were relatively expensive in terms of average yearly wages, as was the lifetime cost per mile; and the automobiles were relatively unreliable. The parallels are clear.

Much information is available on changing costs of evolving systems. The important factors, for the next three decades anyway, generally are changes in technology and in requirements and capabilities; accumulation of experience (or numbers of units built); increasing size of units; increasing rate of production of units; and changes in financial charges and in the buying power of the dollar.

Technology can only improve in our open society. Its future rate of progress is usually taken as a continuation from the past, tempered by any changes in the general rate of advance.

The quality requirements for desalting plants are not apt to change much, and the product will remain water. The accumulation of experience, however, should have some economizing effect.

The decrease of plant and product cost with growing size are related. They result from quantity buying and manufacture, and from the reduction of labor per unit bulk of plant and product. Various types of plants exhibit characteristic reductions of cost with increase in size. Historically, distillation plants of the multistage-flash type have shown modest decreases of unit cost with increasing size, mostly because the heat-transfer area is a major cost. Because optimum tube size changes but little with plant capacity, an increase in plant size means more of the same kind of tubes, rather than, say, larger tubes that are cheaper per unit area of heat-transfer surface. There has been no experience with vapor-compression units. Expensive compressors exist that should become substantially cheaper per unit of capacity as they are made in increasing sizes. However, vapor-compression distillers also have many tubes and will probably be combined with multistage-flash-type processes as hybrid plants. Consequently, the costs of combined plants should behave like those for multistage-flash plants. Electrodialysis, reverse osmosis, and ion exchange should have characteristics like distillation because plant capacity for those processes is increased by adding more small units.

The manufacture of a large number of identical units (mass production) can greatly reduce unit costs. It is unlikely that a family automobile could be produced as one of a kind for even thirty times its present price. It is equally unlikely that a million identical desalting units would be mass-produced. There is, however, some likelihood that a hundred could be built on a production-line basis as airplanes are built. The shared costs of tooling, design, supervision, production, and marketing can result in dramatic reductions in cost per unit.

Although the trends of interest rates are not easily predictable, their effects on costs and the balance between justifiable investment in plant equipment and fuel are predictable. Roughly, product cost increases only from five to ten times as fast as the interest rate. Judging by worldwide interest rates, it is likely that the rate in the United

States will remain, for the foreseeable future, around 8 per cent. Thus, there is little chance that change in water cost is likely to occur from change of interest rate.

A recent study,[4] based on known performance of advanced distillation equipment and on estimates of power from breeder reactors that will begin to produce in 1990, indicates that at the turn of the century water should cost between 10 and 15 cents per thousand gallons (or $33 to $49 per acre-foot in 1970 currency) in capacities from 1 to 2 billion gallons per day—or about 1 to 2 million acre-feet per year. These figures appear to be in line with present trends in distillation technology. Since competitors of distillation will have to undercut these figures if their processes are to be adopted, water costs, if they change by the turn of the century, should be less in terms of today's currency.

Water costs from smaller plants, though higher, would be reduced correspondingly and should find acceptance in communities that will develop near salt-water sources.

There was a time when the cost of fuel was a major reason why desalted water was not economically competitive with runoff water. Now, fuel cost is relatively minor because of increased efficiency in the use of energy and increased capital investment to obtain this efficiency. Present trends of energy costs toward a third of their present value, combined with the lowest practical energy requirements tending toward a quarter of their present value, will bring process and equipment changes based on costs of capital.

A potent reason for reducing capital investment is the difficulty of predicting when a plant will become obsolete in a period of very rapid technological advance. In case of an overestimation of economical plant life, the resulting unfortunate financial position would be the less difficult the smaller the outstanding obligations.

Consequently, with low energy costs prevailing and small investments being desirable during the development period of desalination, the process that costs least per unit of capacity under given conditions may take over the field. Of the processes in sight, electrodialysis and reverse osmosis are the most likely to succeed. Materials such as cellu-

4. "Nuclear Power and Water Desalting Plants for Southwest United States and Northwest Mexico," a preliminary assessment conducted by a joint United States-Mexico-International Atomic Energy Agency study team, September 1968.

lose acetate, of which their membranes are made, are relatively cheap. Consequently, mass production and improved shipping and assembly methods should reduce membrane prices by at least a factor of 10. Whether reverse osmosis or electrodialysis takes the lead would depend on the relative costs of containments for the membranes, of pumps for reverse osmosis and electrical supplies for electrodialysis, as well as the life of the membranes and the production rate per unit area in the two processes. In any case, for distillation to remain competitive with greatly improved reverse osmosis and electrodialysis plants, a breakthrough would be necessary in materials to reduce heat-transfer equipment costs to roughly a tenth of their present values.

Since projected costs of distilled water will be lower than those of alternate means of augmenting California's water supply by 1980, and competitors to distillation may produce cheaper water with smaller investments, it seems reasonable that desalination will supply much of the large shortage projected for about 2020. It is also evident that the existing impounded-water projects of the state will operate more cheaply than other sources.

There is already some urgency in finding the way to proceed in desalination as a solution to California's water problems. Valuable contributions toward improving water quality in southern California could be made now by perhaps two billion-gallons-per-day (BGD) and several hundred-million-gallons-per-day (MGD) desalting plants. The biggest plant in the United States is the 2.6-MGD-capacity Key West distiller. The world's largest facility being built under a single contract in the Middle East consists of several units with a combined capacity of 30 MGD. By comparison, fifty square miles of irrigated crop land or a good-sized California city such as Oakland may use 100 to 300 MGD. Thus, to make meaningful contributions, we will have to learn how to make bigger plants economically.

Recently, the emphasis in the question of a desalted-water supply for California has shifted from whether to use desalination, to when and at what rates. The need to control salt build-up in the Colorado River and areas served by it is with us now. Tests and studies are now being made on alleviating the worsening situation by desalination. Some cities, such as Los Angeles and San Diego, would profit from less salty water but, with full implementation of the California aqueduct system, their situation will probably be tenable to the turn of the century. If increased demands exist in other places sooner, or generally in California after the year 2000, the cost of desalination will be an important factor in justifying the satisfaction of the demands.

To know the costs and capabilities of desalting shortly after 2000, operating experience should have been gained on plants with 1-BGD capacity by that time. This schedule would call for learning to build a plant of this size during the 1980's, preceded by experience in the 100-MGD range during the 1970's. Experience with 50-MGD technology is being gained in the operation of the Interior Department's Office of Saline Water distillation test module at Chula Vista, California. A prototype is being considered by the state and federal governments for the Santa Barbara area, to be operative around 1976. Thus, it appears that an aggressive program of experimental plants operating on the most promising processes could make economical desalting available in time.

To allay doubts or confusion about future water costs that may be caused by the wide discrepancies between bids and projections by manufacturers and estimates and projections by nonmanufacturers, we should note that the first represents what is taking place, and the second what could take place. The federal government set up the Office of Saline Water in the Department of the Interior to try to minimize this discrepancy in a growing industry of great potential importance to the country. Their efforts have been singularly successful in advancing desalination technology by funding research and development, which has reduced desalting costs dramatically. Their demonstration-plant program has done much to shorten the lead time between the discovery of improvements and their incorporation into plants. However, the problem of lead time, although the picture is improved, remains, largely because of our business procedures.

It is true that the desalted-water cost, relative to the general price structure, is virtually certain to decrease during the next three decades. Desalting is an emerging technology with growth and cost-reduction probabilities in general similar to those experienced by the automobile, aircraft, and nuclear-power industries. It is also true that progress toward possible price reductions will be slow unless much of the risk of plant improvement is borne by those who will benefit from lower prices, rather than by plant builders. Capital investments—and thus stated water costs—for commercial desalting plants about to be built reflect the fact that no construction company can afford to gamble that innovations will satisfy contractual performance guarantees.

Nor can a potential plant owner justify the risk of building a plant so much larger than any before that no one knows for sure that it can be built as planned. In addition, it would appear imprudent to undertake such a high-risk venture when there is no guarantee that a precedent-setting plant would not be operating at a loss—long before its payout period was over—because of advancing technology and changing times. It would be small comfort to the owner of the first plant that it was his public-spirited pioneering that had enabled competitors to build much more economical plants and take over his market.

It appears that this impasse should be resolved by the general public. We have become used to plentiful cheap water from natural sources. If we wish to continue receiving this service, we should assume the risk in developing the technology. The public should build the first big plants through their federal agents, principally the Office of Saline Water, into whose province falls the building of large experimental plants. One is currently planned for California by the Office of Saline Water with cooperation from the California State Department of Water Resources.

Unfortunately, such plants have been called "demonstration plants." In the past, they did not demonstrate what can be done but tended to be conservative, with high product cost. These plants were instrumented and supervised more expensively than production plants, and were often run intermittently and at conditions other than optimum for experimental purposes, and suffered frequent modifications. Costs of their product have appeared in publications, thus adding to the confusion caused by divergent views of desalination costs. Early plants should be considered as experimental, and results should be so marked.

Since all desalination methods still consume many times the ideal minimum energy, means of reducing energy requirements in actual plants should continue to be sought. The above discussion of energy-saving in distillation shows that increased effectiveness of heat transfer should bear fruit. For example, a remaining temperature difference that is uneconomically large is caused in flash evaporators by failure of the vapor to release itself as readily as indicated by simple thermodynamic theory. Continuing vapor-release studies should improve multistage-flash distillation.

Vapor-compression performance would be substantially increased by improved compressor efficiency. Pertinent studies in compressor components and materials should lead to reduced costs of some hybrid plants.

The early development of improved nuclear-fission power reactors would reduce energy costs. Research on nuclear fusion to speed its adaptation to power production would be a major step forward.

Since the development of the membrane processes may depend on more knowledge of how fluids and salts pass through membranes, research on these topics should be very worthwhile. The dependence of membrane performance on conditions close to them recommends studies on fluid flow and salt movements near the membranes.

Selective removal of one or two species of chemicals, such as plant poisons, from otherwise good water by ion exchange or a membrane (or other) process would be extremely valuable for reclaiming irrigation water, and should be studied vigorously.

It appears now that limitations on the cost, suitability, and durability of materials are the most important obstacles to cheaper water. The production of materials with desirable properties would be one of the most worthwhile goals. New heat-transfer surfaces are needed to avoid pollution and corrosion problems and to reduce costs. These should have favorable heat-transfer properties. Similarly, better reverse osmosis and electrodialysis membranes are needed.

The related problem of water treatment to prevent corrosion and scale formation, reduce noncondensable gases in condensers, and enhance heat transfer give much scope for valuable water-chemistry research.

The Office of Saline Water research program, carried on in cooperation with the Oak Ridge National Laboratory and many other governmental and private laboratories, continues to contribute significantly. The state of California has a desalination group in the Department of Water Resources and a large desalination research program in the University of California.

Since 1900 research has reduced the cost of desalted water by more than a factor of 10. The incorporation of tested improvements into plant designs should reduce sea-water conversion costs by another factor of 3 or 4 — to the 20-to-25 cent per kilogallon range in medium sizes, or 10-to-15 cent range if very large plants could be built now. With all the possibilities for cost reduction now under investigation, one should expect another factor-of-2 reduction in 1970 dollars by the year 2000. The costs of brackish-water desalting, including waste-water reclamation, also should be reduced significantly.

Consequently, although inflation may mask apparent cost reductions, real progress will be made by early in the next century, and desalted water will be cheaper than other means of water-supply augmentation. Desalination systems will be adequately supplied by nuclear-power stations and should contribute heavily to the well-being of Californians.

# 8 WASTE WATER RECLAMATION — URBAN AND AGRICULTURAL

P. H. McGAUHEY

The phrase "waste water reclamation" is basically meaningless, or at least misleading. It is used in the title of this chapter because it is in widespread common usage and because it creates an image in the mind of the individual citizen that is detrimental to purposeful resource conservation. What seems unconsciously to underlie abhorrence of the product of water reclamation is the popular notion that domestic waste water is forever "sewage." To overcome this mental roadblock, it is necessary to make it clear that "waste water" as a term comprises the water and the wastes it carries when water is used as a vehicle to transport what is in reality a quite small burden of solids. But the term must not be used to describe the vehicle alone — which is "water." In such a context, "waste water" is somewhat analogous to "freight train," that is, a chain of freight cars loaded with a burden purposefully placed upon and within them. "Water" is analogous to "freight car," that is, simply a vehicle. Few men would think it rational to throw away the freight car when it reaches its destination. Instead, it is unloaded and cleaned up, and may become quite suitable for reuse in hauling a load of breakfast food, although the previous load may have been fertilizer.

That more or less defines the way we have to think and act about water reclamation: water is sent to do a job of transport; then it is unloaded, it is cleaned up, and it is ready again for whatever useful task we may assign it. Of course, some of it is lost through wear each time, but that does not destroy the vehicle. Nor is it identified with, nor would it be identified with, the loads it has hauled in the past.

Given such a concept, be it new or old to the reader, it is possible to evaluate water reclamation from any of several major viewpoints. What follows is an attempt to put into perspective the role water reclamation may play in:

Providing the quantities of water envisioned under the California Water Plan.

Overcoming the effects of the California Water Plan's water transfers on the environment via return flows.

Maintaining the over-all quality of the water resource so that it may be usable under any plan of resource exploitation.

## WATER RECLAMATION AND THE CALIFORNIA WATER PLAN

In considering how the concept of water reclamation herein proposed fits into the California Water Plan, it is necessary to look for a moment at what the Plan is and what it is not. Basically, the California Water Plan is a document detailing how the surface waters of California might be redistributed to make up local deficits and so meet the needs of California during the foreseeable future. Its authors did not consider it a blueprint that, once adopted, must be followed regardless of historical developments, advances in technology, or changes in human attitudes and objectives. It is not a fixed and final plan for coordinating all possible sources of water in an optimum system. Consequently, reclamation of water from urban and agricultural return flows is not specifically called for by the Plan. The Plan may perhaps follow the minimum assumption that Californians will continue their past practice of single use of water; but its authors recognized that if local deficits could be diminished in any manner other than by importation of water, so much the better. What the California Water Plan does do is to show what might be done; and it outlines a logical sequence of projects for the doing. But since the Plan was published, there have been significant changes in human attitudes, in water resource management and development concepts, and in the technology and practice of water reclamation. These changes are worthy of summary here.

To begin with, it is becoming increasingly recognized that the degree to which the Plan must be implemented in the future, and consequently what the cost of water resource development may be, depends upon the extent to which water is reused and on the comparative costs of reuse and of long-distance transport. As the spectrum of high priority demands for public investment broadens, as inflation and taxation take their toll, and as the prospect of a power-consuming lift of water over the Tehachapis becomes more immediate, the idea is emerging that we ought to take stock of the economic and technological feasibility of optimizing the use of local supplies. On the part of the citizenry, this idea often appears in the guise of such provincialisms as the concept that residents of southern California are by the very fact of residence there indicted as evil men, or that the water of northern California is the property of whatever dogs are currently in the manger. But at less passionate and more professional levels throughout the west, other considerations are being given serious thought.

*The amount of water that must be imported into any region to meet its projected needs cannot be determined until it is known how much water is available locally and what can be done to utilize it.*

In this context an inventory of local supplies is needed for such sources as fresh water (both surface and ground water), urban (industrial and domestic) and agricultural return flows, and saline ground waters. An economic and engineering analysis, both for short- and long-term objectives, is then required to relate the economics of reclaiming water from various presently unusable or unused sources to that of transporting water from other areas; and to evaluate the technology involved.

Finally it is necessary to answer two important questions. How are the process wastes from water reclamation to be managed in the environment? What fraction of the local supply may not be recaptured because of other beneficial needs, or because of economic and technological infeasibility?

*Long before political and engineering arrangements can possibly be made to bring water from Canada, or even from long distances within the United States, the need to make use of local supplies regardless of their present quality will become acute.*

*The importation of water to make it possible to continue present wasteful practices is senseless and untenable from any resource-conservation viewpoint.*

This simple point should be obvious, but it is not and needs to be stated.

*Reclamation at higher potentials is a necessary aspect of water reclamation.*

This is to say that everybody's bad habits will have to be corrected. Upstream users of water cannot be relieved of their duty to recycle water just because downstream users may be meeting some of their needs by water reclamation. In the specific case of California, this would mean that southern California would not be expected to reclaim water from agricultural return flows, saline ground water, and urban waste water so that water would be made more plentiful in the upper Colorado River Basin to be used on a once-through basis. Although the question of disposal of reclamation-process brines may be harder to resolve at inland points than at the sea coast, the expectation is that it will have to be resolved.

*Where one local source of water is the ocean, reclamation of water from the sea may relieve some demands on the inland water resources.*

However, this should not obviate the need for reclamation at higher potentials.

*A single use of water before it is discharged to the ocean is a luxury the future cannot afford.*

The thinking here is that sequential use of water in a use-reclamation-reuse series is imperative. Thus, capture at a distant point and transport past thirsty people would not be permitted. An analogy might be drawn from the City of San Francisco, the East Bay Municipal Utilities District, or the City of Los Angeles, all of which take title to water at distant points and conduct it past other municipalities or potential users en route to its single use by the owner agency. It is conceivable that cities of the future may find it necessary to reclaim water from their own waste streams for subsequent use in recreation or agriculture, or for the maintenance of aquatic environments.

All of the foregoing concepts may weigh heavily in decisions related to the California Water Plan as time goes on.

## Current Status of Reclamation in California

Historically, agriculture has been the most common user of waste waters, particularly domestic sewage. Sewage farming dates back for many generations. However, a distinction must be made between the application of waste water to the land and the reclamation of water from waste water. The former represents a device for disposition of sewage effluents under circumstances mutually beneficial to city and to farm. The latter represents an upgrading of the quality of water to the degree necessary to permit its use in some beneficial way, or in all beneficial ways that people wish to establish. In agriculture, historic concepts, the nutrient value of sewage, and the fact that crops can use water of low biological quality has continued to suggest that irrigation is the logical user of reclaimed water. The logic breaks down, however, in many localities, because agriculture is by the very nature of geographical relationships neither near, nor downstream from, the large centers of population producing waste water. This does not mean that water reclaimed from sewage is not used on land in California, but it does mean that some one billion gallons per day of sewage will continue to be wasted into the Pacific Ocean off California until some better answer than irrigation is adopted. A better answer is, of course, being adopted. It involves both industrial cooling and groundwater recharge with water reclaimed from the sewer at upstream locations where residues of the reclamation process may be returned to the sewer for ultimate discharge to the ocean.

Throughout the west and southwest, grasslands, orchards, public parks, and golf courses have quite commonly been irrigated with sewage effluents. Direct reuse of the water for industrial cooling has also been practiced, predominantly in California, Arizona, Texas, New Mexico, Nevada, and Utah. Recreational use of reclaimed water is an emerging practice of particular importance, and groundwater recharge is perhaps the most important evolving practice.

To a very considerable degree, present reuse of water in the western United States is confined to water reclaimed predominantly from domestic sewage. Generally, one pass through domestic use is sufficient to add some 300 milligrams per liter to the original dissolved solids. A single use as industrial-cooling water may approximately double the concentration of dissolved solids. Under current standards, with 1,000 milligrams per liter as the maximum acceptable solids concentration for domestic irrigation use, this means that, unless desalination is practiced, water reclaimed from sewage might be near its limit of usefulness in agriculture at the time of reclamation. This is the case with Colorado River water, which enters southern California and Arizona with 700 to 800 milligrams per liter of dissolved solids before use. If such reclaimed water were used as cooling water, its solids content would rise to a level so high that disposal of the concentrate would become the problem after a few cycles through the cooling tower. Thus, dilution through a groundwater recharge is a popular way to utilize reclaimed water in southern California; and it may continue to be until reclamation comes to include removal of salts as well as degradable organic matter.

The largest and best-known water reclamation project in the west is the Whittier Narrows plant in Los Angeles County. Here 12 million gallons a day of water reclaimed from urban sewers is recharged to the ground water. Plans and construction are under way to reclaim nearly 100 of the 285 million gallons a day of waste water carried in the County Sanitation District sewers in some eleven reclamation plants. Capital needs for this project are estimated at $20 million. Total cost of the reclaimed water is estimated at slightly over $20 per acre-foot.

In December 1966, the extent and cost of water reclamation in southern California was approximately as shown in the Table 8.1.

From these data it is evident that the cost of reclaiming water from urban return flows in existing plants in California is of the order of $20 to $25 per acre-foot at the reclamation plant. Recent estimates[1] by the California State Department of Water Resources for similar reclamation in Ventura County are given in Table 8.2.

These estimates, of course, represent the cost above that of sewage disposal and are at plant site. Cost at the point of use is estimated to average about $10 per acre-foot higher. Nevertheless, costs are highly favorable when measured against the $40 to $60 per acre-foot of imported water foreseen for the future.

Data assembled more than ten years ago[2] likewise reflect a favorable cost ratio for water reclaimed for sewage at various places in the southwest (Table 8.3).

Among the most recent installations in California are the 1,400 acre-feet per year recreation project at Santee and the tertiary plant at

1. State of California, Department of Water Resources, "Reclamation of Water From Wastes: Ventura County," Draft Report of Bulletin No. 80–4, February 1968.

2. P. H. McGauhey, "The Why and How of Sewage Effluent Reclamation," *Water and Sewage Works,* June 1957.

TABLE 8.1.
*Water Reclamation, Southern California, 1966*[a]

| No. of plants | Principal use of reclaimed water | Quantity (acre-feet/year) | Average cost ($/acre-foot) |
|---|---|---|---|
| 9 | Groundwater basin recharge | 238,490 | $20 |
| 13 | Irrigation of recreation areas, parks, and golf courses | 14,590 | $31 |
| 4 | Recreational ponds (fishing, boating) | 11,260 | $19 |
| 4 | Industrial use | 69,500 | $31 |
| 4 | Barrier to sea-water intrusion | 123,800 | $26 |
| 6 | Agricultural irrigation | 5,175 | $20 |
| | TOTAL | 462,815 | $23 |

[a] Estimated from State of California, Department of Water Resources, "Reclamation of Water From Wastes: Ventura County," Draft Report of Bulletin No. 80–4, February 1968.

Lake Tahoe. The Santee project is perhaps the first example of the use of water reclaimed from urban waste water for water-contact sport. The Lake Tahoe installation involves carbon filtration and nutrient stripping of some 5 million gallons per day of treated urban waste water, which is then exported from the Lake Tahoe Basin to an artificial pond, from which it flows for agricultural use. Elsewhere in the Tahoe Basin, treated waste water is being used for golf-course irrigation.

These are but a few of the many instances in which scarcity of supply and the high cost of importing water have led to local reclamation of water from municipal wastes for a variety of uses. No compar-

TABLE 8.2.
*Cost of Water Reclamation, Ventura County*

| Use | Cost ($/acre-foot) |
|---|---|
| Irrigation of parks, golf courses, and selected crops | $5-$25 |
| Industrial cooling | $25-$30 |
| Recreational lakes | about $40 |
| Fish and wildlife culture | about $40 |
| Groundwater recharge by spreading | $0-$20 |
| Groundwater recharge by injection | $100 |

TABLE 8.3.
*Cost of Water Reclamation, Southwest, 1956*

| Location | Use | Cost of new water ($/acre-foot) | Cost of reclaimed water ($/acre-foot) |
|---|---|---|---|
| Golden Gate Park, San Francisco | Irrigation of lawn and shrubbery. Ornamental lake. | 66 | 21 |
| Grand Canyon, Ariz. | Irrigation of lawn | 550 | 120 |
| Los Alamos, N.M. | Cooling water for power plant | 92 | 24 |
| Santa Fe, N.M. | Irrigation of golf course | 75 | 49[a] |
| Carlsbad, N.M. | Irrigation of golf course | N.A. | 25 |
| Las Vegas, Nev. | Irrigation of golf course | 30 | 27 |
| Jal, N.M. | Irrigation of golf course | N.A. | 69 |
| Big Springs, Texas | Boiler feed water | 51-105 | 15[b] |

[a] Includes cost of delivering 3½ miles.
[b] Includes only part of treatment cost.

able reclamation of industrial wastes has developed, even though the amount of water used by industry about equals that of domestic use. The reason is that industrial use tends, through both evaporative losses and product residues, to increase the mineral rather than the organic content of water, and no economically acceptable technology has been developed for reclaiming water from such wastes. This does not mean, however, that industry does not practice in-plant reuse of water to a significant degree. Perhaps the most striking example of such water reuse is at the Fontana Steel Mill in southern California. Here water is passed through five separate water systems until it is finally evaporated in quenching ash. The result is that only some 1,400 gallons of water is used per ton of steel produced, in contrast with the normal amount of 64,000 gallons.

Reclamation of water from agricultural return flows and from saline ground waters is, as with industrial waste waters, largely a problem of partial desalination. Processes based on reverse osmosis, ion exchange, and selective membranes have been developed and used on a small scale, but much remains to be done before they can be applied to the degree necessary for water reclamation. Nevertheless, the large amounts of water in California potentially available locally from agricultural return flows and underground sources suggest that, at some time during the life of the California Water Plan, reclamation of water from these sources will figure in its implementation.

### ENVIRONMENTAL EFFECTS OF RETURN FLOWS

Leaving now the subject of water reclamation as a source of water intimately associated with implementing the California Water Plan, we direct attention to the second of the three objectives of reclamation: overcoming the effects of the Plan's water transfers on the environment. To this problem, a great deal of thought is being directed today along two lines.

*Water reclamation involving various levels of restoration of quality may become necessary for beneficial uses other than urban or agricultural water supply.*

The thinking here is that, as an increasing percentage of the total available water resource is subjected to withdrawal for use, reclamation rather than conventional waste treatment may be necessary to protect the ecosystems of aquatic environments.

*A new public policy will have to be developed in relation to reclamation of water from agricultural return flows.*

There are many who suggest that reclamation of water from agricultural return flows at public expense is a logical extension of the national policy of supplying water for irrigation of crops at a price agriculture can pay and still survive. Assuming that the public policy of minimizing food costs at politically popular levels is unlikely to change, and that the concept of supporting agriculture in the semiarid west is inviolate because of the economy of the region and the variety that western agriculture brings to the national diet, steps toward reclamation of water from irrigation flows as a public responsibility seem inevitable. There are those who fear that industry will be required to upgrade its discharges into San Francisco Bay to an otherwise abnormally high degree simply because there will have to be a margin of capacity in the Bay to assimilate agricultural flows. Those who take this position see it as a natural development in a circumstance where agriculture is economically unable to pay and the public is unwilling to face the consequences of its own long-held policies regarding irrigated agriculture. The state of California, however, does seem to have made the first step toward assuming public responsibility for the results of the California Water Plan's water transfer policy. The San Luis Drain, although not a reclamation project, does acknowledge public responsibility for conducting waste water to the ocean via a system which quarantines it from the remainder of the freshwater resource. Under what circumstances it may go into the San Francisco Bay is a matter of current discussion and experimental study. Although analysis of the San Luis Drain question is beyond the scope of this chapter, a very considerable effort is involved to upgrade the quality of the water in the Drain so as to protect the water resource and the environment. This effort at present falls short of reclaiming water from urban and agricultural return flows, but it carries the seed of such public action in the future.

## Maintaining Quality

Although the San Luis Drain is a good example of public acceptance of responsibility for the quality of water degraded as a result of public policy, it is also clearly an example of the third objective of water reclamation: protection of the water resource itself. At this point, however, definitions become somewhat fuzzy and water reclamation is often more incidental than purposeful; or the term is applied incorrectly to traditional management routines having quite different original objectives.

From a purely conceptual viewpoint water reclamation might be accomplished by removing water from a waste-water stream, leaving some fraction of the stream to continue as a transport system carrying most of the original waste load at a much higher concentration, or by removing the solids load from the stream of water (as in unloading the freight cars previously suggested).

An example of the first of these two is the Whittier Narrows Project noted above. No typical example of the second comes to mind, although sea water conversion by distillation might theoretically be carried to such a degree of recovery. In the practical case, however, the economics and the technological problems of removing dissolved solids from water as dry material become overwhelming, and a highly concentrated liquid comes rather to represent the process waste. Obviously, this waste cannot be discharged to the water resource without doing more harm than if no water reclamation had been undertaken at all. The alternative, evaporation to dryness, raises the specter of economics, scaling of equipment, and other practical problems.

Because of such difficulties, the traditional approach to water-quality management has been through such concepts as pollution control and water renovation rather than what we now think of as water reclamation. Both of these more customary concepts result in reclaiming water, in the sense that the quality of water is reestablished at a level suited to the protection of one or more beneficial uses. Thus, the some degree the water resource is reconditioned or reclaimed, although the process may not have involved purposeful water reclamation as such.

The concept of pollution has historically been associated with the presence in water of impurities at concentrations sufficient to limit the water's usefulness. The first, and most urgent, consideration was to protect the water supply as a public health measure. To this end, the technology of sewage treatment was developed with particular reference to human intestinal bacteria, to the oxygen-consuming properties of water (biological oxygen demand or BOD), and to the water's content of suspended solids. When this spectrum was extended to include toxic chemicals from industry and appropriate further standards were established, pollution control may be said to have been essentially achieved in terms of public health, aesthetics, and the protection of a limited range of aquatic life.

The concept of water renovation originated more recently. It developed as a result of population pressure on a relatively fixed water resource, which required that an ever-increasing percentage of the resource be withdrawn for beneficial use. Thus, more and more the water resource came to resemble in quality the return flows from use. Both to overcome this degradation of quality and to restore a better approximation of the original quality of the water resource, it was conceived that more kinds of pollutants must be removed and in greater amounts. Specifically, exotic organic materials should be removed, and the permissible levels of biological oxygen demand and suspended solids reduced. Likewise, the wastes from industry should be scrutinized and a greater number of types of wastes excluded or drastically reduced in concentration.

Fundamentally, both pollution control and water renovation were directed at the return flows from urban use and to the end of protecting water quality for other beneficial uses. Neither concept came to grips with the question of mineralization of water as a result of use and hence gave little attention to agricultural return flows.

The idea that the user of water should return it to the resource essentially unchanged is now rapidly emerging. The resource values to be protected now transcend beneficial uses as such and include protection of the entire ecosystem, rather than only certain fishes and wildfowl, and the preservation of environmental values of a purely esthetic nature. Some of the first steps toward partial desalination have been taken through requiring or demanding removal of nutrients from urban waste water and, in the case of the San Luis Drain, from agricultural return waters as well. This means that at the present (1970) water reclamation is emerging as a requirement of those who wish to use water beneficially. The objective of maintaining the quality of California's water resources has thus been added to the earlier one of making more efficient use of the state's water resources.

## WHAT CONSTITUTES WATER RECLAMATION

It should now be evident that water reclamation, as contrasted with waste-water treatment or water renovation or pollution control, may be a matter of objectives rather than of any profound difference in the process involved. In current water reclamation practice this is to some degree true. However, the quality of water reached by reclamation is normally considerably higher than the quality resulting from treatment intended to achieve water pollution control goals. An extension of the spectrum of processes is required. Also involved is reclaiming water at some point in the sewer or drain system where it can be put to use, whether directly or by recharge to the ground water. This results in a process effluent separate from the water itself, which is not the case with sewage treatment. No particular quality specification defines when water has been "reclaimed." Under current regulatory agency requirements for various sectors of the water resource, reclaimed water may have to be of better quality than the supply from which it is drawn. For example, in situations where water is imported from one source and ultimately discharged into another stream, it may not meet the standards set for the receiving water in terms of dissolved solids, even though it be restored to its quality when first imported.

Under current public objectives of environmental quality, it is entirely conceivable that water will in the future have to be reclaimed from return flows from urban and agricultural use before it can be discharged to any sector of the water resource. If this occurs, we shall hear no more of pollution control, sewage treatment, water renovation, or the like. Water-quality management will require water reclamation of those who would put water to beneficial use.

# 9 GROUNDWATER UTILIZATION

DAVID K. TODD

Groundwater represents a major water-supply source through-out the world. Historically, the use of shallow dug wells for domestic and irrigation supplies dates from ancient times. Within recent decades, however, technological advances have enabled groundwater at great depths to be utilized. These advances include new methods for investigating groundwater, new drilling techniques for water-well construction, and new pumps for lifting water. Thus, larger and more dependable water supplies are now available in arid and semiarid parts of the world.[1]

Developing groundwater resources has several advantages. Groundwater reservoirs are available without cost and provide a natural distribution system. Further, groundwaters are free from contamination, are not subject to evapotranspiration losses, and possess nearly uniform temperatures. With proper development and management, underground water storage can provide efficient and economic water supplies.[2]

Groundwater occurs in all types of geological formations; however, those that are permeable and have a relatively large storage volume are most important in supplying water to wells for use by man. Formations that yield significant quantities of water to wells are known as aquifers; in California most of these are alluvial deposits of sand and gravel in valley areas.

1. D. K. Todd, "Advances in Techniques of Groundwater Development," in Vol. I, Natural Resources – Energy, Water and River Basin Development, United States Papers prepared for the United Nations Conference on the Application of Science and Technology for the Benefit of the Less Developed Areas (U.S. Government Printing Office, February 1963), in which parts of this chapter originally appeared.

2. "Large-Scale Ground Water Developments," Water Resources Development Center, United Nations (New York, 1960).

Water which is underground is part of the hydrologic cycle. Thus, at some earlier time all groundwater was part of rainfall, streamflow, or a lake. After infiltrating into the ground, the water drains slowly toward some outlet such as a stream, a spring, or a lake. By means of wells and drains man may intercept groundwater and apply it to any of several beneficial uses.[3]

## GROUNDWATER IN CALIFORNIA

Groundwater in California occurs in a variety of rock types. Most of the readily available groundwater is stored in the larger alluvium-filled valleys within the state. Local lithology and structural features influence the size, shape, depth, and permeability of the alluvium-filled areas. The unconsolidated to poorly consolidated water-bearing alluvium of these areas is composed largely of continental flood-plain and fan deposits with some interbedded lagunal sediments in groundwater basins bordering the coast and inland bays.[4]

Figure 9.1 shows the hydrologic subregions of California usually employed in defining the groundwater resources of the state. Groundwater data for each subregion are summarized in Table 9.1. Note that a total of 231 distinct valley-filled areas have been identified as groundwater basins. Also, for the Sacramento and San Joaquin basins, it can be seen that the Central Valley forms the largest single groundwater unit in the state, containing far more usable storage space than all of the lakes and reservoirs of California combined.

## AERIAL PHOTOGRAPHS

As the occurrence of groundwater is related to terrain characteristics, proper interpretation of aerial photographs is often a valuable means of identifying groundwater conditions. Vegetation, land form and use, drainage patterns, erosion, color, and special ground features are apparent on air photographs and indicate subsurface conditions. From studies of air-photo mosaic maps and of stereoscopic photo pairs, drainage and soil maps can be prepared.

3. D. K. Todd, *Ground Water Hydrology* (New York: John Wiley and Sons, 1959); W. C. Walton, *Groundwater Resource Evaluation* (New York: McGraw-Hill, 1970).

4. "Ground Water Basins in California," Water Quality Investigation No. 3, California Division of Water Resources (Sacramento, November 1952).

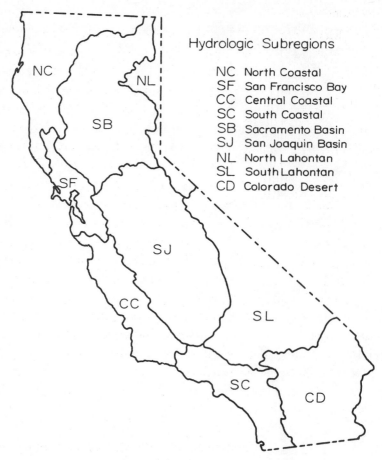

FIGURE 9.1. Hydrologic Subregions of California.

A study in Indiana[5] indicated that air-photo interpretation could be employed to develop a groundwater prediction map. An area was divided into zones of good, fair, and poor water yield based upon air-photo analysis. The classification indicated areas yielding more than 200 gallons per minute as good groundwater areas, areas yielding 50 to 200 gallons per minute as fair groundwater areas, and those yielding less than 50 gallons per minute as poor areas. Examination of well data subsequently confirmed the analysis.

5. R. H. Howe, H. R. Wilke, and D. E. Bloodgood, "Application of Air Photo Interpretation in the Location of Ground Water," *Journal of the American Water Works Association,* Vol. 48, 1956.

TABLE 9.1.
*California Groundwater Data*

| Hydrologic subregion | Number of valley-fill areas | Total area of valleys (sq. mi.) | Usable storage capacity (acre-feet) | Representative well capacity (gallons/minute) |
|---|---|---|---|---|
| North Coastal | 13 | 1,300 | 700,000 | 750 |
| San Francisco Bay | 18 | 2,000 | 1,200,000 | 180 |
| Central Coastal | 24 | 3,500 | 7,600,000 | 500 |
| South Coastal | 44 | 3,000 | 800,000 | 560 |
| Sacramento Basin | 21 | 6,150 | 22,000,000 | 450 |
| San Joaquin Basin | 8 | 13,000 | 80,000,000 | Unknown |
| North Lahontan | 8 | 1,300 | Unknown | 750 |
| South Lahontan | 50 | 13,000 | 720,000[a] | 410 |
| Colorado Desert | 45 | 12,800 | 3,600,000[a] | 200 |
| TOTAL | 231 | 56,050 | | |

SOURCE: "Summary of Ground-Water Data as of 1967, California Region," open-file report, U.S. Geological Survey, Menlo Park, Calif., July 1969.

[a] Storage capacity has been determined for only one valley of the subregion.

The art of air-photo interpretation has progressed to such a point that recognition of types and patterns of vegetation is often a useful indicator of where ground water may be found. It is possible, under certain conditions, to determine from air photos alone where water may be obtained in arid and semiarid regions, the minimum amount that is perennially available, and whether the water is of good chemical quality. Studies by Mann[6] in the southern California desert showed that the interpretation is based on the premise that water of good quality forced to the surface in dry regions will have been pre-empted by phreatophytes, those plants that send their roots down to or near the water table and thus are usually seen growing along stream courses or in other areas where a constant supply of groundwater is available. In contrast, most plants growing in dry regions must depend on precipitation, and they make a picture of dull sparsity in which areas covered by phreatophytes stand out in more vivid luxuriance. Thus, it is true that the amount of water available will govern the size of the vegetated area. A familiarity with the general region and the local plant types may be necessary to interpret air photos with maximum effectiveness. Although such hydrobotanic investigations need subsequent field investigation, it is apparent that this rapid means for

6. J. F. Mann, Jr., "Estimating Quantity and Quality of Ground Water in Dry Regions Using Airphotos," Publication No. 44, General Assembly of Toronto, International Association of Scientific Hydrology (Gentbrugge, Beltium, 1958).

identifying potential groundwater sources can represent a vast savings where new water supplies are needed in large relatively undeveloped areas.

Very often the geologic conditions in a particular area, as well as the associated hydrobotanic conditions, will reveal groundwater situations that can be adequately analyzed from aerial photographs alone. For example, a fault acting as a conduit will show springs where it intersects the axes of the valley. A small spring produces a spot of phreatophytes; a larger spring shows a line of phreatophytes extending downstream. A fault acting as a barrier is shown by a patch of phreatophytes sharply limited by the fault on the down-slope side, and often a strip of dense vegetation marks the overflow. Areas of constriction in dry alluvial channels are frequently marked by large quantities of rising water. In closed desert basins, alluvial fans commonly discharge large quantities of water, and phreatophytes arranged like the spokes of a wheel around the base of an alluvial fan may indicate where groundwater is rising to the surface.

## SEA-WATER INTRUSION

A common problem in groundwater formations located near the coast is that of sea-water intrusion. This may be defined as an increase in the salinity of groundwater over what normally occurs at a given location in an aquifer. Such intrusion is usually the result of acts of man, primarily from concentrated extractions of groundwater in localized areas. The problem is well known along the coasts of the United States; in particular, it has affected the coast lines of Long Island, Florida, Texas, and California.[7] Intrusion is also known along the coasts of Europe, Israel, and Japan.

To control sea-water intrusion, several methods have been suggested, among them reduction or rearrangement of the pattern of pumping, direct recharge, development of a pumping trough adjacent to the coast, maintenance of a pressure ridge above sea level along the coast, and construction of artificial subsurface barriers. Although reduction of pumping may seem to be an obvious method of control,

7. D. K. Todd, "Salt Water Intrusion of Coastal Aquifers in the United States," Publication No. 52. Assembly of Helsinki, International Association of Scientific Hydrology (Gentbrugge, Belgium, 1961).

in many locations legal restrictions and property rights prohibit government agencies from regulating pumping from privately owned wells. Therefore, more costly procedures are necessary, involving one or more of the other methods to control intrusion.

In recent years a comprehensive field test of the pressure-ridge method has been conducted in Los Angeles County, California.[8] The method involves building up a fresh-water pressure ridge adjacent to the coast by means of a line of recharge wells. The internal pressure of the water, technically known as the piezometric surface, along the ridge is raised sufficiently high to repel sea water, causing the recharged water to flow both seaward and landward. By proper control of the height of the ridge, the amount of recharge water wasted to the ocean can be minimized. The ridge consists of a series of peaks at each well with saddles in between. The ridge should be located inland from the saline front to avoid pushing sea water further inland. This method has the advantage of not restricting the usual groundwater storage capacity but has the disadvantage of high initial and operating costs and the need for supplemental water.

In the Los Angeles test, a confined aquifer that had been badly degraded by sea water was selected for study. Nine gravel-packed recharge wells were constructed at intervals of 500 feet, forming a line 4,000 feet long, parallel to and about 2,000 feet inland from the coast line. The piezometric surface along the well line was 6 to 12 feet below sea level and the groundwater contained 16,000 parts per million chloride. Numerous small observation wells were also drilled in the vicinity. Injection of treated fresh water into the recharge wells was begun in 1953. Immediately after recharge had begun, the ridge pressure began to develop, and at the present time the ridge is still successfully being operated and maintained. The combined recharge rate for the nine wells is about 5 cubic feet per second. The amount of water flowing toward the ocean is approximately 5 per cent of the total recharge water, while the remaining 95 per cent flows landward for subsequent replenishment to the groundwater basin. Chlorination of the recharge water has been found necessary to prevent clogging of the wells by bacterial slime. The chloride content of ground water near the

8. "Sea-water Intrusion in California," Bulletin No. 63, California Department of Water Resources (Sacramento, 1958).

recharge-well line dropped rapidly to that of the freshwater content after the injection had become effective.

This investigation demonstrated the technical feasibility of maintaining a recharge line parallel to the coast for control of sea-water intrusion. Subsequently, economic justification of the barrier for protecting the entire groundwater basin indicated that the safe yield of the basin was of such importance that the line was worth extending in both directions so as to protect the entire coastal plain of Los Angeles County. At the present time the recharge-well line is being extended and additional studies are under way for new recharge lines in Orange County.

## ARTIFICIAL RECHARGE

The technique of artificial recharge of underground formations is well known in the United States and in Europe. In recent years considerable attention has been focused upon the importance of increasing rates of artificial recharge in order to provide larger groundwater supplies and also as a means of management of groundwater basins.

Water may be recharged underground by a variety of methods.[9] The surface methods come under the general heading of water spreading, which may, in turn, be subdivided into flooding, basin, ditch or furrow, natural channel, and irrigation types. In the flooding method, water is allowed to spread evenly over large, flat areas. The thin sheet of water spreads at a minimum velocity without disturbing vegetation and soil. Although the cost is minimal for this method of artificial recharge, control of the water is difficult and maximum efficiencies are difficult to obtain.

More common is the basin method, in which water is released into shallow basins formed by excavation or by construction of dikes or small dams. Horizontal dimensions are relatively large, depths being only a few feet. Typically, systems of basins are fed from a nearby surface-water source, allowing one basin to discharge into an adjacent lower basin after it becomes full. The basin configuration can be suited to the local topography so that a system involving many basins can be constructed near flat flood-plain areas bordering surface-water sup-

9. D. K. Todd, *Ground Water Hydrology, op. cit.*

plies. From the lowest basin, excess water is returned to the stream channel. In California, where artificial recharge has been practiced to a greater extent than anywhere else in the United States, basins have been constructed in abandoned stream channels. Usually basins will permit water contact with 75 to 80 per cent of the gross area involved. This method, because of its high efficiency and easy maintenance, represents the favored method of artificial recharge by spreading.

The ditch or furrow method consists of construction of flat ditches paralleling the land contours. Gradients in the ditches must usually be sufficient to carry suspended material through the system; deposition of fine-grained material tends to clog soil-surface openings. The method is most useful for irregular terrain where large, relatively level areas are not available for basin construction.

In the natural channel method, channel barriers are developed to form basins, the primary purpose being to extend the time and area over which waste is in contact with the stream channel. Small dikes of concrete, rock, or simply of the channel material may be constructed in the stream. Quite often these are temporary, requiring only bulldozer work, and may be washed out during the next high-water period.

Finally, the irrigation method consists of spreading excess water on irrigated land. This involves no additional cost or land for the spreading system. The main requirements are availability of water and periods of application in which water will not affect existing crops or when crops are not being grown.

In a typical water-spreading operation the initial recharge rate is high and then decreases rapidly with time to a low minimum value. As the recharge rate decreases, the efficiency of the operation, and therefore the cost of recharging, increases proportionately. Considerable study has been given in recent years to field techniques for increasing the rate of water spreading. Studies by the U.S. Agricultural Research Service have indicated that recharge rates are related to the mean particle size of the soil in which the spreading is occurring. Efforts have been made to increase the soil pore openings by the addition of organic matter and chemicals as well as by growing vegetation on the spreading area. Certain procedures, such as the spreading of cotton-gin trash and the growing of Bermuda grass, have indicated that increased intake rates are possible. Another effective means for controlling the rate of artificial recharge involves alternate wetting and drying of the soil. It has been found that prolonged wetting of a soil exposed to the atmosphere will produce microbial growths which tend to clog the soil surface. Drying kills these growths and reopens the soil pores. Thus, to maintain a high recharge rate, intermittent application of water may prove essential.

Another means for increasing artificial recharge is by detonation of nuclear explosives to improve subsurface conditions for the desired purpose. Two applications are possible in this particular approach. For the disposal of waste liquids, such as radioactive materials, brine, and industrial chemicals, it has been suggested that nuclear explosives could create large underground cavities into which these wastes could be disposed. These cavities would in turn be connected to deep permeable formations, such as abandoned petroleum reservoirs well below any existing groundwater sources. A second application is that of fracturing near-surface impermeable zones and the creation of shallow craters into which water could be disposed for subsequent infiltration and percolation into the ground. Field and laboratory research on this subject to date looks promising; in a few years, perhaps, it will be possible to apply this tool for beneficial purposes to supplement groundwater supplies.

## RADIOISOTOPES

The availability of radioisotopes in recent years has opened up new possibilities for investigation of groundwater resources. An excellent example is the use of tritium for studying the flow and age of ground water. Molecules of water containing tritium, an isotope of hydrogen, act in the same manner as water molecules. Therefore, tritium serves as an excellent tracer, for it can be detected in very low concentrations. In addition, because tritium produced in the atmosphere by cosmic radiation and by thermonuclear explosions is found in rainfall, it is possible by tritium measurements of groundwater samples to ascertain how long water has been underground.

The U.S. Geological Survey conducted a study in New Jersey[10] of the natural tritium in a sandy aquifer adjoining a river. Results

10. C. W. Carlston, L. L. Thatcher, and E. C. Rhodehamel, "Tritium as a Hydrologic Tool—The Wharton Tract Study," Publication No. 52, Assembly of Helsinki, International Association of Scientific Hydrology (Gentbrugge, Belgium, 1961).

showed that concentrations decreased from 120 tritium units at 0.6 meter below ground surface to 1 tritium unit at a depth of 30 meters. This gradient revealed that water more than twenty-five years old existed at the lower level, while water less than eight months underground existed at the water table. This confirmed a hypothesis long recognized from hydraulic studies that ground water occurs and moves in layers, with the youngest water, in the upper layers, moving the fastest. To complete the picture, measurements of the tritium content of the river, whose flow was essentially all base flow from ground water, showed concentrations almost exactly equal to the uppermost groundwater values.

Injections of tritium into groundwater through canals and wells enable groundwater flow to be traced.[11] Field tests have confirmed that tritium can be used as a tracer to ascertain seepage rates from canals. The procedures in working with tritium as a tracer are identical with those using salts and dyes as tracers. Because tritium can be measured in minute concentrations, there is a greater possibility of following tritium after long distances of flow than there is with other previously available tracers.

The availability of radioisotopes has also produced neutron probes. These are recent developments, now available commercially, for the measurement of moisture content in soils above the water table. Neutrons, subatomic particles having no charge and with a mass about equal to that of the hydrogen atom, are slowed by collisions with hydrogen, whereas with other materials of much larger mass the collisions are essentially elastic. Collisions with hydrogen, however, reduce the rate of neutron travel up to one-half; thus, fast neutrons become slow neutrons after contact with material containing hydrogen. Underground, this material would be chiefly water. Therefore, measurements of slow neutrons give a measure of moisture content. The neutron probe is contained in a cylinder which is lowered into a small observation hole in the ground. Radiation is emitted from a radium beryllium source of fast neutrons. The detector is a foil of stable indium-115 which by bombardment by slow neutrons becomes radio-

11. W. J. Kaufman and D. K. Todd, "Application of Tritium Tracer to Canal Seepage Measurements," Tritium in the Physical and Biological Sciences, I, International Atomic Energy Agency (Vienna, Austria, 1962).

active indium-116. This radioactive material can then be measured by means of a Geiger counter.

Important applications for neutron probes include measurement of infiltration rates from applied water and from precipitation. An especially useful benefit is the measurement of need for irrigation by determining critical soil-moisture levels in the root zone. Depths of rainfall penetration and effects of nonhomogeneous layers can also be ascertained easily for the first time.

## WELL-LOGGING

Well-logging is the investigation of subsurface conditions from wells drilled into the ground. Methods of logging are numerous and in recent years improved techniques and new types of logging have extended the possibilities for investigating subsurface conditions. Electric logs which involve the measurement of resistivity of the earth and of potentials within the earth's crust have become standard techniques for studying underground formations.

Radioactive logging can be carried out in cased or uncased holes. Two types of logging are recognized.[12] The first is logging by means of natural gamma rays in the earth. These rays originate from disintegrations of uranium, thorium, and potassium. The relative radioactivity can be used as a rough method of identifying formations and is best done with other supplemental information. Applications of gamma-ray logging include correlation studies and identifications of lithology, formation depths, and bed thicknesses. The second type of radioactive logging is neutron logging. Here, neutrons released from a source placed in the hole can be used for identifying lithology, porosity, fluid type, and formation depths and thicknesses. In practice it is common to carry out the neutron log in conjunction with the gamma-ray log. Most radioactive logging has been done in the petroleum industry; application of the method from oil wells to water wells is now in an early stage.

Other logging techniques now available include current meter logs for measurement of the vertical flow of water inside wells. Often such measurements indicate water movement from one aquifer to

12. P. H. Jones and H. E. Skibitzke, "Subsurface Geophysical Methods in Groundwater Hydrology," *Advances in Geophysics*, 3 (New York: Academic Press, 1956).

another. Such flows are important in establishing recharge to confined formations and migration of saline water into fresh-water aquifers. Also, there are caliper logs, which can be used to determine diameters of holes. Such information indicates formations subject to caving. In other instances such logging can be used to locate well casings or drilling tools. With the availability of television, TV logs have become possible. Portable television cameras and lights of special design are lowered into water wells, and by means of a closed-circuit system the interior of the well casing can be studied in detail. Such studies assist in locating casing breaks and sources of contaminating water, in studying the condition of wells, and in ascertaining the positions of lost drilling tools.

## WELL-DRILLING

The advent of rapid means of drilling deep holes has done much to stimulate groundwater development. As in drilling for oil, the hydraulic rotary method operates by a hollow rotating bit cutting the rock while a mixture of clay and water, or drilling mud, is forced down through the drill rod to carry the cuttings upward in the rising mud. The mud serves the additional purpose of stabilizing the wall of the well, preventing caving and making casing unnecessary. After the drilling is completed, perforated casing is lowered into the hole and the clay lining is washed from the wall by injecting water down the drill rod. Wells can be constructed to depths of about 2,000 feet or even deeper. Diameters up to 18 inches are common, and with reamers diameters twice as large are possible.

The reverse rotary method uses water instead of mud and operates as a suction dredging method. Cuttings are removed by a rotating suction pipe, while the hydrostatic pressure of water within the hole acts against fine-grained deposits to support the wall. The technique is especially useful for large-diameter wells in unconsolidated materials.

Direct rotary drilling using air instead of mud or water to remove cuttings is a rapid and convenient method for small-diameter holes in consolidated and unconsolidated formations. The latest drilling development is a rapid procedure for drilling in hard-rock formations. It involves a rotary-percussion combination with air. Above the rotating bit an air hammer delivers 600 to 1,000 blows per minute to the bottom of the hole. Penetration rates of up to one foot per minute in hard rock have been reported for this method. We appear to be rapidly reaching the stage at which water wells can be drilled within a few hours rather than few days or weeks as was common only a decade ago. As an illustration, some 1,800 new irrigation wells have recently been drilled in the Indus River Basin of West Pakistan. These were 18 to 24 inches in diameter and were drilled to an average depth of 250 feet. Drilling time for most of these was less than 24 hours by the reverse rotary method.

## GROUNDWATER BASIN MANAGEMENT

The concept of groundwater basin management[13] presupposes that a groundwater reservoir will be controlled in terms of inputs and outputs of water. First, this implies some basin-wide type of control over pumping to insure that extraction of groundwater from the basin approximates the average annual replenishment to the basin. Second, control must be exercised over the areal pattern of extraction or recharge. And finally, legal control is involved, in that prescribed water rights of users are established. In the past, most groundwater basin management has been on a trial-and-error basis. Groundwater levels were depressed by excessive pumping, then pumping was reduced to allow levels to rise, and finally levels were depressed again by pumping. Unfortunately, groundwater basins are three-dimensional and nonhomogeneous. It is often difficult to ascertain on an annual basis the amount of water that can be removed or recharged simply by observation of the groundwater level. A groundwater reservoir is entirely analogous to a surface-water reservoir; it cannot be used if the level is to be maintained at the top of the dam at all times. On the other hand, if this water is stored and released so that fluctuations in water levels occur on an annual basis, maximum benefits in terms of water supply, power, flood control, and recreational benefits can be achieved simultaneously. The same applies to groundwater reservoirs. These must be pumped during periods of water need and then recharged dur-

13. "Ground Water Basin Management," Manual of Engineering Practice No. 40, American Society of Civil Engineers (New York, 1961).

ing periods when needs are less and additional supplies are available from other sources.

Ideally, groundwater reservoirs should be managed in conjunction with surface-water supplies. The interrelationship is often referred to as "conjunctive use." Essentially, conjunctive use means that groundwater reservoirs will be pumped during periods when surface-water supplies are limited. At other times, when additional surface-water supplies are available, groundwater reservoirs will be pumped less or not at all and will be recharged both naturally and artificially. This combined water source system usually provides a larger, surer, and more economic water supply than would be available from either source individually. Operationally, conjunctive use requires that the surface and groundwater resources be properly managed in order to have adequate water supplies at all times. It must also be recognized that groundwater levels will fluctuate both seasonally and over a period of years. For example, during an extended drought running for several years, surface-water supplies would be limited and ground-water pumping would be at a maximum. However, in a subsequent period of several wet years, groundwater levels would have an opportunity to recover.

An important new tool for analysis of groundwater basin management is the digital computer. This instrument has been put to work on studies of large, complex groundwater basins. Development and application of techniques suggested by this computer can materially assist water resource managers in preventing groundwater basin exhaustion and in providing for the most beneficial pattern of extraction of ground-water.

An excellent example of the application of the computer is the study of groundwater conditions in southern California. Recent work by the California Department of Water Resources has indicated that this tool is a valuable means for preparing groundwater basin operational programs for future decades.[14] Studies have been carried out on basins which have been subject to withdrawals of water exceeding combined natural and artificial replenishment. As a result, a state of overdraft now exists.

14. "Planned Utilization of Ground Water Basins: Coastal Plain of Los Angeles County," Bulletin No. 104, California Department of Water Resources (Sacramento, September 1968).

For the study of the Coastal Plain of Los Angeles County, basic data necessary as inputs to the computer included boundaries of the groundwater basin, geologic structures within the basin affecting groundwater movement, and physical characteristics such as hydraulic conductivities and storage coefficients. Study of some 5,000 logs of drillers of water and oil wells throughout the area served as the basis for delineating the aquifers. All water-bearing sediments were assigned values of specific yield and hydraulic conductivity.

The study area was divided into eighty-two unit areas, each represented by a nodal point in the model. Equations for groundwater flow along the numerous internodal connections were solved by the computer taking into account the changing conditions of inflow and outflow.

Historical data on replenishment and extraction in the basin were applied to the model to determine whether the computer could actually represent the physical conditions of the aquifers and to measure the groundwater flow throughout the study area. For these tests, data for an eleven-year period were given as inputs to the computer. After some adjustment of the physical factors in specific areas, a representative model was obtained, that is, one that demonstrated water-level changes throughout the basin similar to historical changes.

After the test work on the mathematical model, problems of managing the groundwater basin under future conditions were tackled. Changes could be made in rates and locations of extraction and replenishment. Output data from the model indicated groundwater-level elevation changes with time due to these input variations. This information indicated areas in which extractions should be limited, maximum rates of artificial recharge, and where recharge should be accomplished.

The computer produced a variety of other useful information too. It was found, for example, that reasonable amounts of recharge in the upper areas of the Coastal Plain would not be effective in halting seawater intrusion at the coast twenty-two miles away. It was also ascertained that, because of the physical characteristics of the basin, an adjustment period after any change in input or output would require more than a hundred years before equilibrium would be reached. The information derived from the model served as a basis for preparation of alternative plans of operation to reach optimum utilization of the basin's resources.

Thus, conjunctive use of local groundwater sources and imported surface water supplies can be accomplished in an optimal manner only if a basin is operated under a planned management scheme. The computer cannot only assist in these investigations but can also aid in making management decisions required for operating a basin in the future.

## CONCLUSION

Recognizing that California has outstanding natural underground water resources and that the state pumps more groundwater than any other in the United States, it is important to use these resources to the best economic advantage. Past water projects have not generally done so. However, with a better technical knowledge of groundwater basins and an awareness that feasible dam sites for storage of surface water are rapidly disappearing, a trend toward optimal use of groundwater in conjunction with surface water can be expected in the future.

Furthermore, with a growing need to reuse water, treated waste waters can be artificially recharged into the underground basins for storage and final treatment by natural filtration before reuse. Thus, groundwater can be expected to serve an increasingly important and diverse role in the management of the water resources of California.

# 10 GEOTHERMAL RESOURCES IN THE IMPERIAL VALLEY

ROBERT W. REX

The total natural flow of heat from within the earth to its surface is approximately equivalent to the burning of 1.3 billion barrels of petroleum per year. However, this large quantity of heat is still approximately one hundredth to one thousandth the amount of solar energy reaching the earth's surface from the sun. In spite of this very large quantitative difference, there is a fundamental advantage to geothermal heat. It is naturally and directly accumulated and stored in hot water and then can be tapped in very large amounts in a short period of time.

Solar energy is not readily stored in nature as heat, and the heat of the day is mostly lost at night. The heat of the summer is entirely lost over the winter so, consequently, the seasonal alternations of warmth and cold cancel each other and rarely reach more than fifty feet below the ground surface. Below this depth the natural flow of heat from the interior of the earth is dominant, and ordinarily temperatures rise continuously with depth, reaching very high values within the interior of the earth. Solar energy, however, can be stored in a chemical form as petroleum, coal, and natural gas; and our entire fossil-fuel energy base is dependent on harvesting this chemically stored solar energy.

## The Source of Geothermal Heat

The heat of the interior of the earth is thought to be generated by the decay of naturally radioactive elements over geological time plus

Originally published as "Investigation of Geothermal Resources in the Imperial Valley and Their Potential Value for Desalination of Water and Electricity Production," Institute of Geophysics and Planetary Physics, University of California, Riverside, June 1, 1970.

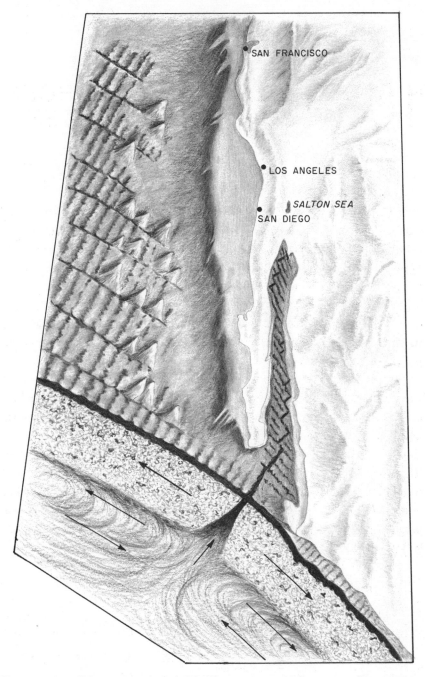

FIGURE 10.1. Schematic relationships between a sea-floor spreading center, a rifting continental area, and the Gulf of California.

a contribution from frictional forces associated with the various circulation patterns of the flowing rocks of the earth's interior.

The crust of the earth shows clear evidence of being dragged along at a speed of one to two inches per year by the interior circulation of the earth; the continental blocks, for example, float like icebergs in an ocean. Areas of current convergence and downsinking accumulate buoyant continents like driftwood floating in a river eddy. Areas of earth interior upwelling are characterized by very hot rocks spreading away from a spreading center or rift (Figure 10.1). Heat flow here is often five to ten times the normal crustal average. The spreading rocks rising from the earth's interior may split open a continent, if one is present at the point, and the opening may be filled with a gulf which eventually will become an ocean. Oceanic drilling by the Deep Sea Drilling Project of the National Science Foundation is showing that Europe and Africa split away from North and South America approximately 140 million years ago by sea-floor spreading. Sea water filled the rift and formed the North and South Atlantic Oceans in the process.

The world-circling main sea-floor spreading rift follows the median line of the Atlantic, where it is called the Mid-Atlantic Ridge, and includes the geothermal area of Iceland. It passes across the Indian Ocean and enters the South Pacific between Antarctica and Australia. A branch runs north into the geothermal area of New Zealand, while the main rift angles northeasterly across the Pacific, where it is called the East Pacific Rise. The crest of the East Pacific Rise passes into the Gulf of California, where rapid rifting of two to three inches per year started about three to four million years ago. The sea-floor spreading has carried Baja California and California west of the San Andreas Fault slowly to the northwest with respect to the mainland. The East Pacific Rise follows the axis of the Gulf of California, passes under the Mexicali and Imperial valleys, and then is obscured by continental crustal features in California. It reappears at the northern end of the San Andreas Fault north of Cape Mendocino, California, and passes on seaward into the northern Pacific Ocean. By inference, the San Andreas Fault is closely tied to the process of sea-floor spreading, but we do not have sufficient data to resolve the details of the forces that control the motion of the San Andreas and its associated faults.

## Mexicali-Imperial Valleys

Sea-floor spreading centers appear to have high heat-flow values extending over a belt at least 50 to 100 miles wide. This hot belt is ordinarily under the oceans and, therefore, rarely seen, although it is over 40,000 miles in extent. California is an exception, and the high values of oceanic heat flow extend into the Mexicali and Imperial valleys. These valleys are occupied by the sedimentary delta of the Colorado River filling a rift basin four miles deep (Figure 10.2). The sands, gravels, silts, and clays of the delta appear to have been deposited primarily over the past 4 million years and in large part consist of the sediments eroded out of the Colorado Plateau at the time of the cutting of the Grand Canyon and the uplift of the Kaibab Plateau. These young water-filled delta sediments have been subject to high heat flow of at least several times the crustal average from the underlying hot rocks. This heat has accumulated in the water-saturated delta sediments, and today there may be as much as 10 billion acre-feet of very hot groundwater in storage in the continuous Mexicali-Imperial valleys. Approximately equal quantities of geothermal reserves appear to exist on each side of the border.

The geothermal resource consists of hot water underground. Temperatures increase linearly with depth (plus or minus 15 per cent) to the maximum depths drilled to date (13,300 feet). In addition, vertical movement of water upward and downward in some areas of the valley produces large variations in temperature gradients. This indicates that major variations can be expected in well depths required to reach economically hot geothermal waters in various portions of the valley. Consequently, there will be wide ranges in costs for wells in different valley locations. Therefore, development of geothermal resources requires that steep temperature-gradient areas be located to indicate optimal areas for steam-field development. Cold areas need to be identified for consideration for waste salt-brine disposal areas.

Geothermal resource development requires consideration of an integrated knowledge of the resource's distribution, quality, disposition, and relationship to human needs, markets, land-use patterns, transportation and distribution systems, pollution factors, and environmental hazards such as ground subsidence and earthquakes.

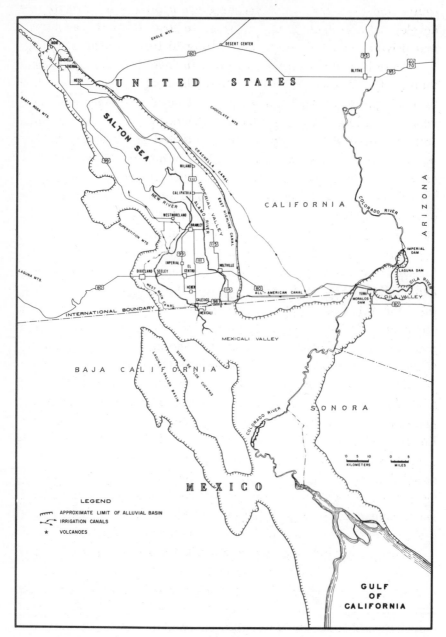

FIGURE 10.2. Index Map of the Imperial Valley.

The Imperial Valley Project of the University of California at Riverside is a multidisciplinary effort to identify the geothermal resource and undertake whatever steps are necessary to evaluate and develop it to the point where appropriate governmental, community, and private industry groups are willing to take over development.

There is a fundamental constraint on developing the geothermal fluids of the Mexicali-Imperial Valley. The heat is stored in a saline brine of approximately 1.5 to 2.5 per cent salinity. This brine is somewhat less saline than sea water and differs from sea water in being sulfate-free, or at least very low in sulfate and free of carbonate. The main anion is chloride, with only little or minor amounts of bicarbonate and sulfate. The cations are sodium, calcium, and potassium.

A special type of hypersaline brine of approximately 25 per cent dissolved solids occurs at the north end of the Imperial Valley in the old salt-sink area now occupied by the Salton Sea. There is no evidence that this highly corrosive salt-saturated brine exists outside the confines of the old salt sink; the normal low salinity, low corrosivity brine found in Mexico is also found over almost the entire U.S. portion of the the Imperial Valley. Unfortunately, early U.S. geothermal drilling occurred in the highly saline, highly corrosive brine in the Salton Sink area and, consequently, generated misconceptions about the nature of the great majority of the U.S. geothermal fluid resource.

Development of a major steam field in Mexico about 25 miles south of Mexicali is under way for electric-power production. A 75 megawatt plant as the first of four modules is under construction by Toshiba Electric Company of Japan. The present well capacity is about 100 megawatts, and an additional 100 megawatts could be quickly developed. Mexican resource estimates have been extremely conservative. Geophysical work on the U.S. side of the border plus satellite and aerial photographs suggest that present Mexican development is less than one per cent of their potential in the Mexicali Valley.

Mexican engineering has incorporated numerous adaptations of New Zealand and Italian geothermal, and U.S. oil field technology. A great deal of original experimentation and innovation has taken place, and the Mexicans are systematically solving the various technological problems associated with harnessing the geothermal resources of the Mexicali-Imperial Valley.

At first glance, it seems hard to understand why the Mexican development program under way to some degree for 8 years has no parallel on the U.S. side of the border. However, there is an evident reason. The Mexicans can dump the hot saline brine coproduced with steam from the geothermal wells into ditches that drain to the Gulf of California. But surface disposal of U.S. saline brines constitutes a pollution hazard to the Salton Sea and, therefore, surface disposal is not acceptable.

The geothermal brine exists in the ground as a hot liquid over 500° F. and at hydrostatic pressures in excess of 2,000 pounds per square inch. When this hot, salty fluid first starts flowing into the well casing, it has less pressure on it and starts boiling in the manner of a geyser. The mixture of steam and boiling brine expands and shoots to the surface at velocities that reach close to the speed of sound. Preliminary calculations indicate that the actual flow is limited by friction in the casing and that larger wells would yield flow rates beyond present values, which are as much as 1,000 tons of steam and brine per hour. Mexican wells appear to cost approximately $100,000 each. Current estimates for U.S. wells of 13 inches inside diameter to an average depth of 5,000 feet put their cost at $250,000 each. The gross revenue of such a well would be approximately $120,000-$240,000 per year (based on $.0029 for steam to produce 1 kw.hr.).

The initial brine heat content of 550-600 B.T.U. per pound permits approximately 20 per cent of the brine to be converted to steam. The remaining 80 per cent of the brine with the same temperature and pressure as the steam is not usable directly for generation of electricity as is the steam. An obvious use of this hot, low salinity brine is in a water desalination plant. There is sufficient heat in the brine to distill nearly all the water left in the brine. The brine chemistry would permit tenfold concentration without causing precipitation of the first major solid (salt) and, consequently, the recovery of water by desalination would reduce by a factor of nearly 10 the quantity of waste brine to be disposed of underground, compared to the Salton Sea type hypersaline geothermal brine where no water desalination appears feasible.

A prime water-deficient area in the southwestern United States is the basin of the Colorado River. The shortages are serious and of a twofold nature. Not only is there insufficient water to meet needs in the basin for the future, but water quality is deteriorating seriously. Geothermal water desalination would produce a distilled water probably of less than 20 parts per million dissolved solids, making an ideal blending material for augmentation and quality maintenance of Colorado River water.

Our present knowledge of the size of the U.S. portion of the basin (Figure 10.3) and the distribution of steep temperature gradients (Figure 10.4) suggest that it is feasible to develop as much as 10-15 million acre-feet per year of geothermal brine production, yielding at least 5-7 million acre-feet per year of distilled water and 20-30 thousand megawatts of electric power.

### ECONOMICS

The average cost of the steam only will probably be about $.15 per million B.T.U. if one allows the producer a reasonable profit. Sale of the steam produced from the raw brine produces revenue which in part can be allocated to the over-all costs of desalination. The economic balance between power and desalination is dependent on the technology employed to take advantage of very low-cost hot water. Present desalination plant designs are optimized for most efficient use of high-cost energy. Geothermal plants probably should be optimized for lowest capital costs. However, there are no current desalination plants designed to take advantage of the special assets of geothermal brines and equipped to cope with their particular problems. These assets include nearly free heat, free pressure, location in the United States in a severe water-deficit area, oxygen-free feedstock, and low sulfate (which is harmful because of its scale-forming tendencies and limits the amount of water that can be recovered from a brine before calcium sulfate scale precipitation). The drawbacks of geothermal desalination include several hundred parts per million of silica in solution, which causes silica scale formation (but much less severe scaling than occurs with the sulfate in sea water), and traces of hydrogen sulfide. Steel, aluminum, and plastics are used in oil-field and refinery technology to deal with the corrosive effects of these same constituents of geothermal brines.

Absence of oxygen and presence of hydrogen sulfide eliminates the necessity to use expensive bronze or brass in the heat exchangers; consequently, there appears to be a considerable sphere for reduction of capital cost in plant design over the present level of sea-water desalination costs.

Preliminary estimates by the Reactor Technology Group of the Oak Ridge National Laboratory suggest that, if electricity were sold at 4.8 mils per kilowatt-hour, water could be produced for 10 cents per 1,000 gallons, a very attractive price. Geothermal power plants cost approximately $120 per kilowatt capacity installed.

### SIZE OF THE GEOTHERMAL RESOURCE

Preliminary studies by our group at the Riverside campus of the University of California of all available geophysical data have made substantial progress. The data include magnetic, heat flow, gravity, seismic, and electric surveys, and electric, sonic, and density well logs. Preliminary interpretation of these data are the basis for Figure 10.3, showing the thickness of water-filled sediment in the Imperial Valley. This map can also be considered a depth-to-basement map. The range of reasonable formation porosities based on well logs, combined with the data in Figure 10.3, give a volume of water in storage on the U.S. side of the border and south of a line running east and west through Westmorland, California. This excludes the hypersaline brine area around the Salton Sea. The volume of available water ranges from 1.6 to 4.8 billion acre-feet, depending on extrapolation of porosities from the well logs. Measured temperature gradients indicate that from 40 to 70 per cent of this water is above 500° F. Consequently, our earlier, cruder geothermal reserve calculations are supported by current work. Further refinement of these values by improved geophysical mapping is needed to determine the details of the total heat reserves as a function of depth. These data are needed to estimate the economics and to plan the management of geothermal field development.

The production of from 10 to 15 million acre-feet per year of geothermal fluids is supported by reserves of hot water sufficient to last from one to three centuries. In addition, the heat stored in the rocks themselves is approximately equal to the heat stored in the geothermal brine. This rock heat could be recovered by injecting sea water underground in cold areas and letting it flow toward the hot areas where, once heated, it would flow into the geothermal wells, flash, and come

# NT. IMPERIAL VALLEY, CALIFORNIA.

| | |
|---|---|
| ▢ | OUTCROP |
| ▢ | < 5,000 FEET |
| ▨ | 5,000 – 10,000 FEET |
| ▨ | 10,000 – 15,000 FEET |
| ▨ | 15,000 – 20,000 FEET |
| ▨ | > 20,000 FEET |

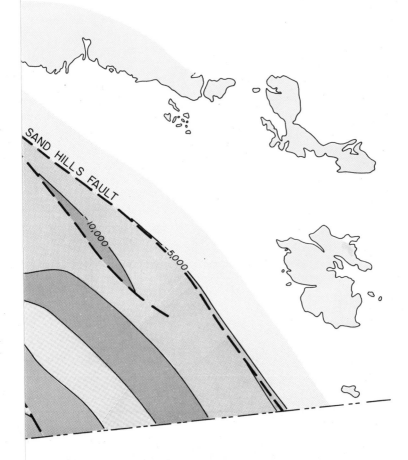

10.3. Thickness of Water-Filled Sediments, Imperial Valley. (This so be considered a depth-to-basement map.)

rosive brine was found. The gradients at the Buttes are no steeper than those at North Brawley and Heber and not much steeper than those at Mesa.

It is expected that steam fields will first be developed at Heber, North Brawley, Glamis, and Mesa while Border, Dunes, East Brawley, Alamo, and other possible prospects not yet delineated will be developed in the future. Each of our exploration programs had disclosed additional field prospects. Much of the flanks of the valley are still unexplored, suggesting that the potential for new fields is larger than now recognized.

Mexican well data indicate that a well located 600 feet away from an observation well may be started and stopped without it being possible to measure pressure changes in the observation well, indicating very high formation productivity. Approximately 125 wells could be located on each square mile of developed geothermal field if this spacing were used. Extrapolating temperature gradients linearly to the depth where 500° F. is calculated yields a measure of the area where 500° F. water should occur within 7,000 feet of the surface. Figuring 125 wells per square mile and a potential field area for 500° F. within 7,000 feet of the surface suggests that from 2,000 to 5,000 wells might be drilled to develop the steam potential of the valley fully.

Groundwater pressure data and stable isotope studies suggest that all the water zones are regionally interconnected and originally derived from the Colorado Basin drainage. Furthermore, high-temperature water is very much more compressible and less viscous than cold water. Consequently, it is suggested that the proposed geothermal wells are capable of tapping all the hot-water resources of the valley even at some distance from the wells.

Location of all reasonable prospect fields is important to assist in planning for water and power distribution in the basin, county land-use zoning, and waste-disposal planning, as well as to insure orderly development of the resource in such a way as to maximize the economic return consistent with protection of the public interest in matters of pollution and maintenance of groundwater pressure.

Fortunately, there is no significant utilization of ground water in the Imperial Valley because of its high salinity. However, farmers in Mexico and Arizona closer to the apex of the delta are pumping shal-

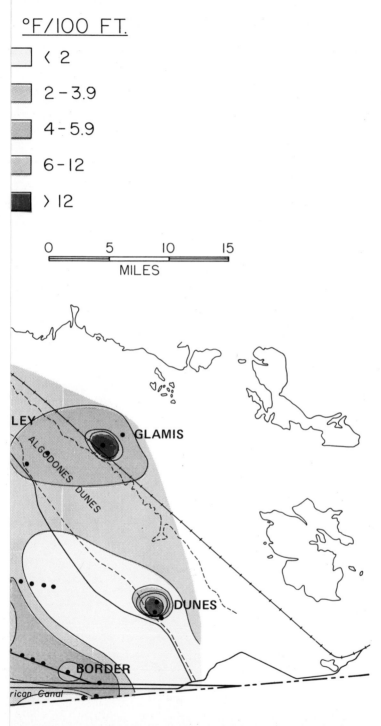

ADIENTS IN °F/IOO FEET
ALLEY, CALIFORNIA.

°F/IOO FT.

☐ ‹ 2

☐ 2 - 3.9

☐ 4 - 5.9

☐ 6 - 12

■ › 12

0       5       10       15
MILES

GLAMIS

DUNES

BORDER

10.4. Temperature Gradients, Imperial Valley. The areas of steepest
ts are suggested as most probable areas for future steam-field develop-
All gradients are measured below the limits of seasonal temperature
tions.

An opportunity created by geothermal fluid withdrawal is a relatively low-cost means of stabilizing the level, salinity, and nutrient balance of the Salton Sea without the need for a major dike-construction program.

Withdrawal of 150,000 acre-feet per year of Salton Sea water of average salinity would lower the level 2 to 4 feet and reduce the surface area exposed to evaporation. Withdrawal of this amount of average Salton Sea water would balance the inflow of salts and stabilize both the salinity and nutrient levels a little below their present levels. We propose pumping the 150,000 acre-feet of Salton Sea water to the northern portion of East Mesa or to the cool area of the Imperial Valley east of Calipatria and injecting it into intermediate or shallow sands. Preliminary order-of-magnitude estimates of the cost of the pipeline, intake works, and pumps for injection and transfer indicate a range of 20 to 25 million dollars. Operating costs and amortization including 8 per cent interest would be approximately $6 million per year. This appears to be a small fraction of the recreational benefits to Riverside and Imperial counties from the Salton Sea. Stabilization of the Salton Sea by this technique would be one of the benefits of development of the geothermal resources of the Imperial Valley.

A possible problem from pressure decline is ground subsidence. Extensive water withdrawal might eventually lead to ground subsidence. Prevention of subsidence is possible by sea-water injection. There is no way at present to calculate with reasonable precision the amount of water withdrawal that will start significant subsidence. Natural subsidence in much of the valley is about one foot per century. However, the East Mesa area actually may be undergoing uplift at present judging from old lake shore lines. We propose establishing a ground subsidence network to monitor ground motion, and in this way to provide early warning as to the need for maintaining increased pressure by sea-water injection. Experience in numerous places in the world indicates that water injection pressure maintenance programs can stabilize ground levels.

## Long Range Back-up

At some stage of geothermal development, the growing water and power needs of the Colorado Basin states and northwestern Mexico will exceed the geothermal capacity of the Imperial and Mexicali valleys. By the time that occurs, the general infrastructure for pressure maintenance and water and power distribution should be constructed and partially or entirely amortized. Diversion of sea water destined for underground injection or nuclear desalination plants would provide additional water and power to fill growth needs. It would also serve as a back-up for the geothermal system in the event that it was unable to meet its projected requirements. This nuclear back-up, coupled with the use of nuclear-plant effluent for geothermal pressure maintenance, eliminates some of the main pollution objections to current nuclear proposals for the lower Colorado basin. The siting of U.S. reactors on U.S. territory also avoids any infringement on Mexican sovereignty.

The lower Colorado River below Yuma is an international navigable waterway by Mexico-U.S. treaty; Yuma used to be a seaport before the damming of the Colorado River. Dredging of a ship canal to bring sea water to Yuma Mesa would not only provide a means of introducing sea water for geothermal pressure maintenance for Mexico and the United States, but it would also open markets for the abundant by-products—potassium chloride, sodium chloride, and calcium chloride—contained by the geothermal brine. The value of these chemicals is low, making it impractical to ship them except by sea. Low-cost calcium chloride shipped by tanker to U.S. east coast cities and to Europe could be used for snow removal and thus provide a major economy to cities such as New York. Preliminary estimates suggest that 37 per cent content calcium chloride brine could be sold in New York City for approximately $5-$6 per ton. Snow removal by this means might become a major continuing saving for many northeastern coastal cities of the United States.

The large-scale production of geothermally produced electricity plus a ship canal might turn northwestern Mexico, southwestern Arizona, and the Imperial Valley into major electrochemical manufacturing centers. The remarkably pollution-free potential for geothermal power makes it particularly attractive for planning new industrial-growth centers for the coming century.

## Summary

In the last analysis the potential for geothermal water and power to provide a pollution-free energy base for the coming century is so large that it must be studied in depth and breadth. It does little good to protest that one energy source or another is excessively polluting the environment if no viable alternatives at all are available. Geothermal energy has the promise of a tremendous potential. However, there are many obstacles to its development, some technical, some political, and some economic. The program at the University of California is directed toward contributing to the solution of these problems. So many things could go wrong that we are faced with a dilemma. The promise is great but there are at least five to six years of hard work ahead to demonstrate full-scale feasibility. Investigative costs are high because the technology needed is highly sophisticated. Water resources in the U.S. economy basically fall in the public domain, but power is split between the public and private sectors. Chemicals clearly belong to the private sector. Safety regulation, environmental monitoring, and land-use zoning are under governmental control. Geothermal energy encompasses all of these areas. Consequently, successful geothermal developments in the Imperial Valley depend on the cooperation and goodwill of all sectors of our society. Without a major cooperative effort on everyone's part, this pollution-free energy source can not be evaluated and, if development is successful, brought to full-scale achievement. It is essential that systematic investigations be made of all of the obstacles to geothermal development. But support for all the necessary programs is not yet available.

Work to date by the Mexican engineers at the Cerro Prieto steam field and by ourselves at the University of California has disclosed no insurmountable technological or economic obstacles. There are, however, many facets of the geothermal resource development that will have to be closely monitored to insure protection of both public and private interests in the region.

The fundamental scientific knowledge needed for and forthcoming from the applied geothermal investigations in the Mexicali and Imperial valleys is of outstanding consequences. There is a major need for deep drilling to 20,000 feet or more to verify the source of the heat, the chemistry of the deep brines, and the size of the deep geothermal reserves. There is some suggestion that valuable metals might occur in solution in the deepest aqueous fluids in the basin. Deep drilling would test this hypothesis.

Successful geothermal development in the Imperial and Mexicali valleys would also provide a technological base for expanded geothermal development in all the western states where there are numerous geothermal steam-field prospects.

## APPENDIX

### GEOTHERMAL RESERVE CALCULATION

An area of 1,800 square miles in the Imperial Valley bounded on the south by the Mexican border, on the north by a line parallel to the Mexican border three miles north of Westmorland, and on the east and west by basement outcrops was evaluated in terms of volume of sediments and volume of contained ground water and connate water. (Connate water is fossil water, thought to have been trapped when the strata in which it appears were laid down.) This evaluation was done by making a 25-square-mile grid over the area and calculating the volume of sediment and the average porosity of each column of sediment from the basement to the surface. A total figure of sediment arrived at was $5.7 \times 10^{14}$ cubic feet. Two parameters were used for calculating the average porosity of each column:

1) On the basis of including all the porosity of all the sediments, a figure of 60 per cent at the surface was linearly extrapolated to a figure of 0 at 20,000 feet in depth. This gave a figure of $2.1 \times 10^{14}$ cubic feet, or $4.8 \times 10^9$ acre-feet of water. This is approximately 1,400 cubic miles of water.

2) The second parameter is that of 20 per cent effective porosity at the surface, extrapolated linearly to 0 at 20,000 feet. This gave a figure of $7.0 \times 10^{13}$ cubic feet, or $1.6 \times 10^9$ acre-feet, which equals approximately 400 cubic miles of contained water.

In summary, depending on the porosity parameters used, we have from 1.6 to 4.8 billion acre-feet and from 400 to 1,400 cubic miles of ground water and connate water contained in the valley sediments underlying the 1,800 square miles investigated to date.

# 11 ENERGY RESOURCES

DAVID L. BOOK

The relation between water and energy consumption is much more intimate that a mere paralleling of growth curves. For example, some industrial processes use up water, instead of just doing something with it, then returning it to circulation. Energy is almost never re-usable; and nearly all of it ends up as heat, so that industrial and population centers are a few degrees warmer than empty countryside.

Many industrial processes use water as a coolant. Availability of coolant water is already a principal factor in industrial-plant siting, especially in the arid west. Most of the water so used is warmed and returned to rivers and reservoirs, which grow warmer in turn. Their temperatures must not increase unduly lest extensive damage to aquatic plant and animal life result and heavy fogs arise. Suppose a limit of 10° F. is arbitrarily imposed on such heating. The total energy use in California in 1970 will be about 5,000 trillion B.T.U.[1] If 500 trillion B.T.U.–10 per cent–ultimately heats water in one way or another, the temperature of 20 million acre-feet would be raised by the maximum acceptable amount. (This amount of water is about 5 times the total for which the State Water Project is designed.)

The figure of 500 trillion B.T.U. is actually conservative, as can easily be seen by considering just one industrial process, thermal

1. "The Future of Power in the West Region, 1970–1980–1990," Report to Federal Power Commission, June 1969, prepared by the West Regional Advisory Committee (whence the more convenient designation "WRAC Report"). Appendix 2, "Energy Supply and Demand," is of especial interest. Most of the data in this chapter given without attribution to source are to be found in the WRAC Report, in particular tables 3, 4, 7, 8, and 9. All numbers for 1969 and subsequent years are, of course, projections. It is this author's opinion that such numbers are very crude approximations, even granting the assumptions used, and are probably good to one or at most two significant figures.

NOTE: In this chapter the following units are employed: 1 kilowatt = 1.34 horsepower = $10^{-3}$ megawatt = $10^{-6}$ gigawatt; 1 kilowatt-hour = 3,412 British Thermal Units (B.T.U.) = $8.60 \times 10^5$ calories; 1 kiloton of TNT = $1.2 \times 10^6$ kilowatt-hours.

generation of electricity. In 1970, California produced about 105 billion kilowatt-hours of electricity by thermal generation,[2] in which heat from fossil or nuclear fuels produces steam which drives turbo-generators. On the average this process is about 35 per cent efficient. In other words, for every kilowatt-hour of electricity, about 6,400 B.T.U. are lost as heat. This means a total of 650 trillion B.T.U. will have to be gotten rid of. Cooling systems account for most of it, with water the principal coolant.

Instead of merely warming water, heat can be used to evaporate it, in cooling towers or by releasing steam after once-through operation of turbines. The 500 trillion B.T.U. mentioned above would vaporize 200,000 acre-feet of water. Water vapor produced this way causes thick fog and sometimes year-round cloud cover, which is usually undesirable. In addition, a significant amount of water is lost. If power consumption continues to rise, there may eventually be a problem in locating enough water to use as a coolant.

Another example of the close links between energy and water supplies is joint water-control/hydroelectric projects. Almost a quarter of all electric power generated in California is hydroelectric. Virtually all of the water stored behind dams or diverted into irrigation systems from open streams comes into use in California as part of a hydroelectric project as well.

As a final example, desalination is highly pertinent. The theoretical minimum energy just for separating salt and sea water at sea-water concentrations is about one megawatt-hour per acre-foot. Practically speaking, at least three times that much energy is needed in any actual working device. This means that if desalination plants produce 10 million acre-feet per year, they would require at least 100 trillion B.T.U. per year just to purify the water — about 2 per cent of the present rate of energy consumption in California. Below, in the section on Alternatives, the subject of nuclear-fueled combination desalination-generation plants will be discussed.

The goals of this chapter are thus to inquire where we get energy,

2. The principal source of data on past and future California electric output has been "Electric Power Survey, Years 1968–1975, for the State of California," prepared by Martin C. White for the California Public Utilities Commission and dated September 15, 1969. (The term of the projections, six years, is comparable for the time required for a generating station to proceed from design to actual operation.) This report contains valuable information on networks, siting, fuels, loads, peak demands, and other topics.

TABLE 11.1.
*Primary Energy Sources, United States, 1965*

| Fuel | Amount (trillion B.T.U.) | Percentage |
|---|---|---|
| Coal | 13,358 | 23.0 |
| Crude oil | 21,337 | 39.6 |
| Natural gas | 16,136 | 30.0 |
| Natural-gas liquids | 1,872 | 3.5 |
| Hydroelectric | 2,086 | 3.9 |

SOURCE: "U.S. Energy Policies: An Agenda for Research," a *Resources for the Future* Staff Report, 1968, p. 7.

what it is used for, how much the state's needs will increase during the remainder of this century, and where the additional energy will come from. All of this will be related to the national energy picture and to the state water situation. Throughout the discussion, one question should be to the fore constantly: When a choice of policies exists, what are the benefits and the costs of each alternative?

## THE ENERGY INDUSTRY

In 1970, the total energy consumption in the United States was about $6.2 \times 10^{16}$ B.T.U., or almost 2 million gigawatt-hours. Energy industries employ about 2 per cent of the nation's labor force and contribute almost 4 per cent to the national income. About 7 cents of the consumer dollar goes to buy energy in one form or another.[3]

It is customary to distinguish between primary and secondary sources of energy. The primary sources are the fossil fuels—crude oil, natural gas, natural-gas liquids, coal—falling water, nuclear fuels, and a few of minor economic importance, such as wood, geothermal and solar sources, winds, and tides. Secondary sources are those produced from primary sources in more convenient forms for distribution or certain uses. Examples are electricity (the most important), gasoline, and coke. Table 11.1 shows the relative importance of the major primary fuels used in the United States in 1965.

Long-term trends show that coal, which in 1900 held 90 per cent of the energy market, has not even doubled in total production since

3. "U.S. Energy Policies: An Agenda for Research," a *Resources for the Future* Staff Report, 1968. The quoted figures are from Chapter 1, "A General View of the Energy Industries," p. 19.

TABLE 11.2.
*Consumption of Primary Energy Resources by Sector,*
*United States, 1965*

| Sector | Amount (trillion B.T.U.) | Percentage |
|---|---|---|
| Industrial | 17,515 | 32.5 |
| Transportation | 12,721 | 23.7 |
| Household and commercial | 11,793 | 21.9 |
| Electrical utilities | 11,110 | 20.6 |

SOURCE: "U.S. Energy Policies: An Agenda for Research," a *Resources for the Future* Staff Report, 1968, p. 10.

then. The rate of increase of hydroelectric-power utilization sped up, then slowed, as all the readily exploitable reserves were tapped. Petroleum products now have captured most of the market. In the past decade, the shares of the total provided by hydroelectricity, oil, gas, gas liquids, and coal have remained almost steady. The only striking change in the near future is likely to be an increasing percentage coming from nuclear fuels.

One-fifth of all the primary fuels consumed goes into making electricity. Table 11.2 shows the principal uses of primary fuels as of 1965. It is expected that the demand for electricity will rise relative to total energy consumption, since modern industry is increasingly dependent on it. Consumption of electricity has doubled every ten years in the country as a whole, and every eight years in California. This is about

TABLE 11.3.
*Energy Content and Average Delivered Price (California) of Principal Fuels*

| Fuel | Energy content (BTU) | 1970 Price (cents/million BTU) |
|---|---|---|
| Electricity, 1 kilowatt-hour | 3413 | 210 (total cost) |
| Natural gas, 1 cubic ft. | 1075 | 35 |
| Fuel oil, 1 barrel | $6.4 \times 10^6$ | 31 |
| Low-sulfur fuel oil, 1 barrel | $6.0 \times 10^6$ | 40 |
| Natural-gas liquids, 1 barrel | $4.4 \times 10^6$ | 82 (propane) |
| Coal, 1 short ton | $2 \times 10^7$ | 45 |
| Wood, 1 cubic ft. | $1.5 \times 10^5$ | 40 |
| U-235, 1 gram | $7.8 \times 10^7$ | 20 |
| Deuterium, 1 gram | $3.2 \times 10^8$ | — |

SOURCE: "The Future of Power in the West Region, 1970–1980–1990," *op. cit.* (in footnote 1); various personal communications; letter dated May 22, 1970, from H. S. Newins, PG&E, to "Mr. Charles Pitts," etc.

twice the growth rate of the Gross National Product, and about eight times that of the population. Conversely, the availability of abundant cheap electric power spurs advances in industrial chemistry and metallurgy. It follows that projections of future needs tend to deal largely with electric power.

To a considerable degree, however, energy needs are flexible. If new supplies of electricity are needed in a given situation, they can be generated from hydroelectric, coal, oil, or nuclear power sources — whatever is cheapest. When new homes or a new transportation system is built, one of the design considerations is cost of power. Gas heating versus oil heating, electric trains versus diesel trains show this clearly. If electrical "needs" are not met, that is, if electricity is so much in demand relative to other sources of energy that its price goes up, then industry will prefer the alternative sources where possible. To facilitate comparison, Table 11.3 presents a summary of the respective energy content and average or typical price for the different types of fuels.

## PROJECTIONS

It is customary to estimate future needs by extrapolating consumption. Most economists agree that this is a poor second best. Needs should be determined instead by determining what public policies will optimize social values and individual welfare. It then might be decided that what we really need might entail a reversal of present trends, rather than their continuance. But policies of this type could be beneficial only in the context of a coherent long-range economic plan, and such planning is unlikely to come to pass in the United States for many years, if at all. Lacking it, we have to fall back on extrapolations of production and consumption curves, total reserves, and unit costs.

The most comprehensive future survey of the western United States covers the years 1970-1990.[4] There are four reasons for studying California's energy needs in the context of a regional picture embracing all of the western states. First, much of California's energy is imported. It may enter in primary form (gas, uranium, oil) or secondary

4. "The Future of Power in the West Region," *op. cit.*

TABLE 11.4.
*Average Cost of Transporting Energy, 1970*

| Form of energy | Means of transportation | Cost per 100 miles (cents/million B.T.U.) |
|---|---|---|
| Nuclear (uranium oxide) | Rail | under .03 |
| Oil | Tanker | .1 to .5 |
| | Pipeline | .4 to 1.6 |
| | Rail | .5 |
| | Truck | 7.4 |
| Natural gas | Pipeline | 1.1 to 2.4 |
| | Tanker (liquefied gas) | .5 to .9 |
| | Rail (liquefied gas) | 2.7 |
| Coal | Slurry pipeline | 1.5 to 3.5 |
| | Rail | 3.6 |
| Electricity | High-voltage AC lines | 3.0 to 9.0 |

SOURCE: "The Future of Power in the West Region, 1970–1980–1990," *op. cit.* (in footnote 1), p. 2–166.

(hydroelectric from Hoover Dam and the northwest, coal-generated electricity from Arizona). Table 11.4 shows average transportation costs for the principal types of energy. In addition, utilities and many large consumers operate across state lines. Their markets are not delimited by political boundaries but follow population. Third, the characteristic problems of California are those of most of the other western states as well: water is usually in short supply, distances between load centers great, and fuel resources remote from the use areas.

Finally, one of the most salient features in the transmission of electrical power in the west is the so-called Western Loop, a system of high voltage lines encircling Nevada (where power consumption is almost zero) and connecting the principal load centers of California with those of the Rocky Mountain states. The Loop permits sharing of load during peak demand periods, planning of maintenance schedules, and possessing reserve capacity for emergency power transfers.

In broad outline, we get energy mainly from hydro installations, natural gas, oil, and coal. This energy is used primarily in industry, as well as in transportation and households. In California, a considerable portion goes to pump water intended for irrigation, industry, and human consumption. Projections indicate total energy consumption in the west will more than double from 1970 to 1990. Electric generation will increase fivefold and thermal generation (nonhydroelectric) will rise by a factor of 10. The increased emphasis on electricity stems in part from the sophistication of modern industry, but also from projecting increased installation of air conditioning and a continuing trend toward service industries. Coal and nuclear energy will meet most of the new needs.

The total estimated exploitable energy reserves in the west are about twenty-five greater than the region's needs projected to 1990. This takes no account of Alaskan and foreign oil reserves, which can be shipped or piped in cheaply, or of nuclear reserves outside the region (in Canada, for instance).

But simple-minded bookkeeping fails to tell the whole story. The harvest of every type of primary energy takes its toll of the environment: flooded valleys, beaches smeared with oil, hillsides gouged away by strip mines. And electric-power plants are among the worst polluters in the country. Fossil-fueled generating plants now contribute 50 per cent of the sulfur oxides and about 25 per cent of the particulates polluting the air.[5] These plants already require about 80 per cent of all cooling water used in industry. In addition, nuclear power raises the specter of the most poisonous kind of pollutants of all.

Right now, there is a shortage of electric power. Blackouts and brownouts occur during peak consumption — as on hot days when air conditioners are turned up — and periods of restricted use are becoming more and more common. Power companies are at the same time encountering strong pressure against building new generating stations on sites near cities or recreational areas. It is getting harder and harder to find places to build on anywhere.

Thus the principal influences on the energy situation are increased demand, especially for electricity, and a countering, growing clamor against pollution and despoliation. They must be understood against a background of discoveries of new supplies, depletion of old ones, and continuing technological progress.

The most important projections are probably those concerned with electricity. California is an importer of electrical energy. Table 11.5

5. Arlene Alligood, "The Power Dilemma: Electricity vs. Environment," *San Francisco Examiner-Chronicle*, May 3, 1970, p. A13. See also *Cleaning Our Environment: The Chemical Basis for Action,* by the Subcommittee on Environmental Improvement, Committee on Chemistry and Public Affairs, American Chemical Society, Washington, D.C. (1969).

TABLE 11.5.
*California Generating Capacity in Megawatts,
1968–1975*

|  | Generation | | Total |
|---|---|---|---|
|  | In-state | Out-of-state |  |
| 1968 | 26.5 | 1.1 | 27.6 |
| 1969 | 27.4 | 2.2 | 29.6 |
| 1970 | 28.1 | 3.7 | 31.8 |
| 1971 | 29.2 | 4.7 | 33.9 |
| 1972 | 30.9 | 4.9 | 35.8 |
| 1973 | 33.9 | 5.0 | 38.9 |
| 1974 | 35.9 | 5.6 | 41.5 |
| 1975 | 36.5 | 5.9 | 42.4 |

SOURCE: "Electric Power Survey, Years 1968–1975, for the State of California," prepared by Martin C. White for the California Public Utilities Commission, Sept. 15, 1969, pp. 26–27.

shows the production capacity available to utilities and public agencies in California from 1968 through 1975. Most of the out-of-state power goes to southern California; it accounts for about one-fifth of the total consumption south of the Tehachapis. Most of the total imported (up to 3 gigawatt-hours per year) comes from Hoover Dam, which allocates two-thirds of its output to California utilities. As a general rule throughout the west, utilization is only about 80 per cent of capacity, to allow for maintenance and reserve needs. But supplies are drawn from all producers at about this 80 per cent rate, so that capacity figures also give a good index of actual consumption.

The Pacific Northwest-Pacific Southwest Intertie agreements are scheduled to bring in new supplies of normal-level and peak energy. The projected sources are the Columbia River Power System, municipal and publicly owned utilities in the northwest, privately owned installations under construction, and Canadian treaty entitlement power. The last is the Canadian share of the benefits of added generation at U.S. plants made available by additional storage behind Canadian dams on the Columbia and Kootenay rivers. The California Department of Water Resources has bought part of the Canadian power rights, which means additional power will simply be fed into the existing network.[6]

One of the problems of supplying electrical power is that the aver-

6. "Electric Power Survey, Years 1968–1975," *op. cit.*, p. 6.

TABLE 11.6.
*Projected PG&E Electrical Production, 1970–1990*

|      | Peak power, gigawatts | Gigawatt-hours per year (in thousands) |
|------|------|------|
| 1970 | 10.8 | 61.0 |
| 1975 | 15.9 | 89.7 |
| 1980 | 23.0 | 130.0 |
| 1985 | 33.5 | 189.0 |
| 1990 | 48.5 | 274.0 |

SOURCE: Telephone conversation, April 16, 1970, with Mr. Ray Perry, PG&E San Francisco Office.

age demand is only about 60 to 65 per cent of the peak rate of consumption. This means that capacity sufficient to meet peak demands is excessive most of the time. The principal peaks occur in midafternoon during the summer months and at dinner time during winter. The heaviest demands in California fall in July and December. It is just during these peak periods that overloads occur, and transmission or generation failures can have the most disastrous consequences. Ties to other generators in California and out of state via the Western Loop help utilities to make up such deficiencies. A second line of defense is load-shedding. If demands begin to place excessive strain on generation facilities, low priority users (irrigation pumping stations, for example) are automatically cut off ("shed") until the balance is restored. Obviously interties, load-shedding systems, and safety margins are closely calculated, so as to serve both profit schedules and the requirements of customers with reliability.

Like the rest of the western region, California's utilities expect to increase output almost fivefold by 1990. Table 11.6 shows a skeleton picture of the anticipated growth in electrical output of the Pacific Gas and Electric Company, which produces three-fourths of the electricity used in the northern half of the state. It supplies private consumers, industry, and the state, including the California Water Project.

Not quite one-fourth of California's power comes from in-state hydroelectric plants. Most conventional hydro sites within the state that can be economically developed already have been. Greater capacity will come largely from addition to existing plants, but this, though it is expected to more than double, will not be important in the overall scheme. Hydro plants are important, however, because they can

TABLE 11.7.
*Electrical Generation in California, by Energy
Source, 1950–1990 (thousand gigawatt-hours)*

|      | Thermal | Hydro | Total |
|------|---------|-------|-------|
| 1950 | 10.9    | 14.8  | 25.7  |
| 1955 | 28.9    | 14.5  | 43.4  |
| 1960 | 47.4    | 17.4  | 64.9  |
| 1965 | 63.7    | 30.5  | 94.2  |
| 1970 | 106.7   | 31.1  | 137.8 |
| 1975 | 174.5   | 32.0  | 206.4 |
| 1980 | 275.8   | 32.3  | 308.1 |
| 1985 | 411.6   | 33.2  | 444.8 |
| 1990 | 567.0   | 36.8  | 603.8 |

SOURCE: "The Future of Power in the West Region, 1970–1980–1990," *op. cit.* (in footnote 1), p. 2–123.

provide peaking power. Water held back behind a dam can be released into spillways and, while the reserve lasts, a higher power level results.

Little of California's additional electrical demands will be supplied by hydro plants; instead, thermal generation will provide most of the increment (Table 11.7). Until recent years, thermal generation in California has been almost all oil- and gas-fired. But it is anticipated that further increases will be satisfied by nuclear generators within the state and coal-fired generators in the Rocky Mountain states (Table 11.8). Almost all production is by public utilities, although some industrial establishments generate their own.

TABLE 11.8.
*Fuels Used for Generation of California's Electricity, 1950–1990*

|      | Natural gas (billion cubic ft.) | Oil (million barrels) | Coal (million short tons) | Uranium oxide[a] (short tons) |
|------|---------------------------------|-----------------------|---------------------------|-------------------------------|
| 1950 | 78.3  | 9.4  | 0    | 0    |
| 1955 | 183.7 | 22.0 | 0    | 0    |
| 1960 | 323.0 | 24.1 | 0    | 0    |
| 1965 | 492.2 | 16.7 | 0    | 14   |
| 1970 | 719.0 | 22.3 | 2.8  | 627  |
| 1975 | 641.0 | 48.3 | 10.8 | 2400 |
| 1980 | 478.0 | 49.4 | 14.7 | 5400 |
| 1985 | 456.0 | 48.6 | 20.0 | 7800 |
| 1990 | 456.0 | 46.0 | 27.8 | 9800 |

SOURCE: "The Future of Power in the West Region, 1970–1980–1990," *op. cit.* (in footnote 1), p. 2–125.
[a] The U-235 in 1 ton of uranium oxide is sufficient to provide about $3 \times 10^{11}$ B.T.U.

TABLE 11.9.
*Western Region Electric Generation, Percentage by Energy Source, 1950–1990*

|      | Natural gas | Oil | Coal | Nuclear | Other | Total Thermal | Hydro |
|------|------|------|------|------|------|------|------|
| 1950 | 13.6 | 6.7  | 1.2  | 0    | 1.0 | 22.5 | 77.5 |
| 1955 | 22.5 | 11.9 | 1.7  | 0    | .4  | 36.5 | 63.5 |
| 1960 | 29.6 | 10.8 | 2.9  | 0    | .3  | 43.6 | 56.4 |
| 1965 | 30.3 | 5.4  | 6.4  | .1   | .3  | 42.5 | 57.5 |
| 1970 | 30.1 | 5.5  | 9.9  | 2.6  | .3  | 48.4 | 51.6 |
| 1975 | 20.3 | 7.9  | 18.0 | 14.1 | .6  | 60.9 | 39.1 |
| 1980 | 12.2 | 5.5  | 19.6 | 32.9 | .7  | 70.9 | 29.1 |
| 1985 | 7.8  | 3.6  | 19.1 | 46.8 | .7  | 78.0 | 22.0 |
| 1990 | 6.3  | 2.5  | 17.2 | 56.9 | .6  | 83.5 | 16.5 |

SOURCE: "The Future of Power in the West Region, 1970–1980–1990," *op. cit.* (in footnote 1), p. 2–127.

By about 1985, nuclear generation is expected to be supplying over half the electricity used in California. The only other major primary source which promises gains is coal. Table 11.9 shows how these two fuels will dominate the picture twenty years hence.

Why should this be so? Mainly, economics. Nuclear fuels are substantially cheaper than fossil fuels. Coal represents over half of the west's proved energy reserves. The west's gas supplies are dwindling fast; ten years more will see them exhausted or severely depleted. And though California's oil fields are expanding, the oil they yield is high in sulfur. Public pressure over pollution is forcing utilities to switch to low-sulfur oil, which must be imported, or somehow to remove the sulfur from domestic oil. Either way, added expense tends to price oil out of competition.

This picture, of course, is simplified to the extreme. There are many complicating factors. For example, each type of fuel has its own strengths and weaknesses, which it will be helpful to note briefly.

*Coal.* Most of the west's coal is in Montana and Wyoming. The deposits in Arizona, though considerably less extensive, are of more importance to California, because of water availability and distances to load centers. Several coal-burning plants are planned or under construction along the Colorado River to serve southern California.

Coal mining has experienced remarkable technical advances which have greatly improved productivity. Highly mechanized strip mines can produce a hundred tons per man-shift, and will do even better with increasing automation. Mine-mouth generating plants have the lowest fuel cost of any in the country, around fifteen to twenty cents per million B.T.U. But strip mining, one of the most destructive ways man has yet found to exploit nature, will possibly run afoul of interests that want to keep the land from being gouged and chewed to shreds.

Another problem with coal is pollution. Untreated soft coal produces foul smoke with a plentiful load of sulfur, ash, and other impurities. It was by banning the use of unsophisticated open coal fires that London did away with its "killer fogs" (like that of 1952) and made its air cleaner than it had been for a hundred years.[7]

Projections indicate that coal prices will remain stable for the next twenty years. Whereas the present rate of consumption is about 23 million tons per year in the west, economically recoverable coal reserves known in these states total about 50 billion tons. In spite of this seeming abundance, it would be desirable to avoid heavy dependence on coal as an energy source. Coal is indispensable in plastics and other chemical industries, being one of the few large-scale sources of carbon and hydrocarbons. Since edible bacteria and yeasts can be cultured on coal and coal derivatives[8] (and, indeed, on crude oil also), we may eventually need coal for food rather than fuel.

*Natural Gas.* Consumption of gas has been rising rapidly, particularly in generating electricity, and particularly in California. Probably before the end of the century (and in any case, sooner than for any other fossil fuel), reserves will decline and natural gas supplies will become tighter. Before about 1950, California supplied most of the gas consumed in the state. Now, even with increases in production, California necessarily imports over half the gas it uses, most of the import coming from Texas and Canada. The Canadian sources will become increasingly important. Prices will tend to rise because of scarcity and transportation charges.

Gas has a number of advantages. It contains less sulfur than do oil and coal. Particulates are not a problem. Gas burns efficiently and is easy to redistribute once delivered. In the generation of electricity, gas turbines are useful for startup and reserve purposes.

7. See, for example, J. R. Goldsmith, in *Air Pollution,* ed. A. C. Stern (New York: Academic Press, 1962), Vol. I, p. 335.
8. See, for example, J. B. Davis, *Petroleum Microbiology* (New York: Elsevier Publishing Company, 1967), ch. 7.

Because gas is so useful, a number of ideas are under investigation to forestall shortages. One is synthesizing gas from coal. Gas produced by synthetic processes costs about twice as much as natural gas, but with improvements and the slackening of natural production these processes will probably become competitive in five to ten years. A second approach is stimulating production in known fields by means of nuclear explosives; this will be discussed below.

*Oil.* It is of crucial importance that the United States is an oil-importing country. Over a quarter of the oil we consume comes from abroad, mostly from countries in the western hemisphere. If international developments should cut off sources in the Near East and Latin America, the price of oil would skyrocket. It would become necessary to augment domestic production or switch to other primary fuels.

As far as California is concerned, pollution is the watchword. California's own crude oil contains about 2 per cent sulfur. Public policy (in the form of air-pollution control laws) is now to use oil with no more than 0.5 per cent sulfur. At the present time about two-thirds of the oil used in the state for electrical generation comes from foreign suppliers, principally Venezuela, Indonesia, Liberia, and North Africa. Low-sulfur oil from the Gulf of Mexico is not competitive with these imports, nor do various stack gas (smoke) treatment processes under development, whose purpose is to remove the sulfur oxides after burning, improve the economic picture. Synthetic fuel oil from coal, oil shale, or tar sands probably will be competitive.

Fuel oil costs for electrical generation will climb by about 20 per cent (the difference in cost between domestic and low-sulfur crude) in the next few years, then level off. Thereafter the rise will be slower. There appears to be no threat of an oil shortage in the world or in the western hemisphere. With the exploitation of the fields on the Alaskan North Slope, the United States could probably be self-sufficient for several decades at the extrapolated rate of national consumption.

Toward the end of the century, technical developments will probably render the Colorado shale-oil deposits accessible. They contain an amount of oil several times greater than the proved reserves of the rest of the world,[9] but at the present time there is no way to exploit them economically.

9. *New York Times,* May 7, 1967 (quoted by Herman Kahn and Anthony J. Wiener, *The Year 2000* (New York: The Macmillan Company, 1967), p. 74.

*Nuclear Power.* Here fuel and operating costs are lower than for fossil fuels, and capital costs (per kilowatt generating capacity) are higher. Therefore nuclear-power stations grow more competitive the larger they are. Nuclear plants are generally in the 500 megawatt to 1 gigawatt (electric output) range—or bigger—for this reason.

Five years ago, California produced no electricity in nuclear plants. Now there are 519 megawatts of generating capacity in stations at San Onofre and Humboldt Bay, and another 3,100 megawatts under construction or scheduled for completion by 1975. Since 1966, new orders for nuclear plants each year have exceeded new orders for conventional plants.

Most of the concepts and techniques that have served to make nuclear power competitive emerged from a vast quarter-century-long research and development program underwritten by the federal government. The government has also accumulated a 50,000-ton stockpile of $U_3O_8$ (uranium oxide or "yellowcake"), which is now available for commercial reactors in case of shortage. Directly and indirectly, uranium prices are fixed in Washington. Critics of nuclear power maintain that these prices are artificially low and conceal a continuing long-term federal subsidy.

Thermal generation using nuclear fuel is in most respects like conventional thermal generation. The reactor heats water, making steam which drives turbogenerators. There are, however, some problems peculiar to the atomic industry.

Concentrated ore (containing at least 75 per cent $U_3O_8$) costs about $8 a pound. Natural uranium is mostly inert U-238, less than 1 per cent being the active fissionable isotope, U-235. Most reactor designs require fuel enriched through concentrating U-235 to a level of several per cent. The enriched fuel is packaged into canisters, slugs, or other convenient shapes, usually by mixing or alloying the uranium metal. Enrichment and fabrication make the cost of the finished fuel elements about triple that of the raw fuel. The fuel elements are radioactive and must be manufactured and handled with a caution not usually accorded to other fuels.

So-called thermal reactors require the use of moderators, substances like carbon or heavy water (deuterium oxide), for their operation. Extreme purity is essential in control rods (which quench the nuclear reaction) and even in structural materials. Many technical problems whose solutions are still unfamiliar to manufacturers and contractors make building a new reactor a kind of R and D problem rather than a routine engineering job. Accidents can irradiate plant employees or release contaminated cooling water into rivers, or even — in the case of control failure — melt down the reactor into an untouchable radioactive ruin, But the safety precautions that the nuclear industry and the federal government have enforced have gained for the industry a nearly perfect record. Reactor-plant personnel are safer than most factory workers. Nonetheless, some scientists have argued recently that the controls on radioactive effluents should be tighter still.[10] Safety statistics have not allayed widespread popular uneasiness.

In the normal course of operation, after about one to several years a reactor needs new fuel elements. These are inserted in place of the old ones, which are processed for any "burnable" material they may hold, then disposed of. Disposal causes serious problems that may prove in the long run to be the limiting factor in the growth of the nuclear-power industry.

The amount of material to be gotten rid of approximately equals the amount of nuclear fuel consumed, and it is extremely radioactive. Radioactive wastes are at once highly toxic and practically indestructible. The only "treatment" known is to store them until the radioactivity has dropped to safe levels. No method thus far proposed — undersea dumping, burial in concrete, storage in liquid form in deep aquifers, ejection into space — is wholly satisfactory. Short-term solutions are out of the question. As an illustration, two of the most dangerous by-products — the isotopes cesium-137 and strontium-90 — have half-lives of about thirty years. After a century of storage, these isotopes still radiate about 10 per cent of the initial level.

After completion of processing for leftover fuel and usable isotopes, reactor wastes take the form of a corrosive liquid or slurry. This fearsome "witches' brew" is heated by the radioactive decay of its constituents to boiling. Even the vapors it emits are deadly. After it has stood

10. J. W. Gofman and A. R. Tamplin, "Nuclear Reactors and the Public Health and Safety," paper presented at the 136th annual meeting of the American Association for the Advancement of Science, Boston, Mass., Dec. 26–31, 1969. It is only fair to note that the views of these authors are controversial and have not found wide acceptance among the scientific community at large.

for a year or two, most of the short-lived unstable isotopes have decayed and the mixture cools somewhat.

At this stage the engineer in charge of waste-processing looks around for a deep hole. But he cannot be satisfied just to bury the wastes; they have to stay buried for at least five hundred to a thousand years.

It is sobering and instructive to recall how frequently power and gas lines and water mains are accidentally broken during construction jobs. Twenty years is often enough time to lose all record of where such cables and pipes were laid. But radioactive wastes must lie safe from accidental unearthing for the next *thousand* years.

Even if the wastes are safe indefinitely from direct contact, there are other problems. Ground water may carry isotopes into rivers or reservoirs or to the ocean where shellfish (for example) can accumulate them. Earthquakes can shift fault lines and flood even dry repositories with unforeseeable consequences. To guard against such possibilities, the wastes should be enclosed in a strong, waterproof, protective casing. Natural salt deposits in abandoned mines afford a measure of protection. Ordinary concrete does not; chemical changes as a result of radioactive bombardment soon weaken it, and thermal stresses and pressure from gases created by nuclear decay in the wastes rupture the concrete shell. But research has produced new types of ceramic to meet this need, and either ceramic casings or salt mines look promising for waterproofing buried wastes.

Finally, there is the problem of getting wastes to disposal sites. Tank trucks and rail cars will carry them along public roadways. How often will collisions or derailments occur? The public is going to have to become nuclear safety conscious if atomic power is to fulfill its projected role, and radiation inspection may well become a familiar fact of life.

Fuel costs will gradually rise in the next ten to twenty years, offsetting savings from improved technology. It is desirable to find a way to burn all the uranium found naturally, not just U-235. Breeder reactors hold out a hope of doing this.[11] They turn U-238 into fissionable

11. For a survey and progress report on breeder development work, see Milton Shaw, "Fast Breeder Reactor Programme in the U.S.," in Proceedings of the London Conference on Fast Breeder Reactors, *Fast Breeder Reactors,* ed. P. V. Evans (Oxford: Pergamon Press, 1967).

plutonium, and thorium (somewhat more widespread than uranium in the earth's crust) into a fissionable form, U-235, of uranium. In fact, breeders will produce a quantity of plutonium or U-233 greater than the quantity of fuel they start with—possibly several times as much. Large-scale breeding would have the effect of increasing the accessible energy in the world's uranium stocks by a factor of 50. Breeders, which have been likened to an intermediate stage between thermal reactor and bomb, are still experimental—and with good reason. An accident in one installation, the Fermi reactor near Detroit, rendered the site unapproachable for two years.

Development will probably yield commercially feasible breeders in ten to fifteen years. They will be very large—1 to 10 gigawatt electric capacity—and will have to be located outside populated areas. At the same time, only a big city can absorb that kind of power output. Where will they go? There are few promising ideas. They might be floated on Texas platforms like those used for offshore oil drilling, but very much larger. They might be put underground or on the ocean floor. Perhaps they will turn out to be reliable enough that people lose some of their chariness, or the population will grow so great that people will become less choosy about where they live.

It is unlikely that there will be any pressure to build power stations using breeders until they are as safe and reliable as thermal reactors. This, in fact, is the major obstacle to their exploitation now. In addition, because of their size, they would be giant heat-polluters. And that may be a more important deterrent to using breeders than nuclear hazards.

Most of the world's known deposits of uranium are in Canada, the Colorado Plateau in the United States, South Africa, eastern Brazil, Australia, Czechoslovakia, and the U.S.S.R. The United States is not an outstandingly uranium-rich country, but it has reserves of over 650,000 tons of $U_3O_8$ in the $10-a-pound-or-less price range. This reserve is several times the total consumption projected for the remaining years of the century. Breeding would enlarge stocks manyfold. In the event of nuclear disarmament, the equivalent of many hundreds of thousands of tons of additional $U_3O_8$, already refined, would be available. Reserves of thorium oxide—about 100,000 tons in the United States, and twice as much in Canada and in India—are known, although to date there has been no great push to locate thorium.

Prospects exist for harnessing the atom by other means as well (see below). Nuclear fuels undoubtedly lie in the mainstream of future energy plans, but that route has recently given indication of snags. First, there is the continuing public fear of contamination or explosion, which has lingered longer than had been anticipated. Second, anti-pollution feeling has created difficulties for all kinds of power plants, and especially for ultralarge nuclear plants with their attendant heat pollution. Third, inflation has made a shambles of early optimistic cost projections and threatened the nuclear plants' vaunted economic superiority. Improvements in conventional plan  design, too, have helped to make the contest closer. All this means that forecasts are especially susceptible to upset, especially if world economic conditions or striking technological innovations take place.

## ALTERNATIVES

Changes in the pattern of energy consumption arise mainly from two causes: increasing affluence and new technology. The first modifies relative demands, the second does this and changes relative availabilities as well. Both operate against a background of exponentially rising population.

The effects of increasing affluence on energy consumption are visible on all sides: more cars, more gasoline used; more electricity, hence more power plants, transmission lines, cooling towers, etc. New demands depend largely on unpredictable changes in tastes, so that it is impossible to make up a comprehensive list in advance. But without being very specific, one can easily predict an upsurge in demands for highly sophisticated secondary fuels. Alongside gasoline and electricity, there will be fuel cells and radioisotope power packs (both already important in the space program), many new kinds of electrical storage, and coal and oil derivatives such as rocket fuel.

Since a new technology takes twenty or twenty-five years to go from basic research to mass production, it is possible to say with some assurance what new types of energy will become commercially available during the next two or three decades. As was indicated, the most important developments will be in the nuclear field. In the decade 1980-1990, breeder reactors will begin to dominate the scene. Their use will guarantee the sufficiency of atomic fuel reserves for at least a century or two while electrical consumption rises exponentially. They will take over most new production, even though extensive supplies of fossil fuels remain, in part because the most readily accessible deposits of coal and oil have already been used. What still is left in the ground costs more to extract.

But suppose some other, cheaper source of power became available. Clearly, it would supersede breeders. Is there such a source?

Yes. It is called thermonuclear fusion, and in a sense is the reverse of the basic process in present-day fission reactors. Instead of heavy atoms splitting, light atoms join together. The fuel used in such fusion reactions is an isotope of hydrogen called deuterium (H-2), which occurs naturally, with an abundance of one atom in 6,500 of ordinary hydrogen. Just as the nuclear reactors now in use may be looked upon as "tame" forms of the atomic (uranium-plutonium) bomb, fusion reactors would be scaled-down hydrogen bombs. The problem lies in reducing the explosion to manageable size, so that the energy produced can be harnessed to generate electricity.[12]

The price of deuterium extracted from water is about $100 per pound. This means that fuel costs would come to about .005 mil per kilowatt-hour of thermonuclear-generated electricity—practically nothing. A thermonuclear generating station would cost about $120 per kilowatt to build—comparable with present conventional-plant capital costs. It would have to be large—5,000 megawatts (electrical) or bigger. But it would contain only a small amount of fuel at any time— less than that required to feed a self-sustaining chain reaction—and so would offer no threat of explosion.[13]

Progress in the controlled thermonuclear reactor program has been slow. The program has been in existence almost twenty years without a successful demonstration model being built. But experiments have gotten better and better results, and it is possible to extrapolate this improvement to conclude that someone will demonstrate

12. For a summary of the technical problems confronting the controlled thermonuclear reactor (CTR) program, see T. K. Fowler and R. F. Post, "Progress Toward Fusion Power," *Scientific American*, 215:6 (December 1966), pp. 21–31.

13. For more details on recent progress in the CTR program, see Amasa S. Bishop, "Recent World Developments in Controlled Fusion," paper presented November 12, 1969, before the Plasma Physics Division of the American Physical Society. Bishop is the recently (1969) retired Assistant Director (for Controlled Fusion), Division of Research, U.S. Atomic Energy Commission.

controlled fusion by about 1975-1978. Several specific lines of research tend to support this projection.

First, a Russian experimental device called "Tokamak" has yielded the best results so far, and a larger improved version is expected to be very close to critical operating characteristics. Second, experiments at the Lawrence Radiation Laboratory in Livermore, California, using another type of design indicate the feasibility of direct conversion—thermonuclear to electrical energy—with efficiencies in excess of 90 per cent. Third, work using high-power lasers to "ignite" deuterium suggest that small pulsed reactors, that is, reactors activated for short bursts rather than for steady output, may eventually be practical. They might put out only a few kilowatts, and hence be useful in a wide variety of industrial applications.

Thermonuclear reactors promise many advantages. The fuel is cheap and easily obtained. Waste products are nontoxic and have very little radioactivity. There is no danger of explosion, nor could such reactors be used to produce material for weapons (as breeders can). A controlled thermonuclear reactor would have high efficiency, about 60 per cent, and would consequently reduce thermal pollution. It could be used as a "plasma torch" to disintegrate trash safely and cheaply. And the raw fuel is incredibly abundant. There is enough hydrogen in the oceans to supply at least $10^{21}$ kilowatt-years of energy. At the present level of consumption, that would handle the world's needs for $10^{11}$ years.

Among other technical developments that could affect the energy picture in this century are:

*Direct Conversion.* Not only in controlled thermonuclear reactors, but in fission and fossil-fuel generation as well, it may be possible to produce electricity without an expensive boiler-turbine-condensor system. A number of approaches—solar cells,[14] thermocouples,[15]

14. A solar or photovoltaic cell is an electronic device which converts light directly into electricity. It has no moving parts. Photovoltaic cells are used in artificial satellites and in solar heat generators. See for example Proceedings of the Seventh Photovoltaic Specialists' Conference, Pasadena (1968).

15. Thermocouples resemble photovoltaic cells somewhat, converting heat directly to electricity with no moving parts. Both are limited theoretically to comparable efficiencies, about 12–14 per cent. See Steven I. Freedman, "Thermoelectric Power Generation," in *Direct Energy Conversion*, ed. George W. Sutton (New York: McGraw-Hill, 1966).

magnetrohydrodynamics,[16] electrogasdynamics[17] — are under investigation, but efficiencies are still low and commercial application is probably a decade off. Any generator running on steam made in a "hot box" has a fairly low efficiency. In theory, direct conversion can utilize primary sources with near-perfect efficiency. But even if utilization became only twice as efficient as it is now (an increase from 35 per cent to 70 per cent), fuel costs would be halved.

*Nuclear Stimulation.* This idea is to use the very cheap, rather unwieldy energy of a nuclear explosion to make a void in gas-bearing formations, then collect the gas that seeps in. Project Gasbuggy, carried out in New Mexico in 1967, demonstrated the feasibility of this technique, but it does not look economic. A twenty-kiloton charge, costing around $400,000, hollowed out a cavity with a volume of two million cubic feet. This hole would have to refill and be pumped out about one million times just to pay for the explosive. There have also been suggestions for using nuclear explosives to extract oil from the oil-shale deposits of Colorado, Utah, and Wyoming. Their feasibility has not yet been shown. Both types of stimulation clearly have special relevance for the western states.

*Nuclear Desalination-Generation Plants.* These are discussed in more detail in the chapter on desalination.[18] They are, of course, of special importance for California. They embody two kinds of economy: economy of scale, and the effciency derived from using heat from the nuclear hot box to run both evaporators and turbogenerators. Breeder or thermonuclear reactors, operating in the 5,000 megawatt range, would introduce further savings.

16. A magnetohydrodynamic generator transforms the internal energy of a gas into electric power in much the same way a turbogenerator does. Moving conducting gas replaces the rotor of a conventional generator. Such systems are thus not truly direct conversion devices, but they share the characteristic of having no stressed moving parts. A magnetohydrodynamic generator producing 10 gigawatts (electric) is quite feasible. To be efficient, however, such a generator requires input gas at high temperatures — 2000° to 3000° K. Few reactors produce temperatures in excess of 1000° K. See Richard J. Rosa, *Magnetohydrodynamic Energy Conversion* (New York: McGraw-Hill, 1968).

17. M. C. Gourdine, "Engineering Aspects of electrogasdynamics," *Transactions of the New York Academy of Sciences,* Vol. 30 (April 1968), p. 804. An electrogasdynamics generator is something like a Van de Graaf generator, except that the belt is replaced with a fast-moving gas stream seeded with ions.

18. For further technical and economic discussion, see *Nuclear Desalination,* Proceedings of a Symposium on Nuclear Desalination held by the International Atomic Energy Agency, Madrid, Nov. 18–22, 1968 (New York: Elsevier, 1969).

There will be other technical developments in the course of time. They will not change the essential nature of the energy industry, which is to take energy-rich materials out of the ground and, after a series of transformations, degrade them into low-level heat. What is wrong with just continuing in this way? To begin with, it is against the public interest and, what is more, it is impossible. Questions of the public interest lead up to fundamental questions about what our goals should be. There are fewer abstractions in deciding whether something is possible or not, but these two kinds of considerations are closely interwoven.

The question arises: What alternative energy resources are there not yet (or inadequately) exploited? But, as is often the case, it is easier to point out weaknesses in the status quo than to describe in detail how to do better.

The trouble is, energy reserves are limited. We may discover new reserves; they too will eventually be exhausted. It may be a long time before this happens, for by increasingly ingenious techniques, by paying more and more to scrape the last crumbs from the bottom of the barrel, we may eke out the supplies a bit longer. But finally, they will all be gone.

With the possible exception of natural gas, none of the fuels discussed here is in danger of depletion in this century. Supplies of coal and oil may last for centuries. But in the long run, this is irrelevant. Sometime, we will have to face the music. The longer matters are allowed to slide and the bigger the "energy mining" industries get, the harder it will be to face the crisis when it comes. It is selfish to insist that such problems belong only to future generations. This kind of thinking has reduced the world's whale population to a few straggling survivors and ruined half the Great Lakes system in our own time.

Our society's priorities are not established in a rational way. Basically, the energy industry works on the profit motive. Firms buy fuels or the right to exploit natural energy sources, then package the energy and sell it to consumers. If demand for a particular energy product increases, or if the raw material it is derived from becomes scarce, the price goes up. If demand drops or new or alternative resources are found, the price goes down.

Government imposes a certain amount of regulation on the industry: air pollution control, control of water utilization and thermal pollution, gas and electric rate boards and commissions, oil import control, control of uranium processing and nuclear-plant siting. No one should overlook the importance of such regulation, but while it modifies drastically the operation of the profit motive it does not affect the basis of the system.

There are, in a sense, two gaps in the system, two kinds of costs incorrectly computed. These are unregulated side effects and damage to future generations. The former have come in for a lot of attention recently. As a result, it appears that such antisocial activities as loosing indiscriminate broadsides of DDT into the environment and using San Francisco Bay, the Great Lakes, and most of our rivers as public sewers will not go unregulated much longer.

Damage to the future can be related to a kind of generalized conservation. People usually recognize that if we chop down all the redwoods or kill all the tigers in the world, our successors will be the worse for it. Our thoughtlessness deprives them of what would be their heritage. What is not so generally recognized is that we may rob our descendants even if we destroy or pollute something worthless, because it may not be worthless to *them*. Throwing atomic wastes into the ocean deeps or depositing them in underground aquifers is short-sighted; our descendants may want to use those deeps or those aquifers, even though we do not. To cite an example closer to home, consider the waning reserves of natural gas, one of our own principal energy commodities. When drillers first began exploiting the oil fields of Texas and Oklahoma, gas was a nuisance. There was no market for it, so the oilman just let it dissipate in order to get to the oil.

The cumulative effect is that the earth "wears man's smudge and shares man's smell," but life goes on. But now industrialization is becoming widespread and world population has topped three billion.

It is necessary to close these gaps, perhaps by legislating financial penalties against antisocial behavior. If there is a tax or a fine for wasting and polluting, conservation and avoidance of pollution become preferable. This happens in an *ad hoc* fashion now. Present legislative measures are inadequate, a scanty patchwork on a structure that developed in another age.

In order to preserve what is left of the environment and our natural resources, it is essential to redefine "progress." Industry turns raw materials into finished goods, destroying the one to create the other. Most goods are ephemeral; they are soon consumed and discarded. If the raw materials are not replenished, the net effect is destruction. Many raw materials are neither effectively unlimited in supply nor replaceable. Fossil fuels and most minerals are this kind of resource. Others, like water, air, sunlight, wood, and ocean salts, can be farmed, that is, managed in a process that does not needlessly exhaust reserves.

It is far from simple to chart a course taking society from the stage of expansive growth to a planned rational biosystem, but it is time to start. Otherwise Earth will change by degrees to a desert planet, and each successive generation will stand helplessly by, regretting the changes.

# PART FOUR

# THE POLITICAL ECONOMY OF WATER RESOURCES

# 12 UNCERTAINTY AND DECISION-MAKING IN WATER RESOURCES

GORDON C. RAUSSER AND GERALD W. DEAN

Uncertainty pervades all dimensions of water resource decision-making, particularly in the investment decisions required in construction. Since these investments are highly durable and generate streams of returns and costs over long periods of time—typically fifty to one hundred years at minimum—uncertainty takes on great importance in the analysis of water resource investment decisions.

The numerous uncertainties affecting the development of water resource systems fall naturally into two familiar and fundamental categories: those related to supply and those related to demand. Uncertainties arising during the construction of the system belong to supply; operational uncertainties can originate in either supply or demand. For example, in this era of rapid technological change, considerable uncertainty exists in the technology of alternative sources of water supply, as in salt-water distillation. Institutional and political uncertainties also pose decision problems both in the construction and the operation of water resource systems. The problems involved in the establishment of the institutional and legal arrangements required for feasible groundwater management serve as an illustration of these uncertainties. Financial uncertainties related to the direct costs[1] of

1. Direct costs are typically referred to as primary costs and indirect costs are equivalent to secondary costs. Primary costs are usually defined as the value of the goods and services needed for the establishment, maintenance, and operation of the project. Secondary costs are simply the costs of further processing and any other costs (above the direct costs) "stemming from or induced by" the project. For further clarification see U.S. Government, Federal Inter-Agency River Basin Committee, Subcommittee on Benefits and Costs, *Proposed Practices for Economic Analysis of River Basin Projects* (Washington, D.C., May 1950; Revised, May 1958).

projects are well known; in fact, direct construction costs are never precisely known until development projects are completed. Indirect costs are many and varied[2] and particularly subject to uncertainty, for example, the possible adverse effects on ecology.[3]

Uncertainties in demand are of a different type than those in supply, in the sense that, typically, heavy investment occurs early in planning while major demands on project outputs generally occur much later. Demands for agricultural, municipal, and industrial water, for recreation and other project outputs, depend critically on rates of population growth, geographic distribution of population, income levels, interregional competition, and other variables largely outside the control of planners. If demand is overestimated, there is danger of the project having unused capacity and becoming a "white elephant." On the other hand, excess demand may result if a project is underbuilt.

The purpose of this chapter is to provide an introduction to some important concepts of decision-making under uncertainty that the authors believe could be usefully applied much more extensively in the water resources field. Hopefully, the discussion will serve a dual role. First, we hope that it will provide the intelligent layman with an understanding and appreciation for the key concepts of planning and decision-making under uncertainty. Second, we hope that it will provide some ideas and useful references for the more technically trained reader, such as economists working in the area of project appraisal. To facilitate reading by these two groups, we have divided the paper into two major sections. The chapter itself is intended primarily for the general reader; the appendix is intended principally for the more technically trained reader. Nevertheless, the appendix is by no means exhaustive or rigorous; the general reader with a little patience can follow most of what is presented. However, the appendix does attempt to illustrate important concepts in a slightly more technical way by diagrams and numerical examples. Despite the dangers involved in

2. See S. V. Ciriacy-Wantrup, "Benefit-Cost Analysis and Public Resource Development," *Journal of Farm Economics,* 37 (November 1955), 676–689.
3. The development of the upper Eel River—the Dos Rios Project—of the California State Water Project is a case in point. There appears a rather high probability that the Dos Rios dam will "distrub the life-support resources of large herds of deer and substantially alter a valuable salmon run in the Eel River, with consequent ecological uncertainties" (D. Seckler, "California Water: A Strategy," A Planning and Conservation League Position Paper, Sacramento, 1970, p. 2).

oversimplifying complex problems, we have chosen to illustrate concepts and tools with reference to recognizable decision problems contained in the California Water Plan.

## TYPICAL APPROACHES TO WATER-RESOURCE DECISION PROBLEMS

A frequently employed approach in water resource planning is simply to ignore uncertainty or risk.[4] That is, both in the theoretical analysis and operation of water resource systems, it is often expedient to act as if consequences of various decisions could be predicted accurately. Such an approach is clearly less tedious than more advanced quantitative methods of investment analysis. Those who employ this deterministic method often argue that since they have used best estimates (that is, the most likely values) of the project's key cost and return variables, the resulting "measure of merit" (benefit-cost ratio, net benefits, or other performance criterion) is an approximation of the "most likely" outcome of a given water resource design alternative. However, in utilizing these single-valued estimates, it is often forgotten that there is only a small likelihood that such estimates will prove accurate. The approach fails to consider explicitly the supply and demand uncertainties surrounding each project alternative and provides the decision maker(s) with no indication of the likely variation about a given project's expected outcome.[5] For example, two projects may have the same benefit-cost ratio based on the most likely values of each component, but one project may be more "risky" in the sense that it is much more vulnerable to possible adverse conditions. This additional information is required before rational choices can be made.

4. The term "risk" has traditionally described situations whose outcomes are based on some known probability distribution (based on objective probabilities or relative frequencies). In contrast, if the probability distribution were unknown, the situation would be described as one of uncertainty. This distinction originated with F. H. Knight, *Risk, Uncertainty, and Profit* (Boston: Houghton Mifflin, 1921). However, if we accept the view that one can always assign probabilities based upon personal judgment, that is, that subjective probabilities exist, the distinction between risk and uncertainty becomes meaningless. Here, therefore, as in modern decision theory, which admits the use of subjective probabilities, the terms will be used interchangeably.

5. There are some conditions under which assumed certainty does provide the correct approach. These conditions have been isolated by Simon, "Dynamic Programming under Uncertainty with Quadratic Criterion Function," *Econometrica*, 24 (January 1956), 74–81, and H. Theil, *Optimal Decision Rules for Government and Industry* (Amsterdam: North-Holland Publishing Co., 1964) and follow from what is referred to as the certainty equivalence theorem. Still other conditions exist which lead approximately to this same equivalence, see E. Malinvaud, "First Order Certainty Equivalence," *Econometrica*, 37 (October 1969), 706–718.

In some water resource decisions, uncertainty is explicitly recognized, typically by such methods as conservative estimation of returns and costs, the addition of a premium to the discount rate, and conservative estimation of the economic life of the project. These approaches have been specifically recommended by the Subcommittee on Benefits and Costs of the Federal Inter-Agency River Basin Committee.[6] The use of conservative adjustments implies that benefit estimates are to be reduced and cost estimates increased in some proportion to the analyst's lack of confidence in the expected or most likely values. Again, there is small likelihood that all estimates will be in error adversely, and consequently this method of compensating for uncertainty obscures important information. For example, decision makers examining a benefit-cost ratio based on these "conservative estimates" have no idea "how conservative" they are. Does it mean that a higher benefit-cost ratio is almost sure to result? How much higher? Moreover, using "conservative" values throughout implies an aversion to uncertainty which is not, and ought not be, necessarily the attitude of public decision makers.[7]

The technique of adjusting the discount rate is a more sophisticated approach to allow for uncertainty. The discount rate is visualized as being made up of two components: a "time component" plus a "risk component." The less certain the outcome of the investment, the higher the "risk component" of the discount rate and therefore the higher the total discount rate itself. Thus, the discount rate varies with the riskiness of the investment. The higher risk discount will of course have the effect of making risky investments less attractive relative to less risky investments.[8] The major disadvantage of this device is the same as the

6. See U.S. Government, *op. cit.*

7. It has been argued that "though conservatism in benefit and cost estimates may not be an appropriate means of counteracting uncertainty in 'expected values,' conservatism is an appropriate countermeasure for the invariably optimistic bias of the technicians who estimate benefits and costs": S. A. Marglin, *Public Investment Criteria* (Cambridge, Mass.: The M.I.T. Press, 1967). This is basically a question of biased benefit and cost estimates, which is an issue separate from the underlying uncertainty of such estimates.

8. For a more complete discussion on the discount rate and related issues, see K. J. Arrow, "Discounting and Public Investment Criteria" in *Water Research,* A. V. Kneese and S. C. Smith, eds. (Baltimore: 1966); O. Eckstein, "A Survey of the Theory of Public Expenditure," in *Public Finances: Needs, Sources, and Utilization* (Princeton, N.J.: National Bureau of Economic Research, 1961), pp. 493–504; J. Hirshleifer, "Investment Decision Under Uncertainty: Applications of the State-Preference Approach," *Quarterly Journal of Economics,* 80 (May 1966), 252–277; and S. A. Marglin, *Approaches to Dynamic Investment Planning* (Amsterdam; North-Holland Publishing Co., 1963).

objection to adjusting benefit and cost estimates—". . . it represents what might be an inordinate aversion to uncertainty."[9]

The third suggestion of adjusting the estimate of the economic life of projects also fails to provide a reasonable approach to the problem of uncertainty. As Marglin points out ". . . there is comparatively little justification for this procedure in any situation, especially in situations where a large number of independent projects contribute to aggregative objectives."[10]

Other traditional approaches which help to recognize explicitly some of the uncertainties involved in water resource decision-making may be classified under the general heading of sensitivity analysis. In its typical form, sensitivity analysis is employed to supplement the assumed certainty approach. The sensitivity of outcomes is measured by varying the values of individual elements one at a time and noting the effect on the performance criteria (measure of merit). This method isolates the outcome effect of over- or under-estimating an element's value and thus suggests the relative importance of accurately estimating each element. However, consideration of each single element alone disregards the fact that all elements will vary somewhat from their estimated values: the actual outcome(s) will be the result of a combination of estimating errors, not the error of just one element.

A natural extension of this approach is to alter the values of several elements (rather than a single element) simultaneously. This extension is frequently referred to as the multiple-case approach and typically takes the form of determining the effect of optimistic, most likely, and pessimistic estimates of all relevant elements of supply and demand. The method results in the establishment of limits on the probable outcomes and the most likely outcome for each possible decision.[11]

9. Other problems associated with the use of this technique include: (1) if the project life is short, variation in the discount rate has very little effect on the outcome, and (2) when a particular water resource design is being evaluated from the standpoint of cost alone (to meet some prespecified demand), increasing the discount rate to reflect cost uncertainty will have an effect opposite to what is intended, i.e., a higher discount rate will lower the present value of costs, with the result that higher risk alternatives are favored. See Marglin, *Public Investment Criteria, op. cit.,* p. 73.

10. *Ibid.,* p. 74.

11. It should be noted that the multiple-case approach can be extended to be consistent with some of the techniques discussed in the appendix. Specifically, if a sufficient number of cases are considered and if values assigned to the elements of supply and demand are varied according to their presumed probability of occurrence, a probability distribution of outcomes can be obtained.

These two forms of sensitivity analysis, although more effective tools in the face of uncertainty than the assumed certainty approach or the adjustment approaches, lack both conciseness and comprehensiveness. Knowledge of how much variation is required in a particular element in order to reverse a decision based on best-estimate values, or knowledge of the range of possible outcomes for a given decision, is of limited value to decision makers if they do not take the next step of estimating the relative frequencies (probabilities) with which these outcomes occur.

In summary, while the traditional methods have features which are useful for dealing with some aspects of uncertainty, all are inadequate in several critical respects. We will argue that decision-making can be improved by a more systematic, complete, and explicit treatment of uncertainty, using certain aspects of decision theory and what has come to be known as research and development (R and D) strategy.

## LESSONS FROM R AND D

Since uncertainty is pervasive in water resource decisions, it may be helpful to recognize the analogy between water resource planning and the general area of research and development (R and D), drawing on the insights developed in this latter field in recent years. R and D strategies explicitly recognize the possibility of reducing or resolving uncertainty as the future unfolds.[12] This possibility becomes relevant when we examine decisions encompassing all aspects of water supply,

12. Some of the relevant literature regarding research and development strategy and its implications for the reduction of uncertainty includes T. K. Glennan, "Issues in the Choice of Development Policies" (Santa Monica: The Rand Corporation, October 1967), reprinted as Chapter 2 in T. Marschak, T. K. Glennan, and R. Summers, *Strategy for R & D* (New York: The Rand Corporation, 1967); A. O. Hirschman, *Development Project Observed* (Washington, D.C.: The Brookings Institution, 1967); B. H. Klein, T. A. Marschak, A. W. Marshall, W. H. Meckling, and R. R. Nelson, *The Rate and Direction of Inventive Activity* (Princeton: Princeton University Press, 1962); T. Marschak, "Strategy and Organization in a System Development Project" (P-1901) (Santa Monica: The Rand Corporation, 1960); T. Marschak, T. K. Glennan, and R. Summers, *Strategy for R & D* (New York: The Rand Corporation, 1967); R. Nelson, "Uncertainty, Learning, and the Economics of Parallel Research and Development Efforts," *Review of Economics and Statistics,* 43 (August 1961), 351–364; R. Nelson, "The Efficient achievement of Rapid Technological Progress," *American Economic Review,* 56 (May 1966), 232–241; and R. Nelson, M. J. Peck, and E. D. Kalachek, *Technology, Economic Growth, and Public Policy* (Washington, D.C.: The Brookings Institution, 1967).

that is, public decisions involving reclaiming waste water, increasing present natural water supplies, desalting sea water, constructing water transportation facilities, and managing underground water supplies. All these entail considerable uncertainties and explicit attempts ought to be made to reduce the magnitude of these uncertainties.

Within an R and D framework, strategies that emphasize sequential decision-making and learning processes, as well as relatively loose interrelationships among the components of the design of the total system, are possible ways of reducing uncertainties. In what follows, the concepts involved are discussed under the general headings of learning processes, loose connections among project components, parallel approaches, and sequential decision-making. Although these four are not mutually exclusive, for purposes of exposition they will be treated separately.

*Learning Processes.* There is considerable uncertainty about future demand for water and still more uncertainty regarding the feasibility of developing alternative sources of water supply. However, these uncertainties can be reduced by explicit attempts to purchase information and knowledge about the phenomena involved, that is to say, by making an explicit attempt to "learn." To illustrate, consider the development of technology necessary to provide salt-water distillation on an economically feasible basis. The primary obstacle to this development is lack of knowledge. Such knowledge is acquired by experiments, research, or experience (commonly referred to as "learning by doing").[13] This concept implies that it might be economically feasible to construct commercial-scale distillation plants even though the costs of water exceed those from alternative sources. What is learned — and the very process of learning — during such construction and operation would likely reduce substantially the technological uncertainties inherent in constructing a sequence of larger and more sophisticated distillers. The higher water costs of distillation can be regarded as an investment in education, which may lead to benefits in the form of

---

13. For an interesting discussion of "learning by doing" see K. J. Arrow, "The Economic Implications of Learning by Doing," *Review of Economic Studies*, 29 (June 1962), 155–173. For some special cases, see W. Fellner, "Specific Interpretations of Learning by Doing," *Journal of Economic Theory*, 1 (August 1969), 119–140.

Cents per thousand gallons

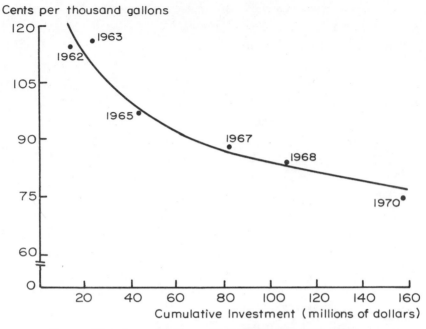

FIGURE 12.1. Learning Curve, Salt-Water Distillation Costs.

improvement in the ability to make good decisions in the future. Even
though constructing distillers now proves more expensive in the short
run than developing alternative sources of water, it may lead more
quickly to feasible distillation processes which in the long run represent the least expensive source of water supply.

Figure 12.1 shows a learning curve for distillation processes based
on available data.[14] This curve represents learning as the product of
experience. More simply, it is a means of explicitly accounting for the
learning process presumed to result from experience. In this example,
(median) cumulative investment by the Office of Saline Water in R and
D, plant construction, and operations and maintenance serves as an
index of experience, while cost per unit of output serves as a proxy for
learning. As Figure 12.1 indicates, between 1963 and 1965, experience
increased slightly less than twofold — in terms of investment, a net
increase of $20.03 million. During this period, cost declined by 19 cents

14. For details on the assumptions, data, and estimation procedures employed in the
derivation of this learning curve, see G. C. Rausser and C. Willis, "Implications of Learning Curves for Saltwater Distillation Processes in the Context of the California Water
Plan" (unpublished manuscript in the library of the University of California, Davis),
1971.

per thousand gallons—roughly 16.37 per cent. From 1965 to 1967, cumulative investment again nearly doubled, leaving a cost reduction of 9.27 per cent (9 cents per thousand gallons). During the interval 1967 to 1970, again cumulative investment nearly doubled—increasing from $81.7 to $157.7 million expenditures. This time, a cost reduction of 14.78 per cent was realized.[15]

Clearly, in the present period, salt-water distillation plants are noneconomic alternatives to the California Water Plan. Costs of distillation are at present in the neighborhood of 70 to 80 cents per thousand gallons, or roughly $230 to $260 per acre-foot (a conversion factor of 326). For aqueducts under the Plan, the estimated cost of Feather River water delivered to southern California is about $60 an acre-foot. Therefore, unless a subsidy exists for some time, charges for water from distillation plants will be prohibitive for most uses. However, if we regard such subsidies as investments in education or learning by doing, a decision to construct distillation plants (prototypes and the like) now or in the near future may represent a feasible alternative. This is particularly evident given projected costs for 1975 of approximately $130 per acre-foot, in 1980 of $59, and in 1990 of $36 per acre-foot.[16] This last figure, even when distribution costs of about $10 are included, implies that portions of the California Water Plan may be unnecessary.

Yet the above discussion fails to reveal the full scope of the learning process. If we define learning as the process of reducing uncertainty, then learning occurs by applying some strategy to allocate effort among different uncertainty-reducing possibilities as development proceeds and knowledge accumulates. Figure 12.1 implies that knowledge increases as larger outputs accumulate. However, other means exist to shift the entire curve downward. This suggests that learning can be influenced by factors other than and in addition to cumulated output.

Supposing that all subjective probabilities have been estimated,

15. The learning curve shown above results from a least-squares fit to the data in double-log form—more precisely, $\log y = \log \alpha + \beta \log X$. This fit produces the result that each time cumulative investment doubles cost per unit declines by 11.98 per cent. For example, if cumulative investment doubles from the 1970 level in some future period, costs would decline to 66 cents per thousand gallons; similarly, if cumulative investment quadruples, costs would become 58 cents per thousand gallons, etc., as long as the values of $\alpha$ and $\beta$ remain constant.

16. See Rausser and Willis, *op. cit.*, for the sources as well as the basis for these projections.

what are these uncertainty-reducing possibilities? How do we improve our estimates of the relevant subjective probability distributions? Can our knowledge be increased by allocating available resources in alternative ways? That is, can the factors that shift the learning curve downward or move us along the learning curve be influenced? What trade-offs are involved?

There is a great variety of techniques for reducing internal uncertainties facing decision makers at the initiation of any development project. These have been isolated by Glennan[17] into six major categories: (1) analysis, (2) test activity, (3) review of design by specialists, (4) testing of physical models, (5) testing of prototype, and (6) testing of production items. Some substitution exists among these various activities and thus the emphasis placed upon different types of activity is an important aspect of development policy.

Analysis activities generally involve mathematical analogs of the physical world. For example, to reduce uncertainties involved in desalting technology, analogs for a wide variety of hypothetical designs for distillation plants can be investigated and preliminary judgments can be rendered on the suitability of alternative designs. Although these mathematical analogs must always abstract from reality, the growth of computer capabilities has allowed more complex analogs to be constructed. It is generally recognized, however, that analysis activities are relatively more useful in the development of highly specialized designs.

The second type of uncertainty reduction — test activity or focused applied research — can be utilized most appropriately after the basic design has been selected for development. Such activity is concerned primarily with questions surrounding the materials, manufacturing techniques, and similar technical inputs to a design. The results of the testing activity are usually employed as inputs to the analysis method of mitigating uncertainties.

Calling upon experts to review designs on the basis of their specialities represents the next method. The usefulness of this method is largely self-evident; the designer seldom has the detailed knowledge necessary to consider all the ramifications of his design. Thus, review groups of specialists ought to be employed and perhaps institutionalized as part of the design process.

17. See Glennan, *op. cit.*

The fourth and fifth categories, model and prototype testing, differ in that the former seriously abstracts from the final selected design. Clearly, these testing categories are not mutually exclusive; nevertheless, it is beneficial to treat them separately. The testing of models typically occurs in a simulated environment. In contrast, testing of prototypes (full-sized or nearly full-sized models) usually takes place in the true physical environment. Prototypes represent first approximations of the final design, and they are expected to be altered as the result of testing. Therefore, prototypes are generally built with a minimum of specialized capital equipment so as to conserve both money and time.[18] Moreover, prototypes may be based on either a subsystem or a collection of subsystems.

In comparing the testing of prototypes to analysis and model testing, it is generally found that a number of disadvantages of the latter two approaches are overcome in the former. Results obtained in testing prototypes do not have to be scaled or calibrated to the physical environment. Also, prototypes have the advantage of being clearly visualized, which allows alterations to be made and tested with greater ease. The major disadvantage in producing a prototype is that it is quite expensive in terms of both resources and time, particularly when it is compared with the first three uncertainty-reducing approaches.

The final approach to uncertainty reduction, testing production items, usually comes into action in the final stages of any development policy. "Cost uncertainties will be nearly fully resolved, reliability will be observed, and producibility will be demonstrated."[19] At this point, most internal uncertainties will have been resolved and virtually all commitments to facilities of some subsystem of the total design will have been made.

If an important advance in the state of the art is being sought and the degree of knowledge available does not provide a guide to an efficient design, testing a full-scale prototype model in a realistic physical environment may be desirable. In such situations, problems of analyses and simulated test activities are, to say the least, difficult. Advances in the technology of desalination and in geothermal projects appear to

18. Such considerations become particularly important in the case of desalting technology and its implications for the transformation of sea water to fresh water and for waste-water reclamation. However, prototype production does not exist (that is, an intermediate stage as a feasible alternative) in water-transfer and storage systems.

19. Glennan, *op. cit.,* p. 10.

fall in this area. In contrast, if the level of desired advance is small and sufficient knowledge exists with respect to performance levels, analysis and model testing may be quite satisfactory, in fact far more efficient than full-scale prototype testing.

The degree to which these various activities complement each other and permit one to be substituted for another suggests that increases in knowledge (uncertainty reduction) can be attained by allocating available resources in alternative ways. For example, prototypes cannot be efficiently built without being preceded by analysis, component testing, and model testing. However, if prototypes are constructed, less analysis and testing of components and models will be required than if testing is first performed on production items. Clearly such considerations depend upon the nature of uncertainty[20] (the degree of impreciseness of knowledge) or the "amount" of learning that must be accomplished as well as the level of interrelationships among components.

*Loose Connections among Project Components.* The desirability of having "weak" interrelationships among the components of the water resource system is closely related to what we saw in the discussion above of learning and reduction of uncertainty. To exploit what is learned in the course of research and experimentation requires maintaining a considerable amount of flexibility regarding the next round of decisions. A loose interrelationship among the components of a system simply implies that the failure of one particular component or group of components will not endanger the remaining components. More specifically, if uncertainty results in any component deviating from its preliminary design specification, it does not follow that other components of the system have to be redesigned. By contrast, a system that entails a high degree of interrelatedness cannot utilize, to the same extent, knowledge acquired by resolving some of the uncertainties present in a particular system. Clearly, if it is desirable to construct a tightly interrelated design, the uncertainty associated with each component should be negligible.

20. This discussion has related entirely to internal uncertainties, factors that can be influenced directly by the decision maker. External uncertainties, for example, water demand uncertainties or the like, are discussed briefly in the appendix. In addition, for the more technically inclined reader, the appendix provides an example of how new information may be combined with existing information using Bayes' formula.

Interrelatedness of components most likely represents a more efficient use of resources than where components are not interrelated. Where major uncertainty exists, however, this is not the case, simply because risks of redesign assume a major role in the analysis. To be sure, it is not difficult to see that trade-offs exist between the degree of interrelatedness of components and the uncertainty surrounding particular components. So far as possible, such trade-offs should be carefully considered during the stages of planning and design. In terms of decision-making, if action results in a highly interrelated system, the value of information derived from prototype tests will most likely be reduced. In these instances, more analysis will be required, since the design of each component will be constrained in part by other components. These imposed constraints in a highly interrelated system suggest that some of the information gained by prototype testing may be difficult or impossible to utilize. However, if components are designed sequentially, those components designed first are less constrained, and hence knowledge based on prototype tests may be utilized. This indicates, of course, that any decision regarding degree of interrelatedness will have some effect on the distribution of effort among uncertainty-reducing activities.

*Parallel Approaches.* Allocating funds in alternative ways as a consideration related to learning or increases in knowledge has been categorized as parallel development efforts.[21] If a particular component involves a high degree of uncertainty, it is possible to hedge some uncertainties through the use of parallel developments. This approach follows naturally from the argument that the typical procedure of isolating the best available estimates and choosing the alternative with the greatest expected net (present) value neglects an important characteristic of the research and development process. That is, "estimates of cost, performance, and development time tend to improve as development proceeds and information accumulates."[22] The possibility of acquiring (at relatively low cost) information that is more precise suggests that it may be economical not to choose one design on the basis of initial estimates, "but rather to initiate parallel development

21. See the works cited above (in note 12) by Marschak *et al.,* Nelson ("Uncertainty, Learning . . ."), and Hirschman.

22. Nelson, "Uncertainty, Learning, and the Economics of Parallel Research and Development Efforts," *op. cit.,* p. 352.

efforts, cutting down the list of competing projects as estimates improve. The best decision to make on the basis of some information may be to delay a final decision until more information is obtained."[23] In other words, the decision to undertake a particular component development need not be viewed as a once-and-for-all decision. Rather, the decision to initiate a project can be viewed as the decision to explore a possibility, aimed at finding out more about the chances of success and the costs and benefits of the project, if it were to be carried through to completion.

The use of parallel developments also suggests that greater flexibility (equivalent to a lower degree of interrelatedness) must be maintained in the rest of the design. To exploit what is learned by using parallel development, as with most other uncertainty-reducing activities, requires that flexibility be maintained toward future decisions. Future systems developments must not depend on the success of any particular development in this parallel approach, since under this strategy it is likely that many component development efforts will fail. Large systems must not be tied to the fate of any one component or group of components. A part of the portfolio of parallel developments thus can be selected to facilitate future choices and future developments of presently perceived alternatives, while part of the same portfolio can aim at expanding the vistas of choices to be made in the future.

To be sure, the above discussion is strictly qualitative and almost tautological in its implication that choices among alternatives are likely to be improved the more information decision makers have available when making their final choice. However, conditions have been derived under which parallel approaches in development seem desirable. For example, Nelson[24] has demonstrated that the factors determining the number of projects that should be run in parallel are "(1) the cost of running a project during the period of competition, (2) the expected improvements in estimates during the period of competition, (3) the difference among the cost and performance estimates of the competing projects, and (4) the design similarities and differences of competing projects" (competition in this context refers to competition among parallel developments for the same component). Nelson's

23. *Ibid.*, p. 353.
24. *Ibid.*, p. 361.

chief result is "if it is possible to reduce uncertainty substantially in the early stages of a development effort, the parallel running of several alternatives may be a very good strategy."

It might be objected that such approaches are strictly limited when it comes to most conventional water resource projects. Although it is true that the intermediate stage of prototype production often implied by the idea of parallel approaches does not usually exist in traditional water resource supply projects, such a result does not hold when the supply's dimensions are expanded. That is, intermediate prototype productions and the use of parallel developments are worth considering in developing efficient desalination technology and groundwater management systems.

*Sequential Decision-Making.* Most investigators of water resource problems recognize that decisions are likely to have consequences that extend over a considerable period of time. Decisions with respect to each of the components of water supply are of this nature, and their consequences are not a single outcome, but rather a sequence of outcomes. Quite typically, many studies consider the central problem to be "whether water resources available at present should be used in the current period or saved for later employment."[25] Such naive conceptualizations are occasionally expanded to take in the possibility of uncertainty resulting in a run of bad luck for a few stages in the planning horizon, a possibility endangering the solvency of the system. More often, however, the question of timing is treated within an environment of certainty. When construction of a system is spread over a considerable period of time, the sequential aspects of decision-making are recognized explicitly. The need for flexibility in the system is introduced by planning early units so that later components can be added, if and when they appear desirable on the basis of additional information. This implies, of course, that the exact timing and design of later components need not be decided when construction of the first units is begun.

Since there is a considerable uncertainty about the ultimate value of water regardless of its source and perhaps still more uncertainty

25. A. Maass, M. M. Hufschmidt, R. Dorfman, H. A. Thomas, S. A. Marglin, and G. M. Fair, *Design of Water Resource Systems* (Cambridge, Mass.: Harvard University Press, 1962), p. 154.

regarding the feasibility of alternative sources of water supply, strategies that emphasize sequential decision-making are generally quite attractive and should play a more prominent role in the analysis of water resource decisions.[26] Sequential decisions permit decision makers to reduce the impact of uncertainties, usually at some cost, on the outcomes of alternative decisions. The possibility of reducing internal uncertainties in each stage of planning implies a two-step decision-making mechanism in each stage, the first step being designed to reduce uncertainties and to buy information through multiple approaches, the second step involving more detailed comparative evaluation of those alternatives remaining. In the development of a system, risk, due largely to technological ignorance,[27] should, and most likely will, result in a major screening of the alternatives in the first step. This screening should utilize research into component developments to attempt to assure that at some point in time there are attractive systems of development possibilities that can be based on reasonably certain components and knowledge. Once the requisite learning has been achieved in the first step, we may proceed with the second step of formal evaluation.

In the context of sequential decision-making and its relationship to learning, loose connections, and parallel components, two general observations appear worthy of some emphasis. First, R and D strategy is inherently sequential and suggests, under circumstances of substantial uncertainty, that "(1) a sequential learning process should be followed, and (2) components of the total system should be relatively loosely interrelated."[28] Moreover, at each stage of the planning horizon, reviews must be conducted and revisions made in existing sub-

26. Aside from the uncertainty-resolving aspects of sequential decision-making, such an approach is, in general, preferred to the once-and-for-all decisions of the type "act now" or "don't act now." For a formal dynamic framework, see S. A. Marglin, *Public Investment Criteria, op. cit.,* demonstrating the desirability of postponing construction for a wide range of cases in which benefit rates of a project depend jointly on calendar time and project age.

27. As Nelson, "The Efficient Achievement of Rapid Technological Progress," *op. cit.,* p. 240, points out, "the major reason why technological uncertainties should and do eliminate many projects from consideration is that the expected cost of the research undertaken and errors made in resolving the uncertainty is very great; given these expected learning costs the project simply is not an attractive gamble at the particular time in question."

28. Marschak *et al., op. cit.,* p. 47.

jective probability distributions on the basis of the knowledge that has been acquired. Thus, the decision makers are regarded as learning or sequentially acquiring knowledge and making a sequence of responses to their changing knowledge.

Second, in their attempts to select a systems design, decision makers in each sequential stage should make judgments about the approximate performance attributes for each of the components or subsystems of the system, as well as set out the degree to which they hope to push the state of the art in each; settle on the degree of component interrelatedness of the design; make decisions about the distribution of effort among the six uncertainty-reducing activities; and make decisions on the number of parallel developments to be employed, if any, on each component.[29]

## Conclusions

The traditional approach of assuming certainty, or some variation thereof, and the typical habit of deciding in advance in favor of the "one best way" can be advantageously replaced by a more experimental approach that allows for learning, flexibility, parallel approaches, and sequential decision-making. California's approach to water resource system designs, as evidenced by the California Water Project, appears for the most part to have ignored the possibility of such an experimental approach. The design of the system is largely restricted to transfers of fresh water from one location to another to eliminate geographically maldistributed water supplies existing now and possibly in the future. Such a single-minded approach may be no longer applicable in the light of changing demands and technology.[30] R and D strategy suggests the desirability of carrying along simultaneously several major alternative lines of experimentation. In the case of water supply, this suggests simultaneous experimentation, in depth, of alternatives such as water transfer, desalination, and underground storage.

For the uncertainties faced in water resource planning and de-

29. A somewhat more technical discussion of sequential (multistage) decision problems is provided in the appendix.

30. Seckler, *op. cit.*, p. 7, for example, characterizes a sequential construction of distillers as providing considerable flexibility in planning, while the existing California Water Plan is defined as a "highly integrated 'lumpy' alternative."

cisions involving the major dimensions of water supply, a number of policy prescriptions have resulted from consideration of R and D strategies. First, rigid specification of performance characteristics should be avoided for fear of excluding component designs which, although no less desirable, are far more feasible than some others. Secondly, considerable flexibility must be maintained among the various components at the outset so as to impart some value to uncertainty-reducing activities. Third, in considering alternative approaches to the development of components, "it may be advisable to try out in practice several approaches until the uncertainties have been sufficiently reduced and to delay until then the decision as the best approach."[31] This last point is crucial, for it reveals the desirability of sequential decision-making. Moreover, it involves a number of trade-offs and in some cases substantial costs; thus, decision makers must be provided with sufficient reason to believe that they will have significantly improved information upon which to base a future decision in order to justify postponement for the time being.

If sufficient justification exists, the introduction of uncertainty and the possibility of reducing it over time will have the effect of forcing rational decision makers to delay major decisions or commitments as long as possible or until adequate knowledge or information is available to make a "best" decision. In addition, under these circumstances, if commitments must be made they will be as small as possible.

31. Hirschman, *op. cit.,* p. 77.

# 13 "160-ACRE LAW"

PAUL S. TAYLOR

Late in the nineteenth century, Congress faced the fact that water and land are separated in the west, not joined together as in the humid belt to the east. It knew that, in anticipation of the coming of water, the thirsty lands had been gathered into the hands of a few — and for a song. As a contemporary California newspaper had observed in 1877:

No one would believe that shrewd, calculating business men would invest their money on the strength of land rising in value while . . . without water. At the same time, purchasers are not lacking who would add it to their already extensive dry domain and the people . . . will find themselves confronted by an array of force and talent to secure to capital the ownership of the water as well as of the land, and the people will at last have it to pay for . . ."[1]

In full knowledge of this setting, the 57th Congress made its decision to give away the western public waters and to finance the cost of storing and moving them to private lands. Simultaneously, it decided to forestall monopoly of the gifts of public waters and subsidies, and to impose public control over private speculation in the windfall profits that would follow in the wake of these gifts. The instrument chosen to achieve these aims, the National Reclamation Act of 1902, also called the Newlands Act, is better known as the 160-acre law. It declares that

No right to the use of water for land in private ownership shall be sold for a tract exceeding 160 acres to any one individual landowner, and no such sale shall be made to any landowner unless he be an actual bona fide resident on such land, or occupant thereof residing in the neighborhood.[2]

1. *Visalia Delta,* May 5, 1877. See also *San Francisco Chronicle,* May 31, 1877.
2. 43 U.S.C. 439.

The United States Supreme Court has stated clearly the principle embodied in the legal language of the statute: it is to insure "that benefits may be distributed in accordance with the greatest good to the greatest number of individuals," and that the "enormous expenditure" for reclamation "will not go in disproportionate share to a few individuals with large land holdings."[3]

The passage of time has obscured this meaning and the motives underlying the law to most of the present generation, but these were crystal clear to Congress as it deliberated in 1902 on the pending reclamation bill. Pleading for its passage, Congressman Frank W. Mondell of Wyoming gave explicit assurance that the bill would guard "against the possibility of speculative landholdings." The bill was drawn, he said, "with a view to breaking up any large landholdings which might exist in the vicinity of government works."[4] Land speculation was to be nipped in the bud.

But past is prologue. Like the United States Constitution, the 160-acre law was enacted a long time ago and it embodies principles that benefit from timely reinterpretation and adaptation to changing conditions. Does the law point only toward the past, or can it serve the future? Will it die or survive? Economic interests and viewpoints are sharply opposed. Large landholding interests — inheritances from the past — eye the speculative gains that emasculation or destruction of the 160-acre law would bring them. Conservationists and educators, on the contrary, are awakening to an opportunity the law offers — by building upon it — to undergird public education financially and to shape a more decent environment.

So, today, more than two generations after the law was enacted, it is under constant pressure from the large landholding interests it was designed to restrain. The magnitude of these landholders can be suggested by figures, unfortunately available in fragments only. A 1947 Federal study in the southern and western San Joaquin Valley found thirty-four owners with three-quarters of a million irrigable acres, an area almost the size of the state of Rhode Island.[5] A much earlier California study had shown thirty-three owners in southern

3. Ivanhoe Irrigation District *v*. McCracken, 357 U.S. at 297.

4. 35 Congressional Record 6677.

5. Hearings before Senate subcommittee of the Committee on Public Lands, 80 Congress, 1 Session, on S. 912, p. 864.

California with nearly 3,850,000 acres, irrigable and nonirrigable alike.[6]

Many interests never have become reconciled to the 160-acre law. Most recently, Governor Ronald Reagan has called it "archaic" and proposed its complete revision in "the public interest."[7] A senior vice president of the Bank of America says that it is a "ridiculous law, fostered by provincialism and eastern political jealousy . . . , subjugating economic realism to petty political tyranny," and he adds, "Maybe this is what causes the seeds of a civil war."[8]

Governor Reagan set up a Task Force on the Acreage Limitation Problem. A "majority of the members," says their report, believe that acreage limitation is "wrong in principle and should be repealed."[9] Despite its open preference for outright repeal, the Task Force made recommendations that follow a different line, but one which, if followed, would come to the same thing, virtual destruction of the 160-acre law. The line bears the name "Engle formula," after its author, Congressman (later Senator) Clair Engle. In the light of past failures to persuade Congress to grant outright exemptions from the law, Engle counseled an indirect approach that was adopted by the Task Force and then embodied in a bill sponsored by Senator George Murphy and four colleagues. Explaining his reason for seeking to attack the law on the flank instead of directly, Engle told Congress: "I grant you, you start kicking the 160-acre limitation and it is like inspecting the rear end of a mule: You want to do it from a safe distance because you might get kicked through the side of the barn. But it can be done with circumspection, and I hope we can exercise circumspection."[10]

The Task Force adopted Engle's circumspect flank attack, seeking to avoid being kicked through the side of the barn by an aroused public

6. California Commission on Immigration and Housing, "Report on large landholdings in Southern California, with recommendations" (1919), pp. 8, 12. The figures include the Southern Pacific railroad's 2,600,000 acres, and the 32 other largest landholdings, ranging in size from 183,000 acres to 15,000 acres.

7. Inaugural address, February 5, 1968.

8. Robert W. Long, Senior Vice-President, Bank of America, *Western Water News*, September 1969.

9. State of California, "Report of Governor's Task Force on the Acreage Limitation Problem" (1968), p. 22.

10. Hearings before the House Subcommittee on Irrigation and Reclamation of the Committee on Interior and Insular Affairs, 84 Congress, 1 Session, on H.R. 104, 384, and 3817 (1955), p. 70.

and an informed Congress. Specifically, the Task Force proposed to allow large landowners, upon making the gesture of returning a portion of the public subsidy given them under the reclamation law, to retain all the water, all the windfall profits from increased land values created by the public investment in water development, and all the rest of the subsidy for all their lands, no matter how many tens or hundreds of thousands of acres they own.

The implication is that, if large landowners double what is paid for water by owners of less than 160 acres, they will have repaid fully the subsidy given them under the reclamation law. The truth lies opposite, as examination of the Task Force's own illustration — water charges on the Friant-Kern Canal — makes clear. Landowners are charged only $3.50 an acre-foot for water from the canal that would cost them $14 if subsidies and special benefits under reclamation law were removed. Even quadrupling (instead of doubling the amount paid by large landowners would be insufficient to recompense the public treasury for the subsidies received, for it overlooks additional subsidies given under the guise of low interest rates, power and municipal water renewals, and flood control contributions.[11]

One of the arguments employed frequently against acreage limitation alleges that limiting farm size to 160 acres impedes the use of large machinery and so promotes inefficiency. The bank official quoted earlier speaks, for example, of the "myth of a small family farm," an "ancient concept . . . tending to inhibit . . . our highly mechanized agricultural industry."[12] The argument finds its most ready acceptance among urbanites unfamiliar with farming practices and the terms of the law. The fact is that American family farms almost from the beginning have used machines much larger than any single farm could afford. They have done, and continue to do, this either through cooperative ownership of the machines or by hiring them on contract to perform a desired operation. The 160-acre law limits land ownership but places no limitation whatsoever on the customary practice of joint use of machines. The inefficiency argument comes from large landholding

11. Hearings on S. 912, *supra*, p. 869. See also "Acreage Limitation," 114 Congressional Record 7420-1.
12. *Western Water News*, September 1969.

interests rather than from families that work their own land, and it is not convincing.

In any event, efficiency is not the real point at issue. To claim efficiency of operation for large landholdings is to obscure the real purposes of those who enacted reclamation law and of those who now seek to destroy it. Large landowners seek for the few the privilege of unlimited gifts of public water, public subsidy to bring water to their lands when they want it, and windfall profits from public investment. Acreage limitation, designed to distribute these gifts equitably among the many, to provide the many with opportunity and with homes, stands in the way of the owners of large tracts.

The subsidies to landowners are generous. Federal taxpayers provide outright about 13 per cent of the cost of the Central Valley Project. By official estimate, irrigation is chargeable with 63 per cent of reimbursable project costs, power with 33 per cent, and municipal and industrial water with 3 per cent. But irrigators are asked to repay only 17 per cent, while power users repay 72 per cent and municipal and industrial water users repay 10 per cent.[13]

By another estimate covering the west, irrigators, that is to say landowners, receive public subsidy ranging from $600 to $2,000 an acre, depending on costs.[14] Using this latter measurement, the 160-acre limitation on water deliveries places a ceiling of between $96,000 and $320,000 upon an individual's permitted subsidy. The attack upon acreage limitation implies that subsidies of these dimensions are ungenerous, that an owner of, say, 120,000 acres, should be allowed a subsidy of from $72 million up to $200 million, as well as the windfall profits flowing therefrom. With the prospect of subsidies of such magnitude if they can circumvent acreage limitation law, large landowners are slow to rely on claimed superior efficiency in order to buy, store, and distribute water themselves at unsubsidized market prices.

The founding fathers of reclamation did take under consideration leaving the program to private enterprise, and they rejected it out of hand. Their grounds for so doing were public policy in the distribution

13. Note, 38 California Law Review 728, 730–32 (1950), citing H.R. Doc. No. 146, 80 Congress, 1 Session (1947), p. 23.

14. Joseph Alsop, "And the rich get richer," citing budget bureau studies: *San Francisco Examiner,* November 24, 1964.

of benefits from a public resource. The House report on the reclamation bill in 1902 said:

> If we were willing to abandon our time-honored policy of inviting and encouraging small individual land holdings, and were prepared to turn over all of the public lands under a large irrigation system to the control of a single individual or a corporation, we could undoubtedly secure the construction of extensive works which can not be profitably constructed by private enterprise under present conditions, but no one contemplates paying so stupendous a price as this for irrigation development.[15]

Nevertheless, opposition to the 160-acre law is an old story and its tactics were thought through long ago. *Business Week* described most of them in May 1944.[16] Repeal of the law or exemptions from it project by project were desired most of all. This tactic succeeded on a few lesser projects but failed on the larger ones.

Then, since the Army Engineers originally were not bound by the 160-acre law, a second tactic was to get the Engineers instead of Reclamation to do the construction. This came to an end in 1944 when Congress extended the law to cover Engineers' projects.[17]

A third approach was to substitute a state for a federal project, the state "paying the entire bill." California has undertaken this experiment.[18] The federal excess land law is not now applied, but this "exemption" rests upon shaky legal foundations. The Interior Department's Solicitor overruled Congressional denial of exemption after six days of floor debate, saying that Congress did "not require the application of Federal acreage limitations."[19] In this way he took it upon himself to confer the exemption. The issue is now in federal court and the final outcome remains uncertain.

Fourth was simply to pump ground water to the surface of one's own land, hoping in this way to avoid enforcement of the excess land law. Since a project delivering surface water inevitably, and often by design, improves groundwater supplies, the 160-acre law should be

15. "Reclamation of Arid Lands," H. Rept. 794, 57 Congress, 1 Session, ser. 4402 (1902), p. 3.
16. "Valley Divided," *Business Week,* no. 767 (May 13, 1944), p. 21.
17. 58 Stat. 891. Public Law 534, Sec. 8 (1944).
18. "Valley Divided," *supra.*
19. 108 Congressional Record 5716.

held to apply equally to both surface and groundwater deliveries.[20] Whether the law actually is applied depends upon those who administer it.

Pressure upon administrators to relax enforcement has at times been astonishingly successful. The Interior Department, for example, ignores the provision of the 1914 statute that obliges the Secretary to require owners of excess lands "to agree to dispose of" the excess "before any contract is let or work begun for . . . construction of any reclamation project . . ."[21] Thus, the Department is investing upward of half a billion dollars to serve an area in which 400,000 acres, or two thirds, is legally ineligible to receive project benefits.

Ignoring the law appears at times to be almost habitual. On the Salt River Valley Project in Arizona, waters are delivered to landownerships of whatever size; only the voting rights of landowners in the water users' association are symbolically limited to 160 acres each.[22] The 1902 requirement that landowners be "actual bonafide residents" upon or "in the neighborhood" is regularly ignored.[23] In California's huge Central Valley Project, the 1926 requirement that excess lands shall not "receive water"[24] is ignored so far as ground water is concerned.

These are but examples. Secretary of the Interior Steward L. Udall in masterly understatement admitted to Congress in 1964 that "the executive branch" has "on occasion exhibited a degree of concern for the excess-land owner which may be difficult to reconcile with the policies embraced by the excess-land laws."[25]

Pressure upon officials to produce nonenforcement is starkly visi-

20. "Valley Divided," *supra*. See also "Westlands Water District Contract," Hearing before Senate Committee on Interior and Insular Affairs, 88 Congress, 2 Session, July 8, 1964, pp. 6, 10, 178, 179.

21. 43 U.S.C. 418.

22. 95 Congressional Record 10126 ff. In 1946 the Bureau of Reclamation reported 165,145 excess acres on completed projects, not including the Salt River Valley Project, and 544, 279 acres on projects authorized or under construction. Neither Army Engineer projects covered by reclamation law nor the Imperial Valley (which in 1964 the Secretary of the Interior said should be covered) were included. Bureau of Reclamation, Land-ownership survey, 1946.

23. 43 U.S.C. 439.

24. 43 U.S.C. 423e.

25. Udall in letter of transmittal to Senator Henry M. Jackson, June 30, 1964, "Acreage Limitation Policy, Study prepared by the Department of Interior pursuant to a resolution of the Senate Committee on Interior and Insular Affairs" (1964), p. xiii.

ble at times. More often it is concealed beneath the surface and is visible only in its results. An instance of strong pressure occurred in 1947 when Congress removed the Commissioner of Reclamation and his Regional Director for the Central Valley Project from the annual appropriation bill, the pretext being that neither was an engineer. They were being punished for supporting before Congress the policy of the President and the Secretary of Interior. But the unexpected re-election of President Harry Truman brought about their restoration to the federal payroll.[26]

Just the same, concealed pressure is more effective than overt, and its product is nonenforcement of law. The intent of the original reclamation statute of 1902 was to provide opportunity for families to make homes on the land. On public land about to be irrigated, the statute charged the Secretary of the Interior with limiting the size of entries to "the acreage which . . . may be reasonably required for the support of a family. . . ."[27]

Ten years later Congress made clear its intent to limit the benefits of reclamation to families on private land as well as on public. The 1912 statute obligates the Secretary to "require the owner of private lands . . . to agree to dispose of all lands in excess of the area which he shall deem sufficient for the support of a family upon the land in question. . . ."[28]

Neither statute has been repealed, and both are part of present reclamation law as recorded in the United States Code. Under pressure, nevertheless, administrators of reclamation have allowed delivery of water to man and wife to serve 320 acres, thus doubling the limit on land intended by Congress. Furthermore, by transfers of ownership or

26. P. S. Taylor, "Excess Land Law: Execution of a Public Policy," 64 Yale Law Journal 477, 501–506.

27. 43 U.S.C. 419.

28. 43 U.S.C. 418. The language of the 1902 statute that limits water deliveries to 160 acres belonging to "any one landowner . . . in private ownership" plainly is intended as a ceiling upon water deliveries to a family, a point the 1912 statute makes abundantly clear. The intent to limit water deliveries to a family rather than to double it, or more depending upon the number of its members, was spelled out in the Columbia Basin Project Act defining "any one landowner" in reference to a "family" consisting of "either of both husband and wife, together with their children under eighteen years of age": 16 U.S.C.A. 835a.

otherwise, owners of private lands claim additional water for 160 acres for each member of a family regardless of how many they are or how old. By administrative, not statutory, determination, owners of excess lands are allowed to operate them with project water for ten years before disposing of them. This retards the availability of project water to the landless and increases benefits derived from the project to those whose holdings exceed the legal limit of water deliveries. The width of this loophole in the legal controls over monopoly of water benefits has never been better expressed than by the chief counsel of the Imperial Irrigation District. "Let us lay the cards on the table . . .," he told Congress. "I will give you my own opinion of [large land-owner] Jack O'Neill's willingness to sign the 160-acre limitation. He thinks if he can get water for ten years on there without having to sell it, he can make enough money out of it so he can afford to sell the land at any old price. . . . that is my candid opinion. . . ."[29]

From the viewpoint of large landowners, nonenforcement, although less welcome than repeal or exemption, is obviously more welcome than enforcement. Its disadvantage to them, as one of their spokesmen expressed it in 1944, is that "landowners cannot rely on continued future nonenforcement."[30] Their fear is that an administration might take office dedicated to enforcement of the law.

That is the essence of the prologue. Until now the interest of the private large landowner in acquiring public water has held the center of the stage. The public interest in managing this resource as it manages forests, parks, waterways, and grazing lands has been overlooked. But now environmentalists and educators are speaking up. They, too, have roots in the past, a different past, and they raise questions: Is the future but to repeat the struggle to capture the water as well as the land? Or is it to take a fresh turn?

In 1967 Allan Temko, environmental critic, warned that the attack upon the 160-acre law "threatens irreparable damage to California's

---

29. Harry W. Horton, statement at hearing before Senate Subcommittee on Irrigation and Reclamation of the Committee on Interior and Insular Affairs, 85 Congress, 2 Session, on S. 1425, S. 2541, and S. 3448 (1958), pp. 87–88.

30. S. T. Harding, statement at hearing before Senate Subcommittee on Irrigation and Reclamation, 78 Congress, 2 Session, on S. Res. 295 (1944), p. 360.

future. This forward-looking law," he said, "coupled with government purchase of excess lands as proposed by Secretary Udall, and urged by the national AFL-CIO, provides a truly effective instrument for rational planning of California in an age of rapid urban growth, and for promoting conservation of open spaces, thus protecting not only agricultural lands but also our expanding cities and new communities."[31]

The following year, the Sierra Club announced its support of "federal purchase of excess lands . . . with the understanding that lands so purchased would be sold or leased under open space regulations."[32]

Soon the environmentalists were joined by educators. Their stake, like that of the large landowners, is in finance. The coming of water to arid land sends values rapidly upward. A study of the first decade of reclamation showed a 759 per cent average increase in the value of improved land.[33] And this remains the guts of the issue. As Secretary of the Interior Harold L. Ickes said, "It is the age-old battle over who is to cash in on the unearned increment in land values created by a public investment."[34]

Educators draw their inspiration from a precedent as old as the nation, grants of public land for the support of education. Between 1803 and 1966, the Bureau of Land Management reports, "the States received grants of public land totalling 228,136,032 acres. Of this total 77,524,126 acres were for the benefit of the common schools and 16,769,198 acres for other schools." As immediately as 1966 "$69,720,-081 were returned to the States" from federal disposal of public lands to "nonfederal interests."[35]

The National Education Association, "representing over one million school teachers throughout the United States," is concerned that the tradition of land grants for education shall be given new life through "water grants for education." The NEA statement of February 25, 1970, reads:

31. 114 Congressional Record 24142.
32. Declaration by Board of Directors, March 17, 1968.
33. Hearings on S. 912, *supra*, p. 204.
34. Secretary of Interior Harold L. Ickes to Frank Clarvoe, editor, *San Francisco News*, October 31, 1945.
35. Dale R. Andrus, Acting Assistant Director, Bureau of Land Management, to Congressman Jeffery Cohelan, July 3, 1968.

We believe that the acquisition of large areas of arid and semi-arid land by large corporations with the obvious intent to irrigate it by water developed at public expense to be a clear violation of "The National Reclamation Act of 1902." . . . All land of this nature should be purchased by the Secretary of Interior . . . at the pre-water price in conformity with the 160 acre per individual owner regulation. This is not alone the problem of those States with arid and semi-arid areas. Tax dollars from all the citizens of the United States were used to provide the water for irrigation and the disposal of irrigable land should be available to the public and the revenues from the operation should be returned to the public coffers. In keeping with the tradition established by the "Northwest Ordinance," the "Morrill Acts" and others it would be most appropriate to direct the revenues to satisfy a pressing need—the financing of public education.[36]

The National Wildlife Federation reflects the present generation's enlarging conception of conservation and of environment. Addressing the Water Resources Council in 1968, the Federation expressed its "belief that a ground swell of public opinion is developing for support of strong enforcement of the Reclamation Act," and it endorsed government purchase of excess lands "particularly if the funds accruing from resale are used for education and conservation." It emphasized that "project planning must include provisions for some of the divested properties to go into parks, recreational areas, greenbelts and other conservation areas," and it proposed that "lands could be acquired for schools, colleges, nature study areas, and other educational features."[37]

The 160-acre law goes even deeper than environmental planning, finance, conservation, and education, fundamental as these are. It penetrates to the very vitals of our society and touches upon the stability and democratic character of our institutions.

Theodore Roosevelt, who personally inspired the 160-acre law that was enacted while he was president, gave these reasons to the Commonwealth Club of California in San Francisco:

36. Statement of Dr. John M. Lumley, Assistant Executive Secretary, National Education Association, on Use of Water Resources, February 25, 1970.

37. Louis S. Clapper, Conservation Director, National Wildlife Federation, "Statement before National Water Commission, Washington, D.C., November 6–7, 1969," p. 8.

I wish to save the very wealthy men of this country and their advocates and upholders from the ruin that they would bring upon themselves if they were permitted to have their way. It is because I am against revolution; it is because I am against the doctrines of the Extremists, of the Socialists; it is because I wish to see this country of ours continued as a genuine democracy; it is because I distrust violence and disbelieve in it; it is because I wish to secure this country against ever seeing a time when the "have-nots" shall rise against the "haves"; it is because I wish to secure for our children and our grandchildren and for their children's children the same freedom of opportunity, the same peace and order and justice that we have had in the past.[38]

38. *Transactions of the Commonwealth Club* 7 (1912–13), 108.

# 14 LEGAL ASPECTS OF CONJUNCTIVE USE IN CALIFORNIA

## STEPHEN C. BIRDLEBOUGH AND ALFRED WILKINS

Optimum use of a groundwater basin depends greatly upon artful administration which takes into account the specific technical and political conditions of the particular basin.[1] It follows that no single structure of legal or equitable rules has significance in every such basin. The California courts, recognizing this, have held that in deciding disputes between water users within a groundwater basin, a primary responsibility of the trial judge is to permit the equitable development of the physical solution that will serve the greatest number of beneficial users of water affected.[2]

Historically, the law governing underground water in California has evolved in response to the water users' increasing technical and financial capacity to utilize the underground basins, or aquifer systems, that hold the groundwater supply. The first and most simple use was extraction of water which had naturally collected in such basins, and the first half-century of legal development regarding groundwater centered on this situation. Later, water users discovered how to combine the use of groundwaters naturally collected in a basin with the use of imported water which percolated, both accidentally and by design, into the basin; this so-called conjunctive use, practiced increasingly in southern California in the 1950's and 1960's, has been the source of important recent developments in California law relating to

1. Krieger and Banks, "Groundwater Basin Management," 50 California Law Review 56, 58: a study of the law and procedure governing use of imported waters conjunctively with locally available underground supplies, primarily in southern California.

2. California Water Service Co. *v.* Sidebotham & Sons, 224 Cal. App. 2d 715, 731.

underground waters. An extension of the conjunctive use concept is the use of underground basins as long-term storage reservoirs; water is artificially supplied to the basin so that it may be taken out during years of scarcity and even exported outside the area of the basin. At present, long-term underground storage is not widespread, so the legal questions affecting such storage are still somewhat speculative; they do not appear unmanageable, however.

In both conjunctive use and long-term storage, water-supply agencies must obviously be concerned with control of water placed in the basin. Such control depends, first of all, on engineering analysis of the way in which water moves underground through the water-bearing gravels of the basin; secondly, it requires an authoritative record of the quantities of water that each significant water user has historically pumped from the basin; and thirdly, it must rely upon some effective restraint to prevent any user from removing improper quantities of water from the basin. Once these conditions are established, the basin can be operated like a bank. Given the information about the physical characteristics and status of the basin and "deposits and withdrawals" by each user, those managing the basin can keep a continuing statement of the water available to each user and agency. By the use of appropriate legal and economic constraints, such as judicial orders, pumping charges, and tax incentives, the storage and withdrawal of water can be equitably regulated and financed.

A definitive listing or determination of the water "rights" of major landowners and water agencies whose land lies above the basin in which the water is stored should be (but seldom is) obtained before initiating a system of conjunctive use or storage. If the making of this register is delayed, distinguishing usage dependent upon imported water from usage customary before the water was added to the basin will prove to be very difficult. Usually it is best to initiate such a determination concurrently with importation of water, since substantial cooperation among water users is essential to economical solution of the issues involved.[3]

One way of obtaining such a determination is termed "basin-wide adjudication," a somewhat cumbersome legal procedure developed in

3. Krieger and Banks, *supra*, 62, 66.

southern California between 1937 and 1965.[4] The procedure is illustrated by the adjudication of water rights in the West Coast Basin
which underlies the Pacific Coastal region of Los Angeles County. In
1945 three of the water-supply agencies pumping water from the basin
commenced legal proceedings against more than 500 other individuals
and agencies also pumping water from the basin. The action was intended to determine groundwater rights in the basin and to prohibit
excessive pumping, for the water table was falling and this threatened
mineralization of the water supply and intrusion of salt water from the
Pacific Ocean. The trial court referred the fact-finding aspects of the
case to the state agencies which had expertise in the field of water
resources.[5] These agencies were to determine the characteristics of the
basin and the actual historic withdrawals of water by the various
users. After some years of study, these state agencies submitted factual
reports. Based upon these reports, the major litigating water agencies,
controlling over 80 per cent of the water rights in the basin, reached an
agreement calling for entry of a judgment to manage the basin effectively. Available water in the basin would be allocated in proportion
to the historic extractions by each water user. Future increases in total
withdrawals of each water user would be prohibited, unless supplies
of water to the basin were increased. There was to be an exchange-pool
arrangement whereby water users with insufficient water rights to
meet their needs could "rent" underground water entitlements from
users having an alternative source of imported water. The State Department of Water Resources was to be appointed watermaster to control withdrawal of water from the basin, under continuing supervision
by the court.

Because the total of all the adjudicated rights was greater than the
safe yield of the basin, that is, the amount of water the basin would
yield under conditions of scarcity, the court provided for gradual re-

4. The Raymond Basin adjudication was instituted by the City of Pasadena in 1937
and is summarized in the case of City of Pasadena v. City of Alhambra, 33 Cal. 2d 908;
see note, 37 California Law Review (1949) 713. It was followed by the West Coast Basin
adjudication, summarized in the Sidebotham case, supra.

5. In 1945 this agency was the Division of Water Resources in the State Department
of Public Works. In 1956 the Division's functions were transferred to the newly created
Department of Water Resources and State Water Rights Board. The latter agency has
since been renamed the State Water Resources Control Board.

duction in the use of water from the basin by each rights holder. All were prohibited from extracting more water than their adjudicated rights, subject to certain provisions for carry-over from one year to the next, emergency withdrawals, and exchanges under the exchange-pool provisions.

Overdrafts in the West Coast Basin were very serious, and had existed since 1920. It was therefore impractical to establish priorities as between water users. Determinations were instead made that the long-standing overdraft had created prescriptions of water rights affecting users, that all users stood on an equal footing, and that any reduction of water use would be ordered on a pro rata basis.

In basins where no serious overdraft has existed for any considerable time, the courts must consider existing water rights, which, in uncontrolled basins, fall into three classifications: overlying rights, appropriative rights, and prescriptive rights.[6] The overlying landowner's water right is considered analogous to the rights of a riparian owner on a surface stream. The owner has the right to pump water from the aquifers underlying his land for use on the land overlying the basin or watershed. Such a right cannot be sold separately from the overlying land; water pumped pursuant to such right must be for the beneficial use of the overlying land, and other interested water users are entitled to prohibit the use of such water elsewhere.[7] Each overlying owner may use only his reasonable share where the total supply of an aquifer is insufficient to meet the needs of all. For a basin beneath an urban development, these overlying rights might be relatively insignificant to the adjudication process because few urban residences rely upon individual wells. For a rural basin, they could be of substantial importance.

Appropriative rights may be obtained for any water occurring naturally within a basin and not needed for the reasonable beneficial use of users with other established rights. Overlying users enjoy priority, however, and the rights of an appropriator are limited to surplus waters within the basin. The appropriative right depends upon the actual pumping of water for beneficial use on land under other ownership than that on which the well is located. Most municipal ser-

6. Witkin, *Summary of California Law*, 1146.
7. Erwin *v*. Gage Canal Co., 226 Cal. App. 2d 189.

vices and water companies supplying domestic water were established for the exercise of such appropriative rights. In a dispute about appropriative rights during periods of shortage, the latecomer among appropriators must yield to those preceding him, insofar as the predecessor's use of water is reasonable for the purpose of the appropriation.[8]

Prescriptive rights come into existence when appropriations of ground water are made to the detriment of other overlying or appropriative holders of water rights and continue for more than five years. Generally, when a basin has been in a state of overdraft for more than five years, some prescriptive rights come into existence.

Litigation to establish water rights and achieve control of water distribution has always been expensive and time-consuming. This has been true with regard to surface waters as well as underground waters, and despite the substantial services available from agencies such as the California Water Resources Control Board.[9] Because of the experience obtained in several adjudications during the 1960's dealing with underground basins, recent emphasis has been upon the creation of basin-wide water districts empowered to control extraction and distribution of water throughout a basin as soon as outside sources of water become available. These districts can control water rights by proceeding with judicial determinations where agreement cannot otherwise be reached. They are authorized to levy taxes, including pumping taxes, to charge for the sale of water, to exchange water, and to initiate actions to adjudicate the rights of pumpers within their boundaries.[10]

As long ago as 1933, the state legislature sepcifically gave the Orange County Water District the power to carry out such functions, and the experience of this district in the management of its groundwater basins is worthy of study. The Orange County district has the power to construct, purchase, or lease necessary water works or facilities to replenish the underground water basins within the district, and to augment the supplies of the district. Recently it has been fur-

8. See Orange County Water District v. Colton, 226 Cal. App. 2d 642.

9. For a discussion of the problem from the viewpoint of the individual water producer, see Reis, "Legal Planning for Groundwater Production," 38 Southern California Law Review 484: a description of the problems and alternatives which confront a user of water from an overdrawn groundwater basin in California.

10. See, for example, Water Replenishment District Act, California Water Code §§ 60220 et seq.; county Waterworks District Act, California Water Code § 55335.

ther authorized to provide for reclamation, purification, treatment, and control of water for the beneficial use of persons or property within its boundaries.

The district maintains three funds: a General Fund, a Replenishment Fund, and a Water Reserve Fund. The General Fund, from which general administration expenses are paid, was generated in a recent year from an ad valorem tax of $0.08 per $100.00 of assessed valuation within the district. The Replenishment Fund, obtained from the pumpers within the district, is used to spread and percolate into the underground basin raw water purchased from the Metropolitan Water District. All sizable wells within the district are required to register and semiannually to report the amount of water extracted. These figures are then compiled to form the basis for the Replenishment Fund levy made by the Board of Directors each year. The levy for 1968-1969, for example, was $13.30 per acre-foot for water used for purposes other than irrigation. The Water Reserve Fund is currently generated by an ad valorem tax of $0.09 per $100.00 and is used primarily for large capital outlay projects.[11]

During the fiscal year 1968-1969 a total of 288,413 acre-feet of water was produced or obtained within the district. Groundwater constituted 178,792 acre-feet of the total, supplemental water 94,513 acre-feet, and all other water 15,108 acre-feet.[12] In 1944 water levels within the basin were considered high enough to prevent the intrusion of water from the Pacific Ocean, but between 1944 and 1956 these levels dropped drastically, allowing sea water to intrude. Proper management of the basin from 1953 to 1965 raised its water levels to the 1944 average, even though during much of that period rainfall was considerably below normal. In those years approximately 1.6 million acre-feet of Colorado River water was spread and stored within the district's boundaries. By February 1970, basin levels were even higher than those of 1944. And all this was achieved in one of the most rapidly growing areas in the nation, at a cost to users of from $29 to $35 per acre-foot.

Since the California Water Plan could deliver water to the San

11. Orange County Water District, *Revised Audit Report,* June 30, 1969.

12. Orange County Water District, *Engineer's Report on Water Supply and Basin Utilization,* 1970.

Joaquin Valley in excess of anticipated demand for many years, the possibility of storing such water against future need and against a dry cycle has been suggested.[13] Given a shortage of long-term storage facilities in the areas to be served by the California Water Plan, one logical place to store water is underground. Such storage would have the incidental benefit of raising water tables in those basins in which the water is stored and improving local pumping conditions during periods of storage. In addition, loss by evaporation, such as would occur above ground, would be largely avoided.

The only restriction on the right to store water in any given basin would appear to be that overlying owners be compensated for any damage resulting from abnormal changes in the water table. Such storage is not generally viewed as a trespass, as long as no damage results to the basin's landowners. Krieger and Banks conclude that "the underground may be used for storing imported water, and without having to compensate overlying owners in the absence of actual damage."[14]

Such a long-term underground water storage plan could, it seems, be operated in California by the State Department of Water Resources without modification to the existing contracts between the state and purchasers of water from the State Water Project. These contracts now provide that charges for supplemental conservation facilities will be paid by all contractors as a portion of the Delta Water Rate when such facilities become necessary.[15] It would appear that the cost of placing water underground and later extracting it from the underground basins could be capitalized and treated in exactly the same way as the costs of constructing conventional reservoirs. Control over water placed underground could be exercised in any one of a number of ways. For example, districts could be formed, or the Department of Water Resources could be authorized by legislation to effect control. Unwarranted withdrawals from a basin might be controlled by making a direct and substantial charge upon any user removing water in ex-

13. Krieger and Banks, *supra,* 58.

14. *Ibid.,* 70. So long as no local waters are in effect removed, and water levels are not lowered or excessively raised by such storage activity, the overlying owners would not be damaged; if water levels are adversely affected, however, liability would follow. See Trussau *v.* San Diego, 172 Cal. App. 2d 593.

15. See California Department of Water Resources, "Standard Provisions for Water Supply Contracts," 1962, Art. 22.

cess of his rights where imported water is being stored. Penal sanctions could be used against overt withdrawals contrary to whatever regulations were in force.[16]

From the legal standpoint, then, long-term storage of excess water underground and its subsequent utilization by authorized users seems to be feasible. Engineering, economic, and other constraints on such development should govern the extent of basin utilization, rather than any legal problems per se.

In general, it may be said that the legal aspects of conjunctive use of surface and underground water supplies prove comparable in nature and complexity to the legal aspects of conventional water supply plans. More important, whether the requirements are for long-term or short-term storage for such conjunctive use, sufficient legal precedent and practical experience with underground water storage now exists to permit formulation of plans for such utilization. Carrying such precedent into the years and problems ahead, such storage appears to offer an alternative approach to solving certain water problems in California.[17]

16. See California Penal Code, Section 499, prohibiting theft of water from existing utilities.

17. Further pertinent references to the problem of groundwater use are "Recapture of Reclamation Project of Groundwater," 53 California Law Review 541 (a critique of plans and the absence of plans for the use of waters reaching the underground basin from Reclamation projects, with emphasis on the San Joaquin Valley); "Cost of Depletion of Groundwater," 18 Stanford Law Review (1966) 1229 (a study of certain fringe benefits from "mining" of underground water supplies); and Wiel, "Law and Science and Groundwater," 13 Southern California Law Review (1940) 377 (an early study of efforts to manage underground basins in California). For other states, see (Arizona) R. E. Clark, "Groundwater Management," 6 Arizona Law Review (1965) 178; (Colorado) R. J. Moses, "Law of Groundwater," 11 Rocky Mountain Mining Law Institute (1966) 277; Moses and Vranish, "Colorado's New Groundwater Laws," 38 University of Colorado Law Review (1966) 295; List, "Who Pays When the Well Runs Dry," 37 Colorado Law Review 402; (Oregon) "Rights to Groundwater in Oregon," 311 Oregon Law Journal 317.

# 15 EVALUATION PROCEDURES OF THE U.S. ARMY CORPS OF ENGINEERS: THE DOS RIOS PROJECT

LOWELL D. WOOD

Water project evaluation by the U.S. Army Corps of Engineers and other federal agencies seeking Congressional appropriations applies some of the theorems of welfare economics to individual projects in a process known as benefit-cost analysis. Since economic evaluation of such projects is essentially concerned with the efficient use of resources, that specialized division of economics known as welfare economics, which provides theory for the analysis of questions of economic efficiency, is what those charged with evaluation turn to.[1]

Benefit-cost analysis provides a comprehensive method of examining the economic characteristics of a project, even though its use in some areas remains an unsolved problem. In addition, the benefit-cost technique leaves the analyst considerable freedom to choose his assumptions.[2] Despite the abuses and distortions of the benefit-cost ap-

1. Otto Eckstein, *Water Resource Development: The Economics of Project Evaluation* (Cambridge: Harvard University Press, 1958); Allen V. Kneese, *Water Resources, Development and Use* (Kansas City: Federal Reserve Bank of Kansas City, 1959); John V. Krutilla and Otto Eckstein, *Multiple Purpose River Development Studies in Applied Economic Analysis* (Baltimore: The Johns Hopkins Press, 1958); Roland N. McKean, *Efficiency in Government Through Systems Analysis with Emphasis on Water Resources Development* (New York: John Wiley and Sons, 1958).

2. Literature dealing with the uses, abuses, and limitations of benefit-cost analysis is abundant. See Eckstein, *op. cit.;* S. V. Ciriacy-Wantrup, "Benefit-Cost Analysis and Public Resource Development," *Journal of Farm Economics,* XXXVII, No. 4 (November 1955), 676–689; Richard J. Hammond, "Convention and Limitation in Benefit-Cost Analysis," *Natural Resources Journal,* VI, No. 2 (April 1966); M. M. Kelso, "The Criterion Problem in Decision Making for Public Investment," in *Water Resources and Economic Development of the West,* Conference Proceedings, Committee on Economics of Water Resource Development of the Western Agricultural Economics Research Council, Report No. 15, December 7–9, 1966.

proach and even though its influence in the decision-making process is limited, there is substantial merit in its application to such analysis as of water resource development proposals. Debate continues, however, on the extent to which resources should be employed in benefit-cost analysis.[3]

The Sacramento-San Joaquin Delta is the focal point for all water activities, including runoff, export, import, releases from upstream storage, and all the rest, for the Central Valley Basin. Both the Federal Central Valley Project and the State Water Project, the two components of the California Water Plan, withdraw water from the Delta. These agencies rely on upstream reservoirs and the unregulated flows occurring in the Delta for their water supply. Logically, then, water supply yields are measured in the Sacramento-San Joaquin Delta area.

Flows of water in the Delta vary widely according to prevailing hydrologic conditions. During some years, Delta flows are greater than export requirements; however, during periods of extremely low rainfall and subnormal runoff, flows in the Delta are greatly reduced and are less than sufficient for all requirements.

The Corps of Engineers proposed a multiple-purpose dam and reservoir complex on the Middle Fork of the Eel River at Dos Rios. The Eel River Basin, approximately 140 miles long and 40 miles wide, lies in the North Coast area of California, and encompasses an area of 36,000 square miles. The main stem of the Eel flows in a northwest direction and empties into the Pacific Ocean fifteen miles southwest of Eureka, California. Water from the Dos Rios Reservoir would be transferred from the Eel Basin to the Sacramento Basin by tunnel. This water would then become part of the water supply for the California Water Project.

The proposed Dos Rios Dam would provide flood control, adequate water for in-basin needs, water for export to state facilities, recreation benefits, and small amounts of hydropower, primarily for in-basin needs. Its benefit-cost study shows that the construction of a multiple-purpose dam reservoir and conveyance tunnel is economically justified. This chapter briefly examines some of the results of the Corps' study.[4]

3. See Ciriacy-Wantrup, *op. cit.,* and Hammond, *op. cit.*

4. U.S. Army Corps of Engineers, *Eel River Basin California: Interim Report on Water Resources Development for the Middle Fork Eel River* (San Francisco: U.S. Army Corps of Engineers, 1967), p. 48. For a more detailed analysis, see Lowell D. Wood, "An Eco-

Emphasis will be primarily on flood control and exported water benefit-evaluation, and the implications of this evaluation upon a search for possible alternative projects.

In evaluating the benefits and costs of a project, it is essential that specific economic conditions with and without the project be projected. Benefits can be claimed only if they can be shown to derive from the project under consideration, though it is often difficult to identify benefits with specific projects where these projects are additions to an existing system. Nevertheless, the principle is sound that benefits claimed should develop from the project being evaluated.

## FLOOD CONTROL BENEFITS

Flood control and prevention benefits for the Dos Rios Project are the value of inundation damages prevented and land-enhancement values created with the project established.

Preproject conditions for evaluating flood control benefits for the Dos Rios Project assume that the authorized, but as yet unbuilt, Federal Delta Levee Flood Control Project is completed.[5] The Corps was responsible for the economic evaluation of this proposed project, which calls for approximately thirty-five miles of levees on both sides of the Eel River, the Salt River, and the east bank of North Bay. This system is designed to handle a flow equal to the peak discharge of the December 1955 flood; that is, it is meant to be capable of confining a discharge of 600,000 cubic feet per second in the Eel River Delta with three feet of freeboard. But when the December 1964 flood exceeded the 1955 flood by a considerable amount, it was obvious that the levee system designed could not handle the discharge. Further studies indicate that any levee system in the Eel River Delta that could handle more than 600,000 cubic feet per second flow would be too costly to build, because extensive relocation of U.S. Highway 101 and the railroad bed of the Northwestern Pacific Railroad Company would be necessary.

nomic Analysis of the Planning and Evaluation Procedures Employed by the United States Army Corps of Engineers with Particular Reference to the Proposed Dos Rios Project in Northern California" (unpublished Ph.D. thesis, University of California, Berkeley, California, 1969).

5. U.S. Congress, House Committee on Interior and Insular Affairs, *Eel River, California,* House Document No. 234, 89th Congress, 1st Session (Washington, D.C.: Government Printing Office, 1965).

A study of the flood-control aspects of the Federal Delta Levee and Dos Rios reveals an interesting contradiction. House Document No. 234, supporting construction of the levee system, emphasizes that flood storage in reservoirs alone is not an economic solution to the flood problems in the Eel River Delta area.

> It was determined that protection by reservoirs or reservoirs with channel improvements, at this time is not practical nor economically feasible. However, it has been determined that a high degree of flood protection by channel improvements in the Delta area together with recreational facilities is economically justified. . . .
> Preliminary evaluation of flood control storage required to provide a satisfactory degree of protection in the Delta area indicate the cost to provide this storage in multiple-purpose or single-purpose reservoirs would exceed all potential benefits. Thus, the selection of a plan of improvement was limited to consideration of improvements on the channel through the Delta flood plain.[6]

While flood-control benefits in the Dos Rios report were derived after assumption was made that the Federal Delta Levee Flood Control Project was constructed, the Dos Rios report includes the following statement, indicating that the proposed reservoir could provide adequate flood-control benefits even if there were no levee system.

In order to determine the possible effect of staging the levee construction relative to the reservoir, benefits were also computed for the proposed reservoir alone, assuming the Delta levees were not constructed. Only the Delta Reach is affected by this assumption. In this Reach, benefits for the reservoir alone were found to be slightly higher for the 50-year study period than the benefits for the adopted condition of the reservoir with authorized levees assumed constructed in advance of the reservoir. Benefits attributable to the reservoir for the 100-year period were found to be practically the same for conditions with and without levees.[7]

House Document No. 234, published for the Corps in 1965, states that the cost of flood protection for the Eel River Delta in multipurpose reservoirs would exceed all potential benefits. Therefore, it says, the levees should be built, and not the reservoirs. The Corps' own Dos Rios Report, in 1967, states that benefits for the proposed Dos Rios Reser-

6. *Ibid.*, pp. 9, 52.
7. Corps of Engineers, *Eel River Basin: Interim Report, op. cit.*, p. E–24.

voir alone, without the levess being constructed, would be slightly higher than the benefits for the levees plus the reservoir, and that therefore the flood-control storage in Dos Rios Reservoir is justifiable, even if the levees are not constructed. The cost of flood control by multi-purpose reservoirs exceeded all potential benefits in the early report. In the latter report, with only *slightly* higher flood-control benefits for the multipurpose reservoir alone, flood control by reservoir construction is seen as justifiable. The Corps is concerned with multipurpose reservoirs in both instances; therefore, the flood-control purpose should be evaluated on the basis that the benefits of flood protection are at least equal to the cost of including that purpose in the multipurpose project.

This contradiction illustrates an incorrect application of the with-and-without principle in the Corps' evaluation of the Dos Rios project. Analysis of land-enhancement benefits for the Eel River Delta by the Corps in the two reports further substantiates the claim that application of the principle was incorrect.

House Document No. 234 estimated the average annual land-enhancement benefits of the Federal Delta Levee Flood Control Project at $342,000 in 1963 prices. When that 1963 value is divided by the factor 0.9175, the resulting figure ($373,000) is an estimate of average annual land-enhancement benefits in terms of 1967 prices.[8]

In the Dos Rios report, issued two years later, the Corps estimated that average annual land-enhancement benefits for the combined projects (levees and Dos Rios) in the Eel River Delta would be $260,000 for a 50-year project.[9] Average annual land-enhancement benefits from the federal levees alone amounted to only $40,000, according to the Dos Rios report. Thus, with the Dos Rios project in place, total average annual land-enhancement benefits come to $113,000 less than was originally claimed for the levees alone.

The Federal Delta Levee Flood Control Project was marginal to begin with, that is, its benefit-cost ratio was close to unity. If the projected average annual land-enhancement benefits are merely $40,000 instead of $373,000, the project is clearly uneconomical and should not

8. The factor 0.9175 was developed using the Consumer Price Index for all items, with 1963 = 106.7 and 1967 = 116.3, given 1957–1959 = 100 (U.S. Bureau of the Census, *Statistical Abstract of the United States, 1949–1968,* 89th Edition, 1968, p. 347.

9. Corps of Engineers, *Eel River Basin: Interim Report, op. cit.,* p. E–21.

be built. Furthermore, the Corps failed to include interest charges during the construction period for the Federal Delta Levee Project, though they were included, as required, in the Dos Rios evaluation. A construction period of seven years (same as Dos Rios) and an interest rate of 3¼ per cent would accumulate $2,068,000 interest for the levee project during construction. This omission of interest charges during construction underestimates average annual costs and increases the benefit-cost ratio. If the project was marginal to begin with, this omission was not only incorrect, but it was a critical consideration in the project's winning appropriations from Congress.

If the federal levee project cannot be justified economically, then the underpinning of the Corps' flood control analysis for the Dos Rios Project is suspect. Since the levees were assumed in place as part of their preproject conditions, if the levees are not built the present analysis is inappropriate. The brief and contradictory statement of benefits accruing to the reservoir alone in the absence of the levees is not a satisfactory solution to this dilemma. The whole of the resulting flood-control benefit analysis is incomplete and incorrect.

Furthermore, the Corps claimed flood-control benefits amounting to $36,000 annually for preventing floods in Round Valley, the site of the Dos Rios Reservoir. "Round Valley would form part of [the] reservoir of [the] proposed project. Therefore, [the] project can be credited with [the] elimination of flood damages."[10]

This interpretation of the with-and-without principle is conceivably possible. Without the project, damage-causing floods occur in Round Valley; with the project, there will be no further flood damages in Round Valley. However, preventing flood damages by permanently inundating an area hardly seems to be an appropriate flood control measure. Flood control benefits in these circumstances should not be claimed for Round Valley.

## WATER-SUPPLY BENEFITS

The discussion that follows can be better understood if a clear picture of the hydrological situation is kept in mind. Both the Central Valley Project and the State Water Plan base their yield studies on the ability of the runoff in the Sacramento-San Joaquin Delta to meet

10. *Ibid.,* p. E–57.

expected requirements, given a recurrence of the driest cycle experienced to date, namely, that of the period 1928-1934. The amount of water available for export during that period is taken as a reasonable measure of the firm yield which would be available at all other times. In other words, the critically dry period, hydrologically, defines the firm yield of the system. Since firm annual-yield measurements are based on the driest runoff cycle, nonfirm flows exist in the Delta during all other than the driest years.

Without additional construction of storage and delivery projects, beginning in about 1990 the State Water Project, in approximately seven years out of every thirty, will require in excess of 900,000 acre-feet of water per year to meet expected requirements. During the other twenty-three years, very little additional water will be required under expected conditions.[11] If 900,000 acre-feet of water are required in seven out of thirty years, then the amount of water required on the average over the thirty years will be much less than 900,000 acre-feet.

Since the California Department of Water Resources and the Corps have emphatically declared their belief that Dos Rios would meet these expected water shortages, we can, therefore, take the annual longtime average export of the Middle Fork Eel River Runoff prepared by the Engineering Consultants to the Senate as an indication of the additional water supply necessary to meet expected requirements. The longtime average annual export of water from this project is estimated to be 400,000 acre-feet per year.

TABLE 15.1.
*Proposed Disposition of Middle Fork Eel River Runoff*

|  | Longtime average | Maximum acre-feet | Minimum acre-feet |
|---|---|---|---|
| Annual inflow | 1,000,000 | 2,250,000 | 170,000 |
| Annual fisheries release | 217,000 | 217,000 | 217,000 |
| Annual export | 400,000 | 1,300,000 | — |
| Spill | 303,000 | — | — |
| Evaporation | 80,000 | — | — |

SOURCE: California Senate Committee on Water Resources, *The Dos Rios Project* (Sacramento: California Senate, 1969), Appendix 4-8.

11. Wood, *op. cit.*, p. 300.

Even with a project that is capable of annually releasing 900,000 acre-feet during the seven-year critically dry period, it is possible that agricultural water deliveries could be curtailed in exceptionally dry years. This eventuality was foreseen by those responsible for drawing up the Standard Provisions for Water Supply Contracts, in that the contracts provide "an allowable reduction in the agricultural use portion of the minimum project yield, due to drought, of not to exceed 50% in any one year, nor a total of 100% of any one year's supply in a series of seven consecutive years."[12]

In summary then, without Dos Rios or some other source not now identified, the State Water Project will be short 400,000 acre-feet of water on a longtime average annual basis by 1990. Moreover, this source must have the potential of delivering up to 1,300,000 acre-feet of water in some years, and in other years no deliveries will be required.

## WATER BENEFITS EVALUATION

The Corps estimated the average annual water-supply benefits accruing to the Dos Rios project to be $26,100,000. Water-supply benefits contribute 90 per cent of the average annual tangible benefits for the entire project. This figure, $26,100,000, is derived by multiplying 900,000 acre-feet (the Corps' estimate of water made firm by the Dos Rios Project) by $29 per acre-foot (the estimated unit benefit for water).

Since the Dos Rios project will neither develop nor export 900,000 acre-feet of water annually, on a longtime basis, this is an incorrect estimate of water-supply benefit. The Corps has overestimated the water-supply benefits by neglecting to consider carefully the with-and-without principle.

It is clear that the actual volume of water developed and delivered from the Dos Rios project to the State Water Project to offset expected deficiencies is a project benefit and that these releases have economic value.[13] These long-run average annual releases, as has been indicated above, amount to 400,000 acre-feet, not 900,000 acre-feet as claimed by the Corps.

12. California Department of Water Resources, *Bulletin No. 141: Water Supply Contracts,* Vol. I (Sacramento: 1965), p. 18.

13. Discussions with Professor S. V. Wantrup, University of California at Berkeley, were very helpful in conceptualizing the water-supply benefit problem as outlined.

It is true that if Dos Rios becomes an integral part of the system the firm annual yield of the system is increased by 900,000 acre-feet. This is an engineering concept, however, that results from having storage capacity available at Dos Rios that can make releases to the State Water Project during a recurrence of the critical dry cycle. In all other years, the excess of nonfirm flows in the Delta are available for utilization. These nonfirm flows amount to 500,000 acre-feet on a long-time average annual basis. But these flows are available without Dos Rios; they occur in the Delta now. These flows have considerable economic value and will be used without the development of the Dos Rios project. The value of these nonfirm, unregulated flows is increased, however, by their being made dependable (firm) with the Dos Rios project. How much more preferable in a quantitative sense is a problem!

The Corps failed to consider this problem in its analysis. It included the full value of all water firmed up, both in the Delta and actually exported from Dos Rios in the benefit stream of the project. The implication is that the 500,000 acre-feet of nonfirm, average annual flows of water in the Delta have zero value without Dos Rios.

U.S. Bureau of Reclamation contracts in the Friant-Kern and Madera Canal service areas indicate that the relative price of nonfirm and firm water is about $1.50 to $3.50 per acre-foot respectively. These contracts indicate the nonfirm water is worth about 43 per cent of the value of firm water.[14] If this relationship is valid, then the value of the nonfirm flows in the Delta without Dos Rios would be about $12 an acre-foot. With Dos Rios, these same flows can be made firm and their value then assumed to be $29 an acre-foot. Thus, with the project, these flows have increased in value by $17 an acre-foot.

Water-supply benefits for Dos Rios can now be estimated as follows:

(400,000 acre-feet × $29) + (500,000 acre-feet × $17) = $20,100,000.

Water-supply benefits as calculated by the Corps contribute 90 per cent of the average annual tangible benefits from the entire Dos Rios Project. We have suggested here that the Corps incorrectly overestimated these benefits. If water-supply benefits are reduced by $6,000,-000 annually, the benefit-cost ratio is likewise substantially reduced. This procedure is justifiable; however, it must be pointed out that the

14. Wood, op. cit., p. 66.

value of the nonfirm Delta flows is a crucial variable, and the estimate used in the example is not meant to be taken as the final value. Effort should be expended to develop reliable estimates of the value of the nonfirm Delta flows.

## CONSERVATION

The Dos Rios development proposal has met with considerable opposition from conservation groups. Every economic readjustment creates many diverse consequences. Given the level of economic and physical development in California today and the far-ranging extent of human settlement, it is difficult to conceive of a water development project that could be built anywhere without causing serious personal, environmental, and social problems.

Recent public policy reflects a growing demand for the use of resources to provide "quality of life" experiences. Public interest in the creation of the Redwoods National Park, the Bay Area Conservation and Development legislation, and President Nixon's campaign to improve our environment attest to this demand. Expected technological advances will tend to change the demand for productive resources as synthetics and substitutes become available. The long-run effects of continued technological advances given current taste patterns implies that resources used in a manner to improve the quality of life have an appreciating value. Resources used in the traditional manufacture of goods and services will depreciate relative to previous uses. It is to be doubted, however, that technology will become so advanced that wonders of nature will be duplicated or extinct species resurrected.[15]

The demand curve for resources that have few or no substitutes, and that are, therefore, unique, is highly inelastic. The nature of an inelastic demand function implies that the implicit price of a unique resource is increased sharply as the quantity of the resource is reduced. Given inelastic demand, the increase in price will be proportionally greater than the decrease in quantity. Thus, each unit of a unique resource lost to society has a proportionally higher implicit price; that is, higher social costs result from the removal of units of a unique resource.

15. John V. Krutilla, "Conservation Reconsidered," *The American Economic Review,* LVIII, No. 4, September 1967.

The Corps' Dos Rios proposal attempts to mitigate environmental effects created by the project. The proposed mitigation measures have not only not been widely accepted, but they have received considerable adverse attention. Society appears to have moved ahead much faster in its concern about the environmental effects of development than has the Corps. It may be time for planning officials of the Corps to note the magnitude of the support and the increasing public demand for quality of life considerations. For if the following statement, taken from the Supplemental Data prepared by the Corps in answer to criticism of Dos Rios, is representative of the Corps' attitude toward ecological and environmental aspects, then there is danger of professional, physically oriented planners substituting the standards of their profession for public objectives.

The Round Valley portion of the reservoir has already lost its natural ecology through farming and other endeavors of man, and should not be considered a true ecological loss. Actually, the ecology of the area will be protected from further depredation of man as a result of the project.[16]

This ignores the social costs of permanently inundating Round Valley, costs that would be very high. In recognition of this fact, the state has taken a stand against flooding the valley and the matter remains moot.

The number of miles of open-flowing rivers has been significantly reduced over time. The costs to society involved in transforming sections of the free-flowing rivers into reservoirs becomes higher with each mile of open river that is removed. Mile after mile of upstream spawning grounds for anadromous fish have been inundated by new reservoirs. As a result, anadromous fish are found in fewer and fewer rivers. Given the limited supply of upstream spawning grounds and the inelastic demand for these resources, each mile of upstream spawning grounds that is removed incurs higher social costs. Thus, developers of water projects that transform unique resources should be obligated to make a clear demonstration that the social benefits of a project exceed its social costs.

16. U.S. Army Corps of Engineers, *Eel River Basin California.* Supplementary Data on Dos Rios Dam Project for Joint Senate-Assembly Hearing on 17 October 1968, Sacramento, California (San Francisco: U.S. Army Engineer District, San Francisco, 1968), Section 4-4.

The adverse effects of resource development cannot be fully mitigated; however, these effects can usually be compensated if adequate funds are available. An affluent society, concerned with improving or maintaining quality of life experiences, can affort higher costs, social or pecuniary, for necessary mitigative measures. The cost estimate for such measures suggested by the Corps is conservative when viewed in this light. The Corps has been willing to negotiate in this respect, however.

## ALTERNATIVES

It has been shown that the Corps' economic evaluation of the Dos Rios project is incorrect, because of an erroneous application of the with-and-without principle. The Corps' approach to a search for alternative solutions to the water problem of the State Water Project also is suspect for the same reason.

This search is made manageable when the water-deficiency problem facing the State Water Project without Dos Rios is restated. A project capable of diverting 400,000 acre-feet of water on a longtime average annual basis, with storage facilities able to deliver up to 1,300,000 acre-feet of water in any one year or 900,000 acre-feet annually in any seven-year period could, together with nonfirm flows in the Sacramento-San Joaquin Delta, meet the expected deficiencies of the State Water Project. When preproject conditions are viewed in this light, the dismissal of almost all conventional water development sites in the Central Valley by the Corps and the Department of Water Resources, because they do not develop 900,000 acre-feet of additional water on a longtime average annual basis, is wrong. The dismissal of possible sites for this reason is illustrated by this quotation from Mr. William R. Gianelli:

It should be pointed out that the Paskenta-Newville and Cottonwood Creek developments are not true alternatives to the Dos Rios project. Together they would develop only 500,000 of the required 900,000 acre-feet of additional supplies necessary to fulfill water service contract commitments.[17]

17. William R. Gianelli, "Statement of the Department of Water Resources on the Dos Rios Project," Statement given before the State of California Committee on Water Resources and the Assembly Water Committee, Sacramento, California, October 17, 1966, p. 7.

Obviously, if Dos Rios can export 400,000 acre-feet of water on a longtime average annual basis, and by so doing firm up the water commitments of the State Water Project, so could any other project of similar magnitude. A project or combination of projects that will make available approximately 400,000 acre-feet of water annually and also provide adequate storage capacity for cyclical dry periods for a wide range of annual deliveries may be considered as an alternative to Dos Rios.

The Assembly Water Committee dismissed some projects as alternatives to Dos Rios because they do not provide necessary flood control or necessary water.[18] We have shown that the Dos Rios flood control measures proposed by the Corps are of questionable value. Mr. Gianelli states that the same reservoirs dismissed by the Assembly Water Committee have a combined total export yield of 1,032,000 acre-feet.[19] Furthermore, a study for the Reclamation Board of the State of California by the Ralph M. Parsons Company concludes that the Dutch Gulch, Farquhar School, Paskenta-Newville, Wing, Mill-Deer, and Bella Vista projects are economically justified, that they would provide significant flood protection for the Central Valley, and that they are capable of producing 800,000 acre-feet of water for export annually.[20]

Apparently, the search for alternatives to the Dos Rios Project was superficial. When the State Water Project's conditions are clearly understood, it is evident that the potential for fulfilling the additional water requirements of the Project exist in the Central Valley through conventional development. Since this water can be developed without incurring the cost of constructing a twenty-one-mile tunnel, it will be cheaper. Limiting alternatives to those including storage in the Eel River Basin is clearly an unnecessary constraint. The Department of Water Resources has, however, continued this policy in the additional studies requested by Governor Reagan.[21]

18. California Assembly Committee on Water, *Preliminary Comments on the Dos Rios Project* (Sacramento: California Assembly, 1969), p. 7.

19. Gianelli, *loc. cit.*

20. *Sacramento River: Upstream Storage Investigation,* A study for the State of California Reclamation Board by the Ralph M. Parsons Company of Los Angeles and New York, November 1, 1968.

21. John R. Teerink, "Report on Additional Studies of Alternatives Within the Eel River Basin," Presented before the California Water Commission, Los Angeles, California, June 6, 1969.

## Summary

Table 15.2 summarizes the benefit-cost ratios that result under differing assumptions. The annual costs, as estimated by the Corps, are taken as given. Column A omits flood control benefits and adjusts water-supply benefits as developed by this study. Column B contains the Corps' estimate of all benefits except water supply, but includes cost estimates developed elsewhere.[22]

This chapter has dealt with the evaluation procedures of the Corps of Engineers with respect to the Dos Rios Project, and analysis has revealed that the Corps has failed to consider properly conditions with and without the Dos Rios Project.

Comparison of the Federal Delta Levee Project and Dos Rios Project reports reveals several contradictions that make the entire flood control evaluation for Dos Rios suspect. The inclusion of flood control benefits for preventing flood damages in Round Valley by permanently inundating it is clearly an inappropriate application of the with-and-without principle. Water-supply benefits are overstated, and the search for alternatives is unnecessarily constrained by the Corps' conception of water-supply yields with and without Dos Rios. Given the increased emphasis by society for quality of life experiences, and given the inelastic demand function for unique resources, the social costs of such permanent processes as inundating Round Valley and the social costs of transforming natural spawning and rearing grounds for anadromous fish into a reservoir is very high. An affluent society might well contract to undertake adequate mitigative measures for other environmental damages incurred.

TABLE 15.2.
*Benefit-Cost Ratios*

| | Corps | A | B |
|---|---|---|---|
| Annual Benefit: | | | |
| Flood control | $ 1,510,000 | -0- | $ 1,510,000 |
| Water supply | $26,100,000 | $20,100,000 | $20,100,000 |
| Recreation | $ 1,210,000 | $ 1,210,000 | $ 1,210,000 |
| Hydropower | $ 210,000 | $ 210,000 | $ 210,000 |
| | $29,030,000 | $21,520,000 | $23,030,000 |
| Annual Costs: | | | |
| Interest, 4⅝% | $21,973,000 | $21,973,000 | $24,310,000 |
| B/C Ratio | 1.4 | .98 | .95 |

22. Limitation of space precluded analysis of the Corps' cost estimates here. The author's research (Wood, *op. cit.*) resulted in the estimates given in Column B.

# 16 ON THE POLITICAL ECONOMY OF WATER RESOURCES EVALUATION

DAVID SECKLER AND L. M. HARTMAN

Wherever there is a problem of choice, wherever one thing must be given up in order to have another thing, economics pertains. Economics has been called "the pure logic of choice," and it has been defined as the science that studies human behavior in terms of a relationship between ends and limited means which have alternative uses.[1]

This definition does not restrict economic analysis to any particular kind of "end," as so many people—economists among them—are inclined to think. It does not restrict economics to the "materialistic" aspects of life, nor does it refer only to those elements of life bought and sold in the marketplace.

It is, however, fair to say that economics historically has concentrated on a particular subset of the whole broad set of choices. Its almost exclusive concern has been with the production of the maximum amount of goods, consumers' goods, from a given base of resources. The reason is obvious. Man's overriding problem has been to provide a sufficient quantity of goods and services—food, clothing, shelter, transportation, and similar aspects of the satisfaction of material wants—to an expanding population. To this end some of the greatest

Some of this text has been adapted from two previous papers: David Seckler and L. M. Hartman, "The Methodology of Economics in Public Outdoor Recreation Research," *Proceedings, 1967,* Western Farm Economics Association, Fortieth Annual Meeting (Las Cruces, New Mexico, 1967), pp. 274–278; and David Seckler, "Economic Value and Social Welfare: The Dilemma of Economics in the Great Society," published in *An Economic Study of the Demand for Outdoor Recreation,* a collection of papers presented at the Annual Meetings of the Cooperative Regional Research Technical Committee for Project No. WM-59, Report No. 1, San Francisco, May 25–26, 1968.

1. Lionel Robbins, *An Essay on the Nature and Significance of Economic Science,* 2d ed. (London: Macmillan, 1946).

minds of history, not only in economics but also in technology and politics, have bent their efforts.

The results in the economically advanced nations of the world have been spectacular. For example, the United States now has a gross national product of a trillion dollars—$1,000,000,000,000—one-third of the world's total. If growth continues at 4 per cent per year, this amount of GNP will triple in the next thirty years, although population will grow only between 25 and 50 per cent in the same period. These rates could continue through the indefinite future. It is not an exaggeration to say that at some time during the past two decades the developed nations crossed a fundamental threshold in human history: the problem of providing for the basic needs of man has been solved.

But this spectacular accomplishment has not been without its costs. The American economy, based on approximately 6 per cent of the world's population, currently uses approximately 35 per cent of the world's resources. As the economic system makes more demands on the natural system of resources, the costs of finding raw materials for the economic system increase and the environment suffers degradation. For the first time, man has come to recognize that he lives on a rather small, almost wholly self-contained, highly limited planet. He neither creates nor destroys. He merely transforms one thing into another. A question is now raised whose answer would have been regarded as absurdly self-evident only a generation ago: Is rapid economic growth worth-while?

In what follows, two major hypotheses will be advanced. First, modern society is undergoing a fundamental change in the relative values it places on economic activities. Briefly, the emphasis is shifting from production of commodities to preservation and restoration of the quality of life. Second, we shall contend that the traditional means in economics of evaluating resource-development projects—benefit-cost analysis—is progressively losing touch with the values of modern society. Benefit-cost is a commodities-oriented means of evaluation. If we are to evaluate in terms of quality, we must devise a different evaluation process. We shall see that this newer kind of evaluation is much different from the old. It cannot provide "answers." The actual, ruling decision must be a political decision. All that economics can hope to accomplish is to contribute to rational political decisions. This requires a basic restructuring of the economist's role and of the traditional interpretation of his science. Otherwise, as the following discussion will attempt to show, economic evaluation may perversely direct resources away from what society wants, and it may reinforce uses society may wish to change.

## THE AGE OF AFFLUENCE

John Kenneth Galbraith was perhaps the first economist to see clearly the importance of the transition from scarcity to affluence. But his contribution has been misunderstood and even maligned. He does not contend, of course, that we live in an era of plenty where everyone has all he wants. He does maintain that relative priorities have changed and that the foundations and direction of the economic system must be critically examined. As he says:

The family which takes its mauve-and-cerise, air-conditioned, power-steered and power-braked automobile out for a tour passes through cities that are badly paved, made hideous by litter, blighted buildings, billboards and posts for wires that should long since have been put underground. They pass on into a countryside that has been rendered largely invisible by commercial art. . . . They picnic on exquisitely packaged food from a portable icebox by a polluted stream and go on to spend the night at a park which is a menace to public health and morals. . . . Just before dozing off on an air mattress, beneath a nylon tent, amid the stench of decaying refuse, they may reflect vaguely on the curious unevenness of their blessings. Is this, indeed, the American genius?[2]

To make Galbraith's point stand out more vividly, let us divide all commodities into two basic groups. There are the ordinary consumers' goods, the "commodities"—food, clothing, shelter, transportation, and the like. Then there are the "amenities"—clean air and water, open space, quiet, natural beauty, wildlife, outdoor recreation, and similar goods. At one time the central objective of the economic system was to provide a supply of commodities. The supply of amenities was either plentiful or their value in comparison with the urgent need for commodities was trivial. Now, however, the situation in the developed

2. John Kenneth Galbraith, *The Affluent Society* (Boston: Houghton Mifflin, 1958). pp. 198–199.

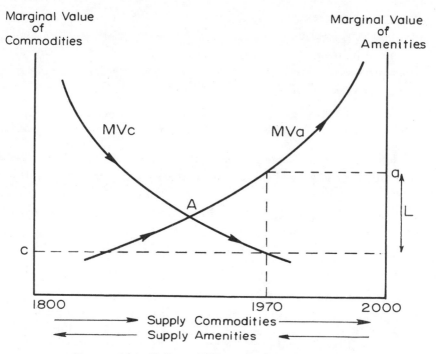

FIGURE 16.1. Values of Commodities and Amenities.

world may be reversed. The spectacular success of the economic system has provided such a massive supply of commodities that their marginal value has been driven very low. But at the same time the system has created increasing demands for the amenities as people strive to escape the frantic atmosphere of the modern industrial order, with its centralization of power complexes in overgrown metropolises, and discover that the supply of amenities has been reduced by the conversion of nature into a resource input to industry.

In Figure 16.1 we summarize this situation. The marginal value of commodities (the value of a little more or less) is indicated by the curve $MVc$. This curve slopes down to the right because of the principle of diminishing marginal value (or "utility"): the more you have of anything, the less the value of each additional unit. Any point of $MVc$ (reading over to the left-hand axis) gives the marginal value of any given amount of the commodity (read on the bottom axis). The marginal value of amenities is given by the curve $MVa$. (We shall discuss how to measure this later.) We have pulled a simple trick with this curve. What we have done, in effect, is draw an $MVa$ graph that looks just like the $MVc$ graph. Then we rotated it through 180° and superimposed it on the $MVc$ graph. Thus, in this figure, while the supply of commodities increases from left to right in the conventional way, the supply of amenities increases from right to left. The $MVa$ curve also decreases as the quantity supplied increases, for amenities also obey the principle of decreasing marginal value.

Now let us analyze what Figure 16.1 shows. We hypothesize that at some time in the past—say the year 1800—the supply of commodities was very low, and thus their marginal value was very high. At that time the supply of amenities was very high and their value correspondingly low. But as time goes on and the present is approached, the supply of commodities grows and the supply of amenities shrinks. Consequently, the value of commodities declines and the value of amenities increases. Eventually a point $A$ is reached where the two marginal values are equal. But we may have passed beyond even that point to the condition indicated for 1970 on the graph.

The importance of the point $A$ is this: Any movement beyond that point is irrational, in the sense that the marginal value of commodities is less than the marginal value of amenities. For the point 1970, for example, the marginal value of commodities is $c$, that of amenities $a$. It follows that if the production of a unit of commodities destroys a unit of amenities in the situation shown in this graph, we are in a net-loss situation. Producing one more unit of commodity brings a gain of $c$ but a loss of $a$; the net marginal loss is, therefore, $a - c$, or $L$.

If this is the case, it would be rational to reduce the amount of commodities and increase the supply of amenities back to the point $A$. At this point social welfare would be maximized. However, this course is not being followed. As time goes on, we push ever further to the right. We become progressively irrational as we move inexorably onward from the social optimum, blindly grinding out commodities at the expense of amenities.

## The Market System

The free market system has been appropriately likened to a vast, highly complex, social machine which, operating through its system of price signals, orders and integrates all the multifarious actions of individuals in an economy. No one who has seriously studied the difficulties of centralist socialism can fail to appreciate the true wonder of the free market. Had it been deliberately invented, it would certainly stand as one of the great accomplishments of the human mind.[3]

But, like all machines, the market is specialized. There are very real limits to what it can do and what it cannot do; and, like all social institutions, it tends to acquire a certain momentum of its own and become self-justifying. It is clear that modern man has been able to create machines, social and physical, to conquer scarcity. It is not at all clear that he has conquered his machines. The genie has been one of the popular fantasies of man since time immemorial, the all-powerful slave who in the end enslaves his master.

The possibility that the machine would take control was once explored by Norbert Wiener,[4] the father of cybernetics and thus of automation. Wiener imagined a day when a large sophisticated computer would be able to keep in intimate touch with the day-to-day activities of every individual in society. The computer would know what each individual considered "success." It could then play a "game" with all individuals simultaneously, in which it would manipulate each individual's environment so that the only way he could succeed would be by acting in a way prescribed by the computer. Each man would go through life making choices; he would fail or succeed according to the choices he made. But only those who chose to act in the way prescribed by the machine would find success. Thus, by manipulating the range of choice, permitting persons either to choose within that range or fail, the computer would control a society duped into the illusion of choice.

Wiener's nightmare seems a comfortably remote possibility. But if we regard it as an analogy of what can happen—as a "model" of social institutions—we can see that something very like it has in fact been the condition of man through his history. Any given age has its own criteria of success. Certain kinds of behavior are permitted, others ruthlessly suppressed. At the very least, behavior outside the range of the acceptable choices of the moment is undertaken at great peril. In this way, people are progressively mapped "into the system."

The difference between Wiener's computer and social systems is, of course, this: Man creates his own system; and thus, he creates the

3. Frederick A. Hayek, "The Use of Knowledge in Society," *American Economic Review,* Vol. XXXV, No. 4 (September 1945), pp. 519–530.

4. Norbert Wiener, *The Human Use of Human Beings* (Garden City, N.Y.: Doubleday, 1954), Chapter X.

ultimate paradox. No outside malignant force destroys his freedom
but rather he himself. Consider, for example, the Victorians of latter-
nineteenth-century England. It is clear that they had a vastly different
range of choice from that of modern man. Whether it was better or
worse we need not say. But it is certain that the change in the range of
choice from the Victorian era to our own was not of any man's choosing.
The transition was brought about as the unintended consequence of
the day-to-day activities of the Victorians and their successors. Thus,
it does not in the end matter if one deplores the prevailing system or
if one admires it. Everyone contributes to its maintenance and to its
eventual destruction. And neither is the direct product of human
choice.

     E. J. Mishan, a leading contemporary economist, characterized
the contemporary illusion of choice in these terms:

Business economists have ever been glib in equating economic
growth with an expansion of the range of choices facing the individual; they have failed to observe that as the carpet of "increased
choice" is being unrolled before us by the foot, it is simultaneously
being rolled up behind us by the yard. We are compelled willy-nilly
to move into the future that commerce and technology fashions for
us without appeal and without redress. In all that contributes in
trivial ways to his ultimate satisfaction, the things at which modern business excels, new models of cars and transitors, prepared
foodstuffs and plastic objets d'art, electric tooth-brushes and an increasing range of push-button gadgets, man has ample choice. In all
that destroys his enjoyment of life, he has none. The environment
about him can grow ugly, his ears assailed with impunity, and
smoke and foul gases exhaled over his person. He may be in circumstances that he will never enjoy a night's rest at home without
planes shrieking overhead. Whether he is indifferent to such circumstances, whether he bears them stoically, or whether he writhes
in impotent fury, there is under the present dispensation practically
nothing he can do about them.[5]

## The Problem of Value

     The past few years have thus witnessed a fundamental shift in
relative value from commodities to amenities. As we have seen, the
powerful market mechanism serves very well with respect to commodi-

     5. Ezra J. Mishan, *The Costs of Economic Growth* (New York: Praeger, 1967), pp.
85–86.

ties, but it also impels us willy-nilly into the progressive destruction of amenities. It would seem to be expedient for us to examine the values we hold and the way in which we evaluate alternative social policies so that we will be led in the desired direction. No better area exists to illustrate the shift in social objectives from those of scarcity to affluence than water resources.

Not long ago that evaluation of water development projects meant simply evaluation in terms of their relative contribution to the following objectives:

1) Irrigation, drainage, and reclamation of land
2) Hydroelectric power generation
3) Water transportation
4) Industrial and municipal use
5) Flood control

These five could, in turn, be easily collapsed into one overriding objective, to maximize the value of commodities produced, or Net National Product (NNP). True, there were certain subsidy elements or income distribution effects, but these were either neglected or greeted with chagrin by economists. Also, it was recognized that flood protection may save lives; but with a rather surprising candor it was said that it is not sensible to evaluate this effect in terms of dollars and cents. Now, however, things have changed, and certain economists have found that a human life is worth something like $75,000. These minor points aside, it is fair to say that the project was deemed best which contributed with greatest increment to NNP.

Today, project evaluation means something quite different. We are now asked to evaluate water in terms of such additional objectives as:

6) Regional development
7) Outdoor recreation
8) Conservation of wildlife and scenic beauty
9) Urban location
10) The distribution of income

It can hardly be denied that these criteria mark a very perceptible shift in our interest in water resources. NNP is no longer the sole objective. Indeed, expenditure of resources on objectives in this second list often decreases NNP; yet this is a price public administrators and hence, presumably, the people are willing to pay. How do we evaluate these objectives?

First, a very important philosophical point must be understood: Value is not a property *of* objects in themselves; it is an attribute we assign *to* objects. As with water above, it is not the intrinsic value of water that is important; it is the value that people put on it (in that marginal area where the values of different commodities — or amenities — compete) that is important. People must make evaluations, and this, of course, makes economic values a function of the other values one has and thus makes it relative. When the Lord looked out on His work and saw that it was good, He enjoyed a prerogative not given to any mortal. We must always ask: Good for what? And good for whom?[6]

This leads to the second point. Different policies can be evaluated only insofar as they relate to the *same* standard of value. The policies must have a common "numeraire" (any unit of account held by two or more entities brought together for contrast) and they can have a common numeraire only insofar as they have a common property. For example, the statement "three apples plus two oranges" is meaningless. It is meaningless because it poses a relation ("plus") in terms of two different properties. However, the statement "three fruit plus two fruit" is meaningful; it means there are five fruit. Denoting some common property, the "numbers" make sense; without a common property, they do not. We shall call this the *numeraire principle* for purposes of easy reference.

The numeraire principle holds for all relations; thus, it holds for evaluations, which are relations of value. Two alternatives can be evaluated only insofar as they relate to a common standard of value.

Now, let us inspect our list of water development objectives in the

6. This line of thought could be extended to an examination of economists' peculiar (almost Freudian) horror of "passing value judgments" as though such words as "cost," "benefit," "efficiency," "optimum," and the like were purely positive, divorced of value connotations, We do not have the space to do so here, but we cite the following observation by an eminent philosopher: "A valuation of any type is always an empirical proposition. The supposition that values are *a priori* could rise only through confusion between apprehension of meaning itself and apprehension that this meaning has application in a particular instance. An apprehension of the nature of value, or of some species of value, is *a priori*; just as the apprehension of the essential nature of hardness is *a priori*: but an apprehension that something, or some kind of thing, has value, is empirical, just as the apprehension that a thing is hard is empirical. And it is only apprehensions of this latter sort which are valuations." C. J. Lewis, *An Analysis of Knowledge and Valuation* (La-Salle, Ill.: Open Court Publishing Co., 1946), p. 380.

light of this principle. The first five easily reduce to one value, namely, NNP. Thus, different projects with different mixes of objectives and different impacts on these objectives can in principle be easily evaluated; they satisfy the numeraire principle. The second list of five, however, appears to be literally a horse of a different color. To take one example: The distribution of income is not reducible to the value of NNP. Redistribution of income may increase NNP or it may decrease it. This may be considered a "benefit" or "cost" of redistribution, but there is nothing in it to tell us whether it should be done or not. That decision rests on some other value than NNP. With NNP as one value and something else, say, equity, as another, the numeraire principle is violated, and the determination of over-all "gain" becomes ambiguous.

Much of the same can be said of the other objectives in the second list. The life of a condor or of a blue whale is considered valuable in other terms than NNP. A congenial atmosphere, mental and physical, is perhaps a major ingredient of psychic wealth but not of NNP, and so on. At least that is how it appears on first inspection. We shall see if it stands up to closer analysis.

It is a fundamental assumption of economics that goods are subjectively evaluated by individuals who develop consistent preferences for various combinations of these goods. Thus, it is assumed that the individual can evaluate the marginal satisfaction (or utility) to himself of an increment of a good and compare it to the marginal satisfaction of another good and that this holds true for all conceivable goods. In brief, it is assumed that all goods are related by the *same* standard of value whatever one calls it—"utility" or "satisfaction" (or even that unknown value providing "indifference").

Now this is a very strong assumption. A few economists—a very few—are not prepared to accept it.[7] Rather, they say there are, even within an individual mind, different standards of value such that goods can be compared only within certain sets defined by a common standard of value but not across these sets. This leads to a theory of "lexi-

7. See Nicholas Georgescu-Roegen, *Analytical Economics; Issues and Problems* (Cambridge: Harvard University Press, 1966); *idem*, "Utility," *International Encyclopedia of the Social Sciences*, Vol. 16 (1968 ed.), pp. 236–267; Tapas Majumdar, *The Measurement of Utility* (London: Macmillan, St. Martin's Press, 1966); I. M. D. Little, *A Critique of Welfare Economics* (London: Oxford University Press, 1960).

cographic" ordering within the mind which, however interesting and important, would lead us too far afield here. The point can be made without going that far (although the direction is the same).

The advantages of this fundamental assumption become clearer, if we consider the mind of some person contemplating the various delectations open to him. If his means are limited, he will rationally choose that set of activities yielding him the highest utility, choosing goods in such fashion that:

$$\frac{mu_a}{p_a} = \frac{mu_b}{p_b} \quad \cdots \quad = \frac{mu_n}{p_n} \qquad (1)$$

(where $mu_a$ = marginal utility of $a$ and $p_a$ = price of $a$) will maximize his utility; that is, he will choose a combination in which the $mu$ per dollar of limited income is equal among all goods he assumes.

We now come to a very important juncture. If it were not for one thing, an economist observing the behavior of this person could conclude only that he had picked a basket of valued objects — of goods; for the economist *as an observer* has no knowledge of the numeraire this single mind employs in discriminating the value of goods comparatively. The utility, the standard of value, is strictly subjective. But if, as is assumed, the individual's "means" is in the form of money, we have an objective, that is, an observable, numeraire. Manipulation of equation (1) reveals that:

$$\frac{p_b}{p_a} = \frac{mu_b}{mu_a} \quad \cdots \quad \frac{p_n}{p_{n-1}} = \frac{mu_n}{mu_{n-1}} \qquad (1a)$$

Thus, the ratio of prices is equal to the ratio of values. We can never observe relative *values,* but we can observe relative *prices*; and, as in equation (1a), we can deduce an isomorphism between the subjective value and the objective numeraire of relative prices. We can deduce from the fact that an individual is willing to pay more for good $a$ than for good $b$ that he values $a$ more than he values $b$. Prices seem to provide a window through which we can see into the very soul of the individual.

Unfortunately, the analysis of a single individual — a Robinson

Crusoe economy—is a rather trivial exercise. An individual refers only to his own preferences and his own resources to make decisions. In a society of many individuals with different tastes and capabilities, some way must be found to organize and coordinate all these components into a reasonable whole. It is certainly one of the great feats of the human intellect to discover how, under certain conditions, the market system does just that. Prices are set by the intersection of demands and supplies. Their movement "signals" when more than one kind of good is needed and less of another kind. These signals, combined with the profit motive, cause resources to move in and out of the production of goods as demand for them fluctuates.

However, the market is subject to serious limitations; there are economic functions it cannot hope to perform. Perhaps even more serious, because it is less obvious, is the fact that there are functions it performs in an undesirable or misleading fashion. When the market fails to order economic activity in a socially desirable manner, intervention in its operation to make coreections becomes necessary. Throughout what follows below, we shall be concerned, in a broad sense, with the reasons for market failure. We shall see that continuous effort is required to keep the market responsive to the ends we wish to achieve, for it will not automatically serve these ends in their entirety. We shall also see that tuning the market to be responsive introduces some very difficult philosophical and technical problems that require substantial reorientation of the economist's role in public decision-making.

Before one can assert that the market is working well, one must be satisfied with the distribution of income prevailing at the moment. If there is an unequal distribution of income, the market transformation of subjective preferences into objective prices can break down.

As we saw above, if someone is willing to pay more for one good than for another, we can legitimately infer that he values that good more than the other. The same reasoning does not apply between two different individuals with different incomes bidding for the same good. If A is willing to pay more than B for a good, we cannot infer that he values it more. It may simply be that A has more money than B and thus values the amount of money he spends on the good less than does

B. In fact, A may value the good less than does B but be willing to pay more because he has more money to spend.[8]

The ethical implications of this are quite significant. It is one thing to say that the market system allocates goods to the highest valued uses; it is quite another thing to say that it allocates goods to the rich. The former has a certain intuitive appeal; the appeal of the latter is less obvious. This is one problem with the market system: It does not maximize consumers' preferences. Rather, it maximizes consumers' demands — the amount consumers are ready, willing, and able to pay.

But even if we neglect the problem of income distribution (as is usual), the virtue of serving consumers' preferences is not beyond question. Indeed, it is somewhat belatedly becoming recognized, even among economists, that beyond a certain long-since-exceeded "subsistence" level of consumption, preferences are largely constructed in a particular cultural milieu — and of advertisers and others who manipulate preferences.[9]

For example, in an age such as ours, where people are very conscious of their status, very "upward bound," quite insecure about whatever pittance of status they currently enjoy, a major part of economic activity will be devoted to creating symbols of status sufficiently expensive to impress the Joneses. Of course, once such a trophy is acquired, the neighbors are frightened into acquiring something equally, if not more, impressive to keep the usurper in his place. So long as a person's state of contentment is based on his *relative position* vis-à-vis his neighbors, not on his *level* of satisfaction from the consumption of goods, there is no discernible limit to the amount of consumption "necessary." Of course, with each upward turn of sprialing

8. David W. Seckler, "On the Uses and Abuses of Economics in Evaluating Outdoor Recreation," *Land Economics,* Vol. XLII, No. 4 (October 1966), pp. 485–495; also, *idem,* "Analytical Issues in Demand Analysis for Outdoor Recreation: Comment," *American Journal of Agricultural Economics,* Vol. 50, No. 1 (February 1968), pp. 147–150, and the references cited therein.

9. "The problem of a democratic society is not only the problem of creating social choice from individual preferences, it is also the problem of ascribing preferences by means of the most objective means available. We all know how a public can be made to believe that it prefers certain states of affairs; the social problem is to create valid sets of preferences"; see C. W. Churchman, "On the Intercomparison of Utilities," in *The Structure of Economic Science,* Sherman Krupp, ed. (Englewood Cliffs, N.J.: Prentice-Hall, 1966), p. 255.

expenditures, the degree of discontent remains the same. It simply becomes more expensive to maintain it.[10]

If we accept consumers' demands as the appropriate criterion of value, the market system does not always perform well. If certain conditions are present, the system will go awry and lead the production and allocation of goods away from maximizing consumers' demands.

The market system is, in essence, individualistic. Of course, it ties the constituent elements — consumers and producers — together in a system; but these components must be related only by market relations. If they are related in any other way, the market itself is led astray. This type of market failure is a highly technical subject that we cannot hope to treat adequately here. We shall simply discuss two of the more frequent species of such failures.[11]

*Externalities:* These, sometimes also called "spillover effects," occur when production or consumption by A affects the welfare of B either positively or negatively, and no compensation is made. That is, no price is paid for the spillover. For example, A's automobile creates noise and air pollution affecting B's welfare, yet A does not pay B for the costs he incurs. As an example of an external benefit, let us suppose that A so orders the land he owns as to provide an aesthetically pleasing landscape from which B benefits without paying A for his enjoyment. In either case, social costs and social benefits are not equated, and either too much or too little of the good producing the externality is provided.

*Collective Goods:* Some goods are consumed collectively rather than competitively. Over a range of use (which may or may not be limitless), the addition of one more consumer of a good does not reduce the amount of that good available to any other consumer. Thus, for example, the national defense "umbrella" of the United States can (under suitable assumptions) equally serve 100 million or 200 million citizens at no additional cost. For economic efficiency to prevail, prices of goods must equal their marginal cost. In the case of pure collective goods, such as national defense, marginal cost of consumption is zero. Therefore, the economically efficient price is also zero. But if one

10. The classic analysis of all this is, of course, Thorstein Veblen, *The Theory of the Leisure Class* (New York: Viking, 1931).

11. Francis M. Bator, "The Anatomy of Market Failure," *Quarterly Journal of Economics,* Vol. LXXII (1968).

charges a zero price, then, obviously, any firm providing this good would have zero revenue. This establishes the prima facie case for public firms in the case of collective goods.

Other examples of collective goods are highways, bridges, national parks, zoos, museums, and natural "wonders." All are collective goods over a range of use (which does not involve congestion effects). They may have a small marginal cost of consumption but not enough to worry about over this range.

Two very interesting types of collective goods are "option' goods[12] and "existence" goods. An option good is a good like, say, the Grand Canyon. Though a person (for example, an eastern city-dweller) might feel that his chances of visiting this world-famous area are remote, yet he might be willing to pay a considerable sum of money if he had to, simply to keep the "option" of visiting it at some vague time in the future. An existence good sounds as if it could be the same thing, but it is in actuality very different. A farmer in Iowa may *know* that he will never see a blue whale but be willing to pay simply to assure its continued existence. Or he may never even want to see a whooping crane but be willing to pay to preserve it from extinction — to know it exists.

The market tends to underestimate the value of collective goods, because the real, effective demand is less than the sum of the effective demands and the "collective" demands. Because they are collective goods, it is difficult to force payment, to transform all demand into effective demand: "let someone else do it." But as we have seen, it is also economically inefficient to force payment through the market system because this would limit the derived benefits to a less than optimal amount.

Finally, there are certain economic goods — goods, that is, which involve the allocation of scarce resources between competing ends — which are beyond the pale of mere preferences. These are goods which entail ethical choices. Thus, consumption of heroin is prohibited even though there is strong effective demand for its use. Children are made to go to school even though there are strong preferences to other alternatives not only on their part but sometimes on the part of their parents. It is illegal to purchase another's life or death. We expressly

12. Burton A. Weisbrod, "Collective-Consumption Services of Individual-Consumption Goods," *Quarterly Journal of Economics,* Vol. LXXXIII (1964), pp. 471–477.

forbid the services of the courts and of public officials to be allocated by market processes.

Further, we attempt to keep the poor from falling so low that they actually die of privation. The distribution of income is itself an issue of this nature. A very powerful, though until recently somewhat neglected, moral sentiment is the responsibility of the present generation to future generations. It is apparent that feelings of moral responsibility are extended to animals other than humans and even to the inanimate world. The slaughter of animals in an inhumane way or to the point of extinction or the destruction of trees and biological ecosystems excites moral outrage.

Of course, all this can be rationalized in the conventional terms of economic analysis. One gives to the poor, for example, because charity is the highest valued good one can buy at that moment — or some such argument. But a little reflection reveals that such rationalization is hardly valid. It is exactly the conflict between economic and moral values that makes Swift's solution to the Irish potato famine so shocking: Feed the very old and the very young people to the more productive middle ages.[13] Or take another example: Say a man's homestead is to be flooded by a dam. He is offered reasonable compensation, even unreasonably high compensation, and refuses. He may refuse any price. On what ethical basis does one settle this conflict?

Finally, ethical decisions are sometimes necessary to settle the questions of risk and uncertainty that inevitably surround large-scale projects. How safe should a dam be? What are the minimal acceptable levels of risk associated with nuclear desalination operations? If we do not know, for example, the effects of Delta diversions on San Francisco Bay hydrology and, thus, on the life of the people in the Bay area, what essentially moral requirements must be met?

It is a rare water development project that does not contain all these problems. Typically, it creates certain market goods; it also has significant income distribution effects. Water, by its very nature, is rife with externalities, and working with it almost always brings up difficult ethical problems of the kind mentioned. Obviously, there is no

13. Nor can this moral dilemma be explained away on grounds of "the invalidity of interpersonal comparisons of utility." Even the compensation test would fail — that is, we would not consider Swift's program feasible even if the young and the old were willing to sell themselves for these purposes.

price, real or imputed, that can be used to appraise all these different welfare effects of a typical water project. They are not reducible to terms of a common numeraire. What do we do now? Do we simply throw up our hands and say:

> Let the long contention cease!
> Geese are swans, and swans are geese.
> Let them have it how they will!
> Thou art tired; best be still.[14]

Not yet.

## EVALUATION

Our basic thesis is that, during the age of scarcity, the overriding objective of water resource projects was to maximize the production of commodities. Now, however, in the age of affluence, other objectives, such as the redistribution of income and the protection or creation of amenities, have also become important. If we define the "welfare" set as the set of all objectives served by a particular project, we can say that previously the welfare set had, for all practical purposes, but one major objective; it was unidimensional. Now it has many; it is multidimensional. Let us here outline the kind of methodology appropriate to evaluation in terms of a multidimensional welfare set.

We shall begin with an example from the business community, which always seems more down-to-earth than formulations in the area of social welfare. Some time back, economic consultants to large business firms found themselves, to their surprise, in basically the same perplexities as resource economists are beginning to find themselves today.[15]

They began their work by creating a model of the production processes of the firm and the markets it confronted and derived a profit-maximizing solution. When the plan was duly presented to the managers of the firm, it created a good deal of confusion. The managers could not understand what was going on. One thing they could understand: If they followed the program recommended by their consultants,

---

14. Matthew Arnold, "The Last Word," cited in D. H. Robertson, "On Sticking to One's Last," *Utility and All That* (New York: Macmillan, 1952).

15. For Example, see W. J. Baumol, *Business Behavior, Value and Growth* (New York: Macmillan, 1959).

the results would be highly undesirable if not disastrous, not only to the firm but also, and perhaps more immediately important, to their own careers. Extended conversations between management and consultants led to discovery of where the essential problem lay. It turned out that these firms were not solely—or even mainly—interested in maximization of profits. They had other equally important objectives they needed to satisfy. They wanted to grow in terms of sales; they wanted to protect their share of the market, to maintain the value of their stock, to promote a benign corporate image, to keep the government off their backs and labor content, and, especially, to keep the votes of their stockholders. Some of these objectives were complementary, some competitive; none was reducible to the single objective of profit maximization, even in the very long run. In a word, they were operating in a multidimensional welfare set.

The example is worth pursuing a bit further. Figure 16.2(a) presents the ordinary model of the large firm under conditions of monopoly. Assume that the firm has two objectives: to make a profit, and to increase sales. If it were indifferent to sales and wished only to maximize profits, it would set prices at $P$ and sell a restricted quantity of product $Q$. However, since it is also interested in sales, it may lower the price to $P'$ in order to increase sales to $Q'$. In this case, considerably less profit, indicated by the crosshatched area, is achieved. (We are neglecting other strategies, such as maximizing profits and devoting all profits above a certain minimum to advertising to increase sales.)

In Figure 16.2(b) we have drawn the transformation curve $T$ between profits and sales. Up to the point $Q$ of sales, the two objectives are complementary—the more sales, the more profits. After $Q$, they are competitive—one objective must be sacrificed to get more of the other.

In Figure 16.2(c) we have extracted the competitive region of Figure 2(b), the space to the right of $Q$, and inflated it for easy exposition. This space we shall call the "decision space," because it is here that choices must be made between the competing objectives. (A cardinal function of good planning is to design systems that are most complementary in objectives—in other words, to minimize the decision space.) The curves $V$ and $V'$ are "value curves" or indifference curves, the slopes of which indicate the relative values of the two objectives, profits and sales. (The two curves indicate two different sets of evalua-

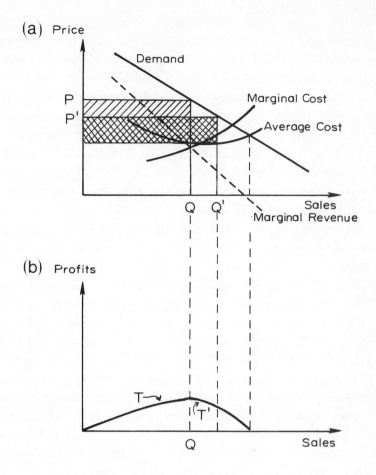

(a) Price

Demand

Marginal Cost

Average Cost

P

P'

Sales

Q   Q'

Marginal Revenue

(b) Profits

T⤳

I(T'

Q   Sales

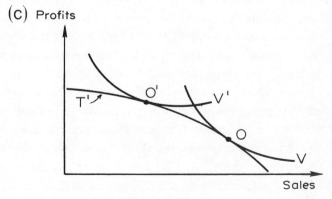

(c) Profits

T'↗

O'

V'

O

V

Sales

FIGURE 16.2

tions.) They are convex to the origin because of the diminishing marginal value of greater satisfaction of each objective. Given the transformation curve $T$ and a value curve $V$ (or $V'$), the optimum mix of profits and sales is found at the point of tangency $O$ (or $O'$).

The moral of the story is clear: In acting as consultant for a firm that entertains multidimensional welfare sets, the economist cannot, in principle, specify the "correct" combination of objectives and their factors. He cannot do so because he does not have access to the crucial information necessary to such specification—the relative values of the objectives, $V$ or $V'$. These values are in the head of the decision maker, and only he can decide the correct combination.

Exactly the same analysis applies to the role of the economist in water resources decision-making. As long as he confronts a multi-dimensional welfare set, he must resign himself to the humble role of adviser. He cannot optimize, because the information necessary to define the optimum—the relative values—is, in principle, subjective. This information is available only to the decision maker, the "superman," who within his single brain combines transformations and values into the necessary grand synthesis, for better or for worse. Here exists the true interface between the two realms of social choice: economics and politics. The economic side is the transformation curve, the trade-off function between competing objectives in the decision space. The political side is the relative values of the objectives, the value curves themselves.

Lest this process be regarded as some kind of mystical and holy union between "expert" and "official," private or public, we hasten to add that, in public-policy questions, the ultimate decision maker is the public. Thus, in this methodology it is not only consistent, it is method-ologically imperative, that the expert bring his work to the people, to go out on the stump. Further, since nothing is purely "objective" in policy questions (for values always influence analysis), it is proper for the expert to attempt to explain what values he has used, that is to say, to show whatever "decision maker" he is addressing what his values are. This demonstration is necessary so that the decision maker may know, through empathy, if he can "trust" the expert's analysis. A good way to communicate values is through dialogue or, less euphe-mistically, argument. Contrary to the usual opinion that the expert should not be "controversial" or an "advocate," we reach the conclusion that, because of value-communication requirements, he must often be so to be objective, that is, he must lay open to observer both his analysis and the values that have influenced it. Candor and honesty are the best assurance of objectivity.

This method of evaluation is commonly known as cost effectiveness. It has several advantages over benefit-cost, one of the most important being that it does not depend upon numeral estimates of either costs or benefits. It therefore permits escape from such absurdities as estimating the "economic value" of a human life. Furthermore, the analyst does not have to pretend to know the numerical value of a day's fishing or of a tree. As someone said, "We have heard so often that you cannot quantify beauty that we tend to forget that you really cannot quantify beauty." Of course, no one denies that you can put a number on anything. The question is: Does that number lead to the kind of choices we wish to make? We think not. Too often, economists, in their zeal to find the market value of amenities, end up like Oscar Wilde's cynic, knowing the price of everything and the value of nothing.

Cost effectiveness requires candor — where nothing is known, it is perfectly all right to say so. This is, indeed, a vital element of decision-making. It leads, for one thing, to a certain salutary caution on the part of the decision maker.

More precisely, the outcome of good economic analysis in water resources should be an assessment of the impact of $n$ alternative designs on $m$ number of objectives. The economist's function is to fill in the cells of the decision tableau of Figure 16.3, each vertical column representing an objective and each horizontal row a number of alternatives.

In the construction of a decision tableau, many of the original objectives can be collapsed into a common numeraire. Thus, as noted previously, some objectives in water resources evaluation (the first five listed earlier) reduce to assessment in terms of contributions to Net National Product. Other objectives, for which the criterion of consumers' demand is relevant but for which no prices exist, can also be reduced to this numeraire through simulation of the market or derivation of imputed prices. For example, some people believe outdoor recreation is "a good like any other good" and should so be evaluated;

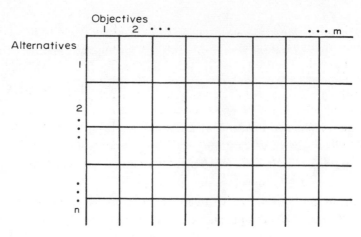

Objectives

Alternatives

FIGURE 16.3.

others — the present writers among them — think not. We might have a column in Figure 3 indicating the relative impacts of $n$ alternatives in terms of the objective of commodity value. But, then, we should need another column assessing the impact of these objectives on the distribution of income or recreation/aesthetic benefits. Perhaps we shall need an ethical column. We shall also need a risk-uncertainty statement for every cell, indicating degree of confidence in the estimate. We may wish to use numbers in the cells or simply words — "fair," "good," "vague," "unknown," "fantastic," or whatever — depending on communication requirements. The important thing is this: In a decision tableau, the outsider can evaluate a *column* — we are using the same standard of value; but only the decision maker can make the over-all evaluation — the *row* evaluations.

Thus, our conception of evaluation is quite different from that of those who employ benefit-cost. They think in terms of dollar values of commodities; the outcome of their analysis is a ratio specifying the dollar value of benefits to the dollar value of costs. The greater this ratio, the better the project. We, on the other hand, consider these dollar relations merely a part of the evaluation process. That dollar benefits exceed dollar costs is neither a necessary nor a sufficient condition in appraising the desirability of projects. Other nondollar, essentially subjective values are always present, and they must be included in the analysis. Without this we come to the kind of vulgar pragmatism described by Abraham Kaplan:

To the ideal of success vulgar pragmatism also adds the ideal of efficiency, the most economic adaptation of available means to given ends. The vulgarization lies in the narrowness with which both means and ends are conceived. Economy implies the conservation of some values whose expenditure is required to achieve others. It becomes a false economy, a mere show of efficiency, when important called human values which are the domain of morality. It characterizes the efficiency on which the fascist states prided themselves: the trains to the gas chamber ran on schedule.[16]

## EVALUATION PROBLEMS IN THE STATE WATER PROJECT

We come at last to the State Water Project, which we can now consider in light of the preceding analysis. The problem is difficult precisely because it involves a multidimensional welfare set. To demonstrate, let us assume that the following are true. First, it is desirable that southern and central California grow in urban population and agricultural output and that water use in that area is at maximum efficiency; and the only way to achieve this desirable result is to supply more water to the region. Second, all known technologies of desalination, groundwater management, etc., are being exploited to their maximum or are relatively too expensive. Last, there exists in the Sacramento Delta-San Francisco Bay region an absolute surplus of water in large quantities serving no use, simply "wasting to sea." Under these assumptions, one could simply perform a benefit-cost analysis on the benefits of southern expansion and the costs of transporting the water through the aqueduct — and arrive at a rather clear-cut, if computationally difficult, decision.

But several basic problems arise as the assumptions are relaxed. To mention only a few: there is no unanimity of opinion on whether further growth or urban population in the south is "good" or "bad" in terms of any standard of value; nor is it clear that agricultural output should be expanded at all. And even if agriculture should be expanded, many object to expansion via large corporate farms and find deplorable

16. Abraham Kaplan, *American Ethics and Public Policy* (New York: Oxford University Press, 1963), p. 37.

the distribution of income consequent to the State Water Plan's serving large landowners.

Now we turn to the Bay-Delta. Enormous uncertainty surrounds the problem of the value of freshwater flows through this area. This uncertainty stems from two sources. First, no one knows precisely what this water does in physical terms. Second, even if this were known, the value of the water in flushing the Bay, preserving wildlife habitats, and performing other ecological functions is subject to debate.

What is known is that, if California and the U.S. Bureau of Reclamation withdraw water in the quantities they contemplate, some time in the near future Delta-Bay inputs of freshwater will have to be augmented by further diversions from the north. And in this cycle, again, the physical-ecological implications of these diversions are not known and, if they were known, there would be no unanimity on their relative values.

In sum, the decision tableau of this vast, complex, and highly integrated system called the State Water Plan is not specified. Even if it were specified, there is no way to evaluate that system objectively. The only conceivable way to make an evaluation is to turn to the subjective preferences of the people, putting it to the vote either directly or through the evaluation of their elected representatives. One fact regarding the State Water Plan is, however, absolutely clear. Neither the public nor their elected representatives have been given the opportunity to evaluate this plan properly. They have not been properly informed of the alternatives to and the consequences of the Plan. Instead, they have been presented with a singular plan of north-south diversions of water as though this were the only feasible approach to the problem. This is contrary to the spirit and meaning of cost-effectiveness. The decision maker must be informed of all the feasible alternatives and the consequences they entail. Without this, it is impossible to make rational decisions.

## Conclusion

Economists tend to neglect the fact that there are not one but two great mechanisms of social choice. Both the market system and the political process convey information about individual evaluations.

Individuals vote for a political decision maker; they presumably do so because they trust his judgment. They vote, in a word, for his subjective evaluations, because his evaluations seem to correspond to their own. This may be called the method of representative empathy. There are, of course, many inadequacies in the political process, but it is not at all clear that this process is more inadequate than the market process. It is always dangerous to compare "model" with "muddle," and it is particularly dangerous to compare an ideal economic model based on a perfectly rational consumer and a perfectly competitive market with a political muddle of corrupt politicians and an irrational and misinformed electorate. Whatever the real merits of the political system are, it is the only means we have of making social choices in a multidimensional welfare set.[17] If the political system does not perform well, it must be adjusted or changed. Either repair the system itself or "kick the rascals out." That is all we can do.

17. We can do no better than repeat some advice Sir Dennis Robertson gave to his fellow economists and to those who must listen to them in a presidential address to the Royal Economic Society in 1947. The address was appropriately entitled "On Sticking to One's Last."

"You will see that my ambitions for my profession are not quite so exalted as my predecessor's. I do not want the economist to mount the pulpit or expect him to fit himself to handle the keys of Heaven and Hell. I want him to be rather brave and rather persistent in hammering in those results achieved within his own domain about which he feels reasonably confident, not too readily reduced to silence by the plea that this, that or the other is ruled out of court by custom, or justice, or the temper of the age. But in the last resort I want him, too, to be rather humble — humbler than some of his great predecessors were disposed to be — content to bow to the judgment of the prophets or even the men of affairs if he is convinced that his case has been properly understood and fairly weighed. In fine, I like to think of him as a sort of Good Dog Tray rather than as a Priest forever after the Order of Melchizedek." Robertson, *op. cit.,* pp. 64, 65.

# APPENDIX

GORDON C. RAUSSER AND GERALD W. DEAN

This appendix is written for the somewhat more technically trained reader who wishes to work toward some operational concepts and tools of decision-making under uncertainty in the water resources field. However, the treatment is intended to be understood by the intelligent layman who wishes to invest a little time in further study. For the professional economist, the appendix is likely to serve primarily as a review and illustration of several more or less well-known concepts, together with references to more sophisticated literature on the various topics.

The limitations of the traditional methods of dealing with uncertainty in problems associated with water resource planning have been recognized for some time.[1] In recent years, considerable effort in the fields of management science and quantitative economics has been devoted to developing improved techniques of analysis under conditions of uncertainty.[2] Operationally, for purposes of water resource

1. A. Maass, M. M. Hufschmidt, R. Dorfman, H. A. Thomas, S. A. Marglin, and G. M. Fair, *Design of Water Resource Systems* (Cambridge, Mass.: Harvard University Press, 1962), pp. 129–158, 273–278.
2. See R. Bellman, *Adaptive Control Processes* (Princeton, N. J.: Princeton University Press, 1961); D. E. Farrar, *The Investment Decision Under Uncertainty* (Englewood Cliffs, N.J.: Prentice-Hall, 1962); K. A. Fox, J. K. Sengupta, and E. Thorbecke, *The Theory of Quantitative Economic Policy* (Amsterdam: North-Holland Publishing Co., 1966), chapter 9, and the references cited therein; D. B. Hertz, "Risk Analysis in Capital Investment," *Harvard Business Review,* 42 (January-February 1964), 95–106; F. S. Hillier, "The Derivation of Probabilistic Information for the Evaluation of Risky Investments," *Management Science,* 9 (1963), 443–457; C. C. Holt, F. Modigliani, J. F. Muth, and H. A. Simon, *Planning Production, Inventories and Work Force* (Englewood Cliffs, N.J.: Prentice-Hall, 1960); A. Madansky, "Linear Programming Under Uncertainty," in *Recent Advances in Mathematical Programming,* R. L. Graves and P. Wolfe, eds. (New York: McGraw-Hill, 1963); J. F. Magee, "How to Use Decision Trees in Capital Investment." *Harvard Business Review,* 42 (September-October 1964), 79–96; H. Raiffa and R. Schlaifer, *Applied Statistical Decision Theory* (Boston: Harvard University, 1961); J. K. Sengrupta, G. Tintner, and C. Millham, "On Some Theorems of Stochastic Linear Programming with Applications," *Management Science,* 10 (October 1963), 143–159.

planning and decisions, the most promising of these techniques involves the direct utilization of probability theory and computer analysis.

As previously noted, the likelihood that all "best estimates" in an analysis will prove to be exactly accurate is extremely small. Since it is the joint effect of variation in all components of supply and demand that will determine a decision's outcome, an analysis technique is required that can allow for this more complex variation. Such a technique must explicitly employ probability theory. Operationally, this involves not only estimating a range of values for each of the most important factors affecting a decision's outcome, but establishing probabilities of occurrence for each of the intervals within that range. The question of dependence or correlation among factors must also be recognized.

Seldom is there sufficient evidence to estimate probability distributions entirely from historical records, experiments, econometric analysis, or other frequency evidence. In some situations, frequency evidence providing the likelihood of occurrence for some factors does exist and is readily available. More often, objective data must be supplemented with expert judgment in order to determine the desired probability distributions. When subjective elements enter the analysis we obtain "subjective" rather than "objective" probability distributions for the various factors. These probability distributions may be based, of course, on "more" or "less" frequency evidence and in this sense might be labeled "more" or "less" subjective.[3] For decision purposes, however, it makes little difference whether an outcome is "known" in terms of a more subjective or a more objective probability distribution.[4]

The approach suggested above differs from the traditional approach in that judgmental elements explicitly enter the underlying assumptions rather than being applied to the final results of the analysis. The subjective probabilities reflect the degree of confidence which an investigator has in the estimates that fall in his area of ex-

3. The amount of frequency evidence that ought to be collected and utilized in the analysis is itself a decision problem. These questions are treated more formally by F. Modigliani and K. F. Cohen, *The Role of Anticipations and Plans in Economic Behavior and Their Use in Economic Analysis and Forecasting* (Urbana: University of Illinois Bulletin, 1961).

4. See S. Reutlinger, "Techniques for Project Appraisal Under Uncertainty," International Bank for Reconstruction and Development Report No. EC-169, August 1968, for a rather complete development of this point.

pertise. No matter how "objective" or "subjective" these probability distributions might be, they illustrate precisely what is unknown as well as what is known regarding a factor's future value. Further, based on the best information available, the *degree* of imperfect knowledge is quantified in the form of probability statements. Such probabilities are introduced in an attempt to "represent ignorance." In contrast to those approaches which consider only the "best estimates," the use of these probability distributions allows a more complete analysis of each decision alternative. In conjunction with the computer, which is employed to enumerate the probable performance outcomes resulting from the combinations of the relevant factors, this approach gives the decision makers a more precise assessment of the risk that may be associated with each decision alternative.

A major result of the R and D philosophy discussed generally in the chapter is that water resource problems should be solved sequentially. The ideas of learning, flexibility, and parallel developments all recognize the fact that one can gain information through time and that "better" decisions can be made on the basis of the additional knowledge gained. Thus, the appropriate conceptual framework for most long-term water resource development problems is sequential or multistage decision-making under uncertainty. However, the concepts and tools needed are more easily illustrated by considering first the single-stage problem which is presented in the following section. The final section of the appendix shows that the multistage problem can be solved by natural extensions of the single-stage problem.

## SINGLE-STAGE DECISION PROBLEMS: BAYESIAN ANALYSIS

The elements of a single-stage decision problem are actions, states, payoffs, probability distributions, and a criterion of choice. These elements are easily illustrated in the following $3 \times 3$ decision table. The decision maker is to choose among three options, or actions, $a_1$, $a_2$, $a_3$. For each action there are three possible states of nature, $\theta_1$, $\theta_2$, $\theta_3$ (for example, recession, stability, or growth in the economy). A given action results in three different outcomes or payoffs (say, net benefits in dollars) depending on which state of nature occurs. The decision maker assigns a probability (objective or subjective) to each

TABLE A.1.
*Decision Table*

| States of Nature | Actions | | | Probabilities $P(\theta_i)$ |
|---|---|---|---|---|
| | $a_1$ | $a_2$ | $a_3$ | |
| | | (payoffs) | | |
| $\theta_1$ | $10 | $20 | $30 | 0.4 |
| $\theta_2$ | 20 | 20 | 25 | 0.4 |
| $\theta_3$ | 30 | 20 | 20 | 0.2 |
| Criterion (Max EMV) | $18 | $20 | $26 | $\Sigma = 1.0$ |

state of nature. Given this information, we need to specify a choice criterion, or measure of performance. In our example, let us assume that the choice criterion is to maximize the long-run average net benefits, that is, the expected monetary value (EMV) of net benefits or weighted average net benefits.[5] Clearly action $a_3$ should be chosen, since it provides an expected value of $26, compared with only $18 for action $a_1$ and $20 for action $a_2$.

With this brief introduction, let us examine these components in more detail.

*Actions (controllable variables) and states of nature (uncontrollable variables):* In any decision analysis, the factors or variables that enter the problem may be typically classified into two major categories: those factors that are external, or are part of the environment in which decision makers must operate, referred to as uncontrollable factors (states of nature), and those that are internal to the development project, referred to as controllable factors (decision variables, or actions). In water resource planning, the demands for water — agricultural, urban, aesthetic, and recreational — and their associated uncertainties fall largely in the uncontrollable category. This results from the fact that the factors influencing demand — weather and its effects on the hydrologic cycle, population growth, the distribution of

5. For example, for action $a_1$ the expected monetary value (EMV) is $18, calculated as follows: ($10 × 0.4) + ($20 × 0.4) + ($30 × 0.2). Many criteria have been suggested to solve problems of this type. However, the expected value criterion (in monetary or utility terms) has been demonstrated to be the only "correct" criterion and includes all others as special cases. See H. Raiffa, *Decision Analysis: Introductory Lectures on Choices Under Uncertainty* (Reading, Mass.: Addison-Wesley, 1968).

population in the area, income levels and distribution, prices, among others—fall largely outside the control of resource planners.

In addition to the uncontrollable demand components, a number of other uncontrollable or external factors should be included in any analysis of alternative water resource designs. For example, those factors related to secondary and external benefits (or costs) should be specified; such factors include the subjective probability distributions in future periods of the existence of unemployed labor, unused capacity, the mobility of labor and capital, land use, useful life of facilities, ecological benefits or costs, and the like.[6] Admittedly, these factors are more difficult to measure than the demand components mentioned above; nevertheless, a respectable analysis of alternative decisions requires their consideration no matter how imprecise our knowledge with respect to measures of these factors. This argument becomes more valid once we recognize the possibility of revising existing information as the future unfolds, and thus revising existing plans.

The question of whether a given factor is controllable or uncontrollable depends critically upon the scope of activity of the public agency making the decisions. If, to take an example, the public agency has responsibility only for transporting and storing natural fresh water, the decision set is quite limited, for it relates to a single dimension of the alternative sources of water supply. Specifically, the factors subject to control revolve around the construction of facilities for water transfer and storage systems (the capital investment) and the operation of the project once it is constructed. In this event, waste-water reclamation, desalting sea water, assisting nature to increase water supplies, and management of underground water supplies fall outside the decision maker's control.

The above framework represents a rather narrow view of the control exercised by public agencies. Public agencies, of one sort or another, are directly concerned with and in large part control the future development of all the major dimensions of water supply. As noted above, groundwater utilization can be effectively managed only on a basin-wide level. This requires the establishment of a management agency to avoid the misuse, abuse, and nonuse of ground water. Moreover, the technological uncertainties associated with waste-water

6. Some of these are, of course, indirectly related to the demand components.

reclamation and desalting sea water suggest that public investment in these fields will most likely represent a major input (perhaps in association with private investment) if success is to be achieved within the near future. In the field of increasing natural water supplies, the discrepancy between private and social costs and returns suggests heavy public-sector involvement. Thus, a comprehensive analysis of public decisions in the development of alternative water resource systems would put most of the major dimensions of water supply under the heading of controllable.[7] This view is in sharp contrast to the current California Water Plan, which is primarily concerned with only a single aspect of water-supply control.

*Payoffs or net benefit calculations (relationships between controllable and uncontrollable variables):* Once the controllable variables (actions) and uncontrollable variables (states) are identified, the payoff or outcome from each action-state pair must be calculated. The following diagram (Figure A.1) illustrates three simple functional relationships relating actions to states; for example, action $a_1$ has three possible payoffs (A, B, or C) depending on whether the state of nature is $\theta_1$, $\theta_2$, or $\theta_3$. Of course, the functional relations may be quite complex and the payoffs may have several dimensions (as will be illustrated in the example below). Also, the usual concern with appropriate measures of benefits, length of planning horizon, discount rates, and so forth, must be faced in the payoff calculations. However, instead of calculating a single "best estimate" of benefits, a different value is calculated for each action-state pair.

The above simplified framework suggests that the cause-effect (stochastic) relationships among the controllable and uncontrollable factors must be specified and incorporated into the decision analysis. These relationships, typically stated as a mathematical model, are based partly on what historical information exists and partly on a priori information or expert opinion.[8] Thus, these relationships are,

7. To reemphasize, by "controllable" we mean that the agency can influence outcomes by its decision (action). This does not mean that the outcome is "certain"; the probabilities of various states of nature may simply change.

8. Formally, this involves statistically estimating the parameters entering each of the algebraic relationships included in the model on the basis of both sample and prior information.

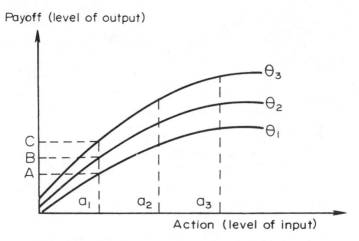

FIGURE A.1. Action-Payoff Relationships.

as are the probability distributions typifying uncertainty, more subjective or less subjective. As the future unfolds, these relationships can
and should be revised on the basis of additional information.

In addition, both the short- and the long-run effects of controllable
variables on external factors should be included (dynamic specification
of the relationships). The importance of such specification can be illustrated by a few examples. A particular water resource design and pricing policy may lead to a rapid development of agricultural land in the
short run which, however, may be phased out of existence in the long
run because of the adverse effects of larger supplies on firm profits.
Again, it is possible for a particular water resource design to remain
viable in the short run, but nevertheless to become less attractive in
the long run because it facilitates rapid population expansion and concentration in a particular metropolitan area. The undesirable effect in
the long run could well be pollution and other environmental anoma-
lies associated with heavily concentrated urban areas.

*Probability distributions over the states of nature:* For each possible action (such as alternative budgets and schedules of construction
in a water resource system), we desire to derive the probability distribution of performance outcomes (payoffs).[9] Essentially, this involves
defining the states and payoffs as above, and then attaching probabilities to the states of nature. Probability distributions generally fall into

9. One could just as well fix some of the performance outcomes and derive the probability distributions of costs and time required to achieve this outcome. The choice of
representation clearly depends upon the situation.

one or two important classes—discrete and continuous.[10] Quite frequently, both types of probability distributions will enter a single
analysis. An attempt to estimate these probabilities for a water resource project clearly requires the knowledge of many disciplines, such
as agronomy, ecology, economics, law, engineering, demography,
geology, hydrology, political science, physics, sociology, and statistics.
The probabilistic approach, by its very nature, forces different experts
to collaborate and interact in preparation of projections or forecasts.[11]

The actual estimation of probability distributions does not necessarily require advanced training in probability theory.[12] In some cases,
it might involve nothing more than stating explicitly the information
that experts have been using all along in making their projections.
For instance, econometric estimates of parameters such as price and
income elasticities also include variances of the estimates, which allow
derivation of the probability distributions of the parameters. In still
other cases, a formal statistical "best" estimate of the probability distribution of an event is neither available nor relevant, for example, the
case of desalination technology. Under these circumstances, the analysis best proceeds[13] by first isolating the limits of the range for a factor's

10. More formally, a random variable that can assume only a finite or countably infi-
nite set of different values is called a discrete random variable, and its distribution is
said to be a discrete distribution in the space of values. Such a distribution is characterized by the assignment of probabilities to all individual values within the set of possible
values, and thus is represented by a function that contains jumps of nonzero amounts at
least at one of the possible values; between possible values, the function is constant. A
random variable and the corresponding distribution are called continuous if the distribution function is continuous and has a derivative at each point, with the possible exception of a finite number of points. In contrast to a discrete distribution, if the distribution
function of a random variable is a continuous function, no single value can have a nonzero probability since a continuous function has no jumps. For a lucid description of the
various forms of discrete and continuous distributions, see A. M. Mood and F. A. Gray-
bill, *Introduction to the Theory of Statistics* (New York: McGraw-Hill, 1963).

11. For a short, interesting discourse on the management of a multidisciplinary
research project, see H. R. Hamilton, S. E. Goldstone, J. M. Milliman, A. L. Pugh, E. B.
Roberts, and A. Zellner, *Systems Simulation for Regional Analysis: An Application to
River Basin Planning* (Cambridge, Mass.: The M.I.T. Press, 1969).

12. Familiarity with the conditions to be satisfied (probability axioms) for some function F(X) to define probabilities should prove useful. These are (1) $0 < F(X) \le 1$; (2)
$F(-\infty) = 0$, $F(\infty) = 1$; (3) $F(X) \le F(Y)$, whenever $X \le Y$; and (4) $\lim_{y \to x^t} F(Y) = F(X)$.

13. For similar views, see Hertz, *op. cit.*; D. G. Malcolm, J. H. Roseboom, and C. E.
Clark, "Application of a Technique for Research and Development Program Evaluation,"
*Operations Research,* 7 (1959), 646–669; T. H. Norton, "On Subjective Probabilities,"
*Chemical Engineering Progress, Symposium Series,* 59 (1963), 49–54; Reutlinger,
*op. cit.*; and B. Wagle, "A Statistical Analysis of Risk in Capital Investment Projects,"
*Operational Research Quarterly,* 18 (March 1967), 13–33.

possible values. These limits on the range of possible outcomes of the event are determined on the basis of historical or other comparable data and experts' collective experience with the event under similar circumstances. The limits selected typically exclude extremely improbable values (such as one chance in fifty or 0.02 probability). The next step is simply to divide the range between extremes into segments or subranges (typically 3 to 5 values each). Finally, each subrange is assigned a probability by (1) ranking the segments on the basis of "more" or "less" likely, and (2) determining the relative magnitudes to be assigned to these likelihoods, such that the sum of the weights equals unity.[14] This process is repeated for each relevant factor for which a formal statistical estimate of the probability distribution is unavailable or irrelevant. In practice, only the most important variables affecting the outcomes need to be treated in a probabilistic framework. The selection of which variables are "most important" is often a priori, or it can be identified by some preliminary sensitivity calculations.

It should be noted that, in some cases, it may be satisfactory to estimate the range that encompasses all likely outcomes and then, on the basis of prior knowledge concerning the form of distribution of the (random) factor in question, directly derive estimates of the parameters for the specific distribution desired.[15] Regardless of method, one of the main points to be stressed is that "it is desirable to avoid 'coloring' these probability judgments by risk preference or risk aversion considerations" (Reutlinger, op. cit., p. 11). Such a possibility appears less likely, using the above approach, than in the case where the investigator is required to summarize a projection of a particular event in terms of a single unique number (presumably the "most likely" value). In this latter traditional procedure, the investigator must disregard much of his knowledge about the event. Moreover, realizing

14. The probability assignment often proceeds by a sequential self-questioning process. For example, what are the chances of a particular subrange of values occurring: 1 chance in 5? 1 in 10? 1 in 20? The resulting probabilities are assigned to a point estimate which is representative in the subrange in question (for example, the mean or midpoint). In this case, of course, the estimated probability distribution is discrete.

15. To illustrate, suppose a beta distribution is logically expected. The mean and standard deviation can then be estimated quite simply by requesting from the expert(s) a pessimistic (p), a most likely (m), and an optimistic (q) prediction. The mean is then derived as $(p+q+4m)/6$, while the standard deviation is $(q-p)/6$. Similar cases of this sort are treated by Wagle, op. cit.

that the unique estimate(s) provided by his analysis will form the only basis for measuring some performance outcome (like present value of net benefits), he may be more apt to provide an estimate that he regards as a proper reflection of the decision maker's aversion toward risk. The probabilistic approach records the information reflecting what experts believe to be the possible outcomes of a particular event and their respective likelihoods and leaves the question of risk preferences where it should be — with the over-all decision maker(s).

If there were only one factor (source of uncertainty) that determined the states of nature, the probabilities of different levels of that factor could be determined by the above methods and applied directly to a decision table such as the one shown in Table A.1. More generally, however, a state of nature must be defined as a complex event comprised of specific levels of several variables. (For example, $\theta_1$ may be some combination of levels of uncertain factors such as "high" population growth, "medium" income levels, "average" weather, and "moderate" inflation.) Given that probability distributions have been estimated for each of the factors independently, we must somehow combine these distributions into over-all (joint) probability distribution(s). Three procedures are available for such a derivation.[16] One is simply to enumerate all possible combinations of the levels of the factors and compute the probability of each combination. This approach is reasonable only for relatively simple problems. Thus, assuming 11 factors, each with 4 possible outcomes, we would have to perform 4 million calculations ($4^{11}$) to enumerate all possible combinations.

For complex problems, a second, more viable procedure is stochastic simulation,[17] based on a simulated sample. For example, consider the case shown in Figure A.2 where three different variables — construction costs, annual revenue, and ecological costs — influence the benefit-cost ratio of a project. Suppose that the three components of Figure A.2 (a, b, and c) are independent. It is then possible to sample values for each component (for example, points $A$, $B$, and $C$) and calculate the outcome (benefit-cost ratio). If this process is repeated a large number of times, each variable will be selected with a frequency that approximately corresponds to its assigned probability. Thus, a

16. See Reutlinger, *op. cit.*, pp. 14–15.
17. For an exposition of this method, see Hertz, *op. cit.*

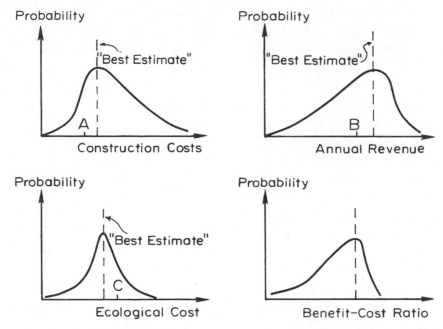

FIGURE A.2. Skewed Probability Distributions for Factors of a Water Resource Decision.

reasonably large sample will result in a close approximation to the actual joint probability distribution such as the benefit-cost ratio in Figure A.2.[18]

Note that for the particular example illustrated by Figure A.2, the various probability distributions of factors are skewed, which implies that the use of "best estimates" for each factor can provide a point estimate of the benefit-cost ratio that is misleading. Thus, the example clearly demonstrates the advantages of the probabilistic approach; the use of 'best estimates" for this example would be unduly optimistic. In more complex cases (such as cases with more variables and where there are correlations or interdependencies among variables), more sophisticated Monte Carlo (random selection) sampling programs must be employed. Computer programs exist for performing the sampling procedures and required computations; the project investigators thus can concentrate their major efforts on estimating the probability

18. Operationally, the sample is considered adequate when the frequency distribution of performance outcome changes an infinitesimal amount as a result of increasing sample sizes. A statistical test is typically employed to determine whether or not additional observations ought to be calculated.

distributions of the major variables, and the relationships among them.

The third available procedure for aggregating probability distributions is to utilize probability calculus to solve directly for relevant characteristics of the joint probability distribution(s). This procedure is based on the application of mathematical expectations to obtain the variance of the estimated probability distributions.[19] This procedure is completely outlined elsewhere,[20] so we shall not discuss its foundations or application here. If the mathematical skills of project appraisers are minimal, the simulation procedure is preferable to the direct mathematical approach. The major limitation of simulation is that the joint probability distribution is specific for only one set of distributions for the several factors. These distributions can, of course, be altered and the sensitivity of the results determined. However, such computations are costly in terms of computer time. In contrast, the mathematical approach can be readily employed to determine the sensitivity of the joint probability distribution, provided that there are relatively few variables and that their individual distributions are tractable mathematically.[21]

The major complication encountered in all approaches is the nonindependence of some random factors. In cases where data exist, and where formal statistical analysis can be utilized, the estimation of correlations (or covariances) among the random factors is a relatively simple matter. However, in cases where such analysis cannot be employed, estimating the extent of correlation between the various probability distributions is likely to prove difficult. For a thorough discussion of this problem, the interested reader is referred to Reutlinger, *op. cit.,* and Wagle, *op. cit.*

*Choice criteria (preference functions):* The specification of actions, states, payoffs, and probabilities provide the elements of a decision table. The question then is how to choose among the actions. Ordinarily, the optimum choice is not at all obvious. To illustrate, let us ex-

---

19. The variance term is typically employed as a proxy variable for uncertainty.

20. See W. Feller, *An Introduction to Probability Theory and Its Applications,* Vol. 1 (New York: John Wiley and Sons, 1957); Hillier, *op. cit.;* and Wagle, *op. cit.*

21. If a larger number of uncertain factors are involved whose estimated probability distributions are reasonably complicated (other than normal), numerical methods are often required, which, of course, takes us back to the simulation procedure.

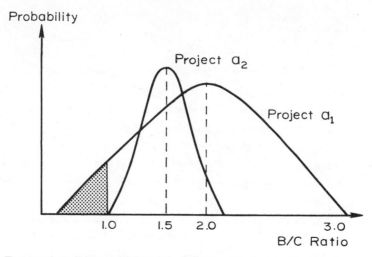

FIGURE A.3. Distributions of Benefit-Cost Ratios for Two Projects.

amine first the case where the benefit-cost ratio (B/C) is deemed the appropriate criterion for measuring that efficiency. Let actions $a_1$ and $a_2$ represent construction of Projects $a_1$ and $a_2$, respectively. Assume that for Project $a_1$, the "best estimate" of the B/C ratio is 2.0, while for Project $a_2$ it is 1.5. The usual analysis selects Project $a_1$ over $a_2$ without question. However, suppose Project $a_1$ is found to be a high-risk project; if things turn out well, it will have a high B/C ratio, but it has a fairly high risk of failure. Suppose that detailed analysis shows that the probability distribution of the B/C ratio from Project $a_1$ (Figure A.3) is as illustrated below, with a mean of 2.0 and a sizable variance. For example, the shaded area under the probability distribution indicates that there is about a 20 per cent chance that the B/C ratio of the project will fall below 1.0. Project $a_2$, on the other hand, is as close to a "sure thing" as one ever finds in the water resources field; it has a mean value of only 1.5 but there is virtually 100 per cent assurance that the B/C ratio realized will exceed unity.

Now that uncertainty has been introduced into the picture, the choice between $a_1$ and $a_2$ is no longer so clear cut. If projects $a_1$ and $a_2$ are "small" (and water resource planners are involved in many such projects), the planners may be willing to ignore uncertainty and pick the project with the highest expected value (highest mean B/C ratio in this case). In other words, the favorable and unfavorable outcomes will "average out" over a series of such projects. On the other hand, assume

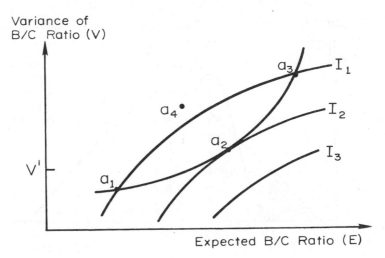

FIGURE A.4. Expectation-Variance Framework.

that $a_1$ and $a_2$ are two alternative approaches to a single massive water project, for example, two general engineering approaches to the California Water Plan. This is a one-shot deal with no chance to "average out" the outcome. In this case, the planners' aversion to risk – or the public's aversion to risk if the question were put to a vote – will enter the decision.

A common conceptual treatment of choice in this situation, assuming that the probability distributions are normal, is the so-called E-V (expectation-variance) framework,[22] that is, in this case, the shape of the distribution is completely determined by knowledge of the mean and variance. To illustrate, assume that for each of four projects or actions ($a_1$, $a_2$, $a_3$, and $a_4$) the mean (expectation) and variance of the B/C ratio is estimated and plotted as shown in Figure A.4. Projects $a_1$, $a_2$, and $a_3$ are on a "efficiency frontier" – defined as the locus of projects with the lowest variance (V) possible for each expected value (E). Project $a_4$ is irrelevant or "dominated" in the sense that there are proj-

22. For a discussion of the limitations of the E-V framework, see G. Hanock and H. Levy, "The Efficiency Analysis of Choices Involving Risk," *Review of Economic Studies*, 36 (1969), 335–346. These are (1) it is relevant for a bounded range only (for example, the rising portion); and (2) it displays increasing absolute-risk aversion everywhere. In addition, these authors demonstrate that the expectation-variance criterion is only a sufficient condition for efficiency dominance. Moreover, if the restricted class of two-parameter distributions is considered, again the mean-variance criterion is only a sufficient condition for efficiency. Of course, the mean-variance criterion is optimal, when the distributions considered are all Gaussian normal.

ects on the efficiency frontier such as $a_2$ with both a higher expected value (E) and a lower variance (V). Curves $I_1$, $I_2$, $I_3$ in Figure A.4 show the preference function of the decision maker(s) in terms of indifference curves. That is, the decision maker is indifferent to alternative combinations of E and V along a given I curve. Curve $I_3$ is preferred to $I_2$ and $I_2$ to $I_1$. Thus, the optimum project is Project $a_2$ which reaches the highest attainable indifference curve ($I_2$ in Figure A.4). The shape of the indifference curves shows risk aversion in the preference function. If there is no risk aversion (or risk preference), the indifference curves would be parallel vertical lines and Project $a_3$, with the highest expected B/C ratio, would be automatically selected—this is the implicit preference function underlying traditional benefit-cost analysis.[23]

A relevant question is: Can such indifference curves (preference functions) be derived or approximated in practice? At the level of the individual decision maker, the answer is probably a qualified "yes."[24] At a group or community level the answer is more dubious, although some would argue that preference functions can be approximated by the legislative process.[25] An alternative approach, which avoids explicit derivation of preference functions (utility functions or indifference curves), is simply to present the "efficiency frontier" to the relevant decision-making group and let it make a direct choice. By making the risks explicit, the risk preferences of the decision makers are called into play and they "reveal" their preferences by their decisions.

It may also be practical to derive special forms of preference functions for problems of this sort. For example, the decision makers may be willing to employ some variant of the "safety-first" principle,[26]

23. It might be argued that decision makers do consider risk by one or more of the informal methods mentioned earlier (using "conservative" estimates, etc.). In fact, these *ad hoc* procedures simply confuse the problem in the sense that when a B/C ratio for a project using such procedures is given, one has no idea whether that value refers to a mean or an expected value, a point on the 10 per cent lower tail of the probability distribution or some other point on the probability distribution.

24. By deriving Von Neumann-Morgenstern utility functions. Given such a utility function, dollar benefits can be converted to utility, utility values replace dollar values in the decision table, and the criterion becomes maximization of expected utility: A. N. Halter and G. W. Dean, *Decisions Under Uncertainty with Research Applications* (Cincinnati: Southwestern Publishing Co., forthcoming).

25. See A. Maass, "Benefit-Cost Analysis: Its Relevance to Public Investment Decisions," *Quarterly Journal of Economics*, 80 (1966), 208–226.

26. See, for example, D. H. Pyle and S. J. Turnovsky, "Safety-First and Expected Utility Maximization in Mean-Standard Deviation Portfolio Analysis," *Review of Economics and Statistics*, 50 (February 1970), 75–81.

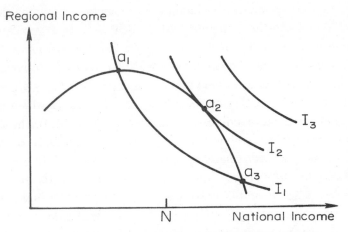

Regional Income

National Income

N

FIGURE A.5. Action Selection with Two Objectives.

which is closely related to the idea of "satisficing" (achieving "satis-factory" levels of goals) in a multiple-goal framework. One form of the "safety-first" principle is to specify a maximum variance that is per-missible ("satisfactory") and then proceed to maximize expected value subject to that maximum permissible variance. For example, suppose decision makers are unwilling to accept any project that has a variance of outcomes greater than $V^1$ in the E-V diagram above. If so, Project $a_1$ will be selected; Projects $a_2$, $a_3$, and $a_4$ all violate this condition.[27]

The above discussion is directed toward explicit consideration of risk in water resource decision-making. The other main deficiency of past practice with regard to preference functions is that a multiple-goal framework has not been used. Public decisions regarding water resource developments are made with a number of broad economic and social objectives in mind. A special Task Force report to the Water Resource Council[28] classifies the broad goals of water resource plan-ning into four categories: (1) national income objectives, (2) regional development objectives, (3) environmental objectives, and (4) "well-being" objectives. Unfortunately, broad goals of this sort are often com-petitive in the sense that a higher level of attainment of one goal can be reached only by reducing the level of attainment of another goal.

27. While the simplest to illustrate, this form of the safety-first criterion is less appeal-ing than other more sophisticated possibilities, see Pyle and Turnovsky, *op. cit.*

28. U.S. Water Resources Council, *Report to the Water Resources Council by the Spe-cial Task Force: Procedures for Evaluation of Water and Related Land Resource Projects,* Washington, D.C., June 1969.

Thus, decision makers have a preference function by which they implicitly weigh the relative importance of the various goals when making choices.[29]

To illustrate simply the problem of choice with multiple objectives, suppose that alternative projects $a_1$, $a_2$, and $a_3$ (Figure A.5) provide different mixes of two competitive goals — say, national income and regional income.[30] Points $a_1$, $a_2$, and $a_3$ are discrete points (actions) on a conceptually continuous "tradeoff" frontier. Again, the conceptual solution would be at Project $a_2$, obtained using a preference function illustrated by indifference curves $I_1$, $I_2$, and $I_3$. Much of the previous discussion concerning the problems of deriving indifference curves in the risk case is also relevant here and need not be repeated.[31] Again, one approach to a multiple-goal preference function may be to employ the "satisficing" ideas indicated above. For example, suppose that the prime objective is to increase regional income. However, planners may be unwilling to maximize regional income if this lowers national income below some level, such as $N$ in Figure A.5. In this case, Project $a_2$ would be selected: it offers the highest regional income of those plans ($a_2$ and $a_3$) which meet the "satisfactory" level N of national income. This framework may be particularly useful where one of the goals

29. The preference function implied in the long-standing procedures used by water resource agencies gives almost complete weight to economic efficiency, since projects with the highest benefit-cost ratio have been preferred. We will not detour here into the voluminous literature which debates the question of which specific form of benefit-cost criterion is most appropriate (benefit minus cost, benefit-cost ratios, maximum internal rate of return, and so forth). All of these alternative criteria are really directed toward finding the best measure of attainment of a single goal: maximum efficiency, expressed in terms of maximizing the national income. This debate, while important, has probably drawn attention away from the still more important fact that decisions should be made within a multiple-goal framework where economic efficiency (maximum national income) is only one of several goals.

30. Of course these may be complementary, as from 0 to $a_1$ (see Figure A.5).

31. The Special Task Force report (op. cit., p. 73) seems to recommend the general approach of showing explicitly the effects of alternate plans with different mixes of objectives, but stops short of specifying a choice criterion, at least at present: "The Task Force believes that a display of project effects in a system of objective accounts would make comparisons more explicit and consequently the judgment process would be improved. Eventually, a more advanced system of optimization based on weighting of the different objectives may be possible of development." See D. C. Major, "Benefit-Cost Ratios for Projects in Multiple Objective Investment Programs," Water Resources Research, 5 (December 1969), 1174–1178, for a suggestion on deriving weights on the two goals of national and regional income such that B/C analysis can be used to solve the choice problem.

TABLE A.2.
*Illustration of Bayesian Approach to Hypothetical
Decision Problems Under Uncertainty*

PART A:

| States of nature (U.S. population) | Actions | | |
|---|---|---|---|
| | $a_1$ Build at slower rate | $a_2$ Build at current rate | $a_3$ Build at faster rate |
| $\theta_1$ Low-Series D | D = S | D < S | D < S |
| $\theta_2$ Medium-Series C | D > S | D = S | D < S |
| $\theta_3$ High-Series B | D > S | D > S | D = S |

PART B:

| States of nature | Actions | | | Original probabilities $P(\theta_i)$ | Revised probabilities[b] $P(\theta_i) = P(\theta_i|Z_1)$ |
|---|---|---|---|---|---|
| | $a_1$ | $a_2$ | $a_3$ | | |
| $\theta_1$   NI[a] | 90 | 89 | 88 | | |
|     CI | 80 | 78 | 76 | 0.4 | 0.7 |
|     CU | 4 | 3 | 3 | | |
| $\theta_2$   NI | 93 | 95 | 93 | | |
|     CI | 86 | 90 | 85 | 0.5 | 0.2 |
|     CU | 5 | 4 | 4 | | |
| $\theta_3$   NI | 96 | 98 | 100 | | |
|     CI | 87 | 88 | 100 | 0.1 | 0.1 |
|     CU | 6 | 5 | 4 | | |
| E(NI) | 92.1 | 92.9 | 91.7 | | |
| E(CI) | 83.7 | 85.0 | 82.9 | $\Sigma = 1.0$ | — |
| E(CU) | 4.7 | 3.7 | 3.6 | | |
| E(NI)$^1$ | 91.2 | 91.1 | 90.2 | | |
| E(CI)$^1$ | 81.9 | 81.6 | 80.2 | — | $\Sigma = 1.0$ |
| E(CU)$^1$ | 4.4 | 3.4 | 3.3 | | |

[a] NI = National Income (index with 100 = maximum rate)
    CI = California Income (index with 100 = maximum rate)
    CU = California Unemployment (in percentage)
[b] Derived using Bayesian analysis as discussed in the text.

cannot easily be expressed in monetary terms but which can otherwise be quantified, for example, recreation days, some index of water
quality, or something similar.[32]

    The two cases just discussed—a single-goal case under uncer-

32. This approach is implied in the recent Special Task Force study (*op. cit.*, p. 71),
where it is stated that "the method of optimizing one objective within specifically prescribed constraints for other objectives is an acceptable approach."

tainty and a multiple-goal case under certainty — are steps in the right direction but still represent somewhat special instances. The most realistic case is where there are multiple goals and where the attainment of each by a given project is measured with uncertainty. Unfortunately, this kind of case does not lend itself easily to graphic analysis. However, the ideas are similar to those outlined above. The following section provides a simple example which incorporates the major ideas of the preceding discussion of a decision framework.

## A Simple Example of a Single-Stage Decision Problem

It is clear that water resource decision problems contain all the elements of a decision table. Decision makers have preference functions; to achieve objectives consistent with the preference functions, they must choose among a range of alternatives (alternative actions); the outcomes (payoffs) of these actions are uncertain and the probabilities of these outcomes can be quantified with objective or subjective information. We now incorporate these concepts in a highly simplified example, yet suggestive of problems in the water resource field.

Probably the major basic decision on the California Water Plan over the next decade is whether to proceed with construction of water storage and conveyance facilities according to schedule (action $a_2$ in Part A, Table A.2), or to "slow down" (action $a_1$) or speed up (action $a_3$) the rate of such construction. A major (but by no means the only) uncertainty affecting the outcome of this decision is the rate of population growth in the United States (and, of course, indirectly, the rate of population growth in California as determined by U.S. rates and migration rates). Let us consider population growth as the single source of uncertainty and define states of nature $\theta_1$, $\theta_2$, and $\theta_3$ as the alternative U.S. Department of Commerce population projections: low (series D), medium (series C), and high (series B) population growth.[33]

Part A, Table A.2 shows schematically the outcomes for the three alternative actions and three possible population levels (states of nature). If $a_1$ is selected and population growth is slow ($\theta_1$), then the demand for and supply of water for agricultural, urban, and industrial

---

33. If more sources of uncertainty were considered, the states would be defined as more complex events and the probabilities assigned to them by one of the methods described earlier.

uses in California are equated at projected water prices, and the project will be paid for by water users. Thus, cell $a_1$, $\theta_1$ in the table shows D = S, or demand for water equals supply of water at given prices. Likewise, if action $a_2$ is taken and $\theta_2$ occurs, or if action $a_3$ is taken and $\theta_3$ occurs, demand and supply of water are equated at given prices (D = S). However, if, for example, action $a_2$ is selected but population growth is only at level $\theta_1$ the project will be "overbuilt" and demand will be less than supply (D < S). In this case, some water would be unused, or prices would be lowered, with the result that water revenues would be unlikely to repay water costs and the general public would be required to finance the difference. On the other hand, if $a_1$ is selected but $\theta_2$ occurs, the project would be "underbuilt" (D > S). In this case, water rationing may be imposed, water prices raised, or other measures taken which would restrict the rate of growth of the California economy below what its potential would be given an adequate water supply.

As discussed earlier, a project such as this has multiple objectives. Suppose they are, for simplification, increased national income (NI), increased California income (CI), and decreased California unemployment (CU). Part B, Table A.2 shows projected values for each of these variables for each action-state combination. Next suppose that demographers estimate subjective probabilities for each state of nature. $P(\theta_i)$. Suppose that, currently, the values are 0.4, 0.5, and 0.1 as shown in Part B, Table A.2. It is now possible to calculate the expected value (or weighted average) of each of the objectives for each action. For example, action $a_1$ has an expected value of national income E(NI) of 92.1, an expected value of California income E(CI) of 83.7, and an expected unemployment rate E(CU) of 4.7 per cent. As indicated in the previous discussion of preference functions, decision makers conceptually have a utility or preference function which depends in some way on the three variables — for example, U = f [E(NI), E(CI), E(CU)]. If an empirical specification of this function could be obtained, the choice of the optimal action would be clear-cut. In practice, unfortunately, utility functions do not abound. A more workable procedure may be simply to present the decision maker (water planner, legislators, or general public, depending on the institutional setting for the particular decision) with the information in Part B, Table A.2. The pros and cons of the various actions can then be weighted in a way that reflects the

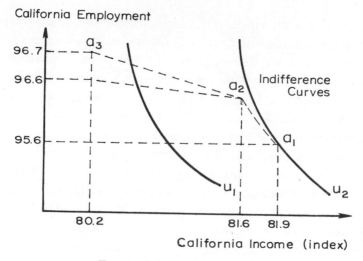

FIGURE A.6. Trade-Off Frontier.

subjective weight applied to the various objectives. Let us imagine an individual decision maker "thinking out loud": "Well, we can just as well dismiss 'building slower' ($a_1$), because by continuing to build at the current rate ($a_2$) we can expect less unemployment and a higher state and national income. Maybe we ought to 'build faster' ($a_3$). But wait a minute! Expected California income would be a lot lower, national income would be down a bit, but unemployment would be virtually the same. I guess we'd better stick to our original schedule ($a_2$)."

Partially to resolve uncertainty, decision makers may revise probabilities on the basis of new information by utilizing Bayesian analysis.[34] To illustrate, suppose a new set of statistics on birth rates in the last year is published. Birth rates continue to show a down trend. Bayesian analysis can be used to combine this new information with the original information in a set of "revised probabilities," as shown in

34. For a standard reference on Bayesian decision-making, see H. Chernoff and L. E. Moses, *Elemenatry Decision Theory* (New York: John Wiley and Sons, 1959).

35. Formally, this involves converting *prior* probabilities to *posterior* probabilities. For example, define $Z_1$ = low birth rates, $Z_2$ = medium birth rates, and $Z_3$ = high birth rates observed in the last year. From historical data, we derive the conditional probability distribution $P(Z_i|\theta_i)$. In effect, we ask: When the true state of nature in the past turned out to be $\theta_i$, what proportion of the time was this preceded by birth rate $Z_i$? Suppose $Z_1$ is observed. Then in Part B, Table A.2, the revised (*posterior*) probabilities

$$P(\theta_i) = P(\theta_i|Z_i) = \frac{P(\theta_i)\ P(Z_i|\theta_i)}{P(Z_i)}$$

using Bayes' formula.

the right hand column of Part B, Table A.2.[35] Suppose the revised probabilities are now 0.7, 0.2, and 0.1 for $\theta_1$, $\theta_2$, and $\theta_3$. A new set of expected values of the three outcomes are now calculated for each action. The decision maker considers the problem anew: "I guess we can now forget $a_3$. It looks like $a_2$ is better in everything but employment and there's not much difference there. But $a_1$ certainly looks a lot more attractive now—it's higher than $a_1$ and $a_2$ in both state and national income. It seems to me that the level of California income is probably more important than unemployment—4.4 per cent still isn't a bad rate and anyway the federal government will probably get the heat on that one rather than us. All things considered I guess I'll push for $a_1$." The preceding statement can be cast in terms of a trade-off frontier between California income and unemployment as shown in Figure A.6. Apparently, this decision maker has indifference curves with the general shape indicated, such that $a_1$ is preferred to $a_2$ and $a_3$.

The above example, hopefully, gives the reader some suggestion of the advantages of explicitly laying out alternatives, possible outcomes, and probabilities. We are aware of the gross simplifications employed to illustrate the approach. However, even such a simple approach may be an improvement over current methods, where a much larger proportion of the problem is based on intuition and vague judgments. An explicit display of outcomes and probabilities pinpoints areas of disagreement and tends to make discussion and debate more factual and rational.

The approach can be made more sophisticated in several ways. One such extension is in the direction of recognizing the sequential nature of water decisions. We therefore now turn to multistage or dynamic planning problems.

## Multistage or Sequential Decision Problems

Water resource planners recognize that current decisions are likely to have consequences that extend over a considerable period of time. The consequences of such decisions are not a single outcome, but rather a sequence of outcomes. While sequential aspects of decision-making are recognized, for example when construction of a system is spread over a considerable period of time, the question of timing is usually treated within an environment of certainty.

S. A. Marglin, in *Approaches to Dynamic Investment Planning*

(Amsterdam: North-Holland Publishing Co., 1963) and *Public Investment Criteria* (Cambridge, Mass.: The M.I.T. Press, 1967), has treated
the case of sequential decision-making under certainty rather completely, with several important results. He demonstrates analytically,
for example, that the economic merit of a project can be improved by
postponing construction and that the postponement may change the
measure of merit for a particular project from an undesirable figure for
construction today to a desirable value for construction at some future
date. K. J. Arrow ("Optimal Capital Policy, the Cost of Capital, and
Myopic Decision Rules," *Annals of the Institute of Statistical Mathe-
matics,* 26 (1964), 21-30), in a generalization of some of Marglin's work,
has demonstrated that in some cases[36] optimal timing of each project
or component increment can be achieved by scheduling construction
the first time the project reveals a positive present value.[37] A. S.
Manne ("Capacity Expansion and Probabilistic Growth," *Econometrica,*
29 (October 1961), 632-649), in still a more general framework, has
shown that optimal construction time is determined by balancing interest costs, loss of benefits, and economies of scale. In fact, if substantial economies of scale exist, it may well be optimal to build ahead of
benefits.

The literature mentioned recognized the possibility of accumulat-
ing additional information through time so that decisions can be
revised sequentially. However, it does not explicitly introduce uncertainty in the form of probability distributions by which decision strategies could be formulated. Moreover, it does not explicitly introduce the
possibility of allocating available resources in such a way as to reduce
or resolve uncertainties. In the following sections, some illustrations
of multistage decision-making under uncertainty are introduced. First
introduced is some general notation that is a natural extension of the
terminology used in the previous single-stage decision table. Then
comes a case of deriving a decision strategy through time. Finally, this

36. Marglin, *Public Investment Criteria, op. cit.,* p. 78, states the rather restrictive
conditions underlying Arrow's generalization: "1. the costs of indivisible projects or
increments are independent, 2. marginal benefits do not increase over time, 3. gestation
periods can be ignored, and 4. the shadow price of capital reflects the appropriate external opportunity cost."
37. Present value is presumed to be the relevant criterion and is always computed on
the assumption that the current benefit rate will continue indefinitely. For this reason,
the resulting decision rule is referred to as "myopic."

is extended to a case where the decision agency or legislative body may allocate resources specifically to reduce uncertainty.

Before setting out the general notation and examples, let us consider a few preliminaries briefly. To simplify the subsequent presentation, we shall assume the first step of the decision-making procedure suggested by the R and D strategy, that is, the means by which (internal) uncertainties have been resolved, is completed, and we are prepared to make a detailed comparative evaluation of the alternatives remaining. That is to say, some alternatives defined as different degrees of component interrelatedness, mixes of uncertainty-reducing activities, and numbers of parallel developments for various components have been eliminated largely on the basis of approximate performance attributes (for each component or subsystem comprising the system design) and the trade-offs involved. Clearly, given the large number of alternatives that might be considered, such a procedure is often necessary to solve the decision problem. Some alternatives will be discarded without detailed investigation and evaluation of their respective expected utilities. Unfortunately, no general methods have been developed for determining ahead of time which decision alternatives these are without generating and evaluating each of them. Thus, given that decision makers consider a small, finite set of alternatives at each stage (from which they will choose one), it does not necessarily follow that the decision strategy chosen is the "best" of all possible strategies that could be generated by considering all possible decision alternatives.

Secondly, our continual reference to decision makers does not imply that we shall consider interagency conflicts in water resource decision-making or groups of individuals that do not have the same preferences for alternative water resource designs and do not agree on the probabilities to be employed.[38] Instead, we assume (again to simplify the exposition) that the decision maker(s) may be treated as an individual in the sense that there is a preference function that can be identified and that needed probabilities can be assessed. Of course, a number of investigators, appraisers, and experts may and should be

38. For such considerations, see T. Marschak and R. Radner, *The Economic Theory of Teams,* Cowels Foundation Monograph for Research in Economics, Yale University (forthcoming).

involved in providing advice, facts, and judgments, but an individual, in the sense outlined above, will make the final decision.

*General notation*: The decision maker must select an element, $a_{ij}$, from a set of actions $a_j = \{a_j\}$ for stage j within the planning horizon, where $i = 1, 2, \ldots, r$, and $j = 1, 2, \ldots, N$. Here r refers to a finite number of decision alternatives or actions and N refers to the number of times periods (stages) for which decisions must be made. The action $a_{ij}$ taken for any stage j is actually a decision for each of several major dimensions of water supply. To illustrate, action $a_{ij}$ may be defined as:

$$a_{ij} = (b_{gj}, c_{hj}, d_{kj}, e_{qj}, f_{mj})$$

where

   $b_{gj}$ denotes the $g^{th}$ alternative with respect to constructing transportation and storage facilities for reallocating fresh water supplies in stage j, selected from the set of alternative decisions $B_j = \{b_j\}$;

   $c_{hj}$ denotes the $h^{th}$ alternative with respect to the development of desalting technology (such as the construction of physical prototypes), in stage j, selected from the set of alternative decisions $C_j = \{c_j\}$;

   $d_{kj}$ denotes the $k^{th}$ alternative with respect to developing the institutional framework for groundwater supply management in stage j, selected from the set of alternative decisions $D_j = \{d_j\}$;

   $e_{qj}$ denotes the $q^{th}$ alternative with respect to the construction of waste-water reclamation facilities in stage j, selected from the set of alternative decisions $E_j = \{e_j\}$;

   $f_{mj}$ denotes $m^{th}$ alternative with respect to assisting nature to increase natural water supplies in stage j, selected from the set of alternative decisions $F_j = \{f_j\}$; and

   $A_j \epsilon R_j$, where $R_j$ is the region to which actions are constrained (based on budget restrictions, etc.).

In summary, the above notation shows that actions are taken in each time period j, and that each action $(a_{ij})$ is defined by specified levels of several subcomponents $(b_{gj}, \ldots, f_{mj})$. Generalizing the earlier example in decision Tables A.1 and A.2, discrete states of nature are now defined for each time period j. The probability distribution associated with the states of each time period $P(\theta_{mj})$ is therefore also

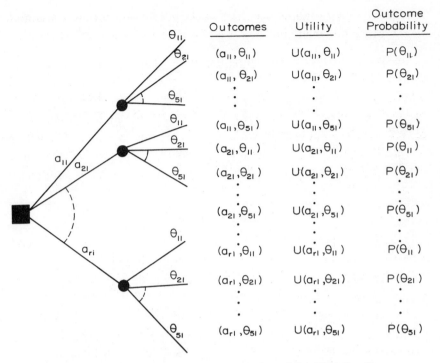

| | Outcomes | Utility | Outcome Probability |
|---|---|---|---|
| $\theta_{11}$ | | | |
| $\theta_{21}$ | $(a_{11}, \theta_{11})$ | $U(a_{11}, \theta_{11})$ | $P(\theta_{1L})$ |
| | $(a_{11}, \theta_{21})$ | $U(a_{11}, \theta_{21})$ | $P(\theta_{21})$ |
| $\theta_{51}$ | | | |
| $\theta_{11}$ | $(a_{11}, \theta_{51})$ | $U(a_{11}, \theta_{51})$ | $P(\theta_{51})$ |
| $\theta_{21}$ | $(a_{21}, \theta_{11})$ | $U(a_{21}, \theta_{11})$ | $P(\theta_{11})$ |
| $\theta_{51}$ | $(a_{21}, \theta_{21})$ | $U(a_{21}, \theta_{21})$ | $P(\theta_{21})$ |
| | $(a_{21}, \theta_{51})$ | $U(a_{21}, \theta_{51})$ | $P(\theta_{51})$ |
| $\theta_{11}$ | $(a_{r1}, \theta_{11})$ | $U(a_{r1}, \theta_{11})$ | $P(\theta_{11})$ |
| $\theta_{21}$ | $(a_{r1}, \theta_{21})$ | $U(a_{r1}, \theta_{21})$ | $P(\theta_{21})$ |
| $\theta_{51}$ | $(a_{r1}, \theta_{51})$ | $U(a_{r1}, \theta_{51})$ | $P(\theta_{51})$ |

FIGURE A.7. Single-Stage Representation of the Decision Tree.

discrete.[39] As explained before, the probability distribution $P(\theta_{mj})$ is actually a joint distribution derived from the probability distributions for each of the relevant factors for which uncertainty exists. Again, extending the simple decision table presented earlier, each action-state pair results in an outcome or payoff in each period. Let us define this outcome as $(a_{ij}, \theta_{mj})$. Assuming that a utility or preference function exists, the utility of each outcome can be denoted by $U(a_{ij}, \theta_{mj})$.

To illustrate the above concepts for one period (let $j = 1$), we introduce a decision tree (Figure A.7). The square box indicates a decision point with r possible actions $(a_{11}, \ldots, a_{r1})$. The circles represent chance events. For example, if $a_{11}$ is chosen, s possible states of nature can ensue $(\theta_{11}, \ldots, \theta_{s1})$. Associated with each action-state pair, there is an outcome, a utility associated with that outcome, and the probability of the state occurring. Suppose $a_{11}$ is chosen and $\theta_{21}$ occurs. The

39. If the underlying distribution is actually discrete, this specification involves no loss in generality; however, if the underlying probability distribution is continuous, the discrete specification will represent some approximation and will be derived by defining discrete intervals for the values of the random variables defining the states of nature.

outcome is then $(a_{11}, \theta_{21})$, the utility of that outcome $U(a_{11}, \theta_{21})$, and the probability of $\theta_{21}$ denoted by $P(\theta_{21})$. Given this information the expected utility of each action can be calculated $-\sum_{m=1}^{s} U(a_{i1}, \theta_{m1}) P(\theta_{m1})-$ and the actions chosen which maximize expected utility. It should be clear that this simplified decision tree is just another way of writing out a decision table. The advantage of a decision tree is that it can be expanded to handle sequential or multistage problems.

*Another example—Decision trees and strategies:* The decision-tree concept is now extended to an illustrative sequential decision problem inspired by the California Water Plan. Formally, we will treat a simple case where r = 2, that is, where only two actions are possible in each stage, where N = 3, that is, where three decision stages are allowed, and where s = 4, that is, where only four states of nature are allowed. The illustration will be simplified further by defining $a_1 = (b_{ij}, 0, 0, 0, 0)$, and $a_2 = (0, 0, 0, 0, 0)$.

Let us assume that water resource planners consider a fifty-year planning horizon. To simplify, assume that major decisions as to the direction of the California Water Plan are made at the beginning of each decade for the next thirty years. The major decision points are thus in 1970, 1980, and 1990. The alternative actions at each of these points (j) are action $a_1$ — continue for the next decade with construction of major water storage and conveyance facilities according to the current California Water Plan; action $a_2$ — complete construction of major water storage and conveyance facilities currently under way but delay for ten years the construction of major new facilities.[40] Again, to simplify, assume that the major sources of uncertainty are the success $(S_1)$ or failure $(F_1)$ of desalination at an "economically feasible" cost level, and the success $(S_2)$ or failure $(F_2)$ of political and legal action by the state to gain public control of pumping from groundwater storage in key areas of the state. Obviously, as has elsewhere been made clear, the success of either or both of these alternatives would greatly reduce or perhaps eliminate reliance on extensive new structures to capture and transport surface water to deficit areas of the state. The water resources decision makers are faced with the possibility of two types

40. Note that the second subscript (j), denoting stages, has been deleted for the sake of simplicity.

of errors. If they continue to build dam and conveyance facilities and desalination or groundwater control become successful, the project may become a white elephant. If they do not build, and desalination and groundwater control fail, the project will be too small to satisfy water demands, and there will be losses to the state in terms of reduced economic growth (perhaps land formerly irrigated may become idled, heavy water-using industries decline, existing supplies will have to be used with less waste, and so forth).

The approach advanced in this chapter involves an explicit recognition of these uncertainties. Each chance event (state of nature) is therefore first identified. In our example, the states refer to success or failure of desalination and control of underground storage within a decade, as follows:

State $\theta_1 = S_1 S_2$ success of both desalination and control of underground storage.

State $\theta_2 = S_1 F_2$ success of desalination, failure of control of groundwater storage,

State $\theta_3 = F_1 S_2$ failure of desalination, success of control of groundwater storage,

State $\theta_4 = F_1 F_2$ failure of both desalination and control of underground storage.

Only at the end of a decade do we know which state has occurred. If $\theta_1$ has occurred (both desalination and control of groundwater succeed), we assume that there is no additional uncertainty during the remaining life of the project. (Recall that we have ignored uncertainty of demand and other factors for purposes of this example.) If $\theta_2$ has occurred (desalination succeeds), then only two states can follow:

$\theta'_1 = S_2 | S_1$ success of groundwater control, given that desalination has succeeded,

$\theta'_2 = F_2 | S_1$ failure of groundwater control, given that desalination has succeeded.

Likewise, if $\theta_3$ has occurred (groundwater control succeeds), only two states can follow:

$\theta''_1 = S_1 | S_2$ success of desalination, given that groundwater control has succeeded,

$\theta''_2 = F_1 | S_2$ failure of desalination, given that groundwater control has succeeded.

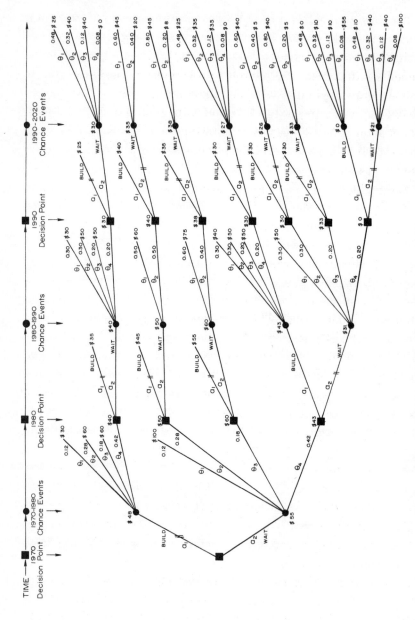

FIGURE A.8. Hypothetical Decision Tree Illustrating Framework for Sequential Decision-Making under Uncertainty for the California Water Plan.

If $\theta_4$ has occurred (both desalination and control of groundwater fail), all four states of nature $\theta_1$ to $\theta_4$ continue to be relevant for the following decade.

The next step is to assign outcomes to each state of nature. In our example, we will assume that these outcomes can be adequately measured in terms of monetary net benefits, that is, the present value of benefits minus costs. Next, probabilities must be assigned to each outcome. As pointed out previously, these are often by necessity subjective. Finally, a criterion for selection of the preferred action at each decision point must be specified. We assume that the decision makers wish to maximize the expectation (weighted average) of the present value of net benefits.

The problem just described is specified completely and solved in the decision tree of Figure A.8. Hypothetical numerical values have been assigned to outcomes ($ million) and probabilities. Possible outcomes are assumed to vary from $100 million to −$100 million. The most favorable outcome would occur if the decision makers choose $a_2$ (don't build) in 1970 and $\theta_1$ occurs (both desalination and control of groundwater succeed) in the decade 1970-1980. In this case, an adequate and economic water supply is generated for future years without additional costly state water development projects. However, the subjective probability assigned to such an occurrence is low (0.12) in our example (that is, 0.4 for desalination and 0.3 for groundwater control, the two events assumed to be independent). The most unfavorable outcome would occur if, in each of the three decision periods, action $a_2$ (don't build) is chosen and $\theta_4$ occurs in each decade (both desalination and groundwater control fail). Such an outcome would result in a disastrous water shortage. Note in the key to Figure A.8, however, that the probabilities of success for the alternative sources of supply (assigned in 1970 by the decision maker) increase over time.

The analytic approach to all problems of this type employs the "backward solution." That is, we start from the "tips" of the decision tree and work backward in time toward the initial decision point. Imagine, for example, that we are at the 1990 decision point on the top branch of Figure A.8. As usual, we are faced with two choices—to "build" ($a_1$) or "not to build" ($a_2$). If we build ($a_1$), the outcome is a certain present value of $25 million in net benefits. If we don't build ($a_2$), there are four possible states of nature ($\theta_1$, $\theta_2$, $\theta_3$, $\theta_4$) with alternative outcomes (net benefits of \$26, \$40, \$40, or \$0 million) and probabilities (0.48, 0.32, 0.12, and 0.08). The expected value of the "don't build" alternative (action $a_2$) is therefore \$30 million (0.48 × \$26 + 0.32 × \$40 + 0.12 × \$40 + 0.08 × \$0 = \$30). The decision maker using the expected monetary net-benefits criterion would therefore select action $a_2$ and "block off" or eliminate action $a_1$. (The latter is indicated in Figure A.8 by the double vertical slashes.)

We can now move back to the 1980 decision point on the top branch of Figure A.8. Here, action $a_1$ has a certainty value of \$35 million and action $a_2$ has an expected value of \$40 million (0.30 × \$30 + 0.30 × \$50 + 0.20 × \$50 + 0.20 × \$30 = \$40). Again, action $a_1$ is blocked off. Moving back to the 1970 decision point, and using the same reasoning, it is seen that the expected value of $a_2$ is \$55 million while that of $a_1$ is only \$48 million. Thus, action $a_1$ is blocked off and action $a_2$ is seen as optimal in 1970. The expected values at each chance point and decision point on the lower branches of the tree are calculated in the same "backward" fashion.

The completed decision tree provides a complete road map or "strategy" for the decision maker; it tells him what to do for every eventuality included in the definition of the problem. Using the expected value criterion, the optimum action in 1970 is $a_2$ (wait, or "don't build"). The next "move" is up to "nature." If $\theta_1$ occurs, no more major construction decisions are required, since desalination and groundwater control insure adequate supplies in future years. If $\theta_2$ occurs, Figure A.8 shows that the best strategy is to pick action $a_2$ in 1980. If $\theta_1'$ then occurs, no further decisions are required — again desalination in the 1970 decade and groundwater control in the 1980 decade insure adequate water supplies. But if $\theta_2$ occurs, the road map says to pick action $a_1$ (build) in 1990. The reader can trade through the decision steps for all other branches of the tree.

A principal result of formal sequential decision analysis under uncertainty is that there is no single "best action" for all time, but rather a "strategy" that is flexible in the sense that decisions in future periods depend on chance events that occur in the interim. The entire problem above is solved at the 1970 decision point. Obviously, only the first step (the 1970 decision) must be taken immediately. But as Figure A.8 makes clear, that step depends on formulating the *entire* decision tree, not just stage 1 data, even though beyond stage 1 it is a "paper plan." In general, new information will become available between 1970 and 1980 that will change the future probabilities. The problem could be formulated again at that time, with 1980 as the first stage in a fifty-year planning horizon and the optimal decision for 1980 derived. This approach is similar to the so-called "rolling plan" idea used in periodically revising economic development plans.

The earlier discussion of multiple goals and preference functions is equally applicable to the example just discussed. Each state-action pair may have associated with it several dimensions of "outcomes" (national income, state income, pollution levels, and similar factors). The decision at each fork in the decision tree requires an explicit or implicit preference function for weighting this multiple outcome.

*Additional complexities:* As we move from the above simplified example closer to a more realistic framework, a number of complexities arise. One such complexity is, of course, that actions $a_{ij}$ include decisions with respect to factors $c_{hj}$, $d_{kj}$, $e_{qj}$, and $f_{mj}$, in addition to $b_{gj}$. For example, in the current period ($j = 1$), the action $a_{i1}$ may represent continuing with the construction of aqueduct systems, delaying construction of the peripheral canal, and delaying East Side development, as well as delaying the development of the Upper Eel ($b_{g1}$); and the construction of two distillation plants for desalting seawater ($c_{h1}$), attempting to establish the institutional framework for management of some portion of the state's underground water supply ($d_{k1}$), the construction of four facilities for waste-water reclamation ($e_{q1}$), and doing nothing with respect to assistance of nature to augment present natural water supplies ($f_{m1} = 0$).

When we include these factors, it becomes clear that the action selected could change our estimate of the probabilities of future states of nature. To illustrate, suppose the action set $a_{ij}$ includes alternative levels of investment by the water agency in desalting technology ($c_{hj}$) and alternative levels of study on the political and legal feasibility of underground water management ($d_{kj}$). In our previous example the (unconditional) states of nature ($\theta_1$, $\theta_2$, $\theta_3$, $\theta_4$) were defined in terms of the "success" or "failure" of these two components. Clearly, heavier investments in $c_{hj}$ and $d_{kj}$ will increase the probabilities of "success." The decision tree for this case would include actions in each time period (stage) with different levels of intensity of investment in $c_{hj}$ and

$d_{kj}$. As we follow out branches of the tree through time, the possibilities of the "successful" states of nature would be assigned higher probabilities for those actions with heavy investments in $c_{hj}$ and $d_{kj}$. This, too, represents an abstraction. That is, the state of nature, $\theta_{nj}$, is a joint event that refers to level of agricultural demand, urban demand, aesthetic and recreational demand, construction costs, operating costs, as well as the degree of success in development of desalting technology, groundwater management, waste-water reclamation, and the like. To be sure, these joint events and their probabilities also depend upon the particular action selected; this dependence refers to the structural relationships defined earlier between controllable and uncontrollable variables.

The complexity introduced in the previous paragraph derives from the lessons of R and D strategy discussed earlier. R and D strategy suggests the use of parallel and loosely related approaches to developing sources of water supply, such as simultaneous investment in water conveyance and storage facilities ($b_{gj}$), desalting technology ($c_{hj}$ at one or more levels of intensity), and underground water management ($d_{kj}$). The decision to invest in a particular component need not be viewed as a "once-and-for-all" decision. Rather, the decision to work with some intensity on a component may be viewed as the exploration of a possibility aimed at finding out more about the chances of success and the costs and benefits of the particular component, if it were completed. T. Marschak, T. K. Glennan, and R. Summers, in *Strategy for R & D* (New York: Rand Corporation, 1967), have formally extended these ideas to the pursuit of approaches with different intensities, isolating the peculiar way such different approaches relate to each other; to the case of many review points and multicomponent parallel developments; and to the case of many-valued preferences.[41] For purposes of water resource decision-making, the implication of these results is that the possibility of considering multiple and parallel approaches aimed at reducing uncertainty (prior to plunging for the one "best" approach) should be explored. As A. O. Hirschman argues

41. See also the work of R. Nelson, "Uncertainty, Learning, and the Economics of Parallel Research and Development Efforts," *Review of Economics and Statistics,* 43 (August 1961), 351–364, and T. K. Glennan, "Issues in the Choice of Development Policies" (Santa Monica: Rand Corporation, October 1967), reprinted as Chapter 2 in T. Marschak, T. K. Glennan, and R. Summers, *Strategy for R & D* (New York: Rand Corporation, 1967).

quite convincingly in *Development Projects Observed* (Washington, D.C.: The Brookings Institution, 1967), development projects are essentially "voyages of technological and administrative discovery" and, as such, require the R and D approach.

Conceptually, the decision tree approach can be used to solve R and D problems of the more complex type described above. However, as Raiffa (*op. cit.*), points out, the decision tree in such a case is likely to become a "bushy mess." Unfortunately, some of the more powerful mathematical tools for solving multistage problems, such as linear and nonlinear programming, are severely limited in handling cases that involve uncertainty.[42] The most viable approaches under uncertainty are probably dynamic programming and stochastic simulation.

Dynamic programming under uncertainty is a formal solution procedure which, at least for some decision problems, allows the derivation of optimal decision strategies.[43] Essentially, the procedure involves restating the complex multistage decision problem as a number of subproblems (one representing each stage within the planning horizon), each of which contains a few controllable or decision variables. The use of dynamic programming as a mathematical technique is too elaborate to be discussed here at any length. However, the solution procedure is analogous to the "backward" solution employed in the earlier decision-tree example.[44]

42. For a discussion of the limitations of "stochastic linear programming," "linear programming under uncertainty," and "chance-constrained programming," see A. J. Charnes, J. Dreze, and M. Miller, "Decision and Horizon Rules for Stochastic Planning Problems: A Linear Example," *Econometrica,* 34 (April 1966), 307–330, and J. K. Sengupta, "The Stability of Truncated Solutions of Stochastic Linear Programming," *Econometrica,* 34 (January 1966), 77–104. These limitations equally apply, but with more force, to the various forms of nonlinear programming under uncertainty.

43. The computational efficiency of dynamic programming is quite high in the cases of quadratic preference functions and state vectors composed of at most two or three components, see Bellman, *op. cit.,* and R. Wilson, "Computation of Optimal Controls," *Journal of Mathematical Analysis and Applications,* 14 (1966), 77–82.

44. For an explanation of dynamic programming techniques, see R. Bellman, *Dynamic Programming* (Princeton, N.J.: Princeton University Press, 1957), and G. Hadley, *Nonlinear and Dynamic Programming* (Reading, Mass.: Addison-Wesley, 1964). For some applications to water resource problems, see K. J. Arrow, S. Karlin, and H. Scarf, *Studies in the Mathematical Theory of Inventory and Production* (Stanford, Calif.: Stanford University Press, 1958), Chap. 2; O. R. Burt, "The Economics of Conjunctive Use of Ground and Surface Water," *Hilgardia,* 36:2 (December 1964), 31–111; J. D. C. Little, "The Use of Storage Water in a Hydroelectric System," *Journal of the Operations Research Society of America,* 3 (1955), 187–199; T. C. Koopmans, "Water Storage in a Simplified Hydroelectric System," *Proceedings of First International Conference on Operations Research,* 1957; and Maass *et al., op. cit.,* Chap. 14.

Unfortunately, generally applicable analytical solution procedures do not exist for certain classes of more complex problems. Thus, stochastic computer simulation is often regarded as the most realistic approach to tracing out the implications of alternative decision strategies. The simulation model can be as complex as a realistic statement of the decision problem requires. Interdependencies among actions and probability distributions can be specified in the model. The probability distribution of the over-all performance criterion can be obtained for a given decision strategy by Monte Carlo sampling methods, that is, by sampling from the relevant probability distributions for each state of nature to obtain the value of the criterion function for a specific computer run. Successive runs with other samples allow approximation of the probability distribution of the particular strategy. Probability distributions for other strategies can be obtained in similar fashion. There is no guarantee that an "optimal" strategy can always be obtained with these methods, but "better" strategies can be derived.[45]

### Summary and Conclusions

It is our major contention that water resource planning and evaluation could be improved by taking explicit account of the uncertainties involved. The approaches advocated and illustrated briefly in this appendix allow for—and indeed encourage—analysis, experience, judgments, and revisions thereof to enter the decision process. We do not underestimate the difficulties of implementing this approach in practice: it would require a substantial investment in systems analysis, computer time, and supporting facilities. However, we are convinced that the required investment would be small compared with the funds currently allocated to engineering and other professional-level work in water resource agencies, and minuscule compared with the total costs of the projects involved. If we can design, engineer, and construct the world's most complex and sophisticated water storage and transfer systems, it does not seem too much to ask that the decision process be analyzed with the same rigor.

45. For a further discussion of simulation in the context of water resource decision, see Maass *et al., op. cit.,* Chaps. 6, 9–12, and Hamilton *et al., op. cit.*

# INDEX

Ackerman, A., 19, 21–22
Acreage limitation, 253. *See also* 160-acre law
Acre-foot, definition, 4 n.
Agriculture, 4, 6
 — and 160-acre law, 254–255
 — import and export products, 55–56
 — income redistribution, 50–51
 — irrigated acreage, 56–58, 71–74, 77–88, 148–149, 169
 — land for, 60–70
 — produce prices, 62–68
 — U.S. Department of, 53, 54
 — use of waste water, 164–165, 167, 169–170
 — water demands of, 49–52. *See also* Crops; Irrigation
Algal bloom, 111–112, 118
Almonds, 66–67
Appliances, household, 38–40
Aqueduct(s), in California State Water Project, 11–13, 16; the California, 12, 13, 15, 49, 58
Aquifer(s), 184–185, 228
Arizona, water use of, 79–82 *passim*

Ballis, G., 24–25
Basins, groundwater. *See* Groundwater basins
Bayesian analysis, 312–331; formula for, 330–331. *See also* Decision-making, mathematical
Benefit-cost analysis, 271–273, 275, 280, 284, 305–306, 319–320, 322; vs quality of life, 286, 304–306
Birdlebough, S. C., 263–270
Blaney-Criddle formula, 78–79, 81
Bollman, F. H., 84–106
Book, D. L., 206–230
Brine, 134–136, 142, 145; by products of, 203; desalination with, 201; disposal of, 151–152, 193, 195, 196, 201; geothermal usage of, 149
Burns-Porter Act, 12, 15

California Aqueduct. *See* Aqueduct, California
California Department of Water Resources, 5, 11–12, 27, 187, 265, 269, 277; predictions for irrigation, 56–58
California, Gulf of, 191, 192
California, southern, water requirements of, 40–41
California State Water Project
 — and 160-acre law, 24–25
 — ecological results from, 26–27, 120–124
 — evaluation of, 307–309
 — facilities of, 12–13, 98–102
 — federal use of, 16
 — financial criticism of, 19–25
 — history of, 5–13
 — purposes of, 13–15
 — size and cost of, ix, 14–17, 206
 — U.S. Bureau of Reclamation and, 5–9, 24–27

California, University of, at Davis, 79; at Riverside, 195, 198, 204
California Water Fund, 15–16
California Water Plan, 48, 235, 241, 268, 269, 272, 315
 — agricultural intent of, 51–52
 — major decision of, 328–331
 — uncertainties in, 233–250, 334–342
 — water reclamation in, 162–164, 168
Canals, 6–7, 12, 13, 14, 16
Cantaloupe, 64
Central Valley Project, ix, 60; 160-acre law in, 255, 257–258; relative to Dos Rios Project, 272, 282; U.S. Bureau of Reclamation in, 5–9; water supply of, 17–18
Chlorination, 179
Ciriacy-Wantrop, S. V., 88, 94, 103, 272
Colorado River, 7, 9, 10, 11, 76, 149, 193, 196–197, 201, 203
Computer analysis, 187, 311, 320, 343
Conservation. *See* Environment, protection of
Cooper, E., 24–25
Cotton, 67–68
Crops, acreage for, 59–62; economic forecasts for, 52–58; feed grains, 55–56, 68; field, 67–68; high value, 49, 60; specialty, 60–68, 70
Crutchfield, J., 94

Dams, in California, 6–7; in California State Water Project, 12–13, 98–101; proposed, 8–9
Dean, G. W., 49–70, 233–250, 310–344
Decision-making, 272, 290–291, 304–305
 — flexibility in, 244–247
 — learning processes and, 239–242
 — mathematical: action payoff, 315–316; choice criteria, 321–328; decision trees, 333–342; research and development strategy, 342–343; sequential problems, 247–249, 331–344; single-stage problems, 312–331, 334–336
 — prototypes of, 243–244
 — public role in, 315, 325
 — under uncertainty, 235–238, 239–250 *passim*; 310–344
 — water problems, examples of, 316, 342
DeHaven, J. C., 19, 23, 39
Delta Cross Channel, 6
Delta Pool, water withdrawal from, ix–x, 9, 10–11, 14, 17, 26, 272. *See also* Sacramento-San Joaquin Delta; San Francisco Bay-Delta System
Demineralization, 148, 150
Desalination, 27, 336–337, 342
 — cost of, 153–158, 240–241
 — definition, 127
 — disposal of salt and sulphur, 150–152
 — generation plants for, 137–138, 149, 152, 207, 226–227

# KEY TO ENDSHEET MAP

RESERVOIRS AND LAKES (EXISTING OR UNDER CONSTRUCTION)

1. Copco Lake
2. Iron Gate Res.
3. Dwinnell Res.
4. Clair Engle Lake
5. Lewiston Res.
6. Lake Pillsbury
7. Lake Mendocino
8. Lake Sonoma
9. Nicasio Res.
10. Lake Hennessy
11. Clear Lake
12. Lake Berryessa
13. East Park Res.
14. Stony Gorge Res.
15. Black Butte Res.
16. Whiskeytown Res.
17. Keswick Res.
18. Shasta Lake
19. Box Canyon Res.
20. McCloud Res.
21. Pit #7 Res.
22. Pit #6 Res.
23. Iron Canyon Res.
24. Lake Britton
25. Tule Lake
26. Clear Lake Res.
27. Goose Lake
28. Eagle Lake
29. Honey Lake
30. Mountain Meadows Res.
31. Lake Almanor
32. Butt Valley Res.
33. Antelope Lake
34. Bucks Lake
35. Lake Oroville
36. Frenchman Lake
37. Lake Davis
38. Little Grass Valley Res.
39. Sly Creek Res.
40. Thermalito Forebay and Afterbay
41. Jackson Meadows Res.
42. New Bullards Bar Res.
43. Bowman Lake
44. Lake Spaulding
45. Scotts Flat Res.
46. Englebright Res.
47. Merle Collins Res.
48. Rollins Res.
49. Camp Far West Res.
50. French Meadows Res.
51. Hell Hole Res.
52. Loon Lake
53. Auburn Res.
54. Folsom Lake
55. Lake Natoma
56. Union Valley Res.
57. Ice House Res.
58. Silver Lake
59. Stampede Res.
60. Prosser Creek Res.
61. Lake Tahoe
62. Lower Bear River Res.
63. Salt Springs Res.
64. Pardee Res.
65. Camanche Res.
66. New Hogan Res.
67. Salt Springs Valley Res.
68. Farmington Res.
69. Woodward Res.
70. Donnells Res.
71. Beardsley Res.
72. New Melones Res.
73. Tulloch Res.
74. Lake Lloyd
75. Lake Eleanor
76. Hetch Hetchy Res.
77. New Don Pedro Res.
78. Turlock Lake
79. Lake McClure
80. McSwain Res.
81. Lake Florence
82. Lake Edison
83. Mammoth Pool Res.
84. Huntington Lake
85. Shaver Lake
86. Redinger Lake
87. Bass Lake
88. Millerton Lake
89. Courtright Res.
90. Wishon Res.
91. Pine Flat Res.
92. Terminus Res.
93. Success Res.
94. Tulare Lake
95. Isabella Res.
96. Buena Vista Lake
97. Mono Lake
98. Grant Lake
99. Lake Crowley
100. Tinemaha Res.
101. Haiwee Res.
102. San Pablo Res.
103. Briones Res.
104. Upper San Leandro Res.
105. San Antonio Res.
106. Calaveras Res.
107. Lake Del Valley
108. Clifton Court Forebay
109. San Andreas Res.
110. Crystal Springs Lake
111. Lexington Res.
112. Calero Res.
113. Chesbro Res.
114. Uvas Res.
115. Anderson Lake
116. Coyote Lake
117. San Luis Res.
118. O'Neill Forebay
119. Los Banos Creek Res.
120. Little Panoche Creek Res.
121. San Antonio Res.
122. Nacimiento Res.
123. Salinas Res.
124. Whale Rock Res.
125. Lopez Res.
126. Twitchell Res.
127. Jameson Lake
128. Gibralter Res.
129. Cachuma Res.
130. Matilija Res.
131. Casitas Res.
132. Pyramid Lake
133. Piru Lake
134. Castaic Lake
135. Fairmount Res.
136. Bouquet Res.
137. Hansen Res.
138. San Fernando Valley Res.
139. Chatsworth Res.
140. Sepulveda Res.
141. Cogswell Res.
142. San Gabriel Res.
143. Morris Res.
144. Santa Fe Res.
145. Whittier Narrows Res.
146. Brea Res.
147. Fullerton Res.
148. Carbon Canyon Res.
149. Puddingstone Res.
150. San Antonio Res.
151. Prado Res.
152. Irvine Lake
153. Villa Park Res.
154. Mojave Res.
155. Silverwood Lake
156. Lake Perris
157. Lake Mathews
158. Railroad Canyon Res.
159. Elsinore Lake
160. Auld Valley Res.
161. Vail Res.
162. Lake Henshaw
163. Sutherland Res.
164. Lake Hodges
165. San Vicente Res.
166. Miramar Res.
167. Cuyamaca Res.
168. El Capitan Res.
169. Murray Res.
170. Sweetwater Res.
171. Lake Loveland
172. Morena Lake
173. Barrett Lake
174. Upper Otay Res.
175. Lower Otay Res.
176. Salton Sea
177. Lake Mead
178. Imperial Res.
179. Senator Wash Res.
180. Laguna Res.

# KEY TO ENDSHEET MAP (continued)

## RESERVOIRS AND LAKES (AUTHORIZED)

181. Butler Valley Res.
182. Knights Valley Res.
183. Lakeport Res.
184. Indian Valley Res.

185. Dixie Refuge Res.
186. Abbey Bridge Res.
187. Marysville Res.
188. Sugar Pine Res.

189. County Line Res.
190. Buchanan Res.
191. Hidden Res.
192. Buttes Res.

## RESERVOIRS AND LAKES (POSSIBLE FUTURE)

193. Helena Res.
194. Schneiders Bar Res.
195. Eltapom Res.
196. New Rugh Res.
197. Anderson Ford Res.
198. Dinsmore Res.
199. English Ridge Res.
200. Dos Rios Res.
201. Yellowjacket Res.
202. Cahto Res.
203. Panther Res.
204. Walker Res.
205. Blue Ridge Res.
206. Oat Res.

207. Sites-Funks Res.
208. Rancheria Res.
209. Newville-Paskenta Res.
210. Tehama Res.
211. Dutch Gulch Res.
212. Allen Camp Res.
213. Millville Res.
214. Tuscan Buttes Res.
215. Aukum Res.
216. Nashville Res.
217. Irish Hill Res.
218. Cooperstown Res.
219. Figarden Res.
220. Little Dry Creek Res.

221. Owen Mountain Res.
222. Yokohl Res.
223. Hungry Hollow Res.
224. Kellogg Res.
225. Los Banos Res.
226. Jack Res.
227. Santa Rita Res.
228. Sunflower Res.
229. Lompoc Res.
230. Cold Springs Res.
231. Topatopa Res.
232. Fallbrook Res.
233. De Luz Res.

## AQUEDUCTS AND TUNNELS (EXISTING OR UNDER CONSTRUCTION)

1. Clear Creek Tunnel
2. Whiskeytown-Keswick Tunnel
3. Bella Vista Conduit
4. Muletown Conduit
5. Corning Canal
6. Tehama-Colusa Canal
7. Putah South Canal
8. Cache Slough Conduit
9. Folsom South Canal
10. Mokelumne Aqueduct
11. Contra Costa Canal

12. South Bay Aqueduct
13. Hetch Hetchy Aqueduct
14. Delta Mendota Canal
15. California Aqueduct
16. Pleasant Valley Canal
17. Madera Canal
18. Friant Kern Canal
19. San Luis Obispo Conduit
20. Whale Rock Conduit
21. West Branch California Aqueduct
22. Angeles Tunnel

23. Los Angeles Aqueduct
24. South Coast Conduit
25. Colorado River Aqueduct
26. San Diego Aqueduct
27. Coachella Canal
28. East Highline Canal
29. All American Canal
30. West Side Canal
31. Santa Rosa Conduit
32. Sonoma Aqueduct

## AQUEDUCTS AND TUNNELS (AUTHORIZED)

33. Stony Canal
34. Folsom-Malby Conduit
35. North Bay Aqueduct
36. Peripheral Canal

37. Pacheco Tunnel
38. Santa Clara Canal
39. Hollister-Watsonville Conduit

40. Coastal Branch California Aqueduct

## AQUEDUCTS AND TUNNELS (POSSIBLE FUTURE)

41. Clear Creek Tunnel #2
42. Trinity Tunnel
43. South Fork Tunnel
44. Cottonwood Tunnel
45. Westside Conveyance System
46. Grindstone Tunnel
47. Stony Creek Conveyance Channel

48. Garrett Tunnel
49. West Sacramento Canal
50. Cache Creek–Sacramento River Canal
51. Knights Valley–Lake Hennessey Canal
52. Sonoma–Marin Conduit
53. Hood–Clay Canal
54. Eastside Canal

55. Contra Loma Canal
56. Tuway Canal
57. Porterville–Bakersfield Canal
58. Sespe Conduit

SOURCES: *California Water Resources Development*, Irrigation Districts Association of California, 1968
and
*Water Resources Development in California*, California State Department of Water Resources, 1970

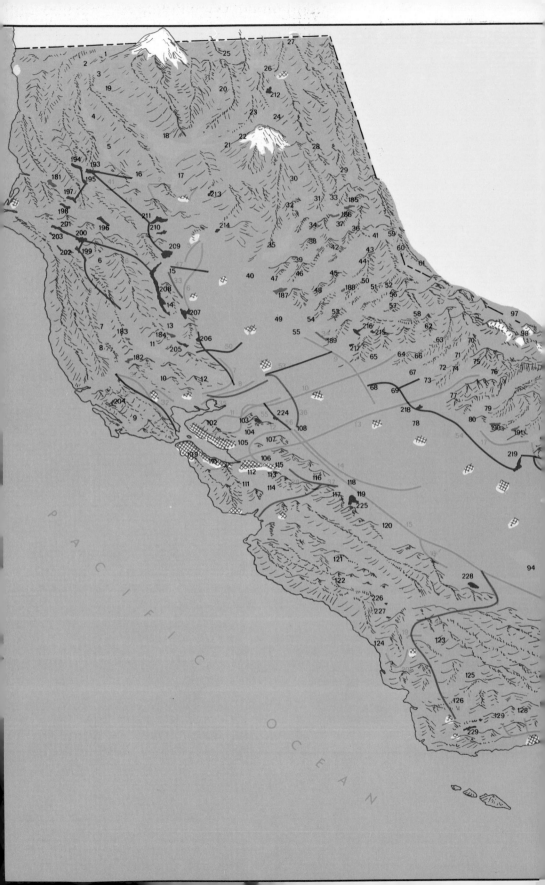